CHURCH AND MINISTRY

Eugene F. A. Klug was professor of systematic theology at Concordia Theological Seminary, beginning in 1960 while the institution was still in Springfield, Illinois. He moved with the seminary to Ft. Wayne, Indiana, and continued his service to the people of God until his death in 2003.

Klug attended Concordia College, Milwaukee, Wisconsin, and Concordia Seminary, St. Louis, Missouri, graduating in 1942. He also earned a master's degree at the University of Chicago in 1941. Klug served as a Navy chaplain during World War II before serving as a campus pastor at the University of Wisconsin, Madison, and as pastor in Kalispell, Montana. Klug spent five years at the University of Illinois, Champaign-Urbana, before embarking on his long tenure with Concordia Theological Seminary.

Awarded the Doctor of Theology degree from the Free University of Amsterdam in 1971, Klug also received the St. Martin of Tours medal for his work on *The Military Chaplaincy under the First Amendment* and his service as Navy chaplain. In addition to *Church and Ministry*, Klug authored *From Luther to Chemnitz: On Scripture and the Word; Getting into the Formula of Concord; Word and Scripture: In Luther Studies since World War II;* and *Lift High This Cross: The Theology of Martin Luther.*

CHURCH
AND
MINISTRY

THE ROLE OF CHURCH, PASTOR, AND PEOPLE FROM LUTHER TO WALTHER

Eugene F. A. Klug

CONCORDIA PUBLISHING HOUSE · SAINT LOUIS

Copyright © 1993 Concordia Publishing House
3558 S. Jefferson Ave., St. Louis, MO 63118-3968
1-800-325-3040 • www.cph.org

Manufactured in the United States of America

Library of Congress Cataloging-in-Publication Data

Klug, Eugene F. A., 1917–2003
    Church and ministry: the role of church, pastor, and people from Luther to Walther / Eugene F. A. Klug.
       p. cm.
    Includes bibliographical references.
    ISNB 0-570-04625-4
    1. Church—History of doctrine. 2. Church. 3. Clergy—History of doctrine. 4. Clergy—Office. 5. Luther, Martin, 1483–1546. 6. Walther, C. F. W. (Carl Ferdinand Wilhelm), 1811–1887. 7. Lutheran Church—Doctrines. 8. Lutheran Church—Missouri Synod—Doctrines. I. Title.
BR333.5.C5K58   1993
262′.041322—dc20 93-25772

2 3 4 5 6 7 8 9 10 11   15 14 13 12 11 10 09 08 07 06

Contents

Foreword

Some may think that *church* and *ministry* are not among current issues that deserve attention. But the term *church* is being applied loosely today to every religious group, regardless of its tenets or spiritual orientation, and religious groups are continuing to proliferate at a rate that defies categorizing or describing them. One such attempt—*Profiles in Belief*—required four volumes, and religious groups continue to appear. Luther's view of *church* is quite diferent, growing out of a unique biblically based concept, with very practical implications for the present.

Likewise, *ministry* has been the subject of much debate in established church bodies, with far-reaching implications for the status and role of those who serve in organized religious groups. How they function depends upon their understanding of *ministry*. Again, Luther's biblically based view has been in need of explanation and definition.

The author mined the voluminous writings of Luther to clarify Luther's understanding of *church* and *ministry* and has shown that, centuries later, Luther's views have shaped specific church bodies such as The Lutheran Church—Missouri Synod and particularly its leading founder, C. F. W. Walther. Even within that body, *church* and *ministry* are being discussed much today. Some Lutheran bodies have viewed these subjects differently, as their history also shows, and the same can be said of other mainline Christian denominations, both Protestant and Catholic.

Part 3 of this book is a major contribution to an understanding of *church* and *ministry*. Because of Luther's massive writings and the need to interpret what the Scriptures say on these subjects, the comments of the three dozen people whom the author interviewed lend great interest and further clarification. Although the interviewees may differ with Luther, amazingly, they agree as to what Luther says about *church* and *ministry*. The same is true of the "other interpreters" in the following chapter.

While the reader may differ with the author's analyses and/or with his interpretation of Luther, the following must be among our overriding common concerns: Biblical teachings related to the issue must be clearly defined without compromise; biblical doctrine needs to be distinguished from the practice or application of doctrine; and information and alternative choices must be carefully considered and clearly understood.

This book is the culmination of years of study and more than three decades of teaching Lutheran theology. It also grew out of years of practical experience in the parish, service with distinction as a United States Navy chaplain in World War II, and membership on various theological committees, such as the Lutheran/Reformed and Lutheran/Methodist Dialogues. Experience and scholarship produced an accomplished theologian with balance and perspective.

In view of present-day efforts to undermine, if not to destroy, the church—and other institutions of society—and in view of the serious discussion of *church* and *ministry* taking place within Lutheranism and other denominations, the significance of this volume is unquestionable.

The Publisher

Preface

Ah, the preface! One could wish that prefaces had never been invented, according to one author. Books used to just start. But we will perforce abide by prevailing custom, albeit with brevity. Such procedure conforms at least to Francis Bacon's dictum that "to use too many circumstances ere one come to matter is wearisome; to use none at all, is blunt."

The subjects of church and ministry remain at the heart of contemporary Christian theology. To say this is not to claim that there is special significance to what follows; it is rather to assert that these two doctrines continue to be the framework within which the rest of Christian doctrine finds its setting, or portrayal. Without quibble the central article of Christian faith is Christ's redeeming work for sinners. Were this great truth' not there, neither the church nor the ministry would have any *raison' d'etre*. But now that by God's grace it is there, the full pertinence and vital place of church and ministry very plainly appear as God's chosen context for proclaiming the Word of reconciliation, the Gospel, to the world.

The Reformation brought all this into focus once more. It was Luther's signal contribution. He spoke for evangelical reform and realignment, not that either Word, or Gospel, or church, or ministry had completely ceased to be; but it was a case of serious distortion, of Christian teaching terribly out of focus.

Christian doctrine is correctly thought of as a unified whole. Luther argues for this point. Christian articles of faith possess an inherent harmony, linked harmoniously together like pearls on the golden strand of the sinner's justification by God's grace for Christ's sake through faith. What this means, among other things, is that no part of Christian doctrine can in reality be touched without in some way involving the rest.

This is especially true of the doctrines under consideration here. Not only are they front and center in contemporary discussion, but church and ministry tend to be misunderstood, often grossly misused, concepts in today's ecumenical milieu. They are in fact key issues for the whole of Christian theology in our day, the framework within which all other articles of faith take their shape, either *on* the side of Scripture, or *to* the side of it.

This Luther saw. His crystal clear teaching on church and

ministry may be viewed as fundamental to the whole Reformation cause. Thus the present volume, which concentrates and pinnacles in Luther's thought in each chapter, is actually more than a narrow, limited look at Luther. As Heiko Oberman reminded me, when I discussed with him the beginning of my task several years ago, it will ultimately have to be a kind of wide, inclusive theology of Luther by its very nature.

Yet there is no presumptive illusion under which I have worked. The individual who claims to having written the definitive, ultimate, or even penultimate "theology of Luther" for all time, universally recognized, is yet to make his appearance. It is likely that he will never appear. The subject is too vast. Both the friends of Luther, who embrace him and stand on his shoulders, and the opponents of Luther, who seek to show his weak spots and cut him down at the knees, be it ever so gently, all demonstrate this fact only, that they are dealing with a man so complex—clear and lucid though he is in every thought! and so vast! even when the monumental Weimar edition of Luther's works is complete the story will undoubtedly go on!!—that they must be frank to admit, that they have only made a beginning. More than that, therefore, cannot be claimed for the present effort.

Moreover, and quite frankly, I have modeled the format of this book after the rightly famous and widely-used and respected work of C. F. W. Walther, *Die Stimme unserer Kirche in der Frage von Kirche und Amt*—usually referred to as *Kirche und Amt*. It appeared first in 1852 and then was reissued in slightly expanded editions several times thereafter, the last in 1911, the centennial of Walther's birth. The doctrines of church and ministry were at the very heart of the identity crisis which he and the struggling band of Saxon Lutheran immigrants confronted in this new land. Were they the church? Could they lay claim to saying that the church was in their midst? Did they have a valid ministry? What in fact was the ministry? To whom did the Keys belong? Walther searched diligently in Holy Scripture, the writings of the fathers, and especially in Luther's ample treatises. They were like gold mines to him. Answers were not long in coming, though the defense of the teaching went on during the ensuing years. The present volume could indeed be dedicated to the memory of this extremely talented consistent theologian, who had so carefully combed through the Word of God and Luther, also through the Lutheran Confessions and some of the great Lutheran teachers of dogmatics. The debt is obvious and readily admitted.

Yet there are some differences unique to my research into the subject. These pertain especially to the greater and more widely ranging concentration on Luther's works. I have tried to mine these even more thoroughly, from all periods of Luther's life and production. Though this claim is made, in comparison with Walther's citations of Luther on the subjects of church and ministry, I will be quick to state that I have found nothing in my research which would demonstrate that Walther either missed any of Luther's accents, or in any way left an incomplete or distorted picture. The facts are rather that one consistent theologian stood firmly on the shoulders of another, Walther on Luther.

If there is any uniqueness, therefore, to my efforts, it will lie in the direction of a portrait of Luther on church and ministry more fully etched, with the addition of some subtle nuances of which he alone was capable, and, hopefully, therefore also a more complete picture of the man and his theology. While I have the temerity to claim, or at least very much hope, that my work might be viewed as a contribution to Luther studies, it was also throughout my purpose to write with the average person in mind. This conformed with the precedent and pattern set by Luther and Walther; they both had great and loving pastoral hearts. Since souls were at stake, neither of them could ever approach any task in merely detached or academic spirit. I have striven for the same goal.

Deus adjuvat

I wish to acknowledge with thanks the efforts of several individuals who helped to get the manuscript ready for publication: Ken Schurb, for assistance with the index; Linda Newman, Beth Thompson, Judy Meyer for the typing; Trudy Behning and Marge Gruber for the camera-ready formatting of the text.

Finally, mention should also be made, with thanks, of the post-doctoral J. W. Behnken award of $10,000, in 1978, courtesy of the Aid Association for Lutherans, Appleton, Wisconsin, which provided the wherewithal for the travel and colloquies sketched in Part III, Chap. 1.

Abbreviations

WA	*D. Martin Luthers Werke:* Kritische Gesamtausgabe. Weimar, 1833 ff.
WA,TR	*D. Martin Luthers Werke:* Kritische Gesamtausgabe. Tischreden. Weimar, 1912 ff.
WA, BR	*D. Martin Luthers Werke:* Kritische Gesamtausgabe. Briefwechsel. Weimar, 1930 ff.
LW	*Luther's Works:* American Edition, ed., J. Pelikan & H. Lehmann. 55 vols. St. Louis: Concordia & Philadelphia: Fortress, 1955 ff.
St.L.	*D. Martin Luthers sämmliche Schriften.* J. Walch, ed. 2nd edition. 25 vols. St. Louis: Concordia, 1880-1910.
Triglot	*Concordia.* The Symbolical Books of the Evangelical Lutheran Church (German, Latin, English) F. Bente, ed., with general introduction. St. Louis: Concordia, 1921. Quotations are from this translation.
KA	Walther, C.F.W., *Die Stimme Unserer Kirche in der Frage von Kirche und Amt.* Zwickau, 1911. Jubilee edition (4th). First published in 1852. (English trans. by J.T. Mueller, Concordia Publishing House, St. Louis, 1987.)
DT	Schmid, Heinrich, *The Doctrinal Theology of the Evangelical Lutheran Church.* Trans., Charles A. Hay. 4th ed. rev. Philadelphia, 1899.

PART I

Chapter 1

What Is the Church?

The Church most simply defined "is, namely, holy believers and lambs who hear the voice of their shepherd." With this statement in the *Smalcald Articles* (III, xii) Luther was right on target with the Scriptures. In characteristically artless and uncomplicated manner he stated the boundaries and told the distinctive properties of Christ's church, His holy body, His faithful fold. Plainly, in this fold there are no imposters, no pseudo-sheep, no unbelievers, no hypocrites. The Lord knows without fail who are His. Of this Holy Scripture leaves no doubt. (John 10:27-29; 11:51f.; 15:6; Rom. 8:9; 1 Cor. 3:16f.; Eph. 1:22f.; 5:23-27; 1 John 2:19).

Referring to the Apostles' Creed in his famous treatise of 1539, *On The Councils and the Church*, Luther states that "the creed clearly indicates what the church is, namely, a communion of saints, that is a crowd (*Haufe*) or assembly of people who are Christians," "a people with a special call," and therefore, "not just *ecclesia* (assembly), but *sancta catholica Christiana*," that is, a holy and catholic Christian church.[1] "He who does not believe and is not holy and righteous, does not belong to the Holy Christian Church."[2] "The church is not wood and stone," states Luther in a sermon for Second Christmas Day, "but the company of believing people, (who) surely have Christ in their midst."[3]

The Lutheran Confessions bear the imprint of Luther's hand, directly or indirectly. The Augsburg Confession (Art. VIII) is a case in point. Its chief author, Melanchthon, draws on Luther's "Great Confession" of 1528 to say that "*the Church* properly is the congregation of saints and true believers."[4] Very early in his career as Reformer, during the crucial years between 1512 and 1519, Luther had come to rudimentary clarity on the Reformation's and Christianity's central article that the sinner is justified before God,

1

sola gratia/fide. He had moved from *theologia gloriae,* the theology of glory, which placed the emphasis on man's efforts in gaining God's favor. Monasticism was the classic example of what Luther came to call the grossest form of idolatry. So subtle was this pious pursuit that its exponents would have been the first to object, deeply offended at the charge. But Luther penetrated through the fictitious veneer and repudiated the system for its gross distortion and obfuscation of Scripture's core teaching, punching through the overlayers to uncover theology of the cross, *theologia crucis,* which focused on Christ's redemptory, vicarious sacrifice for all sins and all sinners. It was the heart of the saving truth which underlay membership in Christ's church.

In his treatise on the Papacy at Rome, 1520, Luther articulated clearly, really for the first time in public writing, the true nature of the church. It was his response to Alveld, Romanist theologian of Leipzig. What is it that makes a Christian? Luther asked. Being with Rome under the papacy? Or being under Christ? Luther squared things with the Scriptures: Christ is the true and only Head of the Church. The church by its very nature must be, and is, a spiritual community, the sum total of believers built upon Christ, its Head. Moreover, Christ does not require anywhere that His church assume an absolute external, visible form or structure, as claimed by Rome. In Luther's mind it was an abuse to call all church affairs and possessions under the Roman aegis "spiritual." The pope cannot give spiritual life and power to his members; not even Peter could do that; only Christ is able, as true Head. How can a mere man, asks Luther, even the pope, rule over a thing whose nature he does not understand?[5]

Rome would like "very much to be regarded as the church," but it was holy merely by its own standards, argues Luther, and was "not entitled to the name 'Christian church' or 'Christian people'" by simple identification. The Holy Spirit sanctifies His people "*per redemptionem, vivificationem et sanctificationem,*" that is, by redeeming, vivifying (regenerating), and sanctifying it. In the Romanist view, on the other hand, you need "just throw a surplice over your head and you are holy in accord with the Roman church's holiness." His stinging satire hit hard at the distorted, sub-standard view of the church, its membership, and its true holiness.[6]

In the Genesis Commentary, completed in late life (1545), Luther pointed to Abraham, Genesis 15:6, as the spiritual leader of the church in that day, and affirmed that already then they who believe were the church.[7] It has to do with the "chief article of our faith," that a man is saved by faith alone (*sola fide*) in the Gospel; for God hears all who plead *sola gratia propter Christum*, by grace alone for Christ's sake, whether in Abraham's house or under some tree, it makes no difference.[8] "We who believe are the church," like Jacob. Believers have the Word and the promise, they have been baptized, and they cling to a promise that will not deceive them. "This is the proper and chief doctrine of the church. It has been handed down by the Holy Spirit. The world and the flesh do not know it. It teaches us that we are lords and heirs of eternal life in no other way than the way in which Jacob was an heir of the blessing."[9]

Jacob's sons were far from models of piety, including especially Judah through whom the promised Messiah would come; but the ancient promise, reaching back to God's gracious Word to Eve (Gen. 3:15), transcended even his unfaithfulness. It persisted because of God's faithfulness. "To be the church and to rule and teach men for their salvation, to be in the people of God and in the number of Abel and the servants of God—this is the primogeniture," to have the birthright in a truly preeminent sense.[10] "The church is not wood and stone but the assembly of people who believe in Christ."[11] The Scriptures which bring us Christ are really in comparison to the Savior Himself but like the "diapers of Christ." This by no means demeans them, but underscores the truth that the Gospel opens up the Scriptures, or is their heart.[12] Only the Scriptures reveal the church's real nature.

Perhaps one of the sharpest, most polemical writings Luther leveled against the corrupt, deceitful pretension of the Roman papacy came towards the end of his life when all hope of a genuinely free council for an impartial hearing of the Reformation's charges had faded. *Against the Roman Papacy, An Institution of the Devil*, 1545,[13] is still offensive to polite ears. The pope "has conjured horse manure into our mouths," Luther snorts, and expects us to swallow that he is supreme lord over all things, secular as well as spiritual; that popes are beyond recall or deposing; and that popes bestow upon kings power to rule. Deep revulsion and disgust stuck in Luther's craw over the effect that such pretentious bombast had upon the church.

Christ's church is cast in a different mold from and quite

unlike Rome's morphology. Christ, Luther stated, has only one church in the world, as we confess in the Creed. It transcends every human machination. Its builder is Christ, and it is very real. "Wherever there is a church, anywhere in the whole world, it still has no other gospel and Scripture, baptism and communion, faith and Spirit, Christ and God, Lord's Prayer and prayer, hope and eternal life, than we have here in our church in Wittenberg." It follows, moreover, Luther asserted, that "everything belonging to the church is equal," except for the gifts which God bestows upon His church and individuals in it variously, 1 Cor. 12 and Rom. 12.[14] "Christendom has no head and can have none except the only Son of God, Jesus Christ" and "the dear Lord knows of no more than one church in the whole world."[15]

To the essence of the church belong these attributes: it is *una*, or one, numerically and in unity; *sancta*, or holy; *apostolica*, or apostolic, built on the apostles' doctrine; and *catholica*, universal or catholic, embracing true believers everywhere throughout the world who are tied to and built on Christ by faith. Luther summed it all up in his extremely popular *Personal Prayer Book* of 1522, in which he described the ingredients of the Christian's faith and life, writing as regards the church:

> I believe that throughout the whole wide world there is only one holy, universal, Christian church, which is nothing other than the gathering or congregation of saints—pious believers on earth. This church is gathered, preserved, and governed by the same Holy Spirit and is given daily increase by means of the sacraments and the word of God.

> I believe that no one can be saved who is not in this gathering or community, harmoniously sharing the same faith with it, the same word, sacraments, hope and love. And that no Jew, heretic, pagan, or sinner can be saved along with this community unless he becomes reconciled with it and unites with it in full agreement in all things . . . I believe that there is forgiveness of sin nowhere else than in this community and that beyond it nothing can help to gain it—no good deeds no matter how many or how great they might be; and that within this community nothing can invalidate the forgiveness.[16]

Nothing compares with the perfect symmetry, unity, wholeness of Christ's church, unless it be God's own essential oneness. Christ is the church's head, and it is His body.[17] Its oneness warrants and suffers no cracks or fissures; for though it has "many members, yet the many members do not divide the unity,"[18] Luther affirms in his *Romans Commentary*. In his "Great Confession" of 1528, on the Lord's Supper, he compares the unity and communion of the earthly elements (bread and wine) and the heavenly (the true Body and Blood of Christ) to "the unity of Christians in one spiritual body of Christ through one spirit, faith, love, and the cross, etc."[19] "But the words used in connection with this sacrament," he wisely cautions, in the same context, "shall and must express with simplicity what they say," lest their meaning be lost by turning or causing them to have some sort of symbolic sense or function.

The church is *sancta*, or holy, because, built on Christ, it draws its holiness from Christ.[20] By and of itself "it knows that it can err and blunder and that it must amend and change such blunder and error according to God's Word, which alone cannot err."[21] Not by one's own work or effort, therefore, but by God's doing it is holy, for "nothing is holy unless it has the Word and name of God."[22] So, when I say, "I believe in the holy church," Luther explains, I am stating that this is true not "if I look at my own person or that of my neighbor, but if I look at Christ, who is the Propitiator and Cleanser of the church; then it is completely holy."[23] This latter statement is recorded in Luther's *Galatian Commentary*, often called the "Magna Charta of Christian Liberty." The word "church" after all is a spiritual word, Luther notes in his *Commentary on the First Epistle of Peter*, and its holiness is tied to these truths: that "you have the Word of God"; that "heaven is yours"; and that "you have become truly pious and holy through Christ."[24] The context is 1 Pet. 2:9, where Christians are declared to be a holy priesthood, because Christ "wants to have a spiritual building, that is, the Christian congregation"; and thus "only those are the holy and spiritual priesthood who are true Christians and are built on the Stone," which is Christ.[25] With reason Luther could say in 1530, as he writes his commentary on Psalm 118 (a psalm he treasured as his own):

I hope that by this time almost everybody knows that whoever prides himself on being a Christian must also take pride in being holy and righteous. Since Christendom is holy, a Christian must also be righteous and holy, or he is not a Christian. All Scripture calls Christians holy and righteous, as does also this verse (20). This is not boastfulness; it is a necessary confession and an article of faith. . . The whole Christian Church is holy, not by its own work but in Christ and through Christ's holiness, as St. Paul says: "He has cleansed her by the washing of water with the Word" (Eph. 5:26). Anyone who hesitates to boast and confess that he is holy and righteous, is actually saying: "I am not baptized. I am not a Christian. I do not believe in Christ. I do not believe that Christ died for me. I do not believe that he took away my sins. I do not believe that his blood has cleansed me, or that it can cleanse me. In short, I do not believe a word of what God has declared of Christ and all Scripture testified." What kind of person thinks or says such things?[26]

Indeed, what person could ever talk that way, to denigrate what God Himself has made holy through Christ's precious blood and sacrifice? The church's and the individual Christian's holiness is real, as real as Christ's atoning sacrifice for sin is real.

The church, moreover, is *apostolica*, not by virtue of fabricated claims of unction or succession flowing to it through some unbroken line from the apostles to the clergy, as a kind of higher spiritual estate, but simply because it is built on the doctrine, or teaching, of the apostles (and prophets). These, Luther says, "are the mountains of God and the cedars of God."[27] Thus Israel was "a shadow of the church to come." Theirs, the apostles' and the prophets', was the God-inspired Word on which the Lord would build His church.

Christ's church is also catholica, catholic or universal, in that it enfolds all true believers. With justice "we are concerned that the authority of the holy catholic church stand unimpaired."[28] Luther's name is often coupled to the tragic dissolution of the unity of the medieval church under the Roman banner. Nothing was farther from the truth. He was no rebel. If he was, he was an obedient rebel who put loyalty to God's Word ahead of party loyalty or ecclesiastical structure. He saw through the fictitious claim to catholicity pretended by Rome. In his "Great Confession" (1528) he expressed the church's existence, or being, as also its true catholicity, in clearest terms. This statement is the immediate precursor for the *Schwabach Articles* of 1529 (October), and these in turn for *Augsburg Confession* Article VII. Hence its great importance and pertinence here.

> I believe that there is one holy Christian Church on earth, that is, the community or number or assembly of all Christians in all the world, the one bride of Christ, and his spiritual body of which he is the only head. The bishops or priests are not her heads or lords or bridegrooms, but servants, friends, and—as the word "bishop" implies—superintendents, guardians, or stewards.

> This Christian Church exists not only in the realm of the Roman Church or pope, but in all the world, as the prophets foretold that the gospel of Christ would spread throughout the world, Ps. 2:8; Ps. 19:4. Thus this Christian Church is physically dispersed among pope, Turks, Persians, Tartars, but spiritually gathered in one gospel and faith, under one head, that is, Jesus Christ.[29]

As Luther herewith expressed the bottom-line meaning of catholicity he placed his finger squarely on the right or Scriptural way of looking upon the church's ecumenicity. There is no other church than the one that is the beloved bride of Christ! The church is as wide and broad as the world is wide and broad; but it is as restricted, singular, and prized as the bride to the Bridegroom. Christ jealously keeps her to Himself, inviolate and inviolable.

The true church is not, as the Romanists boasted, in their "numbers and the strength," not in the appearance of "being the apostles' successors," not in "having governed the church so long," nor because "they cultivate great holiness and the worship of God." Both sides could argue in this way, Luther allows, on who is the true church; but the only arbiter of this question is Christ Himself. Both sides might also claim to have the Holy Spirit, but the true church will be known in accord with Christ's promise: "When the Comforter comes, whom the Father will give you through intercession, you will surely know Him and have Him with you." Why? asks Luther. "Because He will preach solely of Me and will tell you all that I have from the Father." These things you will then "proclaim publicly by word of mouth," and you may then be certain that because you accept and preach this message, you surely have and know the Holy Spirit, who alone glorifies Me through your lips and your office."[30]

Moreover, as Luther adds in the same context, "it will then be found that the great multitude, which boasts of being the church and of having the Holy Spirit, who preaches through it, is a false proclamation and a lying spirit, the devil's church and vessel, even though it decks and adorns itself with names like God, Christ, Holy Spirit, and Christendom."[31] Because of their silencing of the Gospel, the Romanists, may claim "that they are the church and the church cannot err," Luther avers, but the facts are that it was "John Hus and Jerome of Prague," whom they condemned, who "were true and holy members of the holy church."[32] This significant judgment occurs in Luther's commentary on Gen. 6:3 as he distinguishes between the "sons of God" (believers) and the unbelieving "daughters (or children) of men."[33]

It is characteristic, or in the nature, of the royal priesthood of believers, who constitute the church, that they be "prophets or sons and pupils of the prophet." This does not mean, cautions Luther, "that future events be revealed to us," as charismatic or *Schwaermer*-like spirits claim. "For the office of a prophet," Luther states simply, "it is enough that we understand Scripture and are able to teach others and also to help one another with prayers."[34] "Therefore the name 'prophet' belongs equally to all Christians, and he who denies this also denies that he has been baptized and has been instructed through the Word."[35] Men like Elijah and Abraham, as also the inspired prophets of God in the Old Testament, had the Spirit in more abundant and unique manner, Luther allows; but they "did not have a different Spirit," for we have their Scriptures through which the Spirit deals with and instructs us.

Everything turns on the church's relationship to the Gospel. It is this fact which justifies the term universal Christendom, because "the gospel alone is accepted by Christians throughout the world."[36] The citizens of Christ's church or kingdom are earthly, but the kingdom itself is heavenly, not perishable, but enduring. It is "the kingdom of heaven and eternal life, truth and peace, joy, righteousness, safety, salvation, and all good"—because of the Word, which endures, like Christ. It is like silver and gold, not clay.[37]

Knowledge of Christ and church membership go hand in hand "as a result of (God's) promise and because of pure mercy."[38] Adam and Eve were the first members of the church because they trusted God's promise concerning the Messiah.[39] This promise continued down through the patriarchs and God's chosen people, but God's "accidental mercy" reached out to those outside this stem too, for example, outside the stem of Judah.[40] Cain lacked this spiritual blessing because he rejected the promise. It is the believing "church that has the promises of grace which are eternal."[41]

Where faith in the promise is lacking there is no church. The unbelieving heart cannot be in the church, even though it "put on a right and believing face," for "the church is one in spirit," and a perverse heart is turned in on itself (*incurvatus in se*). Unbelievers, or hypocrites, cannot belong to Christ. Those that rejected the Gospel at Christ's time were not in the church. "For the prophets and the Gospels come together in one faith, in one spirit, in one root of truth, in one faith, in one humility," Luther states as he draws Old and New Testament believers together in one entity. "The church dwells in this life in the midst of two mountains," the Old and New Testament.[42] "The body of the church will be full, fat, and crammed with members who are sound and full of faith" through the "efficacy of the Word."

This true church is to be understood, therefore, as a spiritual assembly. But it has its corporeal side or counterpart. However, not every assembly purporting to be the church is really so, but only the believers; thus the wheat without the chaff, a holy kingdom, not a secular realm.[43] The church's holiness, strength, magnificence, which no one really sees but God, has to do with faith. "The reason for this is this rule, that we are not righteous by our works, but righteous works are done by us who have first become righteous" by faith.[44] Its members are sinners still, but sinners who know and trust in the Savior.

Work-righteous "saints" would be intolerable, not to say inconceivable, in Luther's book. "God preserve me from a Christian Church in which everyone is a saint" in a perfectionist, Pelagian sort of way, Luther sighs.[45] "I want to be and remain in the church and little flock of the faint-hearted, the feeble, and the ailing, who feel and recognize the wretchedness of their sins, who believe in the forgiveness of sins, and who suffer persecution for the sake of the Word which they confess and teach purely and without adulteration."[46]

Even more strongly Luther asserts concerning the counterfeit "saints" that Christ "blows them all away." On the other hand, when repentant "sinners enter, they do not remain sinners," for Christ "spreads His cloak over their sins and forgives."[47] The point simply is that Christians, though personally imperfect, are perfect, pure, and righteous in Christ.

Sins are always latent in God's saints; but they do not dominate, even though at times they break out, much to the believing sinner's sadness, discomfiture, remorse, regret. But there is forgiveness with God through Christ! In that forgiveness they live and find strength for holy living.

It is this Word of forgiveness, the Gospel, that builds or creates the church, not the church the Word. Luther notes how God focused Adam's attention on His Word in connection with the trees in the garden of Eden. "Here we have the establishment of the church before there was any government of the home and of the state," by the Word of God.[48] Since the Hebrew word used in Scripture speaks of God "building" for Adam his helpmeet, Eve, it occurs to Luther that she thus becomes an analogy for the church, Christ's bride, which, too, is built by God.[49]

Moreover, God's purposes for His church are far-ranging: "Because the church is established by the Word of God, it is certain that man was created for an immortal and spiritual life."[50] "Not the stones, construction, gorgeous silver and gold make a church beautiful and holy," Luther therefore concludes, "but the Word of God and sound preaching," even as with Abram.[51] Then, as now, and also at David's time, the church must be seen as "established by the fingers of God,"[52] not by the fingers or hands of men.[53]

God's Word may seem like a feeble instrument for building, but it is not. God the Holy Spirit works quietly but effectively through the Word. He will have His children. Yes, "God desires to have children," even though at times it appears as though God were "sterile," and unable to beget children, Luther observes in commentary on Isaiah 66. In fact, "He will have a very large number of children in all nations."[54] It is faith which God's Word prompts, and faith trusts or believes even when it cannot see the reason for doing so, like Abraham.[55]

Those who think that the church consists of certain usages, ceremonies, and orders, are replacing "I believe" with "I see," Luther opines.[56] He reminds his readers that in the Creed we confess, "I *believe*" in the holy Christian Church, the communion of saints.[57] Precisely because of his faith which trusts God's promises, "Abraham is described as a friend of God who talks intimately with Him; and God as his friend is pleased with everything he does."[58] In the same context Luther notes that it was faith in God's Word that determined that only two out of the original mass of people who left Egypt would enter Canaan, Joshua and Caleb.

Nothing is "more precious," "nothing better," in the eyes of God than His beloved, His church.[59] Outside of it there is no salvation, as is the case of "those who forsake the church," since "outside (of it) there certainly is no repentance or remission."[60] Luther is, of course, speaking of the *una sancta*, not some earthly, institutional claimant to such status. He heightens the pitch even more by averring that the true church, the *una sancta*, cannot err and in it there can be no fault. This he states in conjunction with his *Theses Concerning Faith and Law*, 1535,[61] but he repeats it at many places.[62] In thesis 61 he states: "After the apostles no one should claim that he cannot err in the faith, except only the universal church."[63]

It is in the same set of theses that the famous dictum occurs against those who might try to twist the Scriptures against Christ or the faith in any way. "If the adversaries press the Scriptures against Christ, we urge Christ against the Scriptures" (Thesis 49). Lest modern Bible detractors take comfort from this in a wrongful way, they should note that Luther will also reverse the dialectic in favor of Scripture's indisputable authority: "Stick to the Word of God. Ignore every other—whether it is devoid of Christ, in the name of Christ, or against Christ, or whether it is issued in any other way."[64] It is self-evident that Luther connects errorlessness, or faultlessness, to things of God's own special creation, like the Word, and so also the *una sancta*, the holy Christian church; God's own perfection is the warranty in each case. Should anyone try to substitute something else, or claim such errorlessness for an earthly, human agency, Luther advises: "You should answer: It is true, the Christian Church cannot err; but listen, dear friend, let us note which is the true Christian Church ."[65]

In Luther's thinking and writing nothing serves quite as well to portray the church's true nature as the Scripture's own picturesque figures of speech. These graphic etchings immediately conjure up to the mind's eye what it is that belongs to the church's true nature. With his vast knowledge of Holy Writ nimbly at work, Luther leads the reader swiftly and engagingly from one to the other. The church is

Christ's mystical, or spiritual, body[66]
The woman's seed[67]
The Kingdom of heaven[68]
        of God[69]
        of Christ[70]
The bride[71]
    "How great is this ardor"[72]
    "These are great and incomparable words, to hear that Jesus Christ is the Bridegroom and the church is the bride,. . . by which we are made participants."[73]
The widow of Christ—in view of the condition which the church appears to have in the world.[74]
The ark[75]
Canaan, the land of promise[76]
God's pleasure garden—"David. . . paints a fine picture of it. It has His inexpressible treasure: the holy Sacraments, the dear Word, with which it instructs, governs, restores, and comforts His flock."[77]
God's flock[78]
God's dove[79]
Our mother[80]
    "It is our mother hen and we are its chicks."[81]
Sarah[82]
Building, or temple, of the Lord[83]
Royal priesthood[84]
Mt. Zion[85]
Body of Christ, strong and feared by Satan[86]
Hospital[87]
Forsaken spouse, it seems, but the fact is that Christ stands by her[88]
Jerusalem[89]
Vineyard of the Lord[90]

Luther sums up the church's glorious titles in a beautiful commentary on Psalm 65:

> The psalmist gives a number of names to the same church. "Zion," because it observes heavenly things; "Jerusalem," because it has peace and perceives it; "courts," because it is the preparation of future glory and the entrance to it; "house" of God, because God dwells in it; "temple" because God is worshiped in it; "earth," because it is a pilgrim in this life; "river" of God, because it gushes forth from God continually with ever new believers that are born. As from a fountain the waters flow forth constantly, so the saints are born of God in His Words. (Our Fountain is Christ, our Head.) "Fields," because the church has been spread abroad among all nations and made manifest to the whole world; "wilderness," because it despises the things that are in the world; "valley," because of humility; "sheep," because of a constant self-offering and mortification. Again, "the crown of the year of goodness," because it will stand until the end of the world; "tilled field," because it is cultivated and always bears the fruit of merits. You can look for others if you like. Also, the church is likened to "hills," because of the excellence of the righteousness raised above human nature. Add a fifteenth, namely, that is "sprouting," because it is always in bloom and never withers through sluggishness and lukewarmness."[91]

Finally, as regards symbolic names of the church, Luther senses a very interesting allusion or analogy, which ought not be omitted, in Psalm 68:31. "The church" states Luther, "is symbolized by the name 'Ethiopia.'" The reference is self-explaining, "because of the blackness of sin and because the church confesses itself to be black." "The Jews," however, says Luther, "are called Lebanon, because they regarded themselves as white and holy, while the church says: 'I am black but beautiful' (Song of Solomon 1:5), that is, because I acknowledge myself to be black, I am beautiful." The repentant sinner who acknowledges his sin "justifies God in His words (Ps. 51:4) and thus gives glory to God, and by that very fact he is now himself already righteous." He sees the blackness of his heart and says: "I will confess my transgressions to the Lord. And

Thou forgavest, etc. (Ps. 32:5) Therefore to confess sin and to be righteous are the same thing."[92]

Christ will preserve His church. It is very dear to Him.[93] Because it is built on Christ, who is its Cornerstone,[94] the church will endure forever.[95] The false church cannot and will not endure.[96] God's flock and its doctrine persist; God strengthens and upholds it against all foes, against Satan and Satan's kingdom, in all time of trouble.[97] Many claims are made, falsely, by those who "boast of being God's people," or "Abraham's children" spiritually, but the fact is that "only those who hear My Word" are God's children in truth.[98] It is these whom He will preserve. To boast that you are God's creature will not save you. God made the River Elbe, He made apples, He made trees, He made you; but that will not save you. What counts is to belong to Christ by faith in Him. "This is the glory of the church," declares Luther, "that it has no teacher and bishop but Christ who alone rules over His church through His Spirit and His Gospel."[99]

Luther argues at some length in the Large Catechism that the word for church, *ekklesia*, "means really nothing else than a common assembly," or preferably *Gemeinde*, or congregation, "or best of all and most clearly holy Christendom," that is, *eine heilige Christenheit.* He turns away the idea that it should be taken to mean merely *Gemeinschaft*, fellowship. Church in New Testament usage is thus a passive concept, a gathering God has forged.[100] The church is not any sort of gathering, voluntarily assembled and attached. It is Christ's own flock, which He Himself gathers through His Word, "a little group and congregation of pure saints, under one head, Christ, (and) called together by the Holy Ghost in one faith." By that gracious calling Luther believes that he—and every other believer—is "a part and member of the same," and that he shares and is "joint owner of all the goods it possesses," the spiritual treasures of forgiveness and life everlasting.[101]

This gathering or congregation is more than a mere "outward government," Melanchthon explained in the Apology to the Augsburg Confession drawing on Luther's insights. It is a spiritual entity, "the living body of Christ," formed through the regenerating activity of the Holy Spirit. But when it is defined and described as a spiritual realm, lacking apparent and outward physical dimensions or boundaries, Melanchthon affirms that it is as real as God is real. By no means "are we dreaming of a Platonic state," he protests. The church's presence or existence may be spotted or located through its marks, or "signs of the church," Word and sacraments. These do not constitute the church, but they mark where "a fellowship of faith and of the Holy Ghost in hearts" is to be found, the communion or congregation of saints gathered around "the same Gospel or doctrine."[102]

Martin Chemnitz lived in the generation after Luther. Within the Lutheran church he is affectionately known as the "second Martin," a sobriquet accorded him by his Catholic opponents who understood and respected his key role in sustaining the Reformation's thrust. Chemnitz was one of the chief architects of the *Formula of Concord*, 1577, and thus played a pivotal role in helping restore peace and unity to a church severely torn by more than thirty years of bitter theological dissension. He was rightly called a pastors' pastor, since he devoted himself so assiduously to in-service training of the clergy in the Braunschweig territorial church of which he was superintendent. One of the gems issuing from his facile pen was a little handbook on Christian doctrine, the *Enchiridion*. Like Luther, on the subject of the church's essence or nature, Chemnitz notes Scripture's familiar figure of speech in defining the church as the body of Christ over which the Savior is the true Head. Citing Ephesians 1, 4, and 5, also Colossians 2 and 1 Corinthians 12, Chemnitz draws the inevitable conclusion that "he that is not a member of this body, whose Head is Christ, cannot be saved."[103]

John Gerhard, distinguished dean of the orthodox Lutheran theologians of the 17th century, likewise described the church as the "fellowship of those who are welded together by the bond of the Holy Spirit in true faith and in true love." When they are called "saints," Gerhard adds, this by no means should be understood in perfectionist manner, as though in this life Christian believers are ever sinless. The intent is only to underscore the fact that "hypocrites are not really members of the true church, even though outwardly they confess the same faith with the saints and use the same sacraments."[104]

John Quenstedt, Gerhard's nephew and theological heir, repeated the same fundamental emphasis upon the church's true nature as "the sum total of the saints and those who truly believe." For this reason Holy Scripture accords the church affectionate names or titles, states Quenstedt, like "Christ's beloved bride," "Christ's mystical body," "Christ's fold," and "mother not of the dead but of the living, or truly believing."[105]

Abraham Calov, one of Lutheran orthodoxy's sharpest theological minds, nicely disabused people's minds of thinking that there were two churches, one invisible and one visible, "one of saints, the other a mixture." We have to note, says Calov, that the word "church" is "used homonymously, on the one hand, for the total number of believers, (and) on the other hand, for an assembly in which hypocrites are mixed together with believers, "but who do not actually constitute any part of the true church.[106]

The clarity and consistency of these statements in defining the church's true essence are all traceable to Luther, who in turn lived so totally out of the Holy Scripture and its teaching. He was able to translate these concepts into the average man's idiom. None could miss his meaning. "It is plain (from his *On the Papacy in Rome*, 1520) that Christendom is a spiritual community (*Gemeine*) which is to be numbered with the worldly community just as little as minds with bodies and faith with temporal goods." Luther distinguished between the invisible church and the visible, between what he called "a spiritual assembly of souls in one faith" and the external grouping together, for example, of persons who have "assembled together with others at Leipzig or Wittenberg." Of these, says Luther, "I cannot tell at all whether or not" they believe, for true faith is known alone by God who sees and knows the hearts.

"This is the way Holy Scripture speaks of the holy church and of Christendom." The invisible church is "natural, basic essential, and true, (and) we shall call (it) 'spiritual, internal Christendom.'" Thus Luther approved the distinction between the invisible church in which only true believers are present, and the visible church, or "Christendom," to which hypocrites may attach themselves. The latter is "man-made and external, (and) we shall call (it) 'physical, external Christendom.'" It numbers in its midst "all those who are true and real Christians or not," but "it never really exists without some people who are also true Christians," and who are gathered by God through His Word into the first, the internal or invisible community, or congregation (*Gemeine*), of true sheep under the one Shepherd.

Thus in the same context Luther is prepared to "call the two churches by two distinct names," but he intends only to indicate thereby the two ways which we who are limited by our powers to discern faith in the hearts must speak of the church. This is in full accord with Scripture, he believes.[107] Visible Christianity embraces believers and hypocrites alike in its midst; the invisible church is precisely what its name implies, the totality of true believers who are numbered in Christ's holy church.

In America, in the 19th century, it was Carl Ferdinand Wilhelm Walther, who took up the standard of Luther's theology on the doctrine of the church. Known affectionately by later generations as "C. F. W.," Walther was one of the young clergy leaders among the Saxon immigrants of 1839. By the time of his death in 1887, he had come to be recognized as prince of Lutheran theologians in this new land.[108] Numbered in the panoply of his accomplishments are two classics, either of which would have insured his immortality in Lutheran theology, *The Proper Distinction of Law and Gospel* and, recently translated, *Die Stimme unserer Kirche in der Frage von Kirche und Amt.* An abridged version of the latter in English is contained in *Walther and the Church*, edited by Wm. Dallmann, W. H. T. Dau, and Theo. Engelder. In lucid, Luther-like manner Walther set forth nine theses on the doctrine of the church, buttressing each with pertinent Scripture references and salient quotations from Luther and the theologians who followed him. Defining the church's nature Walther stated,

> The Church, in the proper sense of the term, is the communion of saints, that is, the sum total of all those who have been called by the Holy Spirit through the Gospel from out of the lost and condemned human race, who truly believe in Christ, and who have been sanctified by this faith and incorporated into Christ. (Thesis I)

Self-evidently this would exclude everyone "who has not been regenerated," every unbeliever, hypocrite, or godless person (second thesis).[109] Walther's position on the church's true nature thus corresponded precisely with Luther's.

NOTES

1   *LW* 41, 143; *WA* 50, 624f. cf. Explanation to the Ninety-five Theses of 1518, *LW* 31, 216.246; *WA* 1, 608.625; also *Commentary on Psalm 117*, *LW* 14, 22f.; *WA* 31, 240ff.

2   *Commentary on Psalm 118*, *LW* 14, 92; *WA* 31, 164.

3   J. N. Lenker, ed., *Sermons of Martin Luther*. Grand Rapids: Baker, reprint 1983. Vol. I, 170.

4   cf. *LW* 37, 367, for Luther's *Confession Concerning Christ's Supper*, where he states concerning the church: "I believe that there is one holy Christian Church on earth, i.e., the community or number or assembly of all Christians in all the world, the one bride of Christ, and his spiritual body of which he is the only head."—In turn, the *Schwabach--Marburg Articles* of 1529 lean on this same source.

5   *LW* 39, 65-73; *WA* 6, 292-297; *Papacy at Rome*.

6   *LW* 41, 143ff.; *WA* 50, 624ff.

7   *LW* 3, 19; *WA* 42, 561.

8   *LW* 4, 54-65 passim; *WA* 43, 173-181.

9   *LW* 5, 184ff.; *WA* 43, 555f.; cf. *LW* 6, 10; *WA* 44, 6f.

10   *LW* 7, 265; *WA* 44, 496.

11   *LW* 52, 39; *WA* 501, 139.

12   Ibid. cf. LW 7, 281; *WA* 44, 508.

13   Cf. H. G. Haile, *Luther*. New York: Doubleday, 1980, 295ff. for a sharply critical essay of Luther's blast against the papacy.

14   *LW* 41, 358; *WA* 54, 284.

15   *LW* 41, 327.332; *WA* 54, 259.263.

16   *LW* 43, 28; *WA* 102, 393f.; cf. *LW* 37, 275; *WA* 26, 411.

17   *LW* 14, 303; *WA* 5, 40; cf. *LW* 5, 223; *WA* 43, 582.

18   *LW* 25, 106; *WA* 56, 119.

19   *LW* 37, 275; *WA* 26, 411.

20   *LW* 5, 214; *WA* 43, 576.

21   *LW* 13, 383; *WA* 311, 423.

22   *LW* 17, 373; *WA* 312, 550. *Commentary on Isaiah*.

23   *LW* 26, 285; *WA* 40, 445.

24   *LW* 30, 7; *WA* 12, 262.

25   *LW* 30, 52; *WA* 12, 306.

26   *LW* 14, 93f; *WA* 311, 166f.

27   *LW* 11, 197f.; *WA* 3, 608f.

28   *LW* 26, 65; *WA* 401, 131.

29   *LW* 37, 367; *WA* 26, 506. See also Wilhelm Maurer, *Luther und das Evangelische Bekenntnis*, Goettingen: Vandenhoeck & Ruprecht, 1970, pp. 62ff.

30   *LW* 24, 126f.; *WA* 45, 575f. *Sermons on John's Gospel.*

31   Ibid.

32   *LW* 2, 20f.; *WA* 42, 276f.

33   Ibid.

34   LW 3, 364; *WA* 43, 136.

35   Ibid.

36   LW 35, 151; *WA* 102, 90.

37   *LW* 12, 103ff., 66f.; *WA* 45, 212f.; 40, 276f.

38   *LW* 1, 300f.; *WA* 42, 221.

39   *LW* 13, 90; *St. L* 5, 748.

40   *LW* 1, 302; *WA* 42, 222.

41   *LW* 1, 305; *WA* 42, 224f.

42   *LW* 11, 288-291, 324-332; *WA* 4, 135ff., 177ff.

43   *LW* 11, 372ff.; *WA* 4, 239ff.

44   *LW* 11, 264ff.; *WA* 4, 111ff.

45   *LW* 22, 55; *WA* 46, 583.

46   Ibid.

47   *LW* 23, 318; *WA* 33, 510. *Sermons on John's Gospel.*

48   *LW* 1, 103ff., 115; *WA* 42, 79f., 87. cf. *LW* 14, 55; *WA* 311, 84f.

49   *LW* 1, 132; *WA* 42, 99.

50   *LW* 1, 104; *WA* 42, 79.

51   *LW* 2, 334; *WA* 42, 500.

52   *LW* 10, 88f.; *WA* 3, 82.

53   *LW* 13, 301; *St. L* 5, 1003.

54   *LW* 17, 405ff.; *WA* 312, 576f.

55   *LW* 2, 266; *WA* 42, 452. cf. *LW* 13, 286; *St. L* 5, 987.

56   *LW* 27, 85; *WA* 402, 106.

57   *LW* 42, 162f.; *WA* 6, 131f.

58   *LW* 3, 31; *WA* 42, 570.

59   *LW* 4, 6f.; *WA* 43, 139.

60   *LW* 29, 227; *WA* 573, 224f.

61   *LW* 34, 113; *WA* 391, 48.

62   cf. *LW* 41, 194f.; *WA* 51, 479ff.

63   *LW* 34, 113; *WA* 391, 48.

64   *LW* 22, 451; *WA* 47, 165. *Sermons on John's Gospel.*

65   *WA* 28, 263f.; quoted in E. Plass, *What Luther Says*, I, 265.

66   *LW* 25, 53; *WA* 56, 60; *LW* 35, 51; *WA* 2, 743.

67   *LW* 1, 195; *WA* 42, 146.

68   *LW* 1, 233; *WA* 42, 174.

69   *LW* 42, 37ff.; *WA* 2, 95ff.

70   *LW* 1, 240ff.; *WA* 42, 179; *LW* 11, 12f., 226ff.; *WA* 3, 532; 4, 77.

71   *LW* 1, 233; *WA* 42, 174.

72   *LW* 11, 509; *WA* 4, 373f.

73   *LW* 12, 263; *WA* 402, 560f.; cf. also *LW* 15, 193; *WA* 31^2, 588; *LW* 22, 440; *WA* 47, 156; see also Plass, I, 789 & 805.

74   *LW* 31, 237; *WA* 1, 620.

75   *LW* 2, 68.152; *WA* 42, 310.368.

76   *LW* 9, 118; *WA* 14, 643.

77   *LW* 12, 173ff.; *WA* 51, 290f.

78   *LW* 13, 11; *WA* 8, 12.

79   *LW* 13, 14; *WA* 8, 14f.

80   *LW* 13, 14; *WA* 8, 14; *LW* 17, 104; *WA* 312, 342f.; *LW* 26, 441; *WA* 401, 664.

81   *LW* 10, 391; *WA* 3, 446.

82   *LW* 26, 443; *WA* 401, 667.

83   *LW* 13, 269; *WA* 41, 126; *LW* 15, 282; *WA* 54, 40f.; *LW* 16, 76; *WA* 312, 53.

84   *LW* 14, 32; *WA* 311, 251.

85   *LW* 14, 326ff.; *WA* 5, 57f.; *WA* 16, 28f.; *WA* 312, 20.

86   *LW* 15, 242ff.; *WA* 312, 716ff.

87   *LW* 17, 66; *WA* 312, 312.

88   *LW* 17, 237; *WA* 312, 444f.

89   *LW* 18, 119; *WA* 13, 119.

90   *LW* 22, 314; *WA* 47, 43.

91   *LW* 10, 314; *WA* 3, 372.

92   *LW* 10, 350; *WA* 3, 409.

93   *LW* 2, 256; *WA* 42, 444; *LW* 3, 160f.; *WA* 42, 663.

94   *LW* 14, 96; *WA* 311, 173.

95   *LW* 13, 88f., 285; *St. L* 5, 742.

96   *LW* 16, 40; *WA* 312, 28.

97   *LW* 3, 16f., 160f.; *WA* 42, 560. 663; *LW* 6, 52; *WA* 44, 37; *LW* 33, 227. 287; *WA* 18, 743. 782.

98   *LW* 23, 384f.; *WA* 33, 623f.

99   *LW* 16, 212; *WA* 312, 150.

100   Cf. unpublished manuscript, "εκκλησια as a Passive Concept in the New Testament." By Glenn Reichwald, in partial fulfillment of S.T.M. degree, Concordia Theological Seminary, Fort Wayne, Indiana, May 1984.

101   *Triglot Concordia*, p. 691. *Large Catechism*, II, 48ff.

102   Ibid., 227f. Apology of the Augsburg Confession, VII-VIII, 3ff.

103   Martin Chemnitz, *Ministry, Word, and Sacraments. An Enchiridion.* Translated by Luther Poellot. St.Louis: Concordia, 1981, 155.

104   *Loci theologici, de eccl.*, 51. Quoted in C. F. W. Walther, *KA* 5.

105   *Theologia Didactico-Polemica*, IV, 15, 2. Quoted in Walther, *KA* 6.

106   *System. loc.*, VIII, 253f. Walther, *KA* 13.

107   *LW* 39, 68-71 *passim.* cf. St. L, 18, 1015-1020.

108   For Walther's life and work see, among others: Carl S. Meyer, ed., *Moving Frontiers*; Walter O. Forster, *Zion on the Mississippi*; Carl S. Mundinger, *Government in the Missouri Synod*.

109   Wm. Dallmann, W. H. T. Dau, Theo. Engelder, *Walther and the Church.* St. Louis: Concordia, 1938, 56f.

Chapter 2

The Church's Invisible Nature

Since God alone knows the true believers, the church strictly speaking is invisible, except to God. Luther saw merit in retaining the distinction which Augustine made between the invisible and visible church. In no way did Luther intend to imply a double entity, or a dual nature for the church. That was farthest from his thinking. He sought only to underscore what Christ made very clear—for example, in the parables of the wheat and tares, also the net with the good and the bad fish—that the true church according to its essence as "holy believers (or) sheep who hear the voice of their Shepherd," is hidden from all but God. The church's existence, however, cannot be doubted; its reality is more commanding of belief than the sun at noonday. Even though hidden from human eyes as to its limits and boundaries, inner and outer, the church looms up in the world through its telltale markers wherever the Gospel has reached. God's Word can never be without God's church. (Isaiah 55:11) This is a truism oft repeated by Luther. The seeming paradox of being both hidden and seen, invisible and visible, resolves itself simply in God's relationship with believers through the Word of His Gospel on which everything pivots. God's recognition of those that are truly His sheep among the total number of those who profess a connection with the institution(s) called church in this world is an *ipse dixit* for Holy Scripture.

The hiddenness of the church by no means sets it off into the realm of ideas like some make-believe Never-never-land. The church on earth is a living, throbbing, viable entity through the various strands that claim relationship with Christ. Yet God alone knows who in this *corpus mixtum* are really its members, the true believers, since faith is an inner matter, a thing of the heart, known only to God and the believer himself. (Lk. 17:20,21; 1 Pet. 2:5; 2 Tim. 2:19) Faith does not hang on a person's neck externally like a pendant, but is hidden from view and is inward, in the heart. Therefore, only the true Shepherd really knows who His sheep are. (John 19:14)

"How this kingdom of Christ is established in us while we yet live," may be a mystery to man's mind, Luther allows. But,"lest anyone imagine it a visible and physical kingdom," he should be

22

instructed that "it is a kingdom of faith, (and) of peace."[1] Its dimensions God knows. He rules over His kingdom and yet the manner of God's rule over His glorious kingdom, or church, hidden from our eyes, Luther explains in the following passage from his *Commentary on 1st Corinthians*:

> This is a kingdom of faith, in which He rules through the Word, and not in a visible and public manner. It is like beholding the sun through a cloud. To be sure, one sees the light but not the sun itself. But after the clouds have passed, both light and sun are viewed simultaneously in one and the same object. In that way Christ now rules undivided with the Father. It is one and the same Kingdom. The only difference is that it is dark and hidden at present, or concealed and covered, comprehended entirely in faith and in the Word. All that is seen of this is Baptism and the Sacrament, and all that is heard is the eternal Word. These are the only power and might with which He rules and executes everything.[2]

To be sure, now it is like the sun through a heavy cloud layer. "Now it is called Christ's kingdom because we live in it by faith and do not see or hear Him physically as one beholds with the eyes a king of this world in his kingdom with crown and great and grand splendor."[3] But, says Luther, there is no difference between "Christ's kingdom" and "God's kingdom," except that it will be called the latter "when it is no longer hidden but is revealed before all creatures and when faith ends." In either case it is the church. Then Christ will deliver "His whole Christendom openly to the Father into eternal clarity and glory," and "He Himself (will) reign without cloak or cover."[4]

This holy church is His tabernacle. His holy temple is not the one that stands on Mt. Moriah, states Luther, or any other hill, whether at Jerusalem, Rome, or wherever, but the one in which "is hidden every believer."[5] Luther has an extremely fine exposition of God's kingdom, His church, and all that pertains to it in his *An Exposition of the Lord's Prayer*, an early (1519) issue from his pen, written especially for laymen. On the one hand the hiddenness of God's kingdom, or church, may distress us, as though it was as far removed as heaven from earth. But the facts in the matter are that it is as near at hand as God Himself and His Word, or Bethlehem's cradle, Luther points out. Therefore, "if you want to know the kingdom of God, do not go far afield in search of it." "If you wish to have it, you will find it close to you. Yes, it is not only close to you, it is in you." "Christ came to us from heaven to earth; we did not ascend from earth into heaven to him."[6] Yet, even while in the world, the members of Christ's church have an index of whose they are, to whom they belong, and of the faith that is in them and of the church's presence through their sanctification, their striving after godliness. But since that is always imperfect and since the church's holiness results entirely from Christ's righteousness imputed to faith, from its being "thoroughly sanctified in the cross of Christ," it remains for God to know who these are that have been "made right with God," and "how it is in the presence of God, where no one sees except God."[7]

Yet the sheep are a very real part of a very real world, not an imaginary flock in an imaginary world. But we cannot and dare not attempt to draw a line between believers and unbelievers. The true church always remains an article and object of faith.[8] For this reason we confess in the Creed: "I *believe* in the Holy Christian Church, the Communion of Saints." To man's sense and reason the church is invisible; yet he rightly confesses his belief in it and its true existence.

Luther more often than not used the term "hidden," rather than "invisible," to describe this side of the church's nature. The latter term may seem to suggest unreality. That was the farthest thing from his thinking. For Luther the church was very real, flesh and blood, engaged hand to hand in real jousting with the world. But it was not like some kingdom or political entity of the world, as the Romanists conceived of it, headed by the pope, ruled by canon law, defended by weaponry or armies. "The church," Luther said, "is a high, deep, hidden thing which one may neither perceive nor see, but must grasp by faith, through baptism, sacrament, and word."[9]

Many have criticized the use of the term "invisible" in connection with the church's true nature. In an ecumenically oriented age like ours the emphasis is rather on world-wide ecclesiastical super-structures that engage head-on the world and some of its "isms," like Communism and secularism. There is little sympathy, as a result, for definitions of the church which seem to idealize the church or portray it in what appears to be an abstract way. That criticism was present right from the start of the Reformation, and for that matter from the time of Christ and the apostles.

Chemnitz for one is right on target in replying to this criticism, whatever its point of origin: "Eck indeed laughs over this understanding of the word (i.e., church as invisible) and says that this is a 'mathematical church' or a Platonic idea. But let him laugh, if he wants to; that which for us is a truth or concept which cannot be seen, is not a hidden thing for God." Chemnitz cites Col. 3:3, affirming that while by faith our life is hid with Christ in God, it certainly is not therefore a Platonic idea, or, for that matter, a fanatical notion. "The true and holy church of the elect remains invisible in spite of all," Chemnitz states, "particularly when it is described not as a crowd (*Haufe*) of a certain people, as the Jewish or Israelite nation in the Old Testament, but as the catholic (or universal) congregation, which is gathered in all places, all nations, all tongues, and which has accepted the Gospel of Christ in firm faith, has employed his sacraments, and serves under Christ's cross unto life eternal."[10] In so saying he has the mind of Luther.

"We are speaking not of an imaginary church," Melanchthon had written in definition of the church's nature in the *Apology of the Augsburg Confession*, 1531, as though it "is to be found nowhere." As a matter of fact the church "is and abides truly upon earth." But the wicked can have no part of it, even though they might be numbered with it externally, for it is "properly the congregation of saints," or believers.[11] Johann Gerhard reiterated the truth that "the church is spiritual Zion and a heavenly city," even though it exists right here in this world. This is so because "everything spiritual is invisible," and "with human eye it is impossible to discern which are the true worshipers." Their bodies indeed are visible but "not their spiritual natures, by which they belong to the church," and so "the fact remains firm that the church, as a spiritual house, built out of those who are spiritual, is invisible."[12] Abraham Calov concurred, stating that "with the finger," it is possible "to point to the crowd (*Haufe*) in which the church is—where Word and sacraments are in use—but to discern that crowd (*Haufe*) which actually is the church, that is, the communion of believers and saints' is not possible, for it is not visible."[13] We see the people who go to church, John Quenstedt states, "but whether those people are the church, (we) do not know," since "it does not become outwardly evident that these

people are true and living members of the church."[14] When C. F. W.
Walther came to define the church he likewise noted that human
eyes can never judge, know, or discern it in physical dimensions,
limits that are known only to God, and therefore his third thesis
affirmed that "the church in the proper sense of the term is invisible."[15] All of these theologians likewise had the mind of Luther in
support of Scripture's teaching on the church as spiritual body and
kingdom of Christ.

In a notable passage in his *Prefaces to the New Testament*
Luther affirms that the words, "I believe in the Christian Church,"
are "as much an article of faith as the rest" of the declarations of
faith and attest the hidden nature of the church. Because it is
something that only faith apprehends, "this is the reason why natural
reason cannot recognize it, even if it puts on glasses," says Luther.
The church as seen in the world "is a *corpus mixtum*." "The devil
can cover it over with offenses and divisions. God, too, can conceal
it behind faults and shortcomings of all kinds." Therefore the
important thing for faith to acknowledge and confess is that
"Christendom will not be known by sight, but by faith," for "faith
has to do with things not seen." As a matter of fact, "a Christian is
even hidden from himself; he does not see his holiness and virtue,
but sees in himself nothing but unholiness and vice." And for the
"ecclesiocrat" of his day and ours, who dreams of a super-church in
fine ecumenical breadth and dress, Luther has a parting shot: "And
you, stupid know-it-all, would behold Christendom with your blind
reason and unclean eyes."[16] It cannot be done. Only God can see
the church in its real boundaries.

Luther by no means intends with the above limitations to
deny or minimize the inner witness of the Spirit to our spirit that we
are the sons of God through faith in Him and His Word (Rom.
8:16), therefore members of His church. Nor is he minimizing the
truth that, all appearances to the contrary, no fault or error or
wrinkle, even as no unbeliever, can exist in Christ's church, for it is
pure and holy. His brilliant brief against Erasmus, the *Bondage of
the Will* (*De servo arbitrio*) contains a splendid piece on the true
church, which is hidden from man's eyes, *ecclesia abscondita*. Of
it he rightly asserts: "It is impossible for the Church to err." It all
finally comes down to this: "The Church of God is not as common-
place a thing, my dear Erasmus, as the phrase 'the Church of God';
nor are the saints of God met with as universally as the phrase

'saints of God.'" God's true saints are like "pearls and precious jewels, which the Spirit does not cast before swine (Matt. 7:6) but keeps hidden, as the Scripture says (Matt. 11:25), lest the ungodly should see the glory of God. Otherwise, if they were plainly recognized by all, how could they possibly be as harassed and afflicted in the world as they are?"[17]

Because it belongs to God, is formed by God, and safeguarded by God from all sin and evil[18] the true church, which remains hidden, does not err, contains no error, fault, or ungodliness of any kind. In life there is error and failing. In us there is weakness, even in the things we do in worship of God, in expressing our articles of belief, in practice of what we believe to be Christian living. But in God, in what He has given for faith's acceptance—our salvation, the articles of belief, all that is taught in His Word, Law and Gospel, the church which He builds upon His Son, our Savior, Jesus Christ, and every member in it—there is nothing deficient or off the plumbline of His divine wisdom and mercy, for all things are perfect and true in God and in His mighty acts and purposes. This is true also of His holy church. Though now it is hidden from human ken, it is known by Him, even to the very last soul in it, and in it there is utter perfection.

The hiddenness of the church corresponds, of course, to the hiddenness of God Himself as far as human eyes are concerned. Him no man has seen nor can see. (John 1:18; 5:37; Col. 1:15; 1 Tim. 1:17; 6:16) Yet only a fool, Scripture asserts, would therefore deny His existence. The apostle Paul reminds us that God is *deus absconditus*, hidden and inscrutable, especially in His purposes not revealed in Holy Scripture, though these always work eventually for the good of His beloved, His kingdom, or church. (Rom 11:33ff.; 8:28ff.) "He is indeed the God of life, glory, salvation, joy, and peace; and this is the true face of God," Luther states. Moreover, believers "are not scandalized by the counsels of God or offended by the face with which He meets us; for sometimes He wraps it up and hides it, lest we be able to recognize or look upon it." Luther is speaking here first of all about the crosses, trials, afflictions in the believer's life, which spring from the hand of God, and which are inevitably so hard to understand.[19] But we may be sure that God intends everything for our good, Luther assures us, "that you may be humbled, that you may endure and wait for the hand of the Lord and the revelation of His face."[20]

God has His own chosen coverings or veils, the *larvae Dei*, by which He gives us His revelation of Himself and His gracious purposes. Here God speaks plainly as *deus revelatus* and is not hidden, but wants to be known and understood. In the very first chapter of his *Genesis Commentary* Luther urges us not to disdain God at His approach, or in the manner of His revealing Himself to mankind. For Adam and the other patriarchs this came through unique and unusual theophanies, but for us it is through the prophetic and apostolic Word, through Baptism, through the Lord's Supper, and if we try "to reach God apart from these coverings," we exert ourselves in vain.[21] While God indeed is hidden, while His church or kingdom is hidden too, it is evident from God's own drawing back of the curtain from His person and His purposes, that He deigns to be known and approachable. But He is to be approached according to His own ordained way, however simple, humble, and foolish these routes may seem to our thinking. "Let us go to the child lying in the lap of His mother Mary and to the sacrificial victim suspended on the cross; there we shall really behold God, and there we shall look into His very heart," Luther assures us.[22]

So God is both hidden and revealed, a paradox which resolves itself by and through God's Word. The same holds true for His church, which by its very nature is hidden, but which is real and present, wherever His Word is heard and believed, everywhere in the world. Luther is quite right in promising: You will not have to "go far afield in search of it; you will find it close to you; it is in you."

In distinction from the false church, "the true church is hidden," Luther notes with special emphasis; and yet, paradoxically, it is the true church, not the false, which is "banned," "regarded as heretical," "slain," persecuted, vexed, and subjected to all manner of "hardships."[23] It was so in the days of Cain, and it is so now, because the church of the pope, Luther stated, persecuted professed believers. The true church always suffers. But however dark the day or its evils, "God nevertheless has His little church, even though it is small and hidden." Even though He permits it "to be vexed in various ways," it forever remains true of the church that "God is not without His people."[24] In a letter to Margrave Albrecht of Brandenburg, in December 1523, Luther wrote: "The church is built only on Christ. Peter and the popes cannot be this basis or rock. How can Peter or the popes rule or preserve this church, if they cannot know who is holy, can never see this church, (which) Christ alone sees, gathers, and keeps?"[25]

Even though Abraham had God's promise and grounded his life and hope on it, he was surrounded by competing religions claiming authentic existence as God's people. "This, you see, is the way things go in the church and in the kingdom of the world," Luther explains in apt, existential commentary on life in the church on earth. "They are at loggerheads with regard to the promises. The pope and his followers want to be the church of God; the Turk also wants to be the church of God. And yet neither of them is."[26] And God had to assure Abraham, assaulted by doubts about the church's future prompted by those around him and from within his own heart, that He, the Lord, would be his protection, "overwhelm him with a blessing, and from (his) body (bring forth) one who is to be your heir."[27]

The true church on earth will always be vexed and bothered by those who "make this boast (that they) have the numbers and the strength." Moreover, "they give every appearance of being the apostles' successors," and "rely defiantly on (their church's) authenticity, since great and mighty lords, cardinals, bishops, kings, and princes have had a hand in it."[28] But God promises that we shall have His Holy Spirit, with all His promises, if we believe His Gospel. Therefore, Luther urges: "Let us investigate to see who they are that preach correctly about Christ and extol the Baptism, the Sacrament, and the Gospel He gave us." "Then," says Luther, "it will be found that the great multitude, which boasts of being the church and of having the Holy Spirit, who preaches through it, is a false proclamation and a lying spirit, the devil's church and vessel."[29] The true church is known by its loyalty to and fealty under God's promises, His Word.

Now then, though the true church is hidden as to its innermost being, "though it does not appear, it is visible to hope and faith."[30] Faith in God's sure promises is the evidence of things not seen. Christ's resurrection is what makes our faith sure, and thus "this kingdom began the moment He was raised from the dead."[31] It is as real and sure as His resurrection. Luther does not lose sight of Old Testament believers. Already the Old Testament promises made the work of Christ and the foundation of this church sure. In his *Prefaces to the Old Testament* of 1522, Luther wrote: "If you would see the holy Christian Church painted in living color and shape, comprehended in one little picture, then take up the Psalter. There you have a fine, bright, pure mirror that will show you what Christendom is. Indeed you will find in it also yourself and the true *gnothi seauton* (know thyself)."[32]

Meanwhile "the world takes delight in remaining in darkness and restlessness," and "the devil can point to greater martyrs than Christ has, (and) who labor harder to earn hell than Christians work to gain heaven."[33] The kingdom of the world is a kingdom of works-righteousness, and it always stands opposed to Christ's, the kingdom of faith-righteousness. To human eyes it may seem as though "the ungodly perform bigger and more arduous tasks than Christians do," Luther grants. But while Christians suffer during this present time, they "still enjoy a tranquil and peaceful heart, whereas the ungodly know no peace of conscience."[34]

Luther by no means implies that Christian faith is inactive and unproductive; only that it lays its hope entirely on Christ, not on its works. Christ leads His church through no darker doors than He has gone through before, imposes no greater cross-bearing than He has borne for it and all sinners before. Moreover, His church has the assurance, as it makes its ofttimes difficult pilgrimage through this world, that no offense against it shall ever be any different than an offense against God Himself, no more able to overwhelm it than it could God Himself. He promises to preserve it and keep it faithful till the end.[35]

NOTES

1   *LW* 20, 138f.; *WA* 13, 659.

2   *LW* 28, 124; *WA* 36, 568f.

3   *LW* 28, 141; *WA* 36, 592.

4   Ibid.

5   *LW* 10, 125; *WA* 3, 150.

6   *LW* 42, 41ff.; *WA* 2, 98f.

7   *LW* 11, 264; *WA* 4, 112.

8   Carl E. Braaten, *Principles of Lutheran Theology.*   Philadelphia: Fortress, 1983, 43ff.

9   *LW* 41, 211; *WA* 51, 507. *Against Hanswurst.*

10   *Loc. theol.*, III, 117. Quoted in Walther, *KA*, 20.

11   *Apology of the Augsburg Confession*, Art. VII-VIII, 12, 16-20.

12   *Loc. de eccl.*, 151, 73f. Walther, *KA*, 22. (Gerhard's name "Johann" is used here interchangeably with the Anglicized version "John.")

13   *System. loc.* VIII, 264. Walther, *KA*, 27.

14   *Theol. did. polem.*, IV, 15, 2. Walther, *KA*, 28.

15   Dallmann, *et al.*, *Walther and the Church*, 58.

16   *LW* 35, 410f.; *WA*, DB 7, 419f.

17   *LW* 33, 85ff.; *WA* 18, 649f.

18   cf. *LW* 41, 194ff.; *WA* 51, 478f.

19   *LW* 8, 30f.; *WA* 44, 601.

20   Ibid.

21   *LW* 1, 11ff.; *WA* 42, 10ff.

22   *LW* 3, 277; *WA* 43, 73.

23   *LW* 1, 253f.; *WA* 42, 188.

24   *LW* 3, 345; *WA* 43, 122f.

25   *LW* 49, 61ff. passim; WA Br 3, 214ff.

26   *LW* 3, 14f.; *WA* 42, 558.

27   Ibid.

28   *LW* 24, 126f.; *WA* 45, 576.

29   Ibid.

30   *LW* 17, 387; *WA* 31^2, 561.

31   Ibid.

32   *LW* 35, 256f.; *WA* DB 10^1, 105.

33   *LW* 23, 327; *WA* 33, 525f.

34   Ibid.

35   *LW* 31, 98; *WA* 1, 539 *Explanations to the 95 Theses.*

Chapter 3

Treasures and Keys

Christ has entrusted His most treasured possessions, the keys to the Kingdom of heaven itself, to His beloved, the church. It now possesses all the gifts, powers, privileges, offices gained by Christ for it. As His bride, the church shares fully in His riches, all spiritual gifts and blessings, all that has to do with life and salvation. (Matt. 16:15-19; 18:18; John 20, 22, 23; 3:28,29; 1 Cor. 3:21-23; Gal. 4:26; 1 Pet. 2:9)

Christian believers, by faith in Christ and through the forgiveness of sins, have become fellow-heirs with Him. They are a royal priesthood. Theirs are the prerogatives of royal station. The gates of heaven are theirs to enter freely, through Christ's atoning sacrifice and His intercession before God's throne. "The keys," Luther states in his *On the Councils and the Church*, "belong not to the pope (as he lies) but to the church. They belong to the people of Christ and are called 'the church's keys' not the 'pope's keys.'"[1] Thus they are the immediate possession of the believers, singly and together.

The keys have to do with the means of grace. No order of priests or clergy, no world-wide church council, large or small, no church body or synod, and certainly no autocratic figure like the pope, can claim these keys or usurp them from the company of believers, the communion of saints. "The bride," Luther comments on Ps. 8, "possesses all that is Christ's."[2] Chemnitz employs Scripture's figure of the church as Christ's body, and says that Scripture uses it, in order to emphasize how the members of the Body receive all that is necessary for their salvation from the head, who is Christ. Moreover, "whoever is not a member of this Body, of which Christ is the Head, cannot be saved," since the means of grace or ministry of the Word have been given exclusively to it.[3] In the fifth chief part of Luther's *Small Catechism* (expanded version includes Confessions and Keys) it is described as "a peculiar church power, which Christ has given to His Church on earth to forgive the sins of the penitent sinners unto them but to retain the sins of the impenitent as long as they do not repent."

The power possessed by the church is an entirely unique power, states the *Augsburg Confession* (XXVIII, 10), since it "grants eternal things and is exercised only by the ministry of the Word," quite different from secular and civil power which exercises the sword. Human traditions in comparison are "useless services," asserts the *Apology of the Augsburg Confession* (XXVIII, 7.18f.), and "no other word from heaven ought to be sought" than the Word Christ gave to His church, the precious Gospel which proclaims that "we receive the remission of sins freely for Christ's sake."

Such "aid and consolation against sin and a bad conscience" are greatly to be treasured, states Luther in the *Smalcald Articles* (III, viii, passim), since in both private and public absolution it bestows Christ's forgiveness to troubled hearts; "therefore we ought to maintain this point that God does not wish to deal with us otherwise than through the spoken Word and the Sacraments." Rightly in the same context Luther warns against turning inward, away from the outward Word and means of grace: "It is the devil himself whatsoever is extolled as Spirit without the Word and Sacraments."

The *Tractate* to the *Smalcald Articles* (22ff.) observes that the power and right of the church for calling and ordaining "ministers of the church" follows from and is conjoined with the fact "that the keys belong not to the person of one particular man but to the church," and that "wherever the church is, there is the authority (*Befehl*) to administer the Gospel." Moreover, "this authority is a gift which no human power can wrest from the church," for it belongs by Christ's bestowal to the royal priesthood of believers alone and not to any ecclesiastical class or order. (67, 69)

Like Luther before him Martin Chemnitz labeled as "tyrannical claims" whatever usurped "the Keys, that is, the Office (authority) of the Word and the Sacraments" away from the "whole church" to vest them in an ecclesiastical hierarchy.[4] Moreover, when God "calls and sends preachers" He does so not through angels nor any higher power than "through His church or congregation," which is His "dear Bride."[5] Heshusius, loyal follower of Luther, pinpoints this right of governance upon "whoever is truly a Christian believer and a living member of Christ." He goes on to say that called pastors carry out the public administration of the Word "not by their own authority but through the power and command of the church," for "this glorious gift has been entrusted by Christ to the church for bestowal upon the ministers."[6] From this it also follows that "if the preachers do not execute their office as they are obligated to do, or if none are available, then the office returns to the churches whose responsibility it is to bestow it."

John Gerhard described "Christ's beloved Bride" as the mistress of the house which is the church, and "just as a housewife has the keys for opening and locking up the stores of supplies to meet her family's needs," so the "Keys for forgiving and retaining sins, indeed for opening and closing heaven," belong in solemn trust to Christ's church, the congregation of believers at a given place.[7] These are the ones, writes Quenstedt, "to whom Christ Himself has given the Keys of heaven."[8]

In his fourth thesis on the church Walther, like the Lutheran theologians before him, affirms that "this church is the real and sole holder and bearer of the spiritual, divine, and heavenly blessings, rights, power, offices, etc., which Christ has gained and which are available in His church." He points in his seventh thesis to "the visible communions, in which the Word and Sacraments still exist in their essence," as possessors of these powers, not by virtue of name or claim, but "because of the true invisible church of the true believers contained in them."

According to the well-established truth on which these theses are based, Walther contends that we should see how God wants His church to occupy itself with its major task, the preaching of His Gospel. This is His command to the priesthood of believers who are gathered into congregations around the Word here and there at sundry places, and with His command God also gives authority, power, and promised blessing for fulfillment. God has also promised to provide qualified men for the pastoral office called by the church(es) into His service. These, too, are gifts of God to the church, whom He solemnly pledges to equip with necessary gifts for their high calling. Underlying all are the means of grace, the keys, which are the church's foremost possession, God's priceless gift, which it carries within itself as the body of Christ. The church does not receive these keys through an echelon of power, through a certain class of special people, a priestly order; rather those who serve in the pastoral ministry receive their call, authority, and power from the church, or congregation. This is God's will, and this is His order. The pastoral office exists by His command; but it is conferred through the priesthood of believers which is the real and sole holder and bearer of all spiritual gifts.

What Walther taught was cut out of the same piece of fabric first of all with Luther; in fact it was the distillation of Luther's thinking that had been shaped and siphoned out of the seething cauldron of ecclesiastical build-up and papal pretension. "God would not forever bear with this contempt of His Word," is the way Luther described the situation before the Flood, and his judgment was well applicable to Rome's flaunting of God's Word in his day.[9] We were wrong, Luther admitted, for even thinking that we could keep the Word "by remaining in their church." The fact is that when "we keep the Word," then "through the Word (we have) all the advantages of the true church."[10] It all comes down, therefore, to possessing God's pure Word. Where the Word is, there the church is, and they who have the Word are the church. God has spoken with His church through the Word, "promising forgiveness of sins in Baptism, in the Supper of His Son, and in the true use of the keys."[11] In the same context in which he treats of the trusting and believing Abraham, Luther adds: "Thus the church is the pupil of Christ. It sits at His feet and listens to His Word, that it may know how to judge everything, surrounded on all sides by the rays of the Word, (and) may continually walk in joy and in the most beautiful light."[12] It is even so, as we pray in the Lord's Prayer, "Thy Kingdom come," that we ask "that God's kingdom may come also to me and his will be done in me," through His Word.[13]

"When God reveals Himself in some sign, no matter what its nature, one must take hold of Him in it," is Luther's reminder, as he considers the fact that "the Jews had the temple, circumcision, and a definite form of worship." In comparison, "in the New Testament we have the Son of God on the lap of His mother Mary; He suffered and died for us; (and in addition) we have Baptism, the Eucharist, and the spoken Word itself."[14] In all this "the church constantly hears those familiar words: 'Take heart, My son; your sins are forgiven' (Matt. 9:2)."[15] "It is true," says Luther, "that you hear a human being when you are baptized and when you partake of the Holy Supper. But the Word which you hear is not that of a human being; it is the Word of the living God. It is He who baptizes you; it is He who absolves you from sins; and it is He who commands you to hope in His mercy."[16] When one Christian absolves another believing, penitent brother of his sin, "it is there that a brother becomes an angel for his brother." So much do I love God's precious means of grace which He has instituted for me, says

Luther, that even "if God never appears to me visibly," I could not wish for more; in fact "I do not even desire that He do so."[17] There is nothing greater, nothing more reassuring, than to take God at His Word, no matter what the opposition.[18]

When people doubt or question God and His ways of channeling His grace to men, "they are insulting the Holy Spirit," Luther states, "as though He did not know what should be written."[19] Not only the heroics of Abraham, Isaac, and Jacob are detailed for us, but also their failings, as well as the tragic, enormous wickedness in the lives of men like Reuben and Judah and others—all for our learning. It is not the people of Israel, or Jacob, with their commandments, precepts, and arms, which spell out the promise that God sustained through them, but rather the Word concerning the promised Seed, or Messiah. This we now have in "the Word and the Sacraments" which "establish and build the kingdom of Christ."[20]

Here the sword does not belong, as little as it did for the patriarchs, and as little as it belongs to the church militant.[21] Christ does not confuse or coalesce the one sword with the other, the sword of the Spirit, which is the Word of God, with the naked sword of steel, which is the weapon of power in the hands of governments. They err who assay to use the arm of the state to advance the cause of the church, as in some holy crusade. Luther says that he will have none of this; neither should any Christian. "If I were a soldier and saw a priest's banner in the field, or a banner of the cross, even though it was a crucifix, I should run as though the devil were chasing me; and even if they won a victory, by God's decree, I should not take any part in the booty or the rejoicing."[22]

The church is pictured by Scripture not as a troop of soldiers marshaled for bloody conquest, but as "our extremely loving mother hen," gathering its chicks under its wings, says Luther in commentary on Psalm 6.[23] Since the Word is the beating heart of the church, around which it lives and breathes, the sectarian spirits err grievously when "they make Christianity a matter of changing certain externals."[24] They really demonstrate their "ignorance about the kingdom of Christ." In view of the fact that "in the New Testament the proclamation and the Word of God are all-important," and through this means the church flowers and prospers, it ought be seen that "God's wagons," that is, God's strength, lies simply in His mandate to carry His Gospel to the ends of the earth (Matt. 28:19)[25] and not in faddish or "in-thing" ceremonies, customs, or traditions.

When it is said that "the church has the favor and goodwill of the Divine Majesty, of the Father, the Son, and the Holy Spirit," nothing more and nothing less is meant than that by the Word and Baptism "I do not hope for the remission of sins, but I <u>have</u> it forthwith in faith."[26] "I do not believe that Christ is going to suffer for me. No, through faith I am sure that He has suffered for my sins and risen for the sake of my righteousness." What this, therefore, means in a practical and pastoral way, is Luther's point, "is not a mere prayer or wish"; but "it is that by which through the power of the Keys I hand over to you now the remission of sin, the grace and favor of God, in order that you may be able to conclude with certainty that you have God, who is well pleased with you."[27] These are the keys, not that the church has power over the Word, or even "to change the Word, so that the Sacred Scriptures should get their authority from the faith of the Roman Church";[28] but that the Word empowers the church, the congregation of believers which after all is not built on human wisdom and riches but entirely on God's grace, for "it is grace alone that counts."[29] In Luther's *Defense and Explanation of all the Articles* which issued forth directly upon the heels of his dramatic burning of the papal bull, *Exsurge Domine*, threatening his excommunication, the Reformer very clearly supported the Scriptural gift of the keys to all believers, and not to the pope or the clergy estate alone, if at all.[30]

The whole matter concerning the keys and to whom they belong comes down finally to the meaning and proper understanding of Matt. 16:18,19. Very early in his struggle with Rome's distorted views of itself, Luther had written the treatise *Papacy at Rome* (1520). It was an answer to the Romanist theologian, Alveld, of Leipzig. Not only did it clearly state Scripture's teaching concerning the true nature of the church, but it smashed the papal fiction that on the basis of Matt. 16 the keys were given first to Peter, above the other disciples, and then to the pope, as Peter's claimed successor. Citing Matt. 18:18 and John 20:22,23, Luther shows that what Christ says to Peter, He says to all the disciples, and that what He gives to them, He gives to His whole church.[31] In even more brilliant way, Luther expounds the meaning of the above verses in his *Against the Roman Papacy* (1545) and states the only conclusion which is defensible on the basis of Scripture: "The keys were not given to St. Peter alone, much less to the pope alone, but to all the disciples," and so to the church, that is, all true believers.[32]

This means that different from the Old Testament order of things, where the Levites and the house of Aaron were singled out for priestly service, God promised that in the New Testament, through the Spirit's outpouring of faith, "all will be teachers and priests of God"; "all His faithful people are going to be priests."[33] "Faith alone is the true priestly office. It permits no one else to take its place. Therefore, all Christian men are priests, all women priestesses, be they young or old, master or servant, mistress or maid, learned or unlearned. Here there is no difference, unless faith be unequal."[34] The keys are given by Christ to the whole church, not just an element or part thereof.[35]

Luther reminds Christian laymen in his *Open Letter to the Christian Nobility* that it is total fabrication to claim that there is a "spiritual estate" of clergy with special rights and powers, above all others, since "all Christians are truly of the spiritual estate"; and "this is because we all have one baptism, one gospel, one faith, and are all Christians alike; we are all consecrated priests through baptism."[36] The keys, indeed, were given to Peter, but not personally alone, but to you and to me, too, says Luther, and to every lay Christian,[37] for "we, the parish assembly, by virtue of our universal priesthood, have always had and should have the full right and authority" to conduct the affairs of the church,[38] specifically that which pertains to the keys, and the means of grace.

The church, and so the priesthood of believers, stands in closest relationship to the Word of God. Fundamental always is this truth: "The church comes into being because God's Word is spoken; the church does not constitute the Word, but is constituted by the Word." This is a spiritual priesthood of believers, held in common by all Christians, equally; by it each Christian shares the responsibility of proclaiming the Word, of absolving the penitent brother, of calling the servants of the church, the pastors, and of advancing the kingdom of Christ through the Word. It is self-evident, then, that with the establishment of the royal, or universal, priesthood of all believers, ruled by the Word of God alone, "the *outward* priesthood is overthrown," that is, the privileged priestly orders, by whatever name or pretension.[39]

Front and center in the church's task is its handling of the Word of God. "Certainly the first and greatest work in the church is the preaching of the Word," Luther states, and not the "transfer of empires and conferring of world dominions."[40] This is said in sharp criticism of the medieval papacy's scale of values. Luther's *Instructions for the Visitors of Parish Pastors in Electoral Saxony* resulted from his church visitations during the years 1527 to 1529. It was readily apparent that pastors were ill- prepared to cope with the new responsibilities which the Reformation laid on them; the people for their part were also likewise unable to assume fully the role of royal priests.

The instructions, though actually written by Melanchthon, reflect Luther's mind and hand in a pertinent way. They are very practical, down-to-earth guidelines for both pastors and people on faith and life, particularly in helpful distinction of Law and Gospel; but other matters are also treated, including marriage, forms of worship, schools, and civic duty. Foremost is this concern: "While some preach *about* the faith," we ought to be explaining "*how* one shall attain to this faith."[41] Preaching, praying, giving thanks, may be done everywhere, even under the open sky, and often are;[42] also rejoicing and mourning, and, accordingly, it follows that "a Christian leads a double life—the life of the Spirit, and the mortification of the flesh."[43] But genuine worship will always be known by this that it builds up the church[44] and will conform to what God commands, both as to content and also manner and place of worship.[45] The Israelites often forgot this, substituting their ideas and rules for God's Word, their groves for God's temple. Christians are to seek God under the "coverings" (*larvae Dei*) which He Himself has given, the Scriptural Word and the sacraments.

The fundamental meaning and purpose of worship is calling on the name of God, or on the name of Christ.[46] "To build an altar" means the same thing, that is, to hear the Word of God, pray, and bring spiritual sacrifices, as God commanded Abraham to do, not as Abraham might have decided to do on his own.[47] Luther explains that it was for this reason that Abraham's home was a "kingdom of forgiveness,"[48] God's tabernacle, the "ministry of the Word,"[49] the church, "a mound of witness,"[50] a haven where Word and sacraments are preserved,[51] the "ark" of salvation, as for Noah,[52] a house walled about with the Word,[53] "the wagon of God,"[54] the songbird of Christ's righteousness.[55] God's kingdom is to be a kingdom of doers of the Word,[56] whose prayers well up in combined strength together,[57] and whose proclaiming of the Gospel is rightly and effectively set into the context of the Law, thus in salty way "showing the reverse side and renouncing what is not right."[58]

Here too the sacraments are faithfully administered. To Luther Holy Baptism always stood forth as a wondrous miracle of God. This was so especially of infant baptism, as he wrote to Melanchthon in a letter of January 13, 1522: "I see it as a special miracle of God that the article that infants are to be baptized is the only one which has never been denied, not even by heretics."[59] Future events upset this record, as the Anabaptists and Katabaptists appeared on the scene with their sectarian, arbitrary rejection of infant baptism. But their very protest could not overturn God's Word.

Also the Lord's Supper was very dear to Luther's heart, and he certainly did not lower its place in people's lives by declaring that it, too, belonged among the possessions of the universal priesthood. While it was indeed theirs, and not to be distorted nor exploited by tyrannical priests, Luther underscored the fact that its promise was received respectfully by faith, and worshipers ought not brazenly manhandle the Sacrament, as happened under the misguided "enthusiasm" of the so-called "free spirits" and charismatic notions of Karlstadt. In his inimitable way Luther exposed that vulgar popularizing of sacramental usage by observing that "then Herod and Pilate are the chief and best Christians, since it seems to me that they really handled the body of Christ when they had him nailed to the cross and put to death."[60] Here as in all things of true spiritual value Luther's advice was right on target: "No, my dear friends, the kingdom of God does not consist in outward things, which can be touched or perceived, but in faith."[61]

The significance and power of the keys, or means of grace, as God's gifts to His church, can be depicted no more splendidly than to say that thereby heaven's gate is open.[62] "The gates are open to the Gospel, which brings the forgiveness of sins."[63] The Christian's hope is based on God's objective gifts of Word and Sacrament.[64] There is no possible way of articulating the high and powerful role of the church more forcefully than through Luther's trenchant hyperbole, as he boldly, though not brashly, declares that in total outreach "the church quickens more through the spoken Word than Christ Himself did during His ministry."[65] It is indeed so, because this was the Lord's promise to His church, which would literally move mountains of unbelief.

The church always has to do with the Gospel, whereby it erects not St. Peter's church at Rome, but Christ's church, the communion of saints.[66] Christ is King in this church by God's own ordaining,[67] and it follows that outside of His church there can be no forgiveness, no salvation.[68] Christ is the church's firm foundation, or rock,[69] her light,[70] even as He is her head,[71] and no tyrant can prevail against His church, comforted as it is by God's "I am with you." "The church of the faithful is called a spiritual microcosm, so great is the power of the Word."[72] That Word is the Spirit's seed and enfolds a power more mysterious and awesome than the seed in the farmer's field.[73]

The riches of the church are measured by spiritual gifts, which are as strong and mighty as the Rock on which they stand, Christ.[74] The church's boast is not in her external trappings, however rich and fine, but "only of the knowledge of the Lord."[75] As St. Paul wrote to the Corinthians (1 Cor.2:13), it is literally impossible for human nature to think or to speak in spiritual terms, really and truly, until it is within the church of God, or of the household of faith. To be called by the name of God means that we belong to God, and this signifies, Luther says, that we share fully in His power,[76] and like the apostles will conquer the world with the Gospel and thus build Christ's Kingdom.[77] There is no reason to doubt this power with which God equips His church through the Gospel, since God's people shall prevail "as fire prevails over wood and a flaming torch over straw."[78] In comparison with the old priesthood, with its high pretension and boastings, the universal priesthood of believers may seem feeble and weak; yet it is powerful, for it can take a man and make him "sacred and consecrated," "teach and boil him so that he is prepared and sacrificed to God according to the old man, Rom. 12:1," thus made acceptable to God in Christ Jesus.[79]

What is said of the church in general, applies to "the relation of every Christian to his neighbor."[80] Faith ought to call forth obedience with greater devotion, Luther observes, than that with which the fanatics, the Anabaptists, pursue their fanaticism, ready to "surrender everything."[81] In the same context Luther is moved to express deep regret, even disgust, over the shabby treatment which servants, or pastors, in the church were receiving, now that the Gospel had been freely brought to the people. Yet this was not faith's usual posture, for "a willing people ought to act freely," not by compulsion, for it is in the nature of faith that it cannot be coerced.[82]

Power in the church is to be equated with "every good thing
of the Spirit." In his lecture notes on Romans (1:16) Luther wrote:
"To be ashamed of the Gospel is a fault of cowardice in pastors, but
to contradict it and not to listen to it is a fault of stupidity in church
members. This is obvious when the preacher is afraid of the power,
influence, and number of his hearers and is silent concerning the
essential truth and when the unresponsive hearer despises the
lowliness and humble appearance of the Word."[83]   What God
imposes, therefore, what He says in His Word, the church must
declare fully and faithfully.[84]

This has nothing to do with the so-called canonical penalties
which the medieval church loaded on the shoulders of the faithful;
these ought to be discarded and removed.[85] The keys are the *Gospel*
at work; they cannot, therefore, extend to purgatory, Luther notes
already in his *Ninety-Five Theses* (No. 26 and 60), before he had
even discarded the notion of purgatory entirely from the theological
baggage which he had brought along from Romanism.[86] The keys,
which speak forgiveness to the repentant sinner, are by their very
nature restricted to "earth," to man's temporal existence.[87] "By the
ministry of the new priesthood" which Christ worked in and for the
church through His sacrificial death there now is forgiveness.[88] It is
on Christ's merits that the keys rest.[89] For that reason they are a
great treasure, to be loved, of inestimable value for genuine peace
of heart and remission of guilt. They have their rightful place in the
church as its most precious possession, belonging not to Peter alone,
nor to any supposed sacerdotal hierarchy, but to the church, the royal
priesthood of Christ's redeemed followers.

In his sixtieth year the weight of the many burdens,
anxieties, responsibilities was beginning to tell on Luther. Yet his
faith and hope were strong as ever. To his good friend, Wenceslas
Link, he wrote on June 20, 1543:

> For myself I desire a good hour of passing on to God. I am
> content, I am tired, and nothing more is in me. Yet see to
> it that you pray earnestly for me, that the Lord takes my
> soul in peace. I do not leave our congregations in poor
> shape; they flourish in pure and sound teaching, and they
> grow day by day through the ministry of many excellent and
> most sincere pastors.[90]

No more fitting expression of hope and confidence could ever be spoken for the church and its congregations in any day. It must continue so; for to the church belong the keys. They are its priceless possession.

NOTES

1   *LW* 41, 154; *WA* 50, 632.

2   *St. L* 5, 247; cf. *LW* 12, 98ff.; *WA* 45, 204ff.

3   Martin Chemnitz, *Enchiridion.* Handbuechlein der vornehmsten Hauptstuecke der christlichen Lehre. A. L. Graebner, ed. Milwaukee, 1886, 211. cf. Poellot translation, 155.

4   *Exam. Conc. Trid.*, 223a. Cf. Kramer translation, *Examination of the Council of Trent*, II, 15ff.

5   Quoted in Walther, *KA*, 38f.

6   Quoted in Walther, *KA*, 45.

7   *Harm. hist. ev., P. ult. c.* VIII, 426.6. Quoted in Walther, *KA*, 46.

8   *Theol. didact.-pol.*, IV, 12, 2, 402. Quoted in Walther, *KA*, 50.

9   *LW* 2, 23; *WA* 42, 278.

10   Ibid.

11   *LW* 2, 353; *WA* 42, 514.

12   Ibid.

13   *LW* 51, 174; *WA* 301, 100.

14   *LW* 3, 109; *WA* 42, 625.

15   *LW* 3, 155; *WA* 42, 659.

16   *LW* 3, 166f.; *WA* 42, 666f.

17   Ibid.

18   *LW* 3, 174; *WA* 42, 672f.

19   *LW* 7, 10; *WA* 44, 309.

20   *LW* 8, 264; *WA* 44, 773.

21   *LW* 1, 231; *WA* 42, 172.

22   *LW* 46, 168; *WA* 302, 115.

23   *LW* 10, 78; *WA* 3, 71.

24   *LW* 12, 42; *WA* 402, 244.

25   *LW* 13, 16.20; *WA* 8, 16.20.

26   *LW* 5, 196; *WA* 43, 563.

27 Ibid.

28 *LW* 17, 18; *WA* 312, 274.

29 *LW* 22, 190f.; *WA* 46, 701f.

30 *LW* 32, 42-76 passim; *WA* 7, 367-423.

31 *LW* 39, 86ff.; *WA* 6, 309ff.

32 *LW* 41, 317; *WA* 54, 250. For the exegesis on Matt. 16, Matt. 18, John 20, John 21, etc., see also pages 309-327 passim in the same treatise.

33 *LW* 18, 106.109; *WA* 13, 109.111.

34 *LW* 35, 101; *WA* 6, 370. *Treatise on the New Testament.*

35 *LW* 39, 90; *WA* 6, 312.

36 *LW* 44, 127; *WA* 6, 407.

37 *LW* 51, 59; *WA* 2, 248f.; *LW* 49, 28ff.; *WA* Br 3, 23.

38 *LW* 45, 179; *WA* 12, 17f.

39 *LW* 36, 88.148.138.88-120 passim; *WA* 6, 547; 8, 492.486.

40 *LW* 27, 396f.; *WA* 2, 608f.

41 *LW* 40, 274; *WA* 26, 202.

42 *LW* 1, 284; *WA* 42, 210.

43 *LW* 20, 140f.; *WA* 13, 660f.

44 *LW* 54.195f.; *WA* TR 3, 268.

45 *LW* 23, 120; *WA* 33, 185f.

46 *LW* 1, 327f.; *WA* 42, 241.

47 *LW* 2, 284; *WA* 42, 465.

48 *LW* 3, 228; *WA* 43, 38.

49 *LW* 4, 179; *WA* 43, 265.

50 *LW* 6, 80; *WA* 44, 59.

51 *LW* 8, 42; *WA* 44, 609.

52 *LW* 2, 154; *WA* 42, 370; *LW* 30, 115; *WA* 12, 370.

53 *LW* 9, 224f.; *WA* 14, 705; *LW* 17, 318; *WA* 312, 507.

54 *LW* 13, 49; *WA* 311, 196.

55 *LW* 26, 280f.; *WA* 401, 438f.

56 *LW* 51, 71; *WA* 103, 3.

57 *LW* 21, 140; *WA* 32, 415f.

58 *LW* 21, 56f.; *WA* 32, 345.

59 *LW* 48, 370; *WA* Br 2, 426.

60 *LW* 51, 89; *WA* 103, 43.

61 Ibid.

62   *LW* 7, 320; *WA* 44, 536f.

63   *LW* 17, 320; *WA* 312, 507.

64   *LW* 6, 360f.; *WA* 44, 269.

65   *LW* 7, 332; *WA* 44, 546.

66   *LW* 42, 64f. 112; *WA* 2, 117f.

67   *LW* 9, 171; *WA* 14, 673.

68   *LW* 9, 150; *WA* 14, 659.

69   *LW* 11, 477; *WA* 4, 350; *LW* 30, 58,61; *WA* 12, 31f.   315.

70   *LW* 22, 59; *WA* 46, 587.

71   *LW* 23, 218; *WA* 33, 343f.; *LW* 17, 86f.; *WA* 312,329.

72   *LW* 17, 203; *WA* 312, 418.

73   *LW* 17, 309; *WA* 312, 498f.

74   *LW* 16, 54f.; *WA* 312, 37f.

75   *LW* 16, 300; *WA* 312, 221f.

76   *LW* 17, 362; *WA* 312, 541.

77   *LW* 18, 200f.; *WA* 13, 220.

78   *LW* 20, 135; *WA* 13, 656.

79   *LW* 20, 346; *WA* 23, 663f.; *LW* 30, 63; *WA* 12, 317.

80   *LW* 21, 153; *WA* 32, 427.

81   *LW* 23, 356; *WA* 33, 575.

82   *LW* 28, 220; 45, 108; *WA* 26, 7; 11, 264.

83   *LW* 25, 150; *WA* 56, 170f.

84   *LW* 31, 117f.; *WA* 1, 551.

85   *LW* 31, 215; *WA* 1, 607.

86   *LW* 31, 27.31.91; *WA* 1, 234.535.

87   *LW* 31, 93; *WA* 1, 536.

88   *LW* 31, 106; *WA* 1, 544.

89   *LW* 31, 268.255-258.283; *WA* 2, 12.21. From Luther's *Proceedings at Augburg*.

90   *LW* 50, 242; *WA*, Br 10, 335.

Chapter 4

Locating the Church

The church's existence or presence is told by its marks, Word and sacraments. (Mk. 4:26.27; Matt. 13:38; Is. 55:10.11; Matt. 28:18-20; 1 Cor. 10:17; 12:13.) Like an unfurled banner these marks of the church (also known, therefore, as *notae ecclesiae*) are a reliable, foolproof criterion of the presence of the *una sancta*. This is so because of God's promise that His Word will never return void, or without fruit.

Self-evidently the marks of the church do not constitute its essence, or being; for it is believers that make up its body or nature. Who they are is something known only to God. The church, therefore, cannot be said to become visible through the external marks, Word and sacrament, though its presence and location can be definitively spotted through them. One cannot say, there the Word and sacraments are in use and, therefore, we know who the believers are. What we can say, however, is this: because of God's promise connected with the pure preaching of His Word and faithful administration of Baptism and the Lord's Supper, (hence also known as the *notae purae*), we know that there are believers present. This is so even though some impurities or erroneous views or teachings might have entered in. As long as the pure core of the Gospel is present, God will still be gathering sheep, true believers, into His fold, whatever failings, errors, impurities attach themselves to His sheep.

These marks are the vital connecting link between the church in its outward, visible form—congregations, or their indirect derivative, synods or larger church groupings—and the inner, invisible entity or essence, the *una sancta* of believers, known to God but hidden from human eyes as to its exact membership and actual boundaries. It is hidden from all but God. Its existence, however, cannot be doubted. The telltale marks of the church's presence loom up and tell their own tale, wherever the Gospel has reached. God's Word can never be without God's church. (Isaiah 55:11) This is a truism oft repeated by Luther. The seeming paradox of being both hidden and seen resolves itself in God's relationship with believers through the Word of His Gospel on which everything pivots. God's recognition of those that are truly His

46

sheep among the total number of those who profess a connection with the institution(s) called church in this world is an *ipse dixit* for Holy Scripture.

False marks have periodically and consistently put in their appearance among those professing the Christian faith on earth: thus, for example, holiness or perfection of life; claimed powers of healing or speaking in strange tongues; purported apostolic succession through an unbroken line from one generation of bishops or clerics to another, reaching from the apostles, specifically and especially Peter, down to the present; or vaunted monolithic "oneness" under one administrative head, like the Roman pope, or ecumenical super-church with offices at a central location like Geneva, Switzerland. None of these are validly drawn marks taught or promised by the Word of God.

It is a safe rule of thumb to assert that only that can be the mark of church which creates, nurtures, and sustains faith. Only the pure Word of God, the Gospel, and the sacraments of Baptism and the Lord's Supper, the latter sometimes called the "visible Word" because of the elements of water, bread, and wine which God connected with His Word or promise through them, are able to accomplish spiritual regeneration and build the church.

God's means of grace have His own power. In a truly remarkable way they are able to penetrate the hardest of hearts and transcend the most difficult and hostile barriers or borders erected by men. The Gospel, even in its most minimal, elemental form or portion, at least to the extent of the knowledge of God's redeeming work of sinners through Christ, is able to win converts and build Christ's church. Because of this power, which he saw as a wondrously mysterious, miraculous potency, able to blast the fiercest of opposition and strongest of ramparts, Luther states with absolute conviction and certainty:

> God's church is where God's Word resounds, whether it is in the middle of Turkey, in the papacy, or in hell. For it is God's Word which establishes the church. He is the Lord over all places. Wherever that Word is heard, where Baptism, the Sacrament of the Altar, and absolution are administered, there you must determine and conclude with certainty; "This is surely God's house; here heaven has been opened."[1]

In a classic statement, often quoted, the *Augsburg Confession* reinforced Luther's stand:

> For through the Word and Sacraments, as through instru-
> ments, the Holy Ghost, is given, who works faith, where
> and when it pleases God, in them that hear the Gospel, to
> wit, that God, not for our own merits, but for Christ's sake,
> justifies those who believe that they are received into grace
> for Christ's sake. (Article V. Of the Ministry, or Means of
> Grace.)

It should probably be noted here that the words, "where and when it pleases God," have often been misconstrued to mean that God acts in a whimsical, arbitrary sort of way towards mankind, selecting some, rejecting others. That is not the intent of this passage. Rather, the force of this phrase is that we sinners can do nothing to initiate belief, assist it, and, least of all, compel it. God alone is able to draw faith from the human heart and it is by His will, not human effort or initiative, that He accomplishes it through the means of grace. He does not force or compel faith; working by the means of grace is His free choice, and it is a tragic fact that God's benign, earnest purpose is often thwarted by unbelieving hearts.

The seventh article on the nature of the church followed hard on the heels of the statement of the Gospel ministry, with the confessors at Augsburg stating that "the church is the congregation of saints, in which the Gospel is rightly taught and the Sacraments are rightly administered." Moreover, "to the true unity of the Church it is enough to agree concerning the doctrine of the Gospel and the administration of the Sacraments," while usages, rites, and ceremonies need not be demanded or required, since these were instituted by men. It was a good and wise distinction.

Here a comment is in order, to underline what the *Apology* one year later, 1531, made very plain, namely, that the church which is at the center of focus in Augsburg's definition is the *una sancta*, the invisible totality of all believers. Church in Scripture's usage may either have this meaning, or it may be used to designate the outward fellowship of those confessing the Christian faith at a given place, among whom there may be counterfeit, so-called "Christians," who bear the name only but actually are unbelievers. It was the intent of the confessors at Augsburg to point to the church's true nature as "the one holy church (which) is to continue forever," the sum total of true believers. Article VIII on "What the Church Is" displayed this intent.

In its corresponding comments in defense of these articles the *Apology* stressed that this "fellowship has outward marks so that it can be recognized," and then it pointed not at given individuals or offices but at "the pure doctrine of the Gospel and the administration of the Sacraments in accordance with the Gospel of Christ" (Articles VII and VIII, par. 5). "We are speaking," Melanchthon wrote in the same article and context, "not of any imaginary Church," but one which "abides truly upon earth," wherever God's children are found "here and there in all the world, in various kingdoms, islands, lands, and cities, from the rising of the sun to its setting," all who are gathered around "the pillar of the truth," Christ and His Gospel. This disabused people's minds, then as now, of the notion that, when reference was made to the spiritual or invisible entity of true believers, it was something unreal or intangible. The point simply was that only God could lay His finger on who the faithful were or touch them.

"The true marker of the Christian Church," Chemnitz wrote in similar vein, "is not where the largest group (*Haufe*) is," or "where the most powerful, the wisest, the most prominent are," but "wherever these marks are," Word and Sacrament. "Upon this foundation it is built, sometimes gold, sometimes stubble; but wherever the foundation is, there God has his church."[2] As to spotting or locating the church, John Gerhard stated that "the Word of God and the use of the Sacraments are the proper, genuine, and infallible marks" for noting its presence, and the companion truth also obtains, that "where these are pure, the church is pure."[3] Quite correctly, therefore, "the church is looked at in a twofold manner," states J. Benedict Carpzov, either "according to her inner nature," where only believers dwell "in true faith and pure love," or according to "her outward fellowship" where believer and unbeliever "dwell side by side."[4] Carpzov cites the seventh article of the *Augsburg Confession* in support, affirming that the focus in that article is on the nature of the church according to its first, pure, and true sense.

David Hollaz enters into long disquisition on the role which the marks of the church, Word and Sacrament, perform in the outward, external fellowship, particularly in distinguishing the false from the true church. At the same time he notes, however, that in times past the church has survived through "the reading of Scripture alone," even when preaching was forbidden. He also urges, with wise existential counsel, that there may be "certain grades of purity" in the handling of God's truth and that "whole churches are not immediately to be condemned if either the pastor or some few depart from soundness and purity of doctrine," because, as he notes, "the ears of hearers are often purer than the lips of teachers."[5] It is his purpose to affirm that the "church does not immediately cease to exist if the teaching on some articles of religion is not pure." The casual intrusion of error does not frustrate God's building of His kingdom, the church; God will continue to beget and preserve for Himself spiritual children through the Gospel, even when the public ministry has fallen upon bad times and corrupt teaching. Thus the Word succeeds in spite of the departures from the norm.

Walther, too, like his worthy forebears, was ready to grant the church's existence here and there upon the earth, even if and when certain aberrations or faulty teachings existed alongside the pure Gospel. The power of God's redeeming and regenerating Word was never better, nor more forcefully, shown than when in spite of mistaken human accretions, either adding to or subtracting from the pure Word, God was still able to build His church.

Nothing underscored more plainly the inability of men to aid in their salvation than this fact, that even the human errors, as long as they were not so fundamental as to rip out the very heart of the saving Gospel truth, could not sway the ultimate effect of God's mighty working through His designated means of grace, Word and Sacrament. Because of these wondrous instruments of God's working in us, Walther stated we can feel kinship with Jacob who was awed by God's attention and care for him: "Surely, the Lord is in this place; and I knew it not. How dreadful (awesome) is this place! This is none other but the house of God, and this is the gate of heaven."[6]

It was one of Luther's great insights, as he read of God's dealings with mankind in Holy Scripture, to note that God very graciously presented Himself and His Word to man in such a way that man could easily understand and grasp things. Man's physical nature is at home in the dimensions of space, time, and motion, the physical realm around him. God takes the center of the stage in revealing Himself and His purposes to man, at a time and in a

manner of His own choice, but within the limits of man's perception
and cognitive grasp. It is not for man to scramble up to God
somehow, by "ladders" of his own construction, whether to the top
of some physical mountain, or to the top of some mystical mountain
within his own mind or spirit, or combination of the two. It is rather
a case of <u>God</u> using both channels, with which He equipped man in
the creation, and coming to him how and when it pleases Him. This
was so even after man's fall into sin; in fact, all the more so, since
the blessed concourse that existed before between the Creator and
man, undisturbed by sin's barrier, was at an end once man's
rebellion had entered, to despoil the blissful relationship that had
existed in the pristine state. But before sin entered in, God set
certain tangible signs or markers for Adam. The tree of the
knowledge of good and evil would have had such significance,
Luther states, "so that Adam might have a definite way to express
his worship and reverence toward God."[7] This was not self-chosen
on Adam's part, but "a matter of theology," established by God. In
the same way we today have His Word connected with the water of
Baptism, or with the bread and wine in the Supper, Luther notes on
sound Scriptural basis. "It was necessary that man, as a physical
being, also have a physical or external form of worship."[8] So, by
God's own ordaining, "this tree of the knowledge of good and evil
was Adam's church, altar, and pulpit."[9] This was not some form of
primitive or idolatrous nature worship, but simply a fact that resulted
from the Word of God being connected to this particular focal point
by God. The tree, moreover, was "not deadly by nature," but only
"because it was stated to be so by the Word of God."[10]

God has always set certain signs for His church, or His
people. As a result, "the church has never been deprived to such an
extent of outward signs that it became impossible to know where
God could surely be found."[11] It is for man to take, or receive, God
at the point of His approach, and not despise Him or the manner of
His revealing Himself through His Word. "Therefore this gift is
something inexpressible," is Luther's way of emphasizing the
respectful attitude we ought to maintain towards what God is doing
for us, "that God not only deigns to speak to men through the Word
but adds to the Word visible signs of grace, such as Baptism, the
Eucharist, and absolution in the New Testament."[12] Luther's point
is that it should be easy for us to see that "therefore what Baptism
and the Lord's Supper are for us, sacrifice and offering were for

Adam after the promise."[13] Human reason finds plenty to object to
here, but faith listens attentively and trustingly, knowing "such is
always God's way, that He joins some visible sign to the Word."[14]
So, even though God dwells in a light which no man can approach
unto, He has never left man alone and without His gracious Word.

It is rightly stated, therefore, that "we have no silent forms
of worship, but the voice of the Gospel is always heard."[15] Luther
simply stresses that the means of grace by which God channels His
mercy to mankind are very tangible, at hand, and never to be
doubted. Gifts of God they are, that speak loudly, for our salvation.
The gods of the heathen are empty idols who do not speak and have
never spoken. "But the God who has revealed Himself by visible
marks, who has given the Word of promise and has instituted the
sacraments, is the true God and Savior whom we are able to take
hold of and to understand." Therefore, Luther urges, "stay with God
in the category of relation," that is in the relation, or association and
revelation, which He Himself has established for our sakes.[16]

These are God's own *larvae Dei*, the veils or curtains, by
which He wants Himself to be known and understood, tied as they
are to His Word, not to the word of man, not even the pope, who
actually "invents new forms."[17] God made His covenant with
Abraham under the sign of circumcision; He makes His covenant
with us under the ministry of Word, Baptism, the keys. Abraham
might have questioned God about this strange sign, circumcision,
Luther says, "but he accepts it with humility and with thanksgiving."[18] "The concern about the salvation of the heathen he leaves to
God and asks no prying questions about them," and the same holds
for the females among his descendants and why "God (did) not mark
them too by some sign, just as He marked our males."[19] Abraham
rested content with what God had said, with His Word, "and is
intent on doing what he knows has been commanded him." Every
child of God, or believer, needs to bow this same way before God
and His Word.

Jacob, leaving his home because of the vengeful Esau,
discovered through God's revealing of Himself to him in a remarkable dream and vision, that "I find God in this place too."[20]
"Wherever that Word is heard, where Baptism, the Sacrament of the
Altar, and absolution are administered, there you must determine and
conclude with certainty: 'This is surely God's house; here heaven
has been opened.'"[21] This is quite contrary to the way people

usually thought of the church in his day, Luther observes. Then the common belief ran this way: "The chief pontiff is at Rome. Therefore the church is there." On the contrary it ought to be thought of this way, says Luther: "Where God speaks, where Jacob's ladder is, where the angels ascend and descend, there the church is, there the kingdom of heaven is opened."[22] "We acknowledge that the church is among them," Luther says of his opponents, the Romanists, but only because and to the extent that the Word is there, "for if the church is to be the house of God, it is necessary for it to have the Word of God."[23] If the church has everything else, and not the Word, then what it has is in vain, "because Christ and Belial are not in accord; for the bed is narrow, (and) consequently one of the two falls out, and the short cloak cannot cover both, as Isaiah 28:20 says."[24]

"This is the Word of God," is not only a fond idea, or magical incantation, but the truth which God conveys through His chosen means of grace. "I hear a man's voice. I see human gestures. The bread and the wine in the Supper are physical things. At ordination the hands of carnal men are imposed. In Baptism water is water. For the flesh judges in no other way concerning all these matters. But if you look at that addition with spiritual eyes, namely, at whose Word it is that is spoken and heard there, not indeed the word of a man—for if it is the word of a man, then the devil is speaking—but the Word of God, then you will understand that it is the house of God and the gate of heaven." Luther could hardly stress the significance of God's means of grace more emphatically or winsomely. He further underscores the point by stating: "It is an exceedingly important thing when Jacob declares specifically that God's house is found where God dwells with us. He comes first and appears to us on the ladder. He descends and lives with us. He speaks and works in us. Thus the church is established among men when God dwells with men. . . and the Word is taught."[25]

Where God's Word is, there the church is, for "where the Word is taught, there faith is, and where faith is, there are such neighbors" who are "godly people" of all ranks.[26] "When the confession of God and the ministry of the Word sounds forth there, or God is praised and invoked, then it is a temple and a church, even though it is under the open sky, or a tree, or under that oak under which Jacob buried the idols."[27] The heathen might choose similar

"very pleasant spots on the mountains or in the valleys, or near
rivers and trees, to which they lured the people to make sacrifice
under the open sky according to the ritual of the fathers," but the
absence of God's Word meant empty worship; God was not there.[28]
The church is always the pupil of Christ, student of His Word, and
"it does not teach anything except what has been entrusted to it by
Christ."[29]

God withdraws His blessing and His presence where His
Word is despised. Luther believes this happened with the papalists,
"even though they boast of their titles, prestige, large numbers, and
power," and that "God cast them aside for treading His Word
underfoot and persecuting it."[30] This is a very serious matter, one
that sets up a deadly sort of syndrome, for "once God has withdrawn, and once the Word and the grace of God have been taken
away, it is not easily found again," as in the case of the once "very
beautiful church at Rome."[31] In Noah we have a good example of
a man who took God at His Word, not only in the building of the
ark, as commanded, but in leaving it when he was told. "Noah
could have thought differently," Luther states. Since the ark was
his rescue, he might have reasoned this way: "I shall keep it as a
temple or a place for the worship of God; for it has been hallowed
by the Word of God and by the fact that saints, or the church, dwell
in it."[32] But he did not; he bowed before God's Word. The church
in each generation faces a similar temptation with its "monuments,"
its historic mementos, its halls of fame, that it turn these into
idolatrous centers of worship at the expense of denying God's Word.

History tells the story "that the church was gathered only by
the Word, not by force or the sword."[33] It is always the same:
"Wherever one finds the Gospel, Baptism, and the Sacrament, there
is His church, and in that place there are certainly living saints,"[34]
and this is "God's house, where He dwells, be it in the field, in
church, or on the sea."[35] The Word is God's "royal scepter," "the
scepter of His kingdom," both Law and Gospel, by which He rules
in Zion.[36] The Law works its work, the recognition of unrighteousness in ourselves; the Gospel is gentle and soothing, with healing for
sin-filled lives. God has chosen "in His invisible essence" to work
this way "through external, visible signs, of which the preaching of
the Gospel and the Sacraments are the chief ones," the true marks
whereby one can really recognize where the scepter is.[37] "By the

Word alone, therefore, the church is recognized, and in the glory of the Word the reign of Christ is described."[38]

The doctrines or words of men cannot take the place of God's Word. "You must have God's Word to support you."[39] If the church is to "rest on certainty" and skirt empty "beating of the air," it must rest on God's Word which alone can set its footing solidly.[40] The true church delights in God's testimonies, and "she opens her mouth only for purpose of drawing in His Word."[41] What we are dealing with in the church, therefore, is "not the word of teenage girls, but of the bride herself," who is aglow because of her love for the Bridegroom, Christ.[42] Surely we ought not tremble at others' word, while "we are insensitive to the Word of God."[43] Luther puts the bride's, the church's, relationship with the Bridegroom very graphically:

> Therefore stick to the Word of God. Ignore every other word—whether it is devoid of Christ, in the name of Christ, or against Christ, or whether it is issued in any other way. No one dare sleep with the bride or make her pregnant but the Lord Christ alone. If He does not teach or preach or make souls pregnant, all is lost.[44]

The task of shepherding in the church includes proclaiming the Shepherd's Word, as well as "to shout at the wolf and to treat him roughly."[45] "We recognize no other church than the one that heeds the voice of Christ and is baptized."[46] Accordingly, any other voice misleads, and, says Luther, "we know nothing of that church which orders pilgrimages and the wearing of cowls," while "the Gospel demands that we believe in Christ and then love one another."[47] We can be sure that God will gather His people at "any place where Holy Writ is publicly preached and read before a congregation." The hearers may be ever so "turned-off" by a sermon they consider "odd, absurd, and nonsensical." But remember, says Luther, "even His disciples themselves declared: 'What a strange, peculiar, and stupid sermon! Who can remain His disciple or adhere to Him?'"[48] "But so it goes," when Christ seeks to draw men through His Word and promises. But we must not be deterred: "He binds us solely to His Word. He does not want to see the Holy Spirit divorced from His Word."[49]

This was Luther's answer to the high-flying fanatic, charismatic spirits who turn inwardly to their own spiritual experiences or inner wrestlings: "Whenever you hear anyone boast that he has something by inspiration of the Holy Spirit and it has no basis in God's Word, no matter what it may be, tell him that this is the work of the devil. Christ does not bind you to anything but His mouth and His Word."[50] Here is an admonition with serious consequences, if not heeded. "Failure to do this has always given rise in the world to great and terrible errors, idolatries, and schisms."[51] We dare not "run to and fro in search of the Spirit."[52] The church has but one duty, forever and a day, and that is "either adhere to the divine Word or perish and be lost."[53]

Luther's emphasis upon purity of teaching in connection with God's Word is well known. He found himself bound by the Word as revealed by God in Holy Writ. "In matters of doctrine I will let no angel, neither Gabriel or Michael, arise and preach; for they are not God; nor are they the Holy Spirit. I have God's Word for this," Luther states, in evident reference to Holy Scripture.[54] This is the Holy Spirit's book, and as to other sources, "we must disregard these fluttering spirits."[55]

At the heart and core of God's Word are Law and Gospel, the chief articles or doctrines in the Bible. The Law fulfills its necessary function, as it did at Mt. Sinai, when it crushes within man the pretension of righteousness on his own; its proper task is to be God's thunderbolt or hammer to mollify or powder man's innate self-righteous notions about himself.[56] When the Law has thus done its work, the Gospel enters in to lift, quicken, comfort, heal, with the sweet message of forgiveness through Christ. "Unless the Gospel is clearly distinguished from the Law" in this way, "Christian doctrine cannot be kept sound." "But when this distinction is recognized, the true meaning of justification is recognized."

This distinction was to Luther like the continental divide or watershed of all doctrine. "Whoever knows well how to distinguish the Gospel from the Law should give thanks to God and know that he is a real theologian."[57] In self-effacing humility Luther admits: "In time of temptation I myself do not know how to do this as I should"—no doubt because of the propensity of the human spirit to find righteousness in itself. But this is what we must remember at such times:

The way to distinguish the one from the other is to locate the Gospel in heaven and the Law on earth, to call the righteousness of the Gospel heavenly and divine and the righteousness of the Law earthly and human, and to distinguish as sharply between the righteousness of the Gospel and that of the Law as God distinguishes between heaven and earth, or between light and darkness, or between day and night. Let the one be like the light and the day, and the other like the darkness and the night. If we could only put an even greater distance between them. Therefore, if the issue is faith, heavenly righteousness, or conscience, let us leave the Law out of consideration altogether and let it remain on the earth. But if the issue is works, then let us light the lamp of works and of the righteousness of the Law in the night.[58]

For Luther the rule of thumb for distinguishing Law and Gospel was simply that the former differed from the latter as a demand laid upon us differs from a gift given to us. The one drives home the fact of sin; the other bestows God's grace upon conscience so that guilt is gone and freedom in Christ reigns, "on whose account all my sins are forgiven."[59] So both Law and Gospel are important to the sinner; for "how will we learn what Christ is, what He did for us, if we do not know what the Law is that He fulfilled for us and what sin is, for which he made satisfaction?"[60] So, while "we have to preach it (the Law) for Christ's sake," we do not, of course, preach it as a substitute for Christ, not even in the smallest, slightest way.

Against the antinomians, however, Luther also stressed the continuing paedogogical function of the Law, the so-called third use of the Law, in the believer's life, serving him as a pattern of godly living. Thus in the same context where Luther brilliantly set the two apart, like light from darkness, he added: "But in a matter apart from conscience (that is, apart from faith-righteousness or justification), when outward duties must be performed, then, whether you are a preacher, a magistrate, a husband, a teacher, a pupil, etc., this is not time to listen to the Gospel. You must listen to the Law and follow your vocation. Thus the Law remains in the valley with the ass, and the Gospel remains with Isaac on the mountain."[61]

Luther never tired of stressing that the Law itself was good, divine, and holy, even though now its function primarily is negative, constantly accusing the sinner (*Lex semper accusat*), multiplying sin in the human heart. Is the Law, therefore evil, St. Paul asks in Romans 7 and Galatians 3? Luther, drawing on the apostle, answers, "Of course not!" He then adds to his answer: "To put the matter before you by way of a comparison, water is good; but when poured over lime it sets the lime on fire. Is it the fault of the water that the lime becomes hot? Indeed, the lime, which was thought to be cold, is convicted by the water of what it has inside. Thus the Law incites lusts and hatreds, and exposes them; but it does not cure them. But if you pour oil over the lime, it does not become hot. Thus when grace has been poured into our hearts through the Holy Spirit, it extinguishes hatred and lusts."[62] This balm or oil of healing is the Gospel.

If there has been one chief plague in the church, it has been confusion of Law and Gospel,[63] trying to make the one do what only the other can, thus turning their functions around or by denying the further validity or applicability of the Law, for example, in a person's life. Scripture carefully distinguishes between promises and threats, Luther asserts. Moreover, he detected how, against Scripture's plain instruction and injunction, the Roman papacy, in spite of its legalistic, semi-Pelagian, works-righteous theology, had actually lowered the Law's demands. When that happens, and the thunderbolts of the Law no longer strike down the inherent synergistic streak in natural man, even in the believing sinner, the Gospel's promises will seem like "easy promises" and become tasteless, or merely "increase the smugness" in the sinner.[64] It is futile to try to do without the Law; "therefore let us utterly reject the antinomians, who cast the Law out of the church and want to teach repentance by means of the Gospel."[65]

By the same token, there is no hope, no salvation in the Law; and we must understand this very well that "it is one thing to be justified by the Law and another thing to be justified by grace."[66] The first is impossible; the second is God's sure promise. Luther reflects on his youth to draw a vivid example or analogy of how the Law and Gospel work on, or affect, us:

> The same thing happens to us that formerly happened to me in my boyhood and to my companions with whom I used to

gather contributions for our support during our student days.
For when at the time of the celebration of Christ's birthday
in the church we were singing in four voices from door to
door in the villages the usual songs about the boy Jesus who
was born in Bethlehem, it happened by chance that we came
to a country house situated in a lonely spot on the outermost
borders of a village. When the farmer had heard us singing,
he came out of the house and asked in a boorish voice
where we were. "Where are you, you rascals?" he asked.
At the same time he brought out sausages which he intended
to give us. But at the sound of these words we became so
terrified that we all scattered, although we knew no reason
at all for our terror, and the farmer was offering the sausages with the greatest goodwill. It is possible, of course, that
our hearts, beaten down as they were by the constant threats
and the cruelty with which teachers were accustomed to
rage against their pupils, were more likely to be upset by
sudden fright. Finally, however, he called us back from our
flight; and we laid our fear aside, ran up, and took the
contribution he was handing us.[67]

In yet another analogy, Luther urges that we take a lesson
from St. Paul, as he teaches and admonishes Timothy (2 Tim. 2:15),
to learn how "to part the hoof," that is, divide the Word of God
properly. This means laying the Law heavily upon the old nature,
the old man, as upon a jackass, so that the sinful flesh is not free;
and then the Gospel speaks joyfully to the conscience setting it free
according to the new man, the man of faith, who is spiritual.
"Therefore, let the heart become free through the Word of grace, and
let the body become a servant through the law of love; then the hoof
will be properly parted" and we will "chew the cud" in proper
manner.[68]

The Law/Gospel distinction is only one part, though the
principal part, of the concern for purity of teaching in connection
with God's Word. The greatest fault in Cain and in the false
"Cainite church" was the "attack on the sound doctrine" in general,
God's Word as a whole, Luther laments.[69] The Roman church's
failing likewise involved primarily the insinuation of "endless errors
and blasphemous doctrines" into the body of Scriptural teachings,
coupled with audacious branding of all those who opposed such

godlessness as guilty of heresy.[70] It is never "the stones, the construction, and the gorgeous silver and gold that make a church beautiful and holy; it is the Word of God and sound preaching."[71] If in any place in the world, then certainly and especially in the church it should be true that "the teachers try to teach what is certain."[72] In contrast to the papalists who magnify the Law to the neglect of the Gospel, there is "the madness of the antinomians who remove the Law from the church."[73]

Idle speculation, too, is out of place in the church. There are some things that are not answered by God in His Word, and it is best in view of that to keep silence, "lest the church be burdened with a multitude of books."[74] Luther fears that they might possibly lead people "away from reading Scripture itself." We must recognize that everything in Scripture is really important because it is "written by the Holy Spirit for the purpose of establishing faith."[75]

In matters of faith and Christian teaching the primary and principal point is, who is speaking, not what is being spoken. This is the reverse, Luther says, of what obtains in the world and its thinking. "Seneca says: 'Do not consider who is speaking, but consider what is being said.' This rule has a place in the household and in the state; but in the church and in matters of religion it must be turned around, and one must ask who, not what. In the church one must consider who is giving the command."[76] When God speaks as He does in His Word, then we must honor that Word, even as we honor Him, thus fulfilling also the commandments that follow after the first.[77] "No one has the authority to burden the church with new doctrines."[78] All true doctrine is from God, and only from Him. False doctrine, whether that of Arius in the early church, or of Muentzer at the time of the Reformation, runs counter to God's Word. Human traditions do the same. "This was the bane of the church," Luther observes, "for human traditions and ceremonies are very showy and strike the eyes of the people."[79]

The human propensity is always toward the outward splendor that appeals to the mind of man. Thus at Isaac's time the people might well have dismissed the old patriarch as a doddering old fool, and said: "Isaac is a silly old man; he cannot be responsible for anything. Rebecca milks the goats and the cows. Therefore let us establish a different and far more sublime worship of God."[80] There is no alternative to God's Word. "For the Holy Spirit does not come without the Word, but He comes through His lyre; that is,

He wants to come through meditation on the Word or through the spoken words of the father, the mother, or others. Otherwise the devil comes. But, as David, Isaiah, and all Scripture bear witness, the Holy Spirit comes with the Word and through the Word."[81] It is true that "the wheat of the church has always been mixed with tares," but the true church exists because of the pure Word of God.[82] The church and its teachers must be solid and firm as a rock as regards the Word of God. "The Elbe," Luther says, "rushes along; but the rock remains firm. . . Certainty is necessary throughout life, but especially in the teachings of the church."[83]

God has indicated that He intends to dwell "where His Word and honor are," and that is not in some mere "house of wood and stone," but where "His Word, His worship, His office" are present, for through them He has promised to "be with His people and to teach and sanctify them." "That," says Luther, "is what 'God's house' means."[84] That is why it is possible and right to say: "Now where there are people who cling to Christ, there a Christian Church is sure to be."[85] Moreover, God has promised that with the spreading of the Gospel everywhere, and in spite of all appearances to the contrary, He will have a large church, greater than any nation.[86] Nor will its preservation or size be dependent upon anything in us. He will see to its increase and its keeping. Luther sets things into proper perspective concerning God's interworking with His people in this fine statement:

A thousand years ago you and I were nothing, and yet the church was preserved at that time without us. He who is called 'who was' and 'yesterday' had to accomplish this. Even during our lifetime we are not the church's guardians. It is not preserved by us, for we are unable to drive off the devil in the persons of the pope, the sects, and evil men. If it were up to us, the church would perish before our very eyes, and we together with it (as we experience daily). For it is another Man who obviously preserves both the church and us. It is a tragic thing that there are so many examples before us of those who thought they had to preserve the church, as though it were built on them. . . Recently the Anabaptists reminded us forcefully enough how mighty and how close to us the lovely devil is, and how dangerous our pretty thoughts are.[87]

It is good to remember how absolute is our dependence upon God's working and upon His Word. That is the way the situation is and we had best recognize it. Without His Word we are lost and helpless. Around us always are the sectarian spirits, perfectionist or charismatic (or both) in orientation and commitment, who say: "No, we are the heroes who need not worry about our flesh and our thoughts. We are sheer spirit, we have taken captive our own flesh together with the devil, so that all our thoughts and ideas are surely and certainly inspired by the Holy Spirit, and how can he be found wanting?" Luther expresses a rightfully dim view of this shallow, flighty boasting, stating: "Therefore it all has such a nice ending, namely, that both steed and rider break their necks."[88]

This notion, that it is not only God but also man with his energies and innovations that avail for the church's progress and continuance, is also an ongoing plague upon the church. "Everything that God does they must improve." Such leaders sound ever so pious and their programs ever so heavenly minded; but their actions belie their words, "so that there is no poorer, more insignificant and despised disciple on earth than God," the way things work out in the church's life. As a result, "He (God) must be everybody's pupil; everybody wants to be His teacher and preceptor." This self-willed piety and officiousness, Luther states, "may be seen in all heretics from the beginning of the world." Whether you look at "Arius and Pelagius, and now in our time the Anabaptists and anti-sacramentarians, and all fanatics and rebels," the story is always the same: "They are not satisfied with what God has done and instituted, they cannot let things be as they were ordained to be." The tragic story in the church is that "conceit keeps the dance going." However, says Luther, there is comfort in this that "God will not tolerate" this kind of would-be takeover. "He has no intention of being a pupil; they are to be the pupils. . . God can get along without their counsel and rule," and He will.[89] Therefore, the truly pious and proper prayer of each Christian ought to be:

> Dear heavenly Father, speak thou, I am willing to be a fool and a child and be silent; for if I were to rule with my own understanding, wisdom, and reason, the cart would long since have been stuck in the mire and the ship would long since have been wrecked. Therefore, dear God, do thou rule

and guide it thyself; I will gladly put out my eyes, and my reason besides, and let thee alone rule through thy Word.[90]

If that be the prayerful, humble stance of the believer before God, "then things would be right in the church and it would be well governed, and there would be harmony all around." We expect no less in the earthly kingdoms and their management, Luther states. "A city council will not tolerate a fool who frequently gets the whole town into confusion, but casts him out, and the whole country is glad about it. The same thing should happen here in the Christian church; none other should be preached or taught except the Son of God alone."[91] God's injunction to His people, simply and without confusion, is this: "If you have my Word, then stick to it, and pay no attention to anybody who teaches and commands you differently."[92]

The presence of the church, the true church, is not difficult to discover or determine therefore. It will be there "where the pure Word of God is present, where there is the right administration of the Sacraments, where there are people who love the Word and confess it before men." "Where you discover these earmarks," Luther states, "there you may be sure the church exists."[93] Not physical property, or ecclesiastical structures, not even that of the papacy, but Word and Sacraments, these are the church's true and genuine marks.[94] "Just as the banner of an army is the sure sign" by which to distinguish the troops, so God's pure Gospel is the ensign of His church.[95] Where God's Word is, there faith dwells, and there the church is present, whether in forest or field, or wherever.[96] There is no other "proper touchstone," or "reliable yardstick" quite like this.[97] When the church does its proper task, that is, "preaches that Christ, our Bridegroom, was born, was crucified, and died for us," there we can be confident "the church remains" and people confess the Creed truly, "I believe in God the Father, God the Son, and God the Holy Spirit."[98] It is because of God's saving Gospel, and faith in it, that we can say:

We are holy. We are members of a holy fraternity in Wittenberg, in Rome, in Jerusalem, and wherever holy Baptism and the Gospel are. And we do not regard one another otherwise than as saints of God. Even though we are still sinners and many failings always remain in our flesh and blood, He covers up our sins and impurities. Thus we are accounted entirely pure and holy before God, as long as we cling to Christ and His Baptism and rely on His blood.[99]

Many things compete for attention in God's church on earth. It is Luther's sage advice, however, that first and foremost we should "fight and work until we have these necessary things: the preservation of the pure doctrine and faith." There are many legitimate concerns or programs that a church may have, but we need constantly to be reminded that "the Holy Spirit occupies Himself with other matters," and these are, "how to rescue men from sin and death by making them children of God, righteous, and heirs of eternal life; how to build the kingdom of God and destroy the kingdom of hell; how to fight against the devil and overcome him; how to give comfort, strength, and support to a believing conscience."[100]

Luther was never of the opinion that the church on earth could be so pure and free of error that there would be no fault in it, as the sects argued. There was no substitute, of course, for the pure Word of God in all its fulness. Yet, "the true and holy church nevertheless remains," wherever Word and Sacrament are still present; God will be gathering His church even where evil or evil men remain.[101] This by no means is said to minimize the danger and threat from "the lying word" of Satan which works to undo the church and its members.

There are also other signs by which the presence of the church may be known, Luther states, though these in themselves are not to be thought of as reliable as the true marks, Word and Sacrament, since they may in certain instances also be found in the world. Thus, besides the visible sign of the Word, there are in addition cross and suffering, affliction and persecution, which the church regularly bears.[102] The Christian is to put his Savior on, through faith, and become "Christ" to his neighbor, according to Scripture's own injunction. We bear our crosses, imposed by God, after Him. Thus, as we looked at our Savior's lowly poverty, Luther states, "we saw that his poverty teaches us how we are to find him in our neighbor, in the lowliest and the neediest, and that his diapers are the Holy Scriptures."[103] Luther could hardly have stated the need for sanctification in the believer's life more vividly, nor expressed the tie which we have to Holy Writ in more down-to-earth manner.

In his treatise, *Concerning the Ministry*, of 1523, Luther addresses the priesthood of believers, specifically in Bohemia where a crisis of supplying pastors for the pulpits had arisen. His advice bears directly on their emergency. They were to know that since the Word was among them, they should not doubt that the true church was there. They had the true marks of the church, Word and sacraments. Should it be that Rome remained intransigent and refused to supply them with pastors, then, Luther counsels, they should elect a qualified man from their own midst.[104]

A Christian believer's freedom was as wide and broad as God's Word was broad. Preeminent at all times was the Word, higher than any other authority, even the presumptuous papacy. If necessity demanded and no godly clergy filled the pulpits or administered the sacraments, each "father of the household (could at a bare minimum) read the Gospel and baptize," even "if through life they did not dare or could not receive the Eucharist. For the Eucharist is not so necessary that salvation depends on it."[105] The right to call a qualified man into their service inhered in the congregation of believers, the royal priests, as St. Paul already taught in his day, 2 Tim. 2; Acts 18:24ff.; 1 Cor. 14:30; Tit. 1:6ff.[106]

This corresponds to the lengthier and maturer statement which Luther includes concerning the church and its marks in his rightly famous *Councils and the Church*, in 1539. "The holy Christian people are recognized by their possession of the holy Word of God," not straw and stubble; "for God's Word is holy and sanctifies everything it touches."[107] He repeats a familiar tune: "A Christian, holy people must exist there, for God's Word cannot be without God's people."[108] Thereupon, in addition to Word, Baptism, Lord's Supper, and absolution or the Keys, Luther also lists three other marks that identify the presence of the church: "called ministers"; "prayer, praise, and thanksgiving to God" or worship; and "possession of the sacred cross" or "misfortune and persecution, and all kind of trials and evil."[109]

Actually these latter are all in some way contingent upon or derive from the Word, or Gospel, and thus do not actually add anything which is not already there to the *notae purae*, or pure marks of the church. Luther also points to other marks like sanctification of life, which can rightly be expected in the lives of

Christians; but then he adds that "these signs cannot be regarded as reliable as those noted before, since some heathen, too, practice these works and indeed at times appear holier than Christians."[110] Then there are the externals which regularly group themselves around a church, like holidays, certain hours, building, pulpit, font, candles, bells, vestments. Obviously, Luther notes, "Christians could be and remain sanctified without these items." He speaks a special word in behalf of schools, for "we will not have pastors and preachers very long," nor good servants in government and in the schools, etc., if we do not have good schools.[111]

Nothing that Luther adduces here in any way detracts from the single emphasis that God's church is spotted or located by the Word; and while this Word is not the essence of the church—for the church is constituted by people, by believers—it is the sure sign of their presence there. Identifying them, however, is ultimately and finally a precinct which belongs to God alone.

NOTES

1   *LW* 5, 244; *WA* 43, 596. *Genesis Commentary.*

2   *Enchiridion,* 210. cf. Poellot trans., 154.

3   *Loc. Theol.,* XI, 195. Quoted in H. Schmid, *Doctrinal Theology of the Lutheran Church,* 598.

4   *Isagoge,* p. 300. Quoted in Walther, 54.

5   *Examen Theologicum Acroamaticum,* 1307ff. Quoted in Schmid, *DT,* 598.

6   Cf. Walther, *KA,* 54.

7   *LW* 1, 94; *WA* 42, 71.

8   Ibid.

9   *LW* 1, 95; *WA* 42, 72.

10   *LW* 1, 95; *WA* 42, 73.

11   *LW* 1, 248; *WA* 42, 184.

12   *LW* 1, 250; *WA* 42, 185.

13   Ibid.

14   *LW* 1, 329; *WA* 42, 242.

15   *LW* 2, 333; *WA* 42, 499.

16   *LW* 3, 122; *WA* 42, 635.

17   *LW* 3, 123.
18   *LW* 3, 128; *WA* 42, 639.
19   Ibid.
20   *LW* 5, 240; *WA* 43, 594.
21   *LW* 5, 244; *WA* 43, 597.
22   *LW* 5, 244; *WA* 43, 596.
23   *LW* 5, 245; *WA* 43, 598.
24   *LW* 5, 246; *WA* 43, 598.
25   *LW* 5, 248ff.; *WA* 43, 600ff.
26   *LW* 6, 124; *WA* 44, 92.
27   *LW* 6, 250; *WA* 44,185.
28   Ibid.
29   *LW* 2, 356; *WA* 42, 517.
30   *LW* 2, 100; *WA* 42, 333.
31   *LW* 4, 156; *WA* 43, 536.
32   *LW* 2, 112; *WA* 42, 341.
33   *LW* 8, 246; *WA* 44, 759.
34   *LW* 14, 13; *WA* 311, 232.
35   *LW* 14, 103; *WA* 311, 179.
36   *LW* 14, 336; *WA* 5, 65.
37   *LW* 13, 272; *WA* 41, 131.
38   *LW* 16, 32; *WA* 312, 22.
39   *LW* 35, 152; *WA* 102 91.
40   *LW* 13, 140; *StL* 5, 798.
41   *LW* 11, 503; *WA* 4, 369.
42   *LW* 11, 518; *WA* 4, 380.
43   Ibid.
44   *LW* 22, 451; *WA* 47, 165.
45   *LW* 22, 514; *WA* 47, 217f.
46   Ibid.
47   Ibid.
48   *LW* 23, 156; *WA* 33, 244f.
49   *LW* 23, 173; *WA* 33, 274.
50   Ibid.
51   Ibid.

52   Ibid.

53   *LW* 23, 386; *WA* 33, 628.

54   *LW* 23, 349; *WA* 33, 562.

55   Ibid.

56   *LW* 26, 310-313; *WA* 40, 481-486.

57   *LW* 26, 115; *WA* 40, 207.

58   Ibid.

59   *LW* 26, 117; *WA* 401, 210.

60   *LW* 47, 113; *WA* 50, 473. *Against the Antinomians.*

61   *LW* 26, 117; *WA* 401, 210.

62   *LW* 27, 276; *WA* 2, 527.

63   *LW* 3, 77; *WA* 42, 603.

64   *LW* 3, 222-225; *WA* 43, 33-36.

65   *LW* 4, 49; *WA* 43, 171.

66   *LW* 5, 38; *WA* 43, 454.

67   *LW* 7, 335; *WA* 44, 548.

68   *LW* 9, 136; *WA* 14, 650. During his early years Luther occasionally slipped into the allegorical method of Scripture interpretation according to which four senses or meanings were to found in a given passage. Thus, for example, in his lectures on Deuteronomy, he compared the eunuch without testes to the Word of God when it is stripped of the Law and thus becomes ineffective. *LW* 9, 235; *WA* 14, 711. In Luther's behalf, however, it should also be stated that he also very early expressed the opinion that such exegetical method should not be employed to establish doctrine in the church. *LW* 27, 311; *WA* 2, 550.

69   *LW* 2, 30ff.; *WA* 42, 283ff.

70   *LW* 2, 60; *WA* 42, 304.

71   *LW* 2, 334; *WA* 42, 500.

72   *LW* 3, 260; *WA* 43, 61.

73   *LW* 3, 269; *WA* 43, 67.

74   *LW* 3, 305; *WA* 43, 94.

75   *LW* 3, 316; *WA* 43, 101f.

76   *LW* 4, 180; *WA* 43, 265.

77   *LW* 4, 14ff.; *WA* 43, 145ff.

78   Ibid.

79   *LW* 5, 97; *WA* 43, 496.

80   Ibid.

81   *LW* 5, 111; *WA* 43, 505.

82   *LW* 6, 34; *WA* 44, 24.

83   *LW* 8, 212; *WA* 44, 733.

84   *LW* 20, 177; *WA* 23, 519.

85   *LW* 30, 116; *WA* 12, 370.

86   *LW* 3, 66; *WA* 42, 596.

87   *LW* 47, 118f.; *WA* 50, 477. *Against the Antinomians*, 1539.

88   *LW* 47, 119; *WA* 50, 478.

89   *LW* 51, 384ff.; *WA* 51, 118ff.

90   *LW* 51, 388; *WA* 51, 191.

91   Ibid.

92   *LW* 51, 390; *WA* 51, 192.

93   *LW* 13, 90; *St. L* 5, 747f.; cf. *LW* 4, 31; *WA* 43, 157.

94   *LW* 39, 75; *WA* 6, 301.

95   *LW* 39, 305; *WA* 11, 408.

96   *LW* 22, 209; *WA* 46, 718.

97   *LW* 22, 265; *WA* 46, 780.

98   *LW* 22, 269f.; *WA* 46, 783f.

99   *LW* 24, 171. cf. 168-174; *WA* 45, 617. cf. 614-620.

100   *LW* 24, 360f.; *WA* 46, 56f.

101   *LW* 28, 302; *WA* 26, 64.

102   *LW* 1, 255; *WA* 42, 189.

103   *LW* 52, 39; *WA* 101, 139.

104   *LW* 40, 7ff.; *WA* 12, 169ff. The powers of the priesthood of believers is treated at length in Chapter 3 on the Treasures or Keys of the Church, as well as in Part II, Chapters 2 and 4, on the calling of a pastor by the congregation.

105   *LW* 40, 9; *WA* 12, 171.

106   *LW* 40, 37ff.; *WA* 12, 191ff.

107   *LW* 41, 148f.; *WA* 50, 628f.

108   *LW* 41, 150; *WA* 50, 629.

109   *LW* 41, 151ff.; *WA* 50, 630ff.

110   *LW* 41, 166ff.; *WA* 50, 643ff.

111   Ibid.

Chapter 5

The Church and the Churches

It is by divine will and ordering that Christians gather and form themselves into local congregations. Such congregations exist for the purpose of worshiping together, establishing a called ministry, exercising Christian discipline, supervising Christian teaching, and reaching out to the unbelieving world around them, in all of this grounded upon the means of grace. They are properly called Christian churches by reason of the believers present there.

In actual practice counterfeit "Christians" or hypocrites may be mixed among the believers of a Christian congregation. As a result of this existential reality it is proper to say that a congregation bears the name Christian in a synecdochical sense, the whole bearing the name for the part, that is, the true believers present there. The presence of counterfeit Christians, whom God knows, does not cancel out the legitimacy of the Scriptural appellation or title of Christian. Jesus illustrated this with His parables of the tares among the wheat, the rough fish among the good, the five foolish virgins with the five wise, and the proper wedding garment for the king's marriage feast, etc.

The local church has its appointed task from God in connection with the Keys, faithfully to administer Word and Sacrament. It does not have the task of trying to eradicate from its midst those who shield their unbelief. That bailiwick belongs to God who alone discerns the tares from the wheat. Manifest and impenitent sinners, of course, require the church's conscientious efforts at recall and appeal for repentance. Christ has promised the Holy Spirit to His church on earth, to sanctify it and to aid it in its ministry of the Word, which is its high responsibility before God. (Matt. 13:47.48; 25:1.2; 22:2.11; 18:17; Gal. 1:2; 1 Cor. 1:2)

It is proper and Scriptural also to speak of the Christian church on earth in a larger, more general and world-encompassing way, as the sum total of those professing Christian faith in distinction from the non-Christian world. The title "Christian" is applied to church in this sense because of the genuine believers present, thus the whole being named for the part. Different from the congregations which exist with a called pastor by divine right, *jure divino*, at various places, for the ministry of the Word, larger groupings, organizations, church bodies, synods, originate through and by human planning, devising, or wisdom, *jure humano*. They exist normally under covenants, constitutions, or church orders voluntarily agreed upon by member churches. They may indeed serve a good purpose, especially in cultivating and maintaining a godly fellowship of faith, safeguarding pure teaching, training faithful and able clergy, pooling resources in educational and mission pursuits, and many other salutary programs. However, Holy Scripture nowhere indicates a mandate of God for the creation of such organizations, or such super-churches, nor does He dictate or indicate a particular form of polity or government, or structure, or nomenclature. Thus while such groupings into larger church entities may under the exercise of Christian freedom provide efficient structures for doing church work, there is no divine command that they must exist, nor that a congregation must be affiliated with them.

Fellowship of congregations or churches united in faith and practice is not only desirable but also God-pleasing, as New Testament examples show, e.g., the Jerusalem assembly or synod spoken of in Acts 6. In some way, therefore, congregations faithful to God's Word will pursue the goal of cultivating fellowship of faith with those churches, or congregations, where God's Word is purely taught and His sacraments rightly administered according to His institution. Mutual edification results from such God-pleasing inter-action and fellowship of kindred souls. This is so for congregations, even as for individual members in a local congregation. However, the congregation must not be looked upon as in some way incomplete or deficient, nor as a microcosm of which the *Groszkirche*, or large church body, is the appropriate and necessary macrocosm. This distinction is not known in Scripture.

The congregation is complete in itself, as Scripture teaches; for it is the gathering of believers around the Word, under a qualified pastor whom it has called in accord with the will of God, for the sake of ministering the Word in all its fullness to those in its care. In fulfilling its God-given ministry, the congregation is sovereign; it does not derive its authority nor its task from a larger church organization, but from Christ directly. Whatever powers or administrative authority the larger body or grouping of congregations possesses, they have by conferral and consent of the congregations.

Such delegation of powers does not mean surrender by the congregations of the rights and responsibilities they have from God. Nor does such transferral of authority intend to demean the significance of the larger organizations, church, or synods. Walther, for one, showed in his *Uebertragungslehre* how highly he valued them (synodical union or fellowship), stating: "We clearly recognize that without an external union of the orthodox Lutheran clerics and their congregations the unity of the Spirit, and thus the purity in doctrine, cannot be preserved."[1] Nonetheless, the mere fact that it is congregations that establish such bodies, sometimes therefore called *ecclesia representativa*, or representative church, or that congregations may delegate duties to smaller groups within its own entity, for the execution of its work and mission, underscores, not diminishes, the congregation's autonomy under God. It is answerable first of all and in the final analysis only to Him, under His Scriptural Word, as are synods of course also.

There has been considerable confusion on the nature of the church. This has resulted usually from failure to identify, first of all, the *una sancta*, the Holy Christian church, as the body of Christ and company of true believers, known only to God, because it is a fellowship of faith and of the Holy Ghost in the hearts. Whole church bodies are guilty of an externalism, when they identify this true church with themselves, as though they are the sole and entire company of the regenerated, and they alone possess the way to salvation. Some of these have even repudiated the Gospel itself and denied salvation through Christ, thus reverting to cultic heathendom. Obviously these least of all could make the audacious claim of exclusive salvation, for they are actually outside the Christian church. Yet this is not to deny that even there, by reason of the power and efficacy of God's Word, where it is read and heard and believed, there may still be sheep of Christ, true believers in Him and His atoning sacrifice. Luther has captured this whole matter very well in this statement from his *Galatian Commentary*:

Jerome raises an important question here: Why does Paul call "churches" those that were not churches? For Paul, he says, is writing to the Galatians, who had been led astray and turned away from Christ and from grace to Moses and the Law. I reply: When Paul calls them the "churches of Galatia," he is employing synecdoche, a very common practice in the Scriptures.. . . . Even if the church is "in the midst of a crooked and perverse generation," as Paul says to the Philippians (2:15), and even if it is surrounded by wolves and robbers, that is, spiritual tyrants, it is still the church. Although the city of Rome is worse than Sodom and Gomorrah, nevertheless there remain in it Baptism, the Sacrament, and voice and text of the Gospel, the Sacred Scriptures, the ministries, the name of Christ, and the name of God. Whoever has these, has them; whoever does not have them has no excuse, for the treasure is still there.[2]

What distinguishes visible Christianity, whether that be the individual Christian professing his faith in Christ, or the congregation at a given locality, or the larger grouping of Christians or congregations into some *Groszkirche*, is the presence of the Gospel there, also Baptism and the Lord's Supper, with the Holy Scriptures. Luther is quite right in saying so.

The Lutheran confessors at Augsburg (Article VIII "What the Church Is") were at pains to assure loyal Christians that the efficacy of the Sacraments and the Word of the Gospel itself hung on "the institution and commandment of Christ," even if "they be administered by evil men," that is, wolves who give the appearance of sheep. Commenting on and in defense of the same article, Melanchthon in the *Apology* acknowledged that "the church in its wide sense embraces good and evil," while in the narrow, proper sense it is a "fellowship" not of "outward signs" but of hearts, or souls, or individuals in whom the Holy Spirit dwells, who have faith in Christ. To the human eye, therefore, appearances may be quite deceiving, for it is possible that in "this fellowship of outward signs" hypocrites may not only exist but even "bear offices in the church," writes Melanchthon in the same context. In line with this reminder the *Formula of Concord* (Epitome, XII, 9) rejects as erroneous the notion "that that is no true Christian congregation (church) in which sinners are still found." While the church is in the world, evil men will still insinuate themselves into company with the faithful, even as Christ forewarned His disciples in the parables, notably the tares and the wheat.

The redoubtable Lutheran theologian, Aegidius Hunnius, who lived in the generation after Luther, looked seriously upon Christ's promise and, in keeping with it, stated that "hypocrites are

in the church, but they are not of the church."[3]   John Gerhard
stressed the figure of speech, synecdoche, which is present in
Scripture's use of the term "church," namely, that "something is said
of the church as a whole which properly belongs only to a part," that
is, "only the elect and saints, or true believers, in the total number."[4]
Because of the believers present in "the church at Ephesus," states
Gerhard, "one can say that it is a house of God."[5]   By the same
token when one calls the visible church "catholic or universal," it is
said in what should be called "an improper sense," says Gerhard,
"because hypocrites are mixed in."[6] This is "quite different," chimes
in Abraham Carpzov, from the *una sancta*, or church proper in
which only upright believers are, without the admixture of counter-
feits.[7] John W. Baier adds the insight that the term "church militant"
may have the same usage, referring to those who unconditionally are
Christ's, engrafted into Him by faith, or more broadly to the "mixed
group" of the visible entity of professing adherents, among whom
hypocrites or unbelievers may exist.[8]

Walther observes a similar distinction between those who are
truly the saints of God and the various groups of professing
adherents "which consist of good and evil persons, either the general
or world-wide church of the individual divisions of it, namely, the
congregations found here and there, in which God's Word is
preached and the holy Sacraments are administered."[9]   Walther
reiterates that God does not withdraw that glorious name, church,
from them because of the presence of occasional hypocrites, who
cannot be discerned, as little as the disciples were prepared to sift
the tares from the wheat. It is still God's church, as long as some
of His faithful sheep are present, even if it be just His little lambs,
the baptized infants. Christ is the true Shepherd who gathers
believers into His fold.

Walther also recognized that the Scripture refers regularly
to actual, particular congregations, or churches, existing here and
there at given localities. Seldom, if ever, is the church at large upon
earth designated. There is no *Groszkirche*, super-church, which
Christ or His disciples structured on earth, under which the congregations were to exist and, as it were, take their directives. The
individual congregations, to the extent of the genuine believers
present, were co-extensive with the one true church, the communion
of saints or believers. They may include counterfeit "Christians" in
their professed membership, but the true church, the church in the

proper sense is holy and embraces only those who are holy, that is, righteous by faith in Christ, their Redeemer, who has atoned for all sins and who has clothed them in perfect righteousness.

Luther

When Luther says that the Scriptures nowhere state or prove that a certain external church, or ecclesiastical body, has been, or is to be, established,[10] he by no means rules out the existence of individual groupings of Christians in congregations, or larger, e.g., territorial, church organizations, even dioceses. He characterizes God's church on earth as that group, large or small, that "walks in this trust in God's mercy, together with a humble confession of its sins and unworthiness, which hopes that God will grant His pardon through Christ."[11] God's Word has never been without its fruit and thus in earliest times, also by the time of Abraham, "there were many well-established churches in the world."[12]

Luther has in mind first of all the family-unit churches built around the patriarchs and the believing people of God under heads of households.[13] So Abraham gathered a church by the preaching of the Word to his family and servants,[14] as did also Abimelech.[15] The altars they raised were in keeping with God's will and constituted the focal point of worship. This was true also for Jacob and his family. "For when Holy Scripture says that altars were raised, it is just as if it were saying that schools or churches were established where sacred things which belong to the worship of God might be administered: The altars were not erected in the interest of showing spectacles and processions, nor for the sacrifices of Masses, but for the preaching of the Word," Luther comments.[16]

Luther compares the church as it is gathered "into a definite place that is both known and seen" to a bottle into which water is poured. "For the assembly of saints, or the church, is in any case manifest according to the flesh as to where and when they are in existence," Luther stated, thinking of the external nature of the church on earth. Immediately, however, he comments concerning the true church and its hidden nature, portraying this in graphic terms: "But according to the spirit they are placed in storehouses, that is, in hidden places, so that they themselves may not yet see," nor for that matter be seen.[17] This is an apt distinction between the church on earth embracing the sum total of professedly Christian believers and the *una sancta* which is hidden or invisible. For a time "I am a sojourner in the former, that I might be a citizen of the latter,"[18] is Luther's way of describing the pilgrimage of Christians through life. It is "with these gems, these emeralds," in other words, that "God will build His church."[19]

One of Christianity's famous hymns tells of "Jerusalem the golden, O sweet and blessed country, the home of God's elect."[20] Jerusalem, God's church of believers, "was called holy not for the reason that men who lived there were holy, but because of the holy Word of God which ruled there," says Luther, "spiritual Jerusalem, the church of Christ which the Word sanctifies and cleanses."[21] Here the Word of God rules and the church submits itself to it, not setting itself over the Word, judging all doctrine by and according to it.[22]

Faith, fellowship, and fearlessness characterize the child of God "who not only loves the pure doctrine of the Word but takes great pleasure in its propagation and in the growth of the numbers of believers."[23] Armed with the Word of God, those who are Christ's disciples rejoice in the salvation achieved for them by Christ, their Lord, and do not vainly attempt under the Law to work their own, like Sisyphus, in the old Greek story, attempted to roll the rock from the bottom of the mountain to the top, only to have it roll back again just before getting it there.[24]

There was a kind of ingenuous simplicity and wholesomeness that characterized the early church, which in spite of the impact of the Fall made "that age truly a golden one," Luther comments; in fact so much so that "in comparison with it our age hardly deserves to be called an age of mud."[25] When "the world was at its worst," as in Abraham's day when Sodom and Gomorrah were cesspools of moral wickedness, then "at this very time the church was in a most flourishing state and had the saintliest and the most faithful teachers."[26] Household altars, in tents, were the first churches.[27] Then, as now, Luther states, the godless world was blessed by the presence of the church with Word and sacraments.[28]

Luther is under no illusion as regards the general conditions and the times when Joseph lived and his own day, though he is quite blunt in criticizing the populace of contemporary Wittenberg, stating: "I have never seen lazier people than in this region and city." Such lassitude spilled over into the religious arena as well. Then is when Joseph, a good and sound leader, is greatly needed; or to put it in

Luther's graphic way, that is why "the forehead is in front of the back of the head."[29] Parishes need good leaders.

"Like drones," the world "is delighted by the honeymaking of the bees and enjoys it, just as today much gain comes to princes and tyrants as a result of the propagation of the Gospel," also "peace and tranquillity, wealth and safety, which the prayers of the church obtain from God."[30] Luther has touched base here with our American founding fathers, not all of whom were religious, but who recognized the value of Christian influence in the commonwealth and thus wrote into our laws certain guarantees as well as privileges that benefited the churches. Their thinking was not too different from Luther's on this point, though theirs of course was often motivated by simple self-interest. Luther capsuled it well: "Without this church, the world would have perished forthwith."[31] Two hundred years of history have pretty well cemented the truth home, hard and fast, that the Christian church can survive very well in a country like the United States, or any other for that matter; but it is to be doubted whether a democratic form of government like ours could survive at all without the Christian church.

There is a definite continuity between the Old and New Testament churches, is Luther's considered judgment. "For the church, which is now in the morning, began already in the evening, when the synagog was still standing." But when Christ came He "established the church and put an end to the synagog in His life, as also in the Lord's Supper He dealt at the same time with the old and the new Passover."[32] These things ended, so that the new might be raised, that is, the church.[33] Luther does not discount the Old Testament church's existence.

Christ's church is holy, not of itself, but through His Word. "The church today," Luther notes, "even though it prays constantly for the remission of sins, is nevertheless utterly pure and without fault, if you keep your eyes fixed on Word, sacraments, faith and Christ Himself, its Head."[34] This distinguished it from all else. "The wilderness will become a thoroughly cultivated field through the Word and the church,"[35] and it "flourishes inwardly," not with power but with the Spirit, and "it does shine outwardly too, with obedience, love, humility."[36] In comparison with the world around it, the church, Luther says, appears like a handful of people, a fistful of dough, hardly one little biscuit in a whole bakery."[37] But it constantly grows larger, even though outwardly it may seem that "the church is like a ghost town."[38] Its membership, Luther asserts, will actually be very great and "will exceed the total number of Jews," and "will be so wide that it will penetrate to the right and to the left, to the south and to the north, that is, into all the earth; into all cathedrals, pulpits, and temples will come your teaching of the Gospel," is God's promise.[39]

The church's beginning in the New Testament was with John the Baptist's ministry. He testified of the True Light, Christ, who would follow him.[40] We have a well ordered church today, Luther is convinced, because of the faithful apostles who clung to God's Word, "not learned men, not high priests, Pharisees, and scribes, but poor beggars and fishermen, lowly folk, Peter, Andrew, and Bartholomew."[41] Luther customarily spoke of himself, and of all Christians, faithful to God's Word, as lowly "beggars," utterly dependent upon God's largesse, people who need to cling always to God's sacred Word, the Scriptures.

"Outsiders," that is the "uncircumcised," or Gentiles, "were not excluded from the church," Luther points out, and thus "even Job, Cyrus the Persian, the widow of Zarephath, and Naaman the Syrian became members of the church."[42] God's promise to Abraham was that his family would "be the church for the entire world, like a lap and bosom of grace in which all nations, not only your descendants, are to find salvation, provided that they persevere in your faith,"[43] thus "through faith in the Blessed Seed, not through circumcision." Faith like Abraham's in the promise would denote the church's presence, all the way "up to the time of Christ."[44]

There is no other way of salvation "than to walk in simple faith."[45] God's arithmetic counts in each and everyone of those from Abraham's stem and from "outside" who cling to His Word in faith.[46] This meant the Ishmaelites, too, not "because they were born of the flesh of Abraham," but if and when they "sought refuge in grace"; and Luther did "not doubt that Ishmael and many of his descendants were converted to the true church of Abraham."[47] He believed the same might also have been true for the descendants of Cain; that they might be "saved through repentance and through faith in the promise."[48] A man like Abimelech, a contemporary of saintly Abraham, was an example of an "outsider" who shared in God's promise.[49] So also some among the Egyptians at Joseph's time believed the promise "when Jacob or Joseph taught the Word among them";[50] later Ruth and Rahab "were converted (when) they received the Word from the Israelites"[51] and so even the Edomites.[52]

The Gentiles were to be part of Christ's inheritance spoken of in Psalm 16:5, to be included among "My faithful people, My Church," says the Messiah.[53] All nations would flow together in Him, as believers of His Word, not merely as members of an external structure like that "subject to the pope of Rome," who brazenly claims that anyone who is not subject "is not a Christian."[54] "The church will convert the nations not by force but the goodness of the Word."[55] The church would be literally gathered from everywhere, "from all places and conditions, from all walks of life," "by the preaching of the Gospel among all nations throughout the world"; for "this overwhelming of the Gentiles is a spiritual thing, accomplished through the power of the Gospel."[56]

Very early in human history the distinctive roles of state, of government, and church became confused, particularly as the former, alienated from God, nonetheless arrogated spiritual powers to itself, as in the days of Noah when there were giants upon the earth, Genesis 6:4.[57] Under such circumstances and over-reaching by godless secular power, "the church is always a wall against the wrath of God."[58] Abraham's home demonstrated the truth that it served as the cornerstone at this time of both church and state, built on love, ruled by Abraham with patience and love, though at times Abraham and Sarah proved themselves too indulgent and complacent as regards their family members and their conduct.[59] So important a key is the religious life of God's people that without it decay soon set in; and "after the downfall of the church (as at Sodom) came the downfall of the government," or society.[60]

It is evident, then, that God "founded the church" not only for the blessing of those within but also "in order to strengthen the household and the state through the church," certainly not "to destroy the household and the government."[61] By the same token, however, a pious ruler or good government are a boon to the church, "so that the doctrine and the Word of God can be spread." The church prospers under the benign governance of a godly ruler.[62] At times "the three hierarchies" are all in the hand of one man, as with Jacob, "the domestic, the royal, and the priestly."[63] Then the sword of the Spirit, which is the Word of God, and the sword of power—the one the right hand of God, the other the left—are both in the hands of the patriarch who is also foremost in his household. Such an arrangement serves to accentuate the point that God uses the state, or government, in conjunction with the church, for the former "fosters and preserves peace," while "the church has another office, which pertains to the future life" and salvation.[64] A pious ruler's resolve before God is very serious in this regard: "Thou art calling me to perform this service; I will obey gladly. For my part I would prefer to be hidden as a private citizen. But because Thy will and command must be obeyed, I will do my duty in fear and humility."[65]

It is God's will that there be close, even critical, interacting between state and church. But, Luther says, it was a distortion of God's order of things that the Roman church hold both "swords" in its hands. "For a long time now they have joined the sword with the Word in the church and their kingdom," much to the harm of Christ's kingdom, Luther avers.[66] Christian citizens need to be very clear on this: "To the extent that they are Christians they do not wage carnal war," that is, not in the name of the church as in some holy crusade.[67] Luther is by no means a pacifist; but by the same token he resists steadfastly the tendency to make of the church a sword-rattling instrument of death in the name of the Lord. As a citizen a faithful Christian fulfills his civic duties toward his prince, or government, also in bearing arms.[68] Not least, "our Lord God's little remnant, the church, intercedes for the kings and lords," that is, for government, which then "get the benefit of such prayer despite their unworthiness; otherwise things would be in an abominable state."[69]

In the Roman church's view both spiritual and temporal power are taken up into the same hand, something Luther already contested in the 79th thesis of his famous 95 Theses, that "the cross should be emblazoned with the papal coat of arms."[70] From the Coburg, in 1530, Luther wrote to Melanchthon, pressing precisely on this neuralgic point, that bishops had usurped secular authority along with their ecclesiastical, and as a result had brought much evil into both spheres, but especially into the church where the Gospel had grown silent because of this confusion of the church's proper role.[71]

It is in the nature of the church on earth, indeed one of its earmarks, as Luther lists these in his treatise *Councils and the Church*, that it suffer and bear affliction. It is a "suffering and hungering church" in this life; one of the hard things which it must learn is that this happens with "His (God's) approval." This latter is very important, because on the opposite side of the coin is the fact of God's "condemnation of the hypocritical and blood-thirsty" church. God never has forgotten and never will forget His beloved. His severe judgment upon those who work evil in the name of the church "is our comfort, and, as it were, the sugar with which our present hardships must be flavored and overcome."[72] Albeit that the Roman church, with its sympathetic princes, often dealt with those agitating for reform as though they "wished all of us had one neck,"[73] God's faithful people must not be overcome by this heavy burden of suffering.[74] The true church suffers for its faith as Abel did for his.[75] Prayer, also for those who afflict it, is the church's wall and mighty fortress in times of peril.[76] In no way can the church be overcome by the persecution it bears, as long as it remembers that it is because of the very great treasure it possesses, the forgiveness of sins, that the suffering comes.[77]

For the church to adopt a kind of fatalistic logo in times of trial, like "whatever will be, will be," is sinful; such "thoughts are wicked and impious," Luther states.[78] God's way is that the church cling to His Word, no matter what, "for He allows the church to be afflicted and to suffer want in order that it may learn that it must live not only by bread but also by the Word, for the Word is our life and salvation."[79] Satan naturally opposes God and His church at this point, seeking to cause doubts about His Word.[80] Jacob's trouble--filled life can serve us, "for we are reminded here that in our life we should prepare ourselves in the same manner and learn to recognize the church of God in that picture of Jacob's struggle."[81]

It paralleled closely the story of the church at the time of the Reformation, in Luther's opinion, when "contempt, aversion, and hatred for the Word" arose on all sides, even from within the established church, and one might rightly have asked "where the church is" because it seemed to be "nowhere in evidence."[82] Luther reminds us that then it was important to remember that we "must not pay regard to external form but to the Word and to Baptism," which after all are the true marks of the church's presence, even when all else, including its members, are hidden from men's eyes. Joseph's trauma-filled life, like that of Jacob, his father, also serves us in the same way, as "a very beautiful example" of the church under affliction, but still safeguarded by God.[83]

In spite of all, therefore, "the kingdom of Christ is a kingdom of grace and mercy." "Therefore," says Luther, "although He seems to turn away from us, to neglect us, or to cast us off when He sends famine, pestilence, death, and sufferings of every kind," yet we must "acknowledge His goodness and grace even unto death."[84]

Luther finds a parallel between the church's lot and the story which Augustine tells about himself and his mother. "When I was flogged in school and returned home and complained to my mother," Augustine says, "she would laugh about the blows I had received. Nevertheless, she did not wish me ill." So, God's people must learn, too, that their loving Father intends and works them no ill by the afflictions they are called on to carry. We need to remember, Luther says, that "today the world stands and empires are preserved for no other reason than that God gathers a church for Himself in the midst of a perverse nation."[85]

The church sighs to be with Christ, but meanwhile has its bitter Marah to endure.[86] At times, in fact, "Christ seems everywhere to have forgotten the churches throughout the world except the church at Rome," which was "the true spiritual adversary of the spiritual Jerusalem."[87] Beset by troubles, with "every kind of strife and discord," and despised on all fronts,[88] it is still true that "the more the church is oppressed and hemmed in, the more it rises up."[89] God never fails His church in the midst of its earthly turmoil and trial.

Luther traces the church's struggles all the way from Cain's day down to his own and observes that "the church of Satan is everlastingly at war with the church of God."[90] Satan's pattern of attack is always the same, to cause doubt concerning God's Word and the manner of His approach to men, that is, His chosen *larvae Dei*, or veils, as in the New Testament, the Gospels, Baptism, and the Lord's Supper. His angle, even with "very pious people," is to get them to lose sight of "these heavenly blessings" and convince them that "they retain nothing at all," even when they have them.[91] Central to Satan's clever ploy is to see to it that "to the end of the world the false church will be joined to the true church, and false brethren to godly and sincere brethren," side by side.[92] Satan twists things around in such a way, right within the external church, so that it seems "what God says must be false, (and) what they (the pope's party) say must be right."[93] The true church, as a result is often "a frightened people, beset by fear, despair, and sins," much in need of Christ's comforting assurance, "Don't be afraid, I am with you."[94] "The church is and must be the bride of our Lord God,"

Luther affirms, but when, as with Rome, God's Word is opposed by the papal word, then the pretender-church becomes little more than a "repugnant harlot."[95]

It is not as though the church were without warning concerning these matters either, Luther states, for the apostles "have told us in advance" concerning "the final reign of the Antichrist, namely, of the papacy," as well as that "Christendom will be preserved until Christ returns suddenly in His glory and finally frees it from every evil."[96] How clear it is though, Luther contended in his *Explanations to the 95 Theses*, that "the church needs a reformation!" But the kind of reformation it requires is one "which is not the work of one man, or of many men, but the work of God alone," who alone knows "the time for this reformation."[97] Meanwhile God's people must recognize that "when God's word flourished somewhere and His little flock was gathered, the devil became aware of the light, and he breathed and blew and stormed against it with strong, mighty winds from every nook and corner in an attempt to extinguish this divine light";[98] or as Luther puts it at many different places, the Devil was quick to build his chapel next to God's church, to seek to undo it.

The question and claim of primacy between the rival centers of Christianity—Rome and Constantinople specifically—"have endlessly and scandalously" troubled the church, much to Satan's delight.[99] Luther notes that the church at Jerusalem has modestly kept out of the dispute, although "if any church is to have primacy, the church at Jerusalem would have had to be considered as deserving precedence over any other."[100] Next in order would probably have been the Greek churches.[101] Certainly on the basis of Matt. 16:18-19, it is impossible to "prove that the Roman church has a higher rank than other churches in the entire world."[102] In any case Rome's senseless disputing of the question was evidence, Luther held, of a Satanic delusion. "The pope boasts of his succession and on the strength of this right lays claim to the primacy for himself, but we in no wise concede this to him in the church," says Luther.[103]

Christ's church or kingdom is as little invalidated by the presence of hypocrites and evil men in its midst as it was in the days of the patriarchs who were surrounded by false religionists. The true church will always seek pure doctrine, but "hypocrites are always close by," and because they are undercover and are Christians in

name only "they do not fight against and persecute the doctrine," but
sow the seeds of error and false teaching much more cleverly and
covertly.[104] Luther sees a parallel between the papalists of his day
and the sons of Jacob, who had been brought up under godly
influence and "daily heard the Word of God," and yet were like
"spiders (that) sucked nothing but poison from the most beautiful
blossoms and roses."[105]

Luther is quite convinced that, however pious his intention,
"no preacher will ever be able to change or remove everything that
is wrong in the church."[106] Georges Bernanos, in his notable novel,
Diary of a Country Priest, seems to have caught Luther's point
exactly when he writes of the nun of Bruges:

> The mistake she made wasn't to fight dirt, sure enough, but
> to try to do away with it altogether. As if that were
> possible! A parish is *bound* to be dirty. A whole Christian
> society's a lot dirtier. You wait for Judgment Day and see
> what the angels'll be sweeping out of even the most saintly
> monasteries.[107]

It is true in the church on earth that "the great throng cares
nothing about God's Word, nor does it acknowledge it as a blessing
that it can hear this Word without harm or danger."[108] Luther seems
to be speaking for the situation in every century of the church's
history. Shameless sycophants seem always ready to suck the very
life out of the church.[109] This is the situation in the church militant,
Luther states, and "let no one hope for a church that is without
ungodly people, openly or undercover."[110] They are like "noxious
wild branches" on the tree and "they contain no wholesome juice";
in contrast "the Bible is a pure and unadulterated malmsey wine,
yes, a very salutary medicine and cordial," and not at all impure in
any way.[111]

The point is that though error and fault may persist within
the visible church on earth, the true church is still present there by
virtue of the Word and the sacraments.[112] So Luther could claim:
"By the grace of God we here in Wittenberg have acquired the form
of a Christian church," for "in our midst the Word is taught
purely."[113]

Because the pure Word was being taught to a sinful people,
it was true that "the church is indeed holy, but it is a sinner at the

same time,"[114] and it will always survive whatever error or heresy may be present in it.[115] Sins of weakness, or "failings" as St. Paul calls them,[116] are the trademark of a people or an individual who is *simul justus et peccator*, at the same time saint and sinner.[117]

Whatever obstacles beset the visible church on earth, though kingdoms and empires come and go, the true church will abide, even as the Word of God itself.[118] Though persecuted, the church "is not abandoned" and never shall be.[119] In it are both the weak and the strong.[120] One may wonder about the Scriptures at times, "why the Holy Spirit records trifles" as they appear to us; but the truth is that what appears foolish to us is actually "recorded for the comfort of the churches."[121] Because of one godly man, the apostle Paul, God preserved the lives of a whole boatload of people,[122] and, in a similar way, others because of Naaman, Joseph, Jehoshaphat.

Thus the church, though weak and frail to human eyes, is actually a pillar of strength midst its foes.[123] Though "black, undesirable, lacerated, wretchedly afflicted, exposed to the taunts of all men," the church still buds and grows despite all appearances.[124] Its peace has to do with the pure Word of God, and "there is no plague worse for the church than a peace in which the Word of the Spirit and its diligent use are lacking."[125]

God nurtures His sheep, the believers, through His Word, taking them to His bosom,[126] like "a scattered gathering, dispersed here and there by the cross,"[127] but enduring because of the "everlasting covenant" or promise made unto all believers in Christ.[128] Christ is the true and only Shepherd of His church, Luther contended in his set of theses drawn up against the articles of the Louvain faculty, in 1545. Very sharply and pointedly Luther stated in theses 47 and 48:

> There is indeed only one catholic church of Christ on earth, but to that the heretical and idolatrous Louvainists do not belong with their abominable idol, the pope.

> The church of the pope and of the "little masters" is more truly a werewolf, the blood adversary and destroyer of Christ's church.[129]

At the very time, June 29, 1530, when the Confessors were presenting their cause at Augsburg and submitting their Confession to the emperor and their opponents who accused them of heresy and worse, Luther wrote a comforting note to Melanchthon, assuring him that he must not doubt the merits of their case. Above all, he must be sure that "we are the church," not by virtue of any external tie, but because of the Word of Christ on which the Reformation was built.[130] This is still where the matter rests today.

It is also this Word of God which "is the foundation and basis of our assurance" and of every prayer we utter. Because prayer rests on the Word and promise of God to hear every prayer spoken in faith, for that very reason "it is our power and victory in every trial." Luther expresses the wish in this context that he could "call upon God with the ardor with which Judah prays here before his brother," referring to Judah's ardent supplication before Joseph, whom he does not recognize, in behalf of the youngest brother, Benjamin (Gen. 44:18).[131] Worship and prayer are the pulse beat of the church in its life together at a given locality. In many ways, says Luther, "it is somewhat easier to pray" in larger groups, like the congregation, when we all come together to say the "Our Father," supported by each other. When we are alone, however, it is more difficult, for then "the devil fans" thoughts like these "into a bright flame": "You are a despicable person and do not deserve to live. How can you, in the face of this, venture to step before God and call Him Father?" Then it is important to remember that we do not approach God on our own, but in the name and for the sake of Christ, our Savior.[132] "The church," Luther states, "is the inn and the infirmary for those who are sick and in need of being made well," especially in healing from sin; and its glory in large measure is that it may petition God for His help, on the basis of His Word and promise in Christ.[133]

The church orders, forms of liturgy, days and times, are all free matters, Luther stressed; but he was never an iconoclast, and he spoke earnestly in behalf of the churches, or congregations, doing things "in an orderly way," in "orderly, public, reverent assembly," joining together in common worship and prayer, which is the strength of God's church on earth.[134] A people of God that worships in truth is also a loving people; "for faith apprehends the Word and believes the Word; to it then comes love,"[135] love in the home, in the community, in the church. Good works, particularly in the civic realm or society around us, are indeed God's pleasure, Luther says, more excellent than merely to "go into a church, bellow in a chorus, and mumble prayers" like some misguided monks.[136]

Luther leaves no doubt on the question of women being barred from the pastoral ministry by God's ordering of things, but he is hardly a male chauvinist. As a matter of fact, he comes off quite in the opposite corner, appealing for respectful, loving treatment of the wife, or women in general. To the husband he addresses the question, how can "you crush the weak vessel" in a bully's sort of way of showing your authority, in view of the fact that she is a "joint heir of the kingdom of God," one with you "in the same fellowship of Baptism, of all the kindnesses of God, and of the entire church?"[137] Those who are Christ's, members of His church, ought to excel in kindness everywhere in the midst of a perverse world, "for if the world were without godly men, it would not stand."[138]

Regeneration is always followed by renewal, that is, godly, sanctified life, for "when the heart is inwardly justified and at peace through faith in the Spirit, then outward actions soon follow in various ways," in confession of our Lord, in deeds of love, in patient cross-bearing.[139] By no means does this imply that the church is "a perfectly holy society or completely free of flagrant faults and blemishes, as the Papists imagine it to be," says Luther; but nonetheless it strives for righteous living, and "the true church is the one which prays."[140] It errs but is preserved by "her daily petition for 'the forgiveness of sins.'"[141]

Even the building in which the church worships is rightly "termed a house of God," for the reason that it "is dedicated to the service of God,"[142] and love of the neighbor. All bad publicity to the contrary, then as now, Luther was never one to minimize the fact that faith is active in love. "Therefore," he says, "Christ teaches us to make a point of looking for the fruits; it is not enough to boast a great deal of faith and Christ; for where no fruits are in evidence, or where the opposite is seen, Christ will certainly not be present."[143]

For all his expressed hatred for the papalists and their godless doctrines, Luther till the end of his life maintained a genuine affection for the people of the Roman church, as well as the church itself. He stated in his early lectures on *Galatians*, 1519: "I have been compelled to explain myself, in order that they may know that they are mistaken when they cry that I, who love not only the Roman Church but the whole church of Christ with the purest love, am hostile to the Roman Church."[144] He knew, after all, that one day he, too, must die and appear before Christ to "render an account," and always, he said, "I am conscious of being a debtor to the Word, no matter how unworthy I am."[145]

No Christian individually, and certainly not the church corporately as a whole, must ever be "so distracted by the affairs of the churches," or occupied with other business, that there is no time to devote oneself to meditation and study of the Word.[146] We have a tendency, in fact a strong propensity, to follow the example of the Israelites and "chase after pleasant groves," instead of worshiping God as He Himself has ordained in His Word. "Thus," says Luther, "no one of us has been satisfied with his baptism or with the temple where he had the Word of Christ and the sacraments, where he was called, baptized, and absolved; where he had, heard, and felt God speaking with him in His Word." "Instead everywhere chapels and altars were erected," that is, of man's own design and input and meaning, and "the Word and the sacraments were abandoned."[147]

Traditions are a good thing to have and follow in the church, also in the matter of liturgical order, music, and vestments, etc., but never at the expense of supplanting the Word.[148] Vainglory, or triumphalism, in the church is the bane of its life and existence, and "when this poison climbs up to the church or the spiritual realm, the damage it causes is inexpressible," Luther states. "For here the contention is not about learning, genius, beauty, wealth, kingdoms, empires, and the like; but the issue is between salvation and life or perdition and eternal death." And Luther adds with special emphasis that "Paul is very serious about warning those who are in the ministry of the Word about this fault."[149]

The church of Rome as Luther knew it had grown derelict in its ministry to souls. No historian will probably quibble with his observation, given in his notable *Good Works* treatise: "They (the spiritual authorities) behave toward their responsibilities like those mothers who forsake their children and run after their lovers, as Hosea 2 (5) says. They do not preach, they do not teach, they do not restrain, they do not punish, and no spiritual government at all remains in Christendom."[150] The church has too often become a begging institution, for the buildings it wants to build, or the programs it "needs" for its existence. Greediness does not respectfully pass the churches by, to leave them alone. Luther touches a sensitive nerve when in his treatise *On Trade and Usury* he writes:

Beware, therefore, O man! God will not ask you at your
death and at the Last Day how much you have left in your
will, whether you have given so and so much to churches—although I do not condemn this—but he will say to you,
"I was hungry, and you gave me no food; I was naked, and
you did not clothe me" (Matt. 25:42-43). Take these words
to heart, dear man! The important thing is whether you
have given to your neighbor and treated him well. Beware
of show and glitter and color that draw you away from
this.[151]

Luther is speaking for his day as well as for ours, when he
scores severely the argument that "the churches and the clergy do
this," or that "this money is used in the service of God." It would
be best to "leave the name of the church out of it," Luther admonishes, if whatever is gathered is for vainglory, greed, idleness, or
whatever.[152]

In a given church's sphere of responsibility Luther especially
saw children at the center point. He always retained a profound love
for the "little ones," especially that every effort be bent to give them
a good, godly training, "to raise them for God's service," and not
stand in the way of "their ability and desire to learn."[153] Thus
schools, with good, sound educational programs and able teachers,
were always at the top of the agenda for Luther as he thought of the
local community and congregation. No expense ought to be spared
in maintaining and fostering the very best. He spoke in behalf of
what we today would call scholarships or grants in aid for education.
No finer monument could be raised with one's money than to "help
the living" with such scholarship funds. Luther deplores the
lackadaisical attitude of parents and community leaders in his day,
especially in allocating necessary funds. "Now when men are to
establish real schools and real churches, and build the true church,
now all the purses are fastened shut with iron chains."[154] Modern
education, especially Christian education sponsored and supported by
the churches, received its greatest boost and direction from Luther
and the Reformation.

While Luther very often is thinking of the Christian church
in a wide sense, incorporating all those on earth who profess faith
in Christ, he just as frequently has in mind the local congregations
or churches at given places. Thus "Moriah," or the place where God

is worshiped, is "everywhere in the world," that is, "wherever there
is a congregation of the godly."[155] Congregations exist for the sake
of exercising the Keys, Word, and sacraments, Luther states, "for
church assemblies have been ordained for this purpose, that we may
learn concerning God that He is our God."[156] God had His congregation at Mt. Sinai where "the people heard the Law of God."[157]
Here, and also later in Israel's sojourn in the wilderness, the
Scriptures are speaking not of the place where the people assembled
but the assembly itself.[158]

In a broad use of the term "the congregation of God" means
any and all communities of mankind, for God is the Creator and
Father of them all; but "it is only believers who know the article
about creation" and thus God Himself; and these are truly His
congregation, as opposed to the devil's congregations, or assemblies.[159] Those who constitute God's people in any parish are the
true believers, "even though there are many evil and wicked
parishioners in it." This parish "is established by God through His
holy Word for the righteous."[160] It is for their sakes and their
nurture.

Especially in the New Testament do we meet the various
churches or congregations that God established through His apostles,
as in Galatia, at Corinth, and elsewhere.[161] In Galatia particularly
were the congregations "which had been led astray by the false
apostles," and it was the apostle Paul's firm resolve to try to
"convince them beyond any doubt that his Gospel was the true Word
of God." It was not only "his ministry (that) was in jeopardy here,"
but "all the churches that had had him as their teacher."[162] This was
no mere popularity contest. "For," as Luther states, "the issue here
is nothing trivial for Paul; it is the principal doctrine of Christianity,"
the doctrine of justification *sola gratia/fide*.[163]

The Galatian situation was unique in that several congregations were involved. "In other epistles Paul writes to the church of
a single city; here he is writing to the churches of many cities and
of a whole province."[164] In this context Luther refreshes the reader's
mind that the word church "can be used in two ways: both for one
that has no spot or wrinkle and is truly the body of Christ (Eph.
5:17) and for one that is assembled in Christ's name but is without
complete and perfect virtues." The first refers to the *una sancta*; the
second to the church as it is usually found, a congregation of
confessing Christians at a given place, among whom others may be

hypocrites or unbelievers. In the apostle Paul's Letter to Philemon reference is made to Archippus, another of the apostle's co-workers; and this leads Luther to comment: "Undoubtedly there were several churches, different houses in different cities, where ten people who had someone like Archippus would gather."[165]

The exercise of the Keys in the local congregations involved Christian admonition and discipline. Luther notes that this would have been "laid with the consent of the believing congregations upon obvious transgressions."[166] Excommunication was a serious matter, intended not for the hurt of any individual, but for the good of the congregation and the individual as well, whose repentance was always hoped for.[167] This, as well as other matters in the church, including judging of doctrine, lay within the laity's domain, not only the clergy's.[168] Luther faults the Roman church because of its highhanded condemnation of the Bohemian Christians, dismissing them and their appeals with, what Luther calls, "that inane remark of men: 'The church has so ordained,'" instead of seeking "the consent of the church, which is the people of God," under the authority of God's Word.[169] Christian liberty involves or includes also this principle, says Luther, that "neither pope nor bishop nor any other man has the right to impose a single syllable of law upon a Christian man without his consent."[170] Luther, of course, does not exclude here the binding dictums of God's Law, which always stand, but rather the laws of men, or their interpretations.

Confession and absolution are likewise treasures of the people, not intended for tyrannizing of consciences, but for their peace of mind and heart. Luther's considered opinion is this: "I rejoice that it exists in the church of Christ, for it is a cure without equal for distressed consciences." The church in later centuries can only be faulted for having let this important side or application of the Keys slip away, sometimes into the hand of unbelieving, agnostic practitioners and psycho-therapists who really were not equipped to handle a sinner's guilt and need for forgiveness. Concerning the same subject, private and general confession, Luther addressed a *Gutachten*, or theological opinion, to the Nürnberg councilmen, on April 18, 1533. He stated that "absolution may be used in public and in general, and in special cases also in private, just as the sermon may take place publicly, or privately," or forgiveness be spoken "in public to many persons or privately to one person alone," of course unto faith.[172] Luther was countering herewith the mistaken notion, held by the theologian Osiander for example, that argued for *private* confession and absolution as the only right and proper way of practicing church discipline, and which, on the opposite side of the coin, taught that *public* confession and absolution were contrary to the Word of God. Good pastoral care indicated the need for both, according to Scriptural precedent and injunction.

With similarly sound and balanced counsel Luther urges that congregations and pastors place no coercion or legalistic pressure upon people in their attendance at the Lord's Table. A man should desire the sacrament because he feels his sin, under the Law's mirroring, and is eager for the Savior's touch of forgiveness extended to him through His body and blood in the sacrament. Luther deplores the legal framework into which the Roman church had placed it, and exhorts that it be placed once again into a truly evangelical one.

> Then a man no longer heeds the church's command but is happy that he can partake of the sacrament because of his own urging and need, without any command or demand. The pope and all the priests should implant this doctrine and teaching in the people and leave their own precept aside, thus giving everybody a free hand. Then he who for such reasons does not long for the sacrament will not partake of it. Now, however, they stress only their command, and the people throng to it, and great harm is done to Christendom.[173]

In a manner similar to the Scriptural, apostolic usage, Luther sends his greeting to John Brenz, pastor of the congregation at Schwäbischhalle, as well as the congregation itself;[174] gives advice to the pastors and the people of the congregations in Luebeck concerning measures to be taken in introducing the Reformation in that city;[175] and in a number of letters uses the word *ecclesia* to mean congregation, thus indicating its twofold use, either as referring to the *una sancta* or the local congregation (or the visible totality of those confessing the faith).[176] Moreover, it is "when congregations have been set in order (that) then the usage of excommunication can be discussed."[177] Luther is filled with great joy over the reports he has received concerning individual congregations and their pastors, shepherds and sheep prospering under the blessings of the Gospel.[178]

Always the congregation of believers, at places here and there, is the focal point of Luther's concern for the church. He has a true *Seelsorger's* solicitude and concern for the sheep and the lambs of the flock. The integrity of such congregations is a sacred matter, and not even a bishop has "authority to impose on his congregations any statute or ceremony, except with the expressed or silent agreement of the church."[179] This is written in a letter to Melanchthon and Luther goes on to add that "the church is free and lord of all, and the bishops ought not to dominate the faith of the congregations, not burden or oppress the congregations against their will."[180] Rather than "lords of the church," the bishops should see their entrusted position as rising from the congregations whose "servants and stewards" they are. Luther clearly upholds the integrity and God-given authority of the individual congregations in spiritual matters, affirming that in principles of the faith the congregation's governance must remain inviolate, though indeed they are never to act in disregard for fellow Christians and Christian congregations. (Acts 15; 1 Cor. 11:16; 14:36)

NOTES

1   *Walther Speaks to the Church*, 17. Like Walther, Adolf Hoenecke, leading theologian and systematician of the Wisconsin Evangelical Lutheran Synod (hereafter WELS) in its early history, held that Scripture defines *ecclesia* or church in two ways: first, and foundational sense, as *una sancta*, the sum total of believers, or communion of saints, also designated in Scripture as body or bride of Christ; and second, as the congregation of believers (among whom there may be hypocrites) at given geographical locations, like Corinth, Ephesus, etc. But later theologians of the WELS fellowship (John Koehler, John Schaller, August Pieper) took exception to this distinction arguing that "church" properly designates not only local congregations but also larger groupings of believers gathered by the Holy Spirit, like synods or church bodies, and that these exist by divine aegis equally as much as congregations. Thus the Keys, the administering of Word and sacraments, discipline, right to call, etc., are bestowed upon and belong to synods as well as to congregations. Walther, on the other hand (so also Hoenecke), while urging the formation of a synod of congregations joined in the unity of faith and confessional concord, viewed the synod as a voluntary fellowship of congregations and pastors, an *ecclesia representativa*, or representative church body, which exists *jure humano*, hence not required or mandated by God as are congregations. A

synod's existence and agency in Walther's thinking (the position still
held by the church body of which he was a founding father, The
Lutheran Church—Missouri Synod, or LC-MS) are deemed as very
useful, advantageous, and supportive, but as an advisory body only, to
be governed under the constitution and bylaws adopted by its constitu-
tive membership.   Its officials, activities, programs, etc., remain
accountable to the member congregations and their pastors.

2   *LW* 26, 24; *WA* 401, 68f.

3   Quoted in Walter, *Kirche und Amt*, 69.

4   *Loc. de eccl.*, 65. Quoted in Walther, *KA*, 71.

5   Ibid., 79. Quoted in Walther, *KA*, 72.

6   Ibid., 151. Quoted in Walther, *KA*, 72.

7   *Isagog.*, 305f. Quoted in Walther, *KA*, 75.

8   *Compendium Theologiae Positivae*, III, 13, 2. Quoted in Walther, *KA*,
       75f.

9   *Kirche und Amt*, 63.

10   *LW* 39, 69f.; *WA* 6, 296f. *Papacy at Rome*, 1520.

11   *LW* 1, 259; *WA* 42, 192.

12   *LW* 3, 319; *WA* 43, 104.

13   *LW* 3, 321; *WA* 43, 105.

14   *LW* 3, 340; *WA* 43, 119.

15   *LW* 3, 356f.; *WA* 43, 131.

16   *LW* 6, 185f.; *WA* 44, 138f.

17   *LW* 10, 156; *WA* 3, 183f.

18   *LW* 11, 428; *WA* 4, 315.

19   *LW* 17, 243; *WA* 312, 449.

20   *The Lutheran Hymnal*, 613.

21   *LW* 18, 121; *WA* 13. 121.

22   *LW* 23, 231; *WA* 33, 365f.

23   *LW* 26, 378; *WA* 401, 576.

24   *LW* 26, 406; *WA* 401, 617.

25   *LW* 1, 342; *WA* 42, 252.

26   *LW* 3, 234; *WA* 43, 42.

27   *LW* 4, 384f.; *WA* 43, 412.

28   *LW* 7, 62ff.; *WA* 44, 346ff.

29   *LW* 7, 67; *WA* 44, 349.

30   *LW* 7, 68; *WA* 44, 350.

31   *LW* 8, 41; *WA* 44, 609.

32   *LW* 11, 102; *WA* 3, 613

33   *LW* 11, 194; *WA* 4, 49.

34   *LW* 15, 232; *WA* 312, 689.

35   *LW* 16, 280; *WA* 312, 205.

36   *LW* 16; 299; *WA* 312, 221.

37   *LW* 17, 84; *WA* 312, 327.

38   *LW* 17, 186; *WA* 312, 407.

39   *LW* 17, 234f.; *WA* 312, 442f.

40   *LW* 22, 56; *WA* 46, 584.

41   *LW* 22, 229; *WA* 46, 739.

42   *LW* 3, 81.107; *WA* 42, 606.624.

43   *LW* 3, 112; *WA* 42, 628.

44   *LW* 3, 120; *WA* 42, 634.

45   *LW* 3, 128; *WA* 42, 639.

46   *LW* 3, 130-189 passim; *WA* 42, 640ff.

47   *LW* 4, 42f.; *WA* 43, 165f.

48   *LW* 4, 367; *WA* 43, 400.

49   *LW* 5, 52; *WA* 43, 464.

50   *LW* 8, 134; *WA* 44, 677.

51   *LW* 8, 136; *WA* 44, 678.

52   *LW* 9, 236; *WA* 14, 712.

53   *LW* 10, 107; *WA* 3, 106.

54   *LW* 14, 332f.; *WA* 5, 61f.

55   *LW* 16, 123; *WA* 312, 87.

56   *LW* 17, 182; 18, 202.238.253; *WA* 312, 403; 13, 221.318. 328.

57   *LW* 2, 32ff.; *WA* 42, 284.

58   *LW* 2, 51; *WA* 42, 298.

59   *LW* 3, 48-61 passim; *WA* 42, 582-592.

60   *LW* 3, 227; *WA* 43, 37.

61   *LW* 4, 88f.; *WA* 43, 198f.

62   *LW* 3, 78; *WA* 43, 483.

63   *LW* 3, 155; *WA* 43, 535.

64   *LW* 7, 145; *WA* 44, 406.

65   *LW* 7, 181; *WA* 44, 434.

66   *LW* 8, 263; *WA* 44, 772.

67   *LW* 11, 7; *WA* 3, 525.

68   Cf. Luther's several treatises on government, *Secular Authority, To What Extent It Should Be Obeyed*, 1523; *An Exposition of Psalm 82*, 1539; *Whether Soldiers, Too, Can Be Saved*, 1526, etc.

69   *LW* 13, 151; *WA* 51, 204.

70   *LW* 31, 243; *WA* 1, 623.

71   *LW* 49, 382ff.; *WA*, Br 5, 492ff.

72   *LW* 1, 255; *WA* 42, 189.

73   *LW* 1, 261; *WA* 42, 193.

74   *LW* 1, 295; *WA* 42, 217.

75   *LW* 1, 252; *WA* 42, 186f.

76   *LW* 2, 51; *WA* 42, 297.

77   *LW* 2, 320; *WA* 42, 490f.

78   *LW* 5, 173; *WA* 43, 548

79   *LW* 5, 202; *WA* 43, 568.

80   *LW* 5, 204f.; *WA* 43, 568f.

81   *LW* 6, 146; *WA* 44, 109.

82   *LW* 6, 148f.; *WA* 44, 110f.

83   *LW* 7, 129; *WA* 44, 394.

84   *LW* 7, 254; *WA* 44, 487.

85   *LW* 7, 348f.; *WA* 44, 559.

86   *LW* 10, 204; *WA* 3, 242.

87   *LW* 11, 177; *WA* 4, 26.

88   *LW* 17, 176; *WA* 312, 398.

89   *LW* 17, 241; *WA* 312, 448.

90   *LW* 2, 27; *WA* 42, 280.

91   *LW* 5, 145; *WA* 43, 528.

92   *LW* 6, 32; *WA* 44, 23.

93   *LW* 13, 185; *WA* 51, 231.

94   *LW* 17, 89; *WA* 312, 89.

95   *LW* 22, 444; *WA* 47, 159.

96   *LW* 24, 367; *WA* 46, 62.

97   *LW* 31, 250; *WA* 1, 628.

98   *LW* 47, 115; *WA* 50, 475.

99   *LW* 14, 325; *WA* 5, 57.

100   Ibid.

101   *LW* 31, 152.322; *WA* 1, 571.

102   *LW* 31, 280; *WA* 2, 19.

103   *LW* 4, 43; *WA* 43, 166.

104   *LW* 5, 208; *WA* 43, 571.

105   *LW* 6, 358; *WA* 44, 268.

106   *LW* 7, 364; *WA* 44, 570.

107   Georges Bernanos, *The Diary of a Country Priest*.   New York: Macmillian, 1962, p. 15.

108   *LW* 12, 151; *WA* 51, 270.

109   *LW* 14, 283; *WA* 5, 21.

110   *LW* 16, 205; *WA* 312, 145.

111   *LW* 24, 205; *WA* 45, 647.

112   *LW* 26, 25; *WA* 401, 70.

113   *LW* 26, 45; *WA* 401, 103.

114   *LW* 26, 109; *WA* 401, 197.

115   *LW* 26, 140; *WA* 401, 245.

116   *LW* 27, 389; *WA* 2, 603f.

117   *LW* 34, 76; *WA* 303, 342.

118   *LW* 2, 177; *WA* 42, 386.

119   *LW* 3, 70; *WA* 42, 598.

120   *LW* 5, 26; *WA* 43, 446.

121   *LW* 5, 24f.; *WA* 43, 446.

122   *LW* 6, 217; *WA* 44, 161.

123   *LW* 13, 241.273; *WA* 41, 96.132.

124   *LW* 15, 200.349f.; *WA* 312, 611; *WA* 54, 98.

125   *LW* 16, 342; *WA* 312, 256.

126   *LW* 17, 16; *WA* 312, 272.

127   *LW* 17, 264; *WA* 312, 464.

128   *LW* 17, 341; *WA* 312, 524.

129   *LW* 34, 350.357; *WA* 54, 426ff.

130   *LW* 49, 331; *WA* Br 5, 407.

131   *LW* 7, 368f.; *WA* 44, 574.

132   *LW* 24, 386.397; *WA* 46, 78.88.

133   *LW* 25, 263; *WA* 56, 275.

134   *LW* 51, 336; *WA* 49, 592.

135	*LW* 3, 278f.; *WA* 43, 73f.
136	*LW* 4, 209; *WA* 43, 286.
137	*LW* 5, 33; *WA* 43, 452.
138	*LW* 7, 349; *WA* 44, 559.
139	*LW* 9, 184; *WA* 14, 681.
140	*LW* 13, 89; *St. L* 5, 747.
141	*LW* 22, 258f.; *WA* 46, 771f.
142	*LW* 23, 20; *WA* 33, 26.
143	*LW* 24, 264; *WA* 45, 702.
144	*LW* 27, 159; *WA* 2, 449.
145	Ibid.
146	*LW* 3, 3; *WA* 42, 550.
147	*LW* 7, 299; *WA* 44, 521.
148	*LW* 25, 490; *WA* 56, 497.
149	*LW* 27, 98; *WA* 402, 124.
150	*LW* 44, 87; *WA* 6, 255.
151	*LW* 45, 286; *WA* 6, 45.
152	*LW* 45, 306; *WA* 6, 306.
153	*LW* 46, 222; *WA* 302, 531.
154	*LW* 46, 256f.; *WA* 302, 584f.
155	*LW* 4, 101; *WA* 43, 207.
156	*LW* 6, 234; *WA* 44, 173.
157	*LW* 9, 57; *WA* 14, 593.
158	*LW* 9, 229; *WA* 14, 707.
159	*LW* 13, 46; *WA* 311, 193.
160	*LW* 13, 357; *WA* 311, 398.
161	*LW* 26, 63; *WA* 401, 128.
162	*LW* 26, 76ff.; *WA* 401, 146ff.
163	*LW* 26, 106; *WA* 401, 192.
164	*LW* 27, 168; *WA* 2, 456.
165	*LW* 29, 95; *WA* 25, 71.
166	*LW* 35, 382; *WA*, DB 7, 85.
167	*LW* 49, 160; *WA* Br 4, 159.
168	*LW* 36, 15f.; *WA* 6, 500.
169	*LW* 36, 23; *WA* 6, 504.

170   *LW* 36, 70; *WA* 6, 536.

171   *LW* 36, 86; *WA* 6, 546.

172   *LW* 50, 75ff.; *WA*, Br 6, 454f.

173   *LW* 42, 173; *WA* 7, 693f., *Sermon on Worthy Reception of the Sacra-
        ment*, 1521.

174   *LW* 49, 178; *WA*, Br 4, 285f.

175   *LW* 49, 261ff.; *WA*, Br 5, 220f.

176   *LW* 49, 168.201; *WA*. Br 4, 222.508.

177   *LW* 49, 160; *WA*, Br 4, 159.

178   *LW* 50, 170ff.; *WA*, Br 8, 59.99f.

179   *LW* 49, 384; *WA*, Br 5, 493f.

180   Ibid.

Chapter 6

Church Fellowship—Unity

Christ's church is one. There are not many churches. Strictly speaking it is the *una sancta*, the one, holy church of all true believers, the communion of saints. The broken condition of Christendom on earth, sorely divided into denominational groupings, does not destroy the unity and oneness of Christ's fold. It transcends all such division. Also on earth, therefore, Christ's church abides despite the fractured outward appearance. There are not many churches, but properly only one church. The church strictly speaking (*stricte dicta*), embracing all believers, but *only* true believers, is not a different entity from the church as we see and know it in this world. But the latter, broadly speaking (*large dicta*), includes all individuals and groupings who profess Christian faith. That may mean that hypocrites and unbelievers are present, as also faulty or impure teaching and aberrations. But the *una sancta* is and remains pure. Its essence is true believers, who are cleansed by the blood of Christ. In it only true and faultless teaching obtains, as given by God.

Divisions and disunity in the church on earth are not God-pleasing. Neither are false teachings or heterodoxy. Orthodoxy, or right teaching, is not an option, but a God-given directive to the church on earth, not merely an ideal, but a divine mandate. Congregations of Christians at given localities and larger church organizations, like synods, must endeavor to retain God's teaching in its purity and continue "steadfastly in the apostles' doctrine." (Acts 2:42) A congregation, or larger church body, is to be orthodox, striving always to retain God's teaching in all its purity, as given in Holy Writ, free from any admixture that adulterates or detracts from the truth. This is God's will. The unity of the church(es) on earth can only be served and advanced by genuine devotion to purity of teaching and maintaining the "one faith."

Self-evidently a church becomes a caricature of the true church when it tolerates deviations from what God has given purely and plainly. For the sake of the fundamentals of faith still present there, God tolerates continued existence of heterodox churches; but clearly it is not God's will that His Word be in any way adulterated, denied, or reduced. Liturgical forms, usages, and ceremonies are not a matter of orthodoxy, and need not be everywhere alike, as the

100

Lutheran Confessions state. (AC VII)   Since life, either for the individual or the group of Christians, is never perfect and pure, as God's doctrine and Word are,[1] it follows that a congregation, or church body, does not immediately cease to be orthodox by the casual or occasional insinuation of false teaching or practice; but Christian responsibility under and before God's Word demands re-action against such intrusion, forthright confrontation and combating of the false doctrine.

Erring, heterodox churches, therefore, may still be called churches, as long as fundamental Christian beliefs are present there. Countenancing erroneous teaching, however, is to act contrary to God's express will; and Christian believers, individually or as a congregation, are exhorted by God's Word to flee false teaching, to avoid fellowship that compromises faith and pure teaching, and to seek fellowship where God's Word is purely taught and the sacraments rightly administered.   False doctrine is a dangerous, indeed accursed, thing, because it flaunts the truth of God, either unknowingly or in open rebellion, and because it endangers the salvation of individual souls.

Differences in doctrine, therefore, between Christian church bodies on earth cannot be a God-pleasing thing, nor is the church's splintered condition into many denominations. The solution for this disunity and division does not, however, lie in the direction of indifferentism, tolerance, or so-called loving forebearance toward heterodoxy—all of it misguided and wrong—but in humble listening and obedient bowing before God's Word of truth, Sacred Scriptures. This is the posture demanded by God of every devout follower of His and of every church, be it a congregation or a larger fellowship of congregations bearing Christ's name. (Gal. 1:2; Deut. 13:1-3; Matt. 7:15; 24:23.24; Acts 20:30.31; Rom. 16:17.18; 1 Cor. 10:18.21; 2 Cor. 6:14-18; Gal. 5:9; Tit. 3:10.11; Matt.10:32.33; Lk.9:26; Rom. 10:9.10; 1 Cor. 1:10-13; Eph. 4:3-6; 1 John 2:19; Acts 2:42-47)

There is another extreme to be avoided, however.   To oppose God-pleasing fellowship among Christians and churches that are of one mind and united in common confession of Scriptural teaching is sinful separatism, schismatic, and party spirit. Scripture nowhere supports such divisiveness. Those who disturb and divide the church for reasons that are less than fundamental to the faith, for example, on grounds of differences in liturgical or ceremonial practice and custom, or patterns of discipline and life-style, act contrary to God's plea for brotherly love and forbearance. Separatism is sinful because it divides those who ought to be united in Christian fellowship. Often it is generated by personal rivalries, or personal viewpoints, rather than by basic principles or issues. Those involved in it should examine their motives carefully, be willing to repent, to alter course, and be ready to reestablish fellowship quickly with their brethren in the faith.

On the opposite side of the coin, however, unionism, or unionistic alliances or fellowship, must also be recognized as sinful and be avoided like the plague. Unionism occurs when false doctrine is tolerated within a church, or congregation, also when congregations or their larger groupings, or synods, practice fellowship with known heterodox bodies or churches. Such tolerating of and living with false doctrine is against the will of God and, therefore, sinful. It never advances the cause of true unity in the church, since it dilutes purity of teaching. This could be eternally damaging to individual souls, because it refuses to warn the erring brother or the offending church body. Moreover, false doctrine is thus given equal standing with pure, which is a travesty against God's clear and inspired truth recorded in Holy Writ. Compromise with error elevates man's own reason above God's revealed truth. In the style and thinking of Schleiermacher it advances subjective feeling and experience of Christ in one's life above Scripture's objective teaching of faith's content. Piety cannot replace faith's sound base. Nor dare man's finest thoughts preempt authority from God's holy Word. Genuine Christian fellowship has no other basis than agreement in doctrine, a unity based on acceptance of the articles of faith taught by God in His Word.

All such rightful concern for purity of teaching, or orthodoxy, in no way detracts from or minimizes the truth that Christ maintains His true church on earth in spite of all obstacles. The ecumenical endeavors of our day go in the wrong direction, if they fail to confess the truth of God's Word in all its fulness and purity and, by the same token, fail to expose, confront, and address the errors against the Word. What is required now is what has always been required on the part of Christians united in the faith, unequivocal confessional unanimity, as enjoined by the Apostle Paul, "that by the name of our Lord Jesus Christ, ye all speak the same thing, and that there be no divisions among you; but that ye be perfectly joined together in the same mind and in the same judgment" (1 Cor. 1:10). But even when we fail or come short, it is good to remember that God nonetheless accomplishes His purposes in building His church, however divided and scattered and loose the ends may seem to us. Luther has stated this well in his *Confession Concerning Christ's Supper*:

> There is one holy Christian Church on earth, i.e., the community or number or assembly of all Christians in all the world, the one bride of Christ, and his spiritual body of which he is the only head. . . This Christian Church exists not only in the realm of (or under) the Roman Church or pope, but in all the world, as the prophets foretold that the gospel of Christ would spread throughout the world, Ps. 2 (8), Ps.19 (4). Thus this Christian Church is *physically* dispersed among pope, Turks, Persians, Tartars, but *spiritually* gathered in one gospel and faith, under one head, i.e., Jesus Christ.[2]

Luther does not minimize the importance of every true believer allying himself with a congregation, or church body, that teaches God's Word correctly. Orthodoxy is never merely an option, or an alternative. It is God's will, and should be each individual's and each church's goal. The Lutheran church has adopted its Confessions with this in mind. It offers them not as formulations tentatively set forth, but as standards of orthodoxy for safeguarding the articles of faith taught in God's Word, but often debated and doubted; they are rallying flags to which concerned Christians may have recourse when the faith is attacked.

These Confessions propose no new doctrine, no novelties. They present the catholic faith, and thus are genuinely ecumenical documents, originally intended, and still intended, to work confessional unanimity. When these Confessions are called orthodox symbols of Christianity, the Lutheran church is not thereby claiming special status for itself or for its congregations and people, nor that it alone is a saving church, or that its people are all genuine Christians, or that *it* is co-extensive with the *una sancta*. What it does assert is that its doctrine, thus publicly attested and confessed, is in full accord with the Holy Scriptures and the faith once delivered by God through His prophets and apostles. It offers its

Confessions as witness thereto, publicly, and seeks for unity in the church on earth, for genuine fellowship grounded on confessional oneness of faith on all the articles taught in God's Word.

Since the church "is the congregation of saints, in which the Gospel is rightly taught and the Sacraments are rightly administered" (*AC* VII) and "a fellowship of faith and of the Holy Ghost in hearts" (*Apol.* VII & VIII, 5), it must take seriously "the threatenings that there will be wicked teachers and wolves" (Ibid., 22), as also "offense in regard to schism" (Ibid., 23, 49). But it will not be diverted from what God has said; therefore, "though we most earnestly desire to establish harmony," we cannot and will not "cast away manifest truth" in order to compromise with the adversaries of the Gospel (Ibid.). The church stands on this proposition, as Luther puts it in his *Large Catechism* (III, 51ff.), that "outside of this Christian church, where the Gospel is not, there is no forgiveness, as also no holiness," and no church.

"The church can never be better governed and preserved," Luther wrote in the *Smalcald Articles* (II, IV, 9), "than if we all live under one head, Christ," and are "diligently joined in unity of doctrine, faith, Sacraments, prayer, and works of love." The framers of the *Formula of Concord* dismissed the charge that "mere misunderstandings or disputes concerning words" were driving a wedge and dissension into the churches in the period after Luther's death, pointing vigorously to agreement in doctrine as the way to unity in the church and contending that "the opinion of the party in error cannot be tolerated in the church of God, much less be excused or defended" (Preface 9).

The post-Reformation theologians of the late 16th and 17th centuries lent support to these confessional statements. "Doctrine is the principal part of the ministry" of the Gospel, stated Chemnitz, and "those who falsify the doctrine should be forsaken, as the Scriptures state."[3] Moreover, "the true church may lie so hidden, while the other, false crowd prevails and rules," that it may feel like Elijah, all alone.[4] It must not be discouraged or dissuaded, but it must "remain and join in confession with that assembly," Chemnitz avers, "which has the true marks of the orthodox Christian church."[5]

Gerhard finds the true church opposed by the false, either totally, as by non-Christian religions and would-be churches which deny fundamental articles of faith, or partially, where though some articles are wrongly interpreted or taught, the fundamentals necessary for salvation are sufficiently present to justify their being called Christian, and "God is able to nurture and uphold a holy seed."[6] He holds to the formula that "the church is distinguished from heretical communions inside the church through the pure preaching" in conformity with the Word of God.[7]

We must distinguish, says Carpzov, between the church and the false accretions that attach themselves to her, "even as sickness is not the body itself, but only that which attaches itself to and afflicts the body."[8] The church, in other words, is resilient, able to survive in spite of these "ailments."

The chorus of voices among the Lutheran theologians strongly upheld the need for faithful followers of Christ to hold to the pure Word and teaching. Frederick Balduin articulated a principle, which has long obtained within the Lutheran church, that "reception of the Sacrament is a manifestation of faith and doctrine," a criterion for establishing fellowship.[9] Abraham Calov raises the question of whether a person must not seek for the true church and be a member of it. Chief among the reasons for "allying oneself with a church where God's Word is taught purely," he states, is "the command of Christ and his apostles."[10] But an important insight is added by Hollaz who offers very practical advice for the average Christian who might be deeply troubled by the enjoinder to align himself with the church that teaches purely: "We believe that it is not absolutely necessary to know which and where the true visible church is." The papists may have taught that it is impossible to be saved outside of that communion, but Hollaz counsels that "a man can be saved even though he does not know this, as long as he is a member of the invisible church." Quite existentially and in keeping with circumstances as are likely to occur, he adds: "Indeed it may happen that a person die and be saved, even an adult, who does not yet understand what the church is."[11] What he advocates is not unconcern for doctrinal deviations which are plainly present but resilient peace and state of mind which does not trouble itself excessively with every nuance of difference lying beyond his ability to discern.

Walther grants that "the only indispensable requisite for obtaining salvation is fellowship with the invisible Church," but in the every-day encounter with sectarian spirits who detract from the truth the Christian "is still obliged, for the sake of his salvation, to flee from all false teachers and heterodox churches, or sects," and align himself with "orthodox congregations and their orthodox preachers."[12] Readily he acknowledged that "also in erring, heretical congregations there are children of God." Elijah may have thought that he alone in all of Israel had remained faithful, not bowing the knee to Baal, but God assured him that there were at least 7,000 more.

Physically it may be impossible to distinguish the true believers from the mass of unbelievers around them; but spiritually and inwardly there is a difference; faith dwells in their hearts, and they are built upon Christ into a genuine fellowship through the indwelling Holy Spirit. Walther does not forget that the apostle Paul still addresses the churches in Galatia as churches, even though many in their midst had followed "another gospel"; but the apostle does so for the sake and by reason of the true believers who were still numbered there.

Walther recognizes that the Lutheran theologians before him, including Luther, used the title "Lutheran Church" in a twofold sense. On the one hand they meant and contended that their church was co-extensive with the true Christian church, the spiritual mother of true believers, possessing one Spirit, one faith, one doctrine. The claim was never that all in this church were true believers, or that only there could salvation be found. But they were affirming that the doctrines of the Lutheran Church, a name attached to them by their opponents, the papists, was fully in accord with the teachings that God had given through His inspired Word.

On the other hand, with the name Lutheran Church the Reformation confessors, and so also later their theological heirs, were stating their subscription to the public documents, the Lutheran Symbols or Confessions which attested their faith. Here the grounds for their separation from the papistic and sectarian doctrines were given. At the same time that they cited these issues—the grounds for their separation—they very carefully noted that they did not conceive of themselves as the only company of the totally regenerated or saved. Undoubtedly there were true believers wherever God's Word was still heard and the sacraments still administered in their essential conformity with the Word of God. Thus they bore the name Lutheran Church within visible Christianity as an ensign or standard of orthodoxy, because they were committed to God's charge that His Word should be purely taught and His sacraments rightly administered.

This very concern for faithful attention to all that God had given is a trademark of Lutheran theology. The reason is not for orthodoxy's sake alone, but for the sàke of imperishable souls whose salvation depends upon God's promises. These are to be purely taught even as they are purely given in His Word. Therefore, says Walther, "everyone is obliged, for the sake of his salvation, to flee all false prophets and to avoid fellowship with heterodox churches, or sects."[13] This was the mind and thinking of the reformers, the Confessors, and the orthodox theologians.

It is not compatible with the pure Word of God that a person consider it an indifferent matter whether he belongs to a church on earth which rightly and purely adheres to God's Word, or to some erring, sectarian communion. To argue that the main thing is membership in the *una sancta*, the holy Christian church, whether one's fellowship is with this or with that group, evades the issue. One can indeed be a living part or member of Christ's holy church, no matter what group one belongs to on earth, even a heretical church. But, says Walther, no Christian would, or should, argue this way. It is one thing to act in ignorance. But when a person recognizes that sectarian teaching is contrary to the explicit Word of God and still maintains his connection and fellowship with that body, he obviously is acting contrary to God's Word. Admittedly he may still be in the church of the Lord. God alone knows that. But it is incumbent upon him that he also be of the church, that is, in fellowship with that earthly communion where he sees that God's Word is taught in its truth and purity, and the sacraments are administered in accordance with what God has instituted and promised in His Word.

Human opinions and preferences must not take precedence over God's Word under any circumstances. A person does not knowingly and willingly sin because he knows that there will be forgiveness for sin. By the same token he does not knowingly and willingly fellowship with the heterodox because he knows that membership in Christ's kingdom is by faith alone through the Spirit. A child of God seeks always to act in accord with God's command and promises. These supersede all human predilections.

The right and proper way for a faithful child of God to act, therefore, according to Walther, is in accord with God's mandate. That mandate is: "Every Christian is obliged, for the sake of his salvation to profess allegiance, and adhere, to orthodox congrega-

tions and their orthodox preachers wherever he finds such."[14] God's
Word very plainly admonishes believers to keep, cultivate, nurture
the fellowship of faith.   Nothing stands out quite so clearly in
apostolic teaching and apostolic practice. Fellowship in faith was
grounded upon unity and agreement in doctrine, in faithful conformity and unanimity with the revealed Word of God.   Walther,
therefore, quotes Balduin with approval when he states that the
common reception together of the Sacrament of the Altar is the
highest manifestation of such unity.

In his ninth thesis Walther repeats the truism that for the
attainment of salvation only one thing is required, faith in the Lord
Jesus Christ as Savior from sin. He that is built upon Christ by the
Holy Spirit in the heart is thereby in Christ's church and in fellowship with all other true believers, a member of the household of
faith. Accordingly, the statement of Gerhard that he who does not
have the church as his mother does not have God as his heavenly
Father, is to be understood of the true, invisible church, the
communion of saints. External fellowship or membership with the
church on earth does not effect this; only faith in Christ and His
redeeming work can and will. This brings true, inward fellowship
and kinship with Christ and the company of saints.

To argue that outward linking with this or with that
particular body of professing Christians assures a person of salvation
is to detract from that which alone counts before God, the justification of the sinner *sola gratia/fide*, by faith alone in Christ and His
vicarious atonement. Needless to say, this very emphasis, which, is
at the core of the Christian faith, underscores the importance of the
pure Word of God, faithfully preached and taught. God's people
will there be gathered where *His* Word is heard.

No one has ever successfully accused Luther of being a
small man, a bigoted, ego-centric demagogue. If they have, they do
not really know his story, nor the story of the Reformation. No
matter who writes the history of that day, the answer today, if fairly
given, is that Luther was one of history's remarkable men, so
profound in his grasp of the issues that really count in man's life
before God and with his fellowman. Both those who embrace him
and call him their own, as well as those who oppose him and
dissociate themselves from his stance, stand back in due awe before
his impact upon the world in every aspect of its life for the last four
and a half centuries. Various explanations will be given, but the

simplest seems to be this, that seldom, if ever, has a man lived so completely out of the content of Holy Scripture, with such balanced judgment, with such keen insight into the plight of sinful mankind. As a result, friend or foe take their bearing point in telling the story of man in the modern era from the giant who at the Diet of Worms (1521) struck a blow that has resonated throughout life and human history ever since.

It was not the revolutionary character of the man. There was also that in him. He had to take his stand against what he saw to be in violation of God's Word. But he was no simple rebel. He has been called the obedient rebel. If rebel he was, it was only because the papalist system pressed protest and remonstrance out of him. The buildup of oppression in all aspects of life in the name of religion was bound to trigger popular uprising and rebellion. But Luther never catered to the spirit in himself and in other men to seek revenge or righting of wrongs through the multiplying of harm and overt action. On the basis of Holy Scripture his plea was for calm, judicious confrontation of the issues. Those that pertained to life and social ills and abuses he felt could be equitably resolved around the negotiating table by mediation. For Luther the linchpin of the religious issue in the 16th century was the main thing: Rome's religious system had failed at the most vital point of man's life, his standing before God.

Nothing else explains Luther; nothing else explains why he was willing to see western Christianity split, deeply though he felt the pain over it, than his concern for pure teaching in the church. This he knew was Christ's will; this he recognized as the apostolic injunction. To compromise with error was to yield the truth; worst of all, to endanger men's souls.

Luther's opposition to Rome can only be explained, therefore, in religious terms, and that primarily in the confusion concerning Law and Gospel. Man by nature is undoubtedly a born synergist, inclined always to offer his own works and efforts to God as sufficient, in a form of self-justification. This characterizes all natural theologies and/or religions. Moral improvement programs are always more gratifying to man than the Gospel of forgiveness of sins following upon the Law's sharp accusations of unrighteousness and transgression, even in man's so-called most splendid works. If the Law and its demands are softened, in order to put them within man's reach and attainment, it is of course more satisfying to his own ego and pretension of righteousness; but the Gospel in turn becomes offensive, unpalatable, something to be forgotten.

Luther saw that Romanist theology had taken this course. He never doubted, of course, that here and there the Gospel had survived, that there were genuine Christians throughout the system. But works-righteous theology had supplanted faith-righteousness, domestic-righteousness had supplanted alien-righteousness, theology of glory (man's elevating of himself) had supplanted theology of the cross (Christ crucified for men's salvation).

How could this happen, that the Gospel, Christianity's distinguishing doctrine, be shelved into virtual oblivion? Luther's answer was on target: through the papalists' lowering of the Law's demands. "The entire error of the papists," Luther stated, "lies in the fact that they consider the ordinary duties of this life which are commanded in the Decalog easy for them to perform perfectly. Therefore they ascend from the Decalog to their schemes, as though they were going to a higher level."[15] In effect the Romanist system had triggered a scrambling up the cross of each person's striving, meanwhile displacing the One who had hung there for their sakes, for their redemption. God, says Luther, is not our debtor; we are His debtors. "Therefore, if He gives us something, He gives it, not because of a right but out of grace, which He lavishly and richly offers to all who believe His promise."[16] By that promised grace also Ishmael, or any other, could be saved, Luther points out.

The monastic system was but the pinnacling of the wrong kind of focus. It even places a halo around or upon doubt. "Yes," says Luther, "they even teach the propriety of doubt; they say that it is impossible for man to be certain of being in a state of grace and of having the Holy Spirit."[17] But Christ *is* sure, and *He* is holy, and I am built on Him and have His righteousness and the Holy Spirit in my heart, through Word, Baptism, and the Lord's Supper, all of which cement tightly for me God's promised grace.[18]

Luther knew that the Gospel was not totally erased within the Romanist communion, that "faith, the Christian Church, Christ, and the Holy Spirit must also be found among them,"[19] and he asked: "What business have I, then, to preach against them as a pupil preaching against his teachers?" He took this question very seriously, and the answer just as seriously, because he found Rome's official theology leading to "a complete removal of Christ" and describing Him "only as the One who wants to judge me according to my life and my works, whether I have paid or atoned for sin or not." "If I view Him in such a light," Luther states, "I cannot run to Him for help but must flee from Him and seek refuge with Mary and other saints rather than with Christ and His redemption." In deep dismay he adds: "Behold, those are the people who want to be called the Christian Church but cast Christ completely aside. We are expected to obey them and to fear their writ of excommunication rather than Christ Himself."[20]

Luther recognizes, however, that really "there is nothing new about this dispute" and that "it has always been this way from the beginning," ever since the promise of God was given to fallen mankind and mankind disdained God's Word and preferred its own way.[21]

In taking his stand against Rome's heresy, Luther dug deeply into the whole history of the matter, also the innermost recesses of his own heart, asking this penetrating, bothersome question: "Do you suppose that He (God) would leave His church in error for so many centuries?"[22] Cannot others know the Scriptures as well as you, he wondered? That possibility he never doubted, but this we also "know for a certainty," he stated, "that it is an accursed lie that the pope is the arbiter of Scripture or that the church has authority over Scripture."[23] Not even an angel in heaven, nor any apostle would claim that. The church was under Scripture's authority, not vice versa.[24] Therefore, if it is in error, it needs to be rebuked, like any other individual, fanatic or whoever, for no one has "the right to teach whatever he pleases."[25]

Essentially, therefore, Luther's opposition to the pope and the papalists needs always to be seen as a doctrinal issue. Because of the sectarian teachings that had infiltrated Christian theology through the papal office, Luther held that "the pope is the supreme heresiarch and the head of all heretics."[26] "Frightful dissension" had come into the church and into Christian teaching through the papal office, with the elevating of the Roman bishop above simple believers and simple faith, "as though the unity of the church rested on man's person and on superior power rather than on the faith, hope, and love that are in the Spirit."[27]

Such notions of solidarity were contrived and self-erected. The Leipzig Debate, and Luther's preparation for it, helped to clarify for him how gross this fiction was. Against Rome's pretension stood history, the Holy Scriptures, the Councils themselves,

especially Nicaea.[28] In the process and under the cloak of Christian
piety, Rome had become a cover for "notorious godlessness."[29]
Luther can honestly say that he "never intended to attack" the church
as such, not even its hierarchy, but "when I saw all efforts to save
it were hopeless, I despised it, gave it a bill of divorce, and then
turned to the quiet and peaceful study of the Holy Scriptures."[30]
Then as time went on his eyes were opened even more to the
"infamy of Rome."

Luther's struggle with the papalists erupted into full blast as
he defended himself against the church's official listing of forty-one
"heretical or scandalous" errors in his theses. The *Defense and
Explanation of All the Articles* issued from his pen early in 1521,
shortly after he had burned the papal bull threatening his excommunication, December 10, 1520. Events moved swiftly thereafter, till
Luther finally stood at Worms before the notables of church and
empire, and bravely reiterated his total commitment to Scripture's
authority even though it meant challenging papal and conciliar
authority. It seared deeply into his very soul to be told: "Martin,
you finally retreat and flee to the place to which all heretics have
been accustomed to retreat and take refuge, the holy Scriptures."
But he stood his ground and the answer at Worms was not, "Yes, I
will recant," but "I am bound by the Scriptures I have quoted and
my conscience is captive to the Word of God; I cannot and I will
not retract anything."[31]

His heroic stand was probably one of history's most crucial
moments, certainly for Scripture's unassailable authority and for the
right and integrity of the individual conscience. Later, in his
Councils and the Church, of 1539, Luther would argue that, if the
reform of the church did not proceed out of Scriptural loyalty and
dutiful listening to what is there taught by God, it would fail, no
matter how many councils, how much effort, would be devoted to
that enterprise.[32]

Rome's great error was to set the church against Scripture,
as though the former were as much inspired as the latter, perhaps
even more so. "It is not true," Luther averred, "that the church does
not err or sin, for it prays daily 'Forgive us our sins.'"[33] Only the
Scriptures do not err, and "hence, after the apostles no one should
claim this reputation that he cannot err in the faith, except only the
universal church," by which Luther meant the *una sancta*.[34]

Luther was perfectly aware of the kind of exegesis heretics employed to twist Scripture's meaning deliberately to suit their own opinions; and, therefore, in the same set of theses he asserts Scripture's own hermeneutical principle, namely, "if the adversaries press the Scriptures against Christ, we urge Christ against the Scriptures."[35]   He found Rome guilty of obfuscating the Gospel. Inspiration could only be claimed for the Biblical writers who "spoke all things which are contained in the Scriptures by the Spirit of Christ."[36] For Luther it was a considered judgment, buttressed by the Scriptures themselves, that the papacy and those that stood with it, were the true schismatics and heretical spirits. On the grounds of the trademarks Scripture itself revealed Luther was willing to go farther, and term the papacy "the very Antichrist, the final horror." He accepted it as the "verdict of the Lord Jesus Christ" Himself.[37] The sensitive, neuralgic point was the obliteration of the Gospel under papalist dogmas concerning human attainment of righteousness by infusion of power through Christ's and the saints' merits.

"The battle of the church" has thus perpetually been against "the fanatics" who oppose their "pious" thought to the Word of God.[38]   There are no bitterer enemies than those who fall from God's Word, as Eve fell, when she "turned away from God and from His Word to lend her ears to Satan."[39] Yet some are saved in spite of the errors that persist, in spite of the fact, for instance, that "the pope was responsible for the concealment of the forgiveness of sins in the church," and teaching instead this foolish theology: "Mother Mary showed her breasts to her Son, the Son showed His wounds to the Father, and thus man was saved through the intercession, not of the Son but of His mother."[40]

Even Cain understood, Luther states, that he was not merely being driven from his home but also from the church, because of his faithlessness.[41]   People who take their stand against the Holy Scriptures today are in reality "siding with the Cainite church rather than with the holy church."[42]   The true church is troubled and "pressed on both sides" by the false church, because it has "the holy faith and the pure Word," while the false church prefers "to utter prophecies which have their origin in its own head."[43] Thus division in the church came very early,[44] and yet this did not mean that Cain or Ishmael, and the like, could not be saved, if they repented and believed God's promises.

It is really idolatry that slips back into the church when God's Word is disdained. The so-called wisdom of men deems God's Word foolishness; but the true story is really the other way around. "Stupid imitation by the ungodly has always followed upon the faith of the godly, and this has been the source and origin of all misfortune in the church."[45] Luther has evaluated the situation quite correctly, also in this that "the false church is always the persecutor of the true church, not only spiritually, by means of false doctrine and ungodly forms of worship, but also physically, by means of the sword and tyranny."[46] Heretics not only think their own opinions convenient, as Luther wrote to Erasmus,[47] but they also have a penchant for thinking themselves "to be nearest to God" and "to be the people of God."[48] Esau was a prime example of such false religion, who "when his father is away, is king and pope in that church," even though he despised not only his birthright but God's promise of the Messiah as well.[49]

It is Luther's conviction, however, from the examples he finds in Scripture and in church history, that God will vindicate and rescue His true church of believers, and that "all that oppose them will be confounded and lie like mud in the street."[50] In turn he lists as foes of the church, all who in some way have opposed it, whether Jews, Arians, Manichaeans, Pelagians, Muentzer and his crowd, the papalists, Sacramentarians, or the like. It has always been so that "there must be fighting" when the Word of God is doubted, "and it will always seem as though the others had won." "But," says Luther with conviction born of experience, "the Lord is with us, so that the riders who think they have won will be confounded."[51]

The true versus the false church will always be decided on the basis of "who has the promise of Abraham and the faith of Abraham."[52] Precisely this is the evil of the sectarian "reformers," that they "break into the church without a call, boasting about the Spirit and about their heavenly doctrine and under this pretext (become involved in) overthrowing true faith and doctrine," not to mention that they also "lay claim to primacy among evangelical theologians."[53] They cause much confusion in the church. It is significant to note, says Luther, that "the papists and the Anabaptists are harmoniously agreed on this one proposition, over against the church of God, despite their verbal pretenses: namely, that a work of God is dependent on the worthiness of man. For this is what the Anabaptists teach: 'Baptism is nothing unless a person is a believer.' On the basis of this principle, it necessarily follows that none of the works of God are anything if a man is not good."[54] On this ground Luther is ready, in his early lectures on Galatians, to denounce the Bohemian Christians as sectarian, although later he reverses himself on their plight when he comes to understand better the adamant conduct and repudiation of these struggling remnants of faithful believers by the official Romanist camp.[55]

Concerning the Anabaptists and their notion of "believer's baptism," Luther deplores the confusion which they have introduced into the church concerning baptism and faith. They end with emphasis on their own inner spiritual wrestlings and works, much as Rome has done with its work-theology, thus with theology of glory over, and in place of, theology of the cross, in spite of all their preaching concerning Christ crucified.[56] In a letter to his friend Wenceslas Link, May 12, 1531, Luther underscores the need for "baptism to be a matter of certainty," because of the affirming Word of God, not by virtue of or in the strength of the individual's faith, as the fanatics held.

Whatever trouble, turmoil, and dissension the church faced in his day, Luther recognized the hand of Satan in the assault. Even though he did not firmly hold to the view, it was his opinion that it was quite "likely that Adam sinned on the seventh day," and that therefore "Satan now disturbs the Sabbath of the church when the Word is taught."[57] Satan's target, of course, was not merely the day of worship, but the Word itself, causing Eve to doubt, "even as he (Satan) still does in the church."[58] "In the name of the Lord" and "for the welfare of the church," these are still the jingles and angles Satan uses to sow his evil seed in the church and divert people from God's Word. After all, Luther states, what could be worse for the church in any day than leading the people "away from the promise of the forgiveness of sins toward one's own righteousness."[59]

Though the church is never safe from Satan's wily "way of moving, namely, that he creeps in and does not walk erect," nevertheless, says Luther, the church is safe from Satan's total tyranny, for "his malevolence has been broken."[60] A vivid aspect of Satan's design is the idolatrous place in the church's life that Mary had been given as co-redemptrix with her Son; "but," says Luther, "this must not be permitted" and the church must not allow Satan in this way "to deprive her Son of the glory of our redemption and deliverance."[61] This is not the only point of Satan's attack, and the

Agreement in the Word, in what God teaches, is the *sine qua non* of a God-pleasing fellowship. "It is apparent," states Luther, "that true preachers and false preachers, true Christians and false Christians, cannot dwell side by side. Yes, they automatically part company; for the Word or the doctrine divides the hearts. Thus we cannot make common cause with the papist crowd or with the Anabaptists and other sects, nor they with us; for we are as far apart as summer is from winter."[104] Luther spoke these words in his series of sermons on John's Gospel, preached at the *Stadtkirche*, or city church, in Wittenberg; and thus they would have had a particularly pertinent, practical application.

Church fellowship, at altar and in the pulpit, must be based at the very least on agreement in the articles of faith. "A trivial cause," however, should never "separate those who should really be bound with the firmest ties," a thing that often happened in Christendom after the days of the apostles over differences in ceremonies, customs, and traditions.[105] Even when we stand firmly in the pure doctrine, we must still do it with love, genuine love, not "a completely bare, meager, and mathematical love, which does not become incarnate, so to speak, and does not go to work," but the kind of love that "is in the position of a servant."[106]

Ofttimes would-be peacemakers in the church proclaim love to the exclusion of pure doctrine. Luther urges: "We must proclaim concord in doctrine and faith as much as they proclaim concord in life."[107] Both need to be present and sought after. "For Satan is continually attacking both the purity of doctrine, which he seeks to destroy by means of sects and discord, and the integrity of life, which he pollutes through our daily transgressions and offenses."[108] We require God's own attitude. "The Holy Spirit is as generous and kind in bearing with sins and minimizing them as He is unyielding in maintaining and defending the doctrine of faith."[109] A "frightful dissension," therefore, it was in Luther's judgment that caused the sees of Rome and Constantinople to stand apart—as they still do—"just as though the unity of the church rested on man's person and on superior power rather than on faith, hope, and love that are in the Spirit."[110]

This principle always abides: "If the Word of God is present in its purity and is active, the church is there." But by the same token, Luther avers, "if the doctrine is filled with lying, life is hypocritical."[111] False doctrine is dangerous to God's people in the earth-bound that they in effect were asking, "What is heaven if we have flour here?" "Why bother" in other words. But it was all so satanically futile, Luther observes, like "milking the billy goat and holding a sieve underneath."[69]

Like Esau the church has sold its birthright. "The false church feigns godliness merely in order to enjoy the pleasures and honors of this world." Luther's judgment upon the papalist is very severe: "Hence Holy Scripture is pointing out that all people become greedier, prouder, and more carnal when they have lost the blessing than they were before, longing for the red pottage with horrible cupidity, but under the name of Christ and of God and under the title 'church.'"[70]

It is God's way of testing the church that it might "be cleansed by the Word."[71] Every evil in the world, even thorns, should remind us of our sin. Thus, all creation, Luther says, preaches a sermon "charging us with sin," yea, "all the fields, almost the entire creation, is full of such sermons, reminding us of our sin and of God's wrath."[72] In similar way God in Holy Scripture includes accounts like Joseph's temptation by Potiphar's wife, in order that we might learn "to fight and stand against the devil when he assails our faith and chastity as he attacks the faith of Joseph here by means of lust."[73]

When teachings of God's Word are attacked, Luther asks, "what else in the church do you suppose it is but the whirlwind of the wrath of God, through which we are propelled down the same road by so many, so diverse, so changeable, and so uncertain teachings as the countless briefs of the jurists and the opinions of the theologians?"[74] What else is it but the foxes and the little foxes at work, Luther jibes, pointing at the workers of iniquity in government in the first instance and to the church in the second allusion.[75] Yet God preserves His church, however severe the attacks, and sometimes he does it "through just one person," as He did through Paul the apostle, after Barnabas was no longer with him and even Peter had dissembled.[76] Whoever the enemies of the church may be, within or without, "God turns this judgment of theirs upside down and pronounces the sentence on them" who work the evil.[77]

In every generation the question arises, Where is the true church? The unfailing marks remain constant, the pure Word and the right administration of the Sacraments. In accord with these, says Luther, "those who have the Holy Spirit and adhere to the

Word can pass this judgment," no matter what "noble pretense" is made to the contrary.[78] Isaac, for example, "transmitted to his hearers," all that he "had from God, and without a doubt he was a teacher completely free from error," as a result of God's direct prompting and revelation, "one who trained and instructed the church diligently in the Word of faith and truth. . . for the purpose of establishing a church for the sake of his descendants."[79] Jacob stood in similar relationship with God, and thus the vow which he made at Bethel was not "a foolish and godless vow," as though "to placate God by making it, but to give thanks, to glorify God."[80]

These "heroes of the church of God" took God's promises very seriously, e.g., "the hope of the resurrection," and they "had no doubts about the immortality of the soul"; and that "is why they were so greatly concerned about burial," because they did not despise the body as "the most worthless part of man," but had due respect for what God had made, and maintained firm faith "about the resurrection of the body."[81] It was the preaching of the Gospel concerning Shiloh, the Messiah who was to come, that distinguished these patriarchs and the people of God from the other kingdoms around them, for they were "ruled by the Word" and believed God when He sent them forth in this "work that was to be done through preaching."[82]

In the church militant, of course, the struggle against the ungodly world that opposes itself to the church is endless, till glory dawns and things that were unclear now are made known.[83] "The church militant is called the house of David because of Christ's humanity," who by His lineal descent is "wrapped and incarnated in humanity" through David's line.[84] God knows who the just are, who belong to Him; in fact "God alone knows the way of the righteous," Luther states on the basis of Psalm 1:1, something which "is hidden even to the righteous."[85] All things fade and die, including the poets who compose the church's hymns, but "when they (the poets) die, the church survives them and keeps on singing their songs."[86] Kingdoms come and go, the sects rise and disappear, but "the church will not only be multiplied but will abide in the multiplying."[87]

The church always confesses her sins, and those in it live with daily confession and absolution. Because sin continues to beset even the saints of God, "there must be continual forgiveness among Christians, and we continually need forgiveness from God, always clinging to the prayer, 'Forgive us, as we forgive.'"[88] The church existed long before the popes ever came into the picture and cast their shadows; and this is so simply because the Gospel knows no barriers of time or place.[89] "The sects and the heretics have always assailed the true church," but they have not been able to overcome it.[90] Of these, and of the papalists, Luther states that "we are ready to concede that they are in the Christian Church, but not that they are the true members of the church," even though "they have the pulpit, Baptism, the ministry, the Sacrament."[91]

Spiritual knaves or unbelievers are tied to the visible church "just as mouse droppings are found among the pepper or cockleburs among the grain," but "they merely help to fill the bushel," and don't really belong. Heretics detach themselves from the church, or are detached, as a result of their "false doctrine and unbelief." And it should be an accepted truism that "the Christian Church is not the same as a collection of bishops' or cardinals' hats," or any other externalism. "If you want to be the church and bear its name," Luther avers, "you must prove your title," that is, "you must teach correctly, as the holy Christian Church teaches, have your life conform to its life, manifest your faith and the fruits of faith."[92] And if the papalist adversaries "deny our claim to be the Christian Church because we come from Galilee or from Wittenberg," in other words from outside their fictitious "holy" precincts, that will not faze us, Luther says; "we will not wait for their decision, nor will we preach to their liking," but we will "preach about the Man who will give us abundance also after this life."[93]

"We have Holy Writ and the prophets," and it matters little to us that the popes and bishops cry, "We occupy the apostles' office; we are the Christian church," is Luther's firm challenge.[94] The true seed of Abraham, after all, are those who not only have the Gospel but believe it and conform their lives to God's holy will.[95] It was because of Erasmus' preference to remain safely under the canopy of the papal church, exercising meanwhile his skeptical indifference to the text of Scripture, that Luther insisted that a Christian faith worth its weight is one that forthrightly asserts its belief and humble submission under the Scripture's authority.[96]

It is incumbent, therefore, upon the church, upon all its loyal sons and daughters, that Christ be front and center in their lives, that the articles of the catechism be confessed in their lives and with their lips, in other words, that "the pulpit, altar, and baptismal font (be) restored to their proper place, so that—thank God—the form of a Christian church can again be recognized."[97] If that is the proper, singular focus of the church, surely the church must not ape the world in its fascinations and concentrations. Looking critically at the superstructure of the church of his day, Luther could only wonder, "How did they (pope, cardinals, bishops) become the secular lords of all the world?"[98]

Fellowship of believers is a great treasure. God does not intend for His people to be divided into multiple sects and individual camps. Thus Abimelech and Abraham enjoyed a happy relationship because of their common faith, and Abimelech could assure Abraham: "We are not ill-disposed toward you, since we plainly see that God is with you; and we also want to be associated with you in the same church and faith. We want to know and worship your God. Therefore let there be an oath between you and us. Even though we have not been circumcised, yet we want to learn the true faith from you."[99] Thus agreement in the faith was for them the proper fellowship basis, even though certain outward signs and forms varied. Sects and schisms arise from dispute over doctrine and life; they "corrupt the Word (and) keep it from remaining pure."[100]

Unbrotherly nitpicking can, however, cause divisions. "The devil cooks this up in Christendom," says Luther, "and he is so successful at it that finally nothing is left but continual judging in matters of life as well as in matters of doctrine." Luther is not minimizing the importance of either of these areas, but he is scoring the hyper-critical, separatistic spirit, and he rightfully deplores this, stating: "Though the kingdom of Christ is a united, harmonious, and peaceful kingdom both in doctrine and in life, this (spirit) divides it and replaces it with sectarianism, arrogance, and contempt."[101]

If, on the other hand, Christians "willingly practice forgiveness, patient forbearance, and humility in (their) relations with one another, then everything in Christendom would move along correctly and harmoniously, as it should, and God would be with us."[102] The enemies to the outside are easily recognized by the church, and even though they may wreak physical harm, they are not as dangerous as those who work inside. These "do not disturb my body and my goods but let me keep what I have," Luther comments, but they "craftily reach out for the doctrine, to remove the treasure itself from my heart, the dear Word."[103]

church must be aware that "until the Last Day he will rage with such great fury against the church and the Son of God,"[62] primarily in a ceaseless effort to undercut God's Word and its authority and reliability in some way.[63] Familiar is Luther's oft used metaphor that "wherever God builds a church, he (Satan) builds his chapel or tabernacle next to it."[64]

Idolatrous practices have insinuated themselves into the Romanist church, Luther contends, in the name of God, of course, "for wherever Christ builds a temple and gathers a church, Satan invariably has the habit of imitating Him like an ape and inventing idolatrous forms of worship and idolatrous traditions similar to the true doctrine and the true forms of worship," but the meanwhile "belittling the promise" and "obscuring true worship."[65] So, the question, according to Luther, is not "whether there is a church," in that troubled day of the Reformation. "But the issue is: Which is the true church?" Luther responds to that point:

> We are agreed with the pope that there is a church. We believe that there assuredly is a Christian Church. The pope concurs in this. We are as firmly and strongly convinced as they that there must be a Christian Church on earth. But this is the question at issue and the bone of contention: Which is the Christian Church? For the devil and the pope dismember, pervert, and falsify all names.[66]

Luther's concentration is not simply and only on the papalists and their aberrations which have led to the silencing of the Gospel in the midst of the church, laying claim to primacy on the coattails of St. Peter. There is an assault as well from every corner when and where the sectarian spirit intrudes to direct a man inward to his own spiritual wrestlings for salvation, rather than outward to the Savior, the Lord Jesus Christ.[67] Perpetually the human spirit is after its own glory, its own efforts at salvation, this "evil (which) is implanted in the hearts of all human beings." As a result of its influence, says Luther, "if God were willing to sell grace, we would accept it more quickly and more gladly than when He offers it gratis."[68]

That was the sad state of affairs in Romanist theology, and, as a result, people had gotten used to being tied to the rituals and routine prescribed by the church; their religious sentiments were so church for the simple reason that it has "always sought out those who were not powerful in Holy Scripture and who could be easily deceived," thus "the common people," who require the influence of God's pure Word.[112]

The way of false doctrine is not direct assault on the things that God has given, like His Word, Baptism, the Lord's Supper, but indirectly to insinuate some other meaning in connection with them, with what God has said and taught, and to get people to "rely on their own way of life and works" rather than on God's promises in the Gospel.[113] It was in this way that the Scholastics succeeded in slipping Aristotle into the church, to allow "the pseudo philosophy of Aristotle to make its inroads into the church," especially in connection with the Mass.[114]

Fellowship at the Table of our Lord is where Christians manifest unity of faith in a particularly graphic way, for "the sacrament of the holy body of Christ," Luther states, "is a sign of the community of all saints."[115] In a letter to Martin Bucer, January 22, 1531, Luther stresses this point especially, that altar fellowship presupposes unanimity of confession and unity of faith.[116] To that end he exhorts the councilmen at Nürnberg to be solicitous that "pure teaching and preaching are preserved."[117] Digressions from the Word of God were above all other things the reason why the Jews had destroyed for themselves the unique place they had in God's designs for them, Luther points out at length in his notable, and controversial, treatise *On the Jews and Their Lies*.[118] This work is seen in proper perspective when that is borne in mind. For Luther the so-called Jewish question is not racial but primarily theological.

In his *Councils and the Church*, of 1539, Luther underscores with heavy ink the fact that the first four councils of the church had but one objective, to maintain concord and fellowship in the church by defending the faith and unity in confession; indeed the former was to flow from the latter.[119] It was Luther's deepest concern, as it had always been of the people of God, that we "remove the discord from our midst," but never at the expense of doctrine and unity of the faith. Thus as regards the Sacramentarians who had spiritualized the body and blood of Christ out of the Sacrament Luther stated the case for fellowship in the following explicit way:

> We who affirm the presence of the body of Christ would
> have gladly received our opponents into fellowship with us

if they had turned away from their error. Since no kind of an agreement could be reached with them, we decided unanimously that they were outside of the fellowship of the Christian church and that we would not recognize them as brothers and members of the church. This decision seemed so harsh to our opponents that the negotiations almost ended in strife; for surprisingly enough they wanted to have us as brothers. We were amazed at the changeableness of those men who a little earlier in their wailings had ridiculed us as worshipers of a God made of bread and who now sincerely sought our fraternity and fellowship, but we did not abandon the view which we had once and for all decided to uphold. But when our attitude also seemed harsh to the prince, we tempered our view in this way, that we were indeed willing to acknowledge our opponents, Zwingli and Oeclampadius as friends, but not as brothers and members of the church of Christ.[120]

This statement by Luther, taken from the account of the Marburg Colloquy and the Marburg Articles of 1529, was the fruit and climax of a long dispute over the doctrine of the real presence that had raged between Wittenberg and Geneva, between the Lutheran party and the Reformed. It is evident that Luther and colleagues agreed that a sufficient basis for church fellowship between the two communions was lacking. It virtually goes without saying that the situation has not altered. The same disagreement still obtains, in fact has intensified today, if anything. In fact the Reformed leaven has infiltrated to some extent within the churches calling themselves Lutheran; a unionistic spirit has surfaced widely among Lutherans who refuse any longer to consider the differences divisive of fellowship, thus in effect countenancing the Reformed position. Luther undoubtedly would enter a strong demurrer. It was not a case of judging whether they could be believers and be saved, but whether they therefore belonged in the fellowship pledged to the pure Word and right administration of the Sacrament.

Probably there is no more brilliant brief in behalf of pure teaching, and the need of the church to support it at all costs, than in Luther's famous *Galatians Commentary*. Many a theologian has been schooled through the reading of this great work. The church in our day continues to need Luther's finely honed advice and exhortation to the church and its people. Luther's comments follow at length:

> Paul, they said, was a stubborn and quarrelsome man, who was shattering the harmony among the churches on account of some trifle, for no other reason than because he alone wanted to be right. With this false accusation they made Paul detestable in the eyes of many. Others, who had not yet fallen completely away from Paul's teaching, imagined that there was no harm in disagreeing a little with him on the doctrines of justification and faith. Accordingly, when they heard Paul placing such great emphasis on what seemed to them a matter of such minor importance, they were amazed and thought: 'Granted that we have diverged somewhat from Paul's teaching, and that there is some fault on our side, still it is a minor matter. Therefore he should overlook it or at least not place such great emphasis on it. Otherwise he could shatter the harmony among the churches with this unimportant issue.'
>
> Paul answers them with this excellent proverbial statement: 'A little yeast leavens the whole lump.' This is a caution which Paul emphasizes. We, too, should emphasize it in our time. For the sectarians who deny the bodily presence of Christ in the Lord's Supper accuse us today of being quarrelsome, harsh, and intractable, because, as they say, we shatter love and harmony among the churches on account of the single doctrine about the Sacrament. They say that we should not make so much of this little doctrine, which is not a sure thing anyway and was not specified in sufficient detail by the apostles, that solely on its account we refuse to pay attention to the sum total of Christian doctrine and to general harmony among all the churches. This is especially so because they agree with us on other articles of Christian doctrine. With this very plausible argument they not only make us unpopular among their own followers; but they even subvert many good men, who suppose that we disagree with them because of sheer stubbornness or some other personal feeling. But these are tricks of the devil, by which

he is trying to overthrow not only this article of faith but all Christian doctrine.

To this argument of theirs we reply with Paul: 'A little yeast leavens the whole lump.' In philosophy a tiny error in the beginning is very great at the end. Thus in theology a tiny error overthrows the whole teaching. Therefore doctrine and life should be distinguished as sharply as possible. Doctrine belongs to God, not us; and we are called only as its ministers. Therefore we cannot give up or change even one dot of it. (Matt. 5:18) Life belongs to us; therefore when it comes to this, there is nothing that the Sacramentarians can demand of us that we are not willing and obliged to undertake, condone, and tolerate, with the exception of doctrine and faith. . . On this score we cannot yield even a hairbreadth. For doctrine is like a mathematical point. Therefore it cannot be divided: that is, it cannot stand either subtraction or addition. On the other hand, life is like a physical point. Therefore it can always be divided and can always yield something.

Doctrine must be one eternal and round golden circle, in which there is no crack; if even the tiniest crack appears, the circle is no longer perfect. What good does it do the Jews to believe that there is one God and that He is the Creator of all, to believe all the doctrines, and to accept all of Holy Scripture, when they deny Christ? 'Therefore whoever fails in one point has become guilty of all of it.'

Hence this passage (Luther's comments are on Gal. 5:9, 'A little leaven, etc.. . .) must also be considered carefully in opposition to the argument by which they accuse us of offending against love and thus doing great harm to the churches. We are surely prepared to observe peace and love with all men, provided that they leave the doctrine of faith perfect and sound for us. If we cannot obtain this, it is useless for them to demand love from us. A curse on a love that is observed at the expense of the doctrine of faith, to which everything must yield—love, an apostle, an angel from heaven, etc.! Therefore when they minimize this issue in such a dishonest way, they give ample evidence of how highly they regard the majesty of the Word. If they believed that it is the Word of God, they would not play around with it this way. No, they would treat it with the utmost respect (Luther undoubtedly is referring directly to the Holy Scriptures): they would put their faith in it without any disputing or doubting; and they would know that one Word of God is all and that all are one, that one doctrine is all doctrines and all are one, so that when one is lost all are eventually lost, because they belong together and are held together by a common bond.

Therefore let us leave the praise of harmony and of Christian love to them. We, on the other hand, praise faith and the majesty of the Word. Love can sometimes be neglected without danger, but the Word and faith cannot. It belongs to love to bear everything and to yield to everyone. On the other hand, it belongs to faith to bear nothing whatever and to yield to no one. (Luther has *fides quae creditur*, the body of Christian doctrine, in mind, not *fides qua creditur*, personal Christian faith—though of course there is a close connection between the two!) In the issue of salvation, when fanatics teach lies and errors under the guise of truth and make an impression on many, there love is certainly not to be exercised, and error is not to be approved. For what is lost here is not merely a good deed done for someone who is unthankful, but the Word, faith, Christ, and eternal life. Therefore if you deny God in one article of faith, you have denied Him in all; for God is not divided into many articles of faith, but He is everything in each article and He is one in all the articles of faith. Therefore when the Sacramentarians accuse us of neglecting love, we continually reply to them with this proverb of Paul's: 'A little yeast, etc.'

I have said this at some length to encourage our own people and to instruct others, who are perhaps offended by our firmness and who do not think that we have definite and serious reasons for this firmness. Therefore let us not be moved when they make such a boast of their zeal for love and harmony; for he who does not love God and His Word does not count for anything, regardless of what or how much else he may love. Accordingly, Paul warns both preachers and hearers with this statement not to think that the doctrine of faith is little or nothing and that we can play around with it as we please. It is a sunbeam coming down from heaven to illumine, brighten, and direct us. Just as the world with all its wisdom and power cannot bend the rays of the sun which are aimed directly from heaven to earth, so nothing can be taken away from or added to the doctrine of faith without overthrowing it all. . .

With the utmost rigor we demand that all the articles of Christian doctrine, both large and small—although we do not regard any of them as small—be kept pure and certain. This is supremely necessary. . . We can be saved without love and concord with the Sacramentarians, but not without pure doctrine and faith. Otherwise we shall be happy to observe love and concord toward those who faithfully agree with us on all the articles of Christian doctrine. In fact, so far as we are concerned, we shall have peace with our enemies; and we shall pray for those who slander our doctrine and persecute us out of ignorance, but not with those who knowingly offend against one or more articles of Christian doctrine and against their conscience. . .

Therefore, as I often warn you, doctrine must be carefully distinguished from life. Doctrine is heaven; life is earth. In life there is sin, error, uncleanness, and misery, mixed, as the saying goes, 'with vinegar.' Here love should condone, tolerate, be deceived, trust, hope, and endure all things (1 Cor. 13:7); here the forgiveness of sins should have complete sway, provided that sin and error are not defended. But just as there is no error in doctrine, so there is no need for any forgiveness of sins. Therefore there is no comparison at all between doctrine and life. 'One jot' of doctrine is worth more than 'heaven and earth' (Matt. 5:18); therefore we do not permit the slightest offense against it. But we can be lenient toward errors of life. For we, too, err daily in our life and conduct; so do all the saints, as they

earnestly confess in the Lord's Prayer and the Creed. But
by the grace of God our doctrine is pure; we have all the
articles of faith solidly established in Sacred Scripture. The
devil would dearly love to corrupt and overthrow these; that
is why he attacks us so cleverly with this specious argument
about not offending against love and the harmony among
the churches. . .

Therefore I would not want the pope, the bishops, the
princes, and the fanatical spirits to be in accord with us; for
such accord would be a sure sign that we had lost the true
doctrine.   In short, the church must suffer persecution
because it teaches the Gospel purely. The Gospel proclaims
the mercy and the glory of God; it discloses the wickedness
and the wiles of the devil, portraying him in his true colors
and taking away his mask of divine majesty, by which he
has made an impression on the whole world. That is, it
shows that all the forms of worship, religious ways of life,
and monastic orders invented by man, as well as the
traditions about celibacy, special food, etc., by which men
think they can gain the forgiveness of sins and justification,
are all ungodly things and 'doctrines of demons' (1 Tim.
4:1). Thus there is nothing that vexes the devil more than
the proclamation of the Gospel; for this takes from him the
mask of God (*larva Dei*) and shows him up for what he is,
not God but the devil. Therefore, it is unavoidable that
when the Gospel flourishes, the stumbling block of the cross
will follow; otherwise it is sure that the devil has not really
been attacked but has only been gently caressed. If he is
really attacked, he does not remain quiet but begins to raise
a terrible disturbance to create havoc everywhere.

Therefore if Christians want to keep the Word, they must
not be offended or frightened when they see the devil
breaking his reins and running wild, or the whole world in
tumult, or tyrants in a rage, or sects arising. But they
should know for a certainty that these are signs, not of terror
but of joy, as Christ interpreted them when He said (Matt.
5:12): 'Rejoice and be glad.' Therefore may the stumbling
block of the cross never be taken away, which is what

would happen if we were to preach what the ruler of this world (John 14:30) and his members would like to hear, namely, the righteousness of works; then we would have the devil friendly to us, the world on our side, and the pope and the princes kindly disposed toward us. . .

When things come to the point where the Word is about to be cursed or its teaching— and as a consequence, God Himself—blasphemed, then you must invert your sentence and say: 'Blessed be the Word and God! And cursed be anything apart from the Word and from God, whether it be an apostle or an angel from heaven!'

Therefore let us not underestimate the importance of the yeast of doctrine. No matter how little it is, if it is despised, this causes the eventual loss of truth and salvation, and the denial of God. For when the Word is distorted and, as necessarily follows, when God is denied and blasphemed, there is no hope of salvation left. . .

Let us learn to praise and magnify the majesty and authority of the Word. For it is no trifle, as the fanatics of our day suppose; but one dot (Matt. 5:18) is greater than heaven and earth. Therefore we have no reason here to exercise love or Christian concord, but we simply employ the tribunal; that is, we condemn and curse all those who insult or injure the majesty of the divine Word in the slightest, because (Gal. 5:9) 'a little yeast leavens the whole lump.' But if they refuse, let them perish and be banished to hell, and not only they themselves but the whole world with all its godly and ungodly inhabitants, just as long as God remains; for if He remains, life and salvation remain, and so do the truly godly."[121]

Luther's attitude is not arbitrary. It is dutiful bowing before God and His Word. "From all places and conditions," no matter what the circumstances, no matter how deeply Satan has made his inroads into the church and its doctrine, God will still gather His sheep whose "conscience will have been set free through the righteousness of faith."[122] This Luther never doubted. The borders

of God's church transcended the barriers set up by men and their
citadels, even the most resplendent ecclesiastical structures. The task
of the church in any generation, under any conditions, remains ever
the same: faithful preaching of the pure Word. Hence Luther's
sharp enjoinder and barb: "If they do not want to be bishops in
God's name, let them be bathhouse keepers in the devil's name."[123]

History has recorded the accuracy of Luther's rightful
concern. The Word in its rightful meaning is still the church's only
reliable mooring point or anchor. Its God-given function is the
salvation of sinful mankind, of all who will abide its message, Law
and Gospel. Christian fellowship among individuals and larger
groupings worthy of the name is grounded and tied to unequivocal
commitment to that Word. Ecumenical striving which compromises
or softens the base by wilful emasculating of that Word is a travesty
and is destined to fail, let alone bring dishonor upon God's name.
It is one of the unhappy, saddening facts of contemporary religious
life, however, that even among those who agree in confessing
Scripture's inspiration and inerrancy as the Word of God there
should exist differing interpretations of clear Scriptural teaching.
This bane not only nullifies the claimed agreement but, as Luther
has shown, makes genuine fellowship impossible.

NOTES

1   Cf. Luther's treatise, *Against Hanswurst*, *LW* 41, 209-222; *WA* 51,
        503-529.

2   *LW* 37, 367; *WA* 26, 506. Emphasis added.

3   *Examen Concilii Tridentini*, 237a.

4   Quoted in Walther, *KA*, 166.

5   *Enchiridion*, 211 f.; cf. Poellot trans; 155.

6   *Loc. de eccl.*, 126. Quoted in Walther, *KA*, 100.

7   Ibid., 131. Quoted in Walther *KA*, 103.

8   *Isag. in libros symb.*, 874. Quoted in Walther, *KA*, 107.

9   Quoted in Walther, *KA*, 137f.

10   Quoted in Walther, *KA*, 153f.

11   *Exam. theol.*, IV, 1, 35, 1306. Quoted in Walther, *KA*, 172.

12   *Kirche und Amt*, 95.

13   *Kirche und Amt*, 113.

14   *Kirche und Amt*, 144.

15   *LW* 3, 217; *WA* 43, 30.

16   *LW* 4, 42; *WA* 43, 166.

17   *LW* 24, 129; *WA* 45, 579.

18   *LW* 24, 130; *WA* 45, 579.

19   *LW* 24, 304; *WA* 46, 6.

20   *LW* 24, 307; *WA* 46, 9.

21   *LW* 24, 330; *WA* 46, 28.

22   *LW* 26, 15; *WA* 401, 55.

23   *LW* 26, 57; *WA* 401, 120.

24   Ibid.

25   *LW* 26, 66f.; *WA* 401, 132f.

26   *LW* 27, 91; *WA* 402, 114.

27   *LW* 27, 218; *WA* 2, 488.

28   *LW* 31, 309.318; *WA*, Br 1, 420ff.

29   *LW* 31, 336; *WA* 7, 44.

30   *LW* 31, 338; *WA* 7, 45.

31   *LW* 32, 112. 55-159 passim; *WA* 7, 832ff.

32   *LW* 41, 9-53 passim; *WA* 50, 509-547.

33   *LW* 34, 75.68-75 passim; *WA* 303, 341.331-341 passim.

34   *LW* 34, 113; *WA* 391, 44ff.

35   Ibid., Thesis No. 49.

36   Ibid., Thesis No. 57.

37   *LW* 41, 364; *WA* 54, 289.

38   *LW* 1, 22; *WA* 42, 18.

39   *LW* 1, 156; *WA* 42, 117.

40   *LW* 1, 180; *WA* 42, 134.

41   *LW* 1, 298; *WA* 42, 220; cf. *LW* 2, 30; *WA* 42, 283.

42   *LW* 1, 326; *WA* 42, 240.

43   *LW* 1, 320ff.; *WA* 42, 235ff.

44   *LW* 1, 252.291; *WA* 42, 187.215.

45   *LW* 2, 192; *WA* 42, 398.

46   *LW* 2, 214f.; *WA* 42, 413.

47   Cf. *LW* 33, 236; *WA* 18, 749.

48   *LW* 4, 108; *WA* 43, 213.

49   *LW* 5, 102.112f.; *WA* 43, 499.505f.

50   *LW* 20, 303; *WA* 23, 627.

51   Ibid.

52   *LW* 22, 197; *WA* 46, 707.

53   *LW* 27, 100; *WA* 402, 127f.

54   *LW* 27, 148; *WA* 401, 36.

55   *LW* 27, 392; *WA* 2, 605f.; cf. *LW* 36, 23ff.; *WA* 6, 504ff.

56   *LW* 40, 231-261 passim; *WA* 26, 144-174.

57   *LW* 1, 70; *WA* 42, 52.

58   *LW* 1, 146; *WA* 42, 110.

59   *LW* 1, 179; *WA* 42, 134.

60   *LW* 1, 189; *WA* 42, 141.

61   *LW* 1, 192; *WA* 42, 144.

62   *LW* 1, 200; *WA* 42, 149.

63   *LW* 1, 276; *WA* 42, 204.

64   *LW* 21, 212; *WA* 32, 474. cf. *LW* 21, 263; 23, 285; *WA* 32, 517; 33, 454.

65   *LW* 4, 236; *WA* 43, 304f.

66   *LW* 23, 285; *WA* 33, 455.

67   Ibid.

68   *LW* 4, 399; *WA* 43, 423.

69   *LW* 4, 403f.; *WA* 43, 425f.

70   *LW* 4, 408f.; *WA* 43, 429f.

71   *LW* 1, 145; *WA* 42, 109.

72   *LW* 1, 209; *WA* 42, 156.

73   *LW* 7, 90; *WA* 44, 366.

74   *LW* 14, 306; *WA* 5, 43.

75   *LW* 15, 221; *WA* 312, 663.

76   *LW* 26, 113; *WA* 401, 203.

77   *LW* 26, 457; *WA* 401, 684.

78   *LW* 2, 198f; *WA* 42, 401f.

79   *LW* 5, 80; *WA* 43, 484.

80   *LW* 5, 260; *WA* 43, 608.

81   *LW* 8, 140; *WA* 44, 682.

82   *LW* 8, 244; *WA* 44, 758.

83   *LW* 11, 136; *WA* 3, 642.

84   *LW* 11, 548; *WA* 4, 406.

85   *LW* 14, 309; *WA* 5, 45.

86   *LW* 15, 274; *WA* 54, 34.

87   *LW* 17, 327; *WA* 312, 513.

88   *LW* 21, 155; *WA* 32, 427.

89   *LW* 22, 512f.; *WA* 47, 216f.

90   *LW* 22, 524; *WA* 47, 226.

91   *LW* 23, 386; *WA* 33. 456.

92   *LW* 23, 289; *WA* 33, 461.

93   Ibid.

94   *LW* 23, 378; *WA* 33, 615.

95   *LW* 23, 418; *WA* 33, 672.

96   *LW* 33, 19-44; *WA* 18, 603-620.

97   *LW* 47, 53; *WA* 303 307f.

98   *LW* 47, 39f.; *WA* 43, 489.

99   *LW* 5, 87; *WA* 43, 489.

100   *LW* 21, 210; *WA* 32, 473.

101   *LW* 21, 215; *WA* 32, 477.

102   *LW* 21, 222; *WA* 32, 483.

103   *LW* 21, 248; *WA* 32, 505.

104   *LW* 24, 235; *WA* 45, 676.

105   *LW* 24, 246; *WA* 45, 685.

106   *LW* 27, 52; *WA* 402, 65.

107   *LW* 27, 107; *WA* 402, 136.

108   *LW* 27, 109; *WA* 402, 139.

109   *LW* 27, 110; *WA* 402, 140.

110   *LW* 27, 218; *WA* 402, 448.

111   *LW* 28, 303f.; *WA* 26, 64.

112   *LW* 29, 37; *WA* 25, 32.

113   *LW* 30, 170; *WA* 14, 35.

114   *LW* 36, 31; *WA* 6, 509.

115   *LW* 39, 7; *WA* 6, 63.

116   *LW* 50, 6f.; *WA*, Br 6, 25f.

117   *LW* 50, 62f.; *WA*, Br 6, 339f.

118   *LW* 47, 162-253 passim; *WA* 53, 437-501.

119   *LW* 41, 53-124 passim; *WA* 50, 547-624.

120   *LW* 38, 78f.; *WA* 303, 152f.

121   *LW* 27, 36-46; *WA* 402, 45-57; Cf. *LW* 41, 214-219; *WA* 51, 513-522.

122   *LW* 17, 182; *WA* 312, 403.

123   *LW* 34, 52; *WA* 302, 344. In Luther's day the bathhouse keeper was
       also the barber and the bloodletter!

PART II

Chapter 1

What Is the Ministry?

"We have this ministry," writes the Apostle Paul to the Corinthian congregation (2 Cor. 4:1). He is speaking first of all of his office as apostle, chosen of the Lord; but he is enlisting the people's support in the conduct of the ministry in their midst. God has entrusted the means of grace, Word and Sacrament, to all believers, who, as the apostle Peter affirms, are the royal priesthood (1 Pet. 2:5.9). Christ's mandate (Matt. 28:19 and Mark 16:15) makes each Christian a witness for the Gospel to the world around him. The Church is built and preserved through the ministry of the Word. God's people, Luther reminds us, cannot be without God's Word. The church owes its existence to the Word, not vice versa, and "wherever the Church is, there is the authority to administer the Gospel," state the Lutheran Confessions (*SA* Tractate, 67). The world owes its continued existence to the unfinished task of the church in spreading that Word (Matt. 24:14).

However, there are not two ministries, as the above may seem to suggest. Christ establishes only a single ministry for the building of His church through the Word. The mandate which places all believers under the responsibility to make disciples for the Lord is the ground upon which the public pastoral office rests. The term ministry thus has both a wide and a narrow sense. In the first sense it refers to the rights and duties which in connection with the Gospel belong by Christ's ordering to the totality of the spiritual priesthood of believers (1 Pet. 2:9; Matt. 18:17; John 20:23; 1 Cor. 3:21f.). Every Christian, young or old, man, woman, or child, shares in this ministry as a believing, baptized child of God. By faith he is a member of Christ's church and His royal priesthood, possessing all the privileges and responsibilities that accompany that station.

But ministry in the New Testament also has a more restricted, yet proper and pointed sense that refers to the office of the public pastoral ministry. By God's express will, in accord with stated criteria, it is a specially authorized and chartered office into which a qualified man is to be called by the Christian believers

135

gathered at one place in a congregation. The rights and responsibilities of the spiritual priesthood belong to them, but they are not each to administer the means of grace, Word and Sacraments, for themselves publicly, valid and efficacious though this might be; but they are to call, that is, elect, or choose, or appoint, a qualified man to do this in their name and stead.

The called pastor does publicly, by the will of God, what belongs to the ministry of the Word. His is an office specially designated by God, for the sake of the church on earth (Acts 20:24; Rom. 15:16; 1 Cor. 4:1). He is to have a special aptitude to teach and minister beyond the usual capacity of the believers in general (1 Tim. 3:2; 5:21; 2 Tim. 2:2). However, his credentials for functioning stem from the special, particular call of the Christian congregation to perform these duties of ministry in their stead (Acts 14:23; Eph. 4:11; Rom. 1:1). The church, or congregation, does not surrender its rights and responsibilities by calling a pastor. The church, or fellowship of believers, retains "the authority to call, elect, and ordain ministers," as the Lutheran Confessions state (*SA* Tractate, 67), and this authority is a gift "which no human authority can wrest from the Church."

The distinctive nature of the public pastoral office must not be lost, however, as the considerable prerogatives and duties of the general priesthood of believers are asserted and predicated. There is need for affirming this, as Luther showed, because of the Romanist teaching and presumption which funneled and vested these powers into the hands of the ecclesial hierarchy, from pope down through the ordained clergy. Luther never lost sight of the fact that God had established the public pastoral office *through* the congregation's call and *for* its sake. Walther very properly emphasizes the same truth in his theses on the ministry, *Vom heiligen Predigtamt oder Pfarramt*.[1] In the first of his theses, completely in accord with Luther and the Confessions, he states, that "the holy ministry, or the pastoral office (parish pastorate), is an office distinct from the priestly office, which belongs to all believers." In explanation Walther shows on sound Scriptural grounds "that there is in the church an office for teaching, shepherding, governing, etc., which does not belong to Christians by reason of their general Christian calling." Citing 1 Corinthians 12:29; Romans 10:15; and James 3:1, Walther states that even as all were not called to be apostles, so not all were to be pastors or teachers; as the office of apostle was distinct, so also is the pastoral office, to this very day.

In no way does this denigrate the general priesthood of believers, or elevate one person over another; but it does clearly establish the public pastoral office, or the parish pastorate, in distinction from the general priesthood. There is a mutual coinhering and deriving which is to be noted, not a clashing between the two senses in which ministry is understood in Holy Scripture. God is a God of order, and it is by His divine ordering that the particular office of pastor (teacher, elder, bishop, presbyter are synonyms) exists in the church, and for the church.

It is a lofty calling to which God in the first place has called each individual believer of the royal priesthood; it is a lofty office to which these believers by God's explicit mandate call a man into their service for administering the means of grace among them. The ministry of the Word is God's order of things. It is also He who has established the particular office of the parish pastorate in His church among His royal priests.

The Tractate of the *Smalcald Articles* asserts the God-given authority which churches, specifically congregations, have, in the event that the order heretofore followed for the obtaining of pastors, that is, through ecclesial bishops, etc., should cease or become impossible (*SA* Tractate 67). Previous to this declaration of power and authority which resides in God's people, the Tractate had shown convincingly that the pretension of papal power and primacy by divine right (*iure divino*) was totally groundless and without Scriptural warrant, as well as historical basis or precedent (cf. *SA* Tractate, 1-37). Nor should the consciences of the faithful be bound by the godless presumption of the papal office which required recognition of such authority as necessary for salvation (*SA* Tractate, 38-59). Since the authority of the Keys ultimately and first of all belongs to the priesthood of believers, the Tractate concludes that "there are just reasons why we do not obey" Rome's hierarchical, autocratic rule, and why "it is right also to restore this jurisdiction to godly pastors, and to see to it that it is legitimately exercised for the reformation of morals and the glory of God" (*SA* Tractate, 76).

On the basis of Article V in the *Augsburg Confession* Walther notes that the first and primary emphasis of the Confessors was to stress, in the wide sense, the ministry of the Word, the Gospel, by which God builds His kingdom or church of believers.[2]

At the same time there is implicit in this article the establishment of the parish pastorate. Walther insists that what is implicit in the article, that is, the pastoral office, is explicitly expressed in Article XIV of the *Augsburg Confession*, "that no one should publicly teach in the Church or administer the Sacraments unless he be regularly called." Article XXVIII of the same Confession carefully articulates the power of the Keys and to whom they are given stating that this power is exercised by one man, or by several, who have been called into the pastoral office. Thus the ministry of the Word is the property of the general priesthood, but it is performed, under God's careful ordering, by designated ministers who are called into their parish pastorates through the instrumentality of the churches (*AC* XXVIII, 5ff.).

Self-evidently the Gospel ministry, which is the possession and the duty of all believers, is in a very unique way instituted by God the task that belongs to the special office which He has established in His church, the pastoral office, the parish pastorate (*Pfarramt*).

Luther set the direction very early on the doctrine of the ministry, both on the general priesthood of believers, and also on the particular office of the parish pastor. Congregations supportive of the Reformation required pastoral care, because bishops were unwilling to supply them with pastors. This exigency threw Luther back upon the Scriptures for the warrant which established the ministry both in the wide and the narrow sense. To the Christians in Prague, who were facing this exact dilemma, he wrote in 1523:

> Here we take our stand: There is no other Word of God than that which is given all Christians to proclaim. There is no other baptism than the one which any Christian can bestow. There is no other remembrance of the Lord's Supper than that which any Christian can observe and which Christ has instituted. There is no other kind of sin than that which any Christian can bind or loose. There is no other sacrifice than of the body of every Christian. No one but a Christian can pray. No one but a Christian may judge of doctrine. These make the priestly and royal office.[3]

From this position on the general priesthood of believers and their God-given rights Luther never wavered, though as the years went on he more and more came to recognize how the average Christian layperson needed the leadership of dedicated magistrates and princes to guide them, lest anarchy reign. But the basic doctrinal position did not change. He meant it when he said, "here we take our stand." He was referring to the relation of individual Christians to the office of the public ministry. Alongside the doctrine of the royal priesthood with its wonderful prerogatives stood the article on the public pastoral office, or *Pfarramt*. It too had Scripture's full warrant. Luther carefully articulated its relationship to the general priesthood:

> It is of the common rights of Christians that we have been speaking. For since we have proved all of these things to be the common property of all Christians, no one individual can arise by his own authority and arrogate to himself alone what belongs to all. Lay hold then of this right and exercise it, where there is no one else who has the same rights. But the community (*Gemeinschaft* in German, hence a confraternity of spiritual nature, or congregation!) rights demand that one, or as many as the community chooses, shall be chosen or approved who, in the name of all with these rights, shall perform these functions publicly. Otherwise there might be shameful confusion among the people of God, and a kind of Babylon in the church, where everything should be done in order, as the Apostle teaches (1 Cor. 14:40). For it is one thing to exercise a right publicly; another to use it in time of emergency. Publicly one may not exercise a right without consent of the whole body or of the church. In time of emergency each may use it as he deems best.[4]

Luther sets Romanist pretension as regards the vaunted "splendid power of consecration" in the transubstantiation of the elements in the Mass into perspective when he compares it with the wonderful "power of baptizing and of proclaiming the Word," which the average person has, including women. With biting satire he states: "Meanwhile this miracle-working priest changes the nature of the bread, but by no other or greater word of power, and it has no other effect than that it increase his awe and admiration before his own dignity and power. Is not this to make an elephant out of a fly? What wonder workers! In despising the power of the Word they make marvelous their own power."[5]

Like Luther, Martin Chemnitz upheld New Testament teaching on the ministry of the Word, noting that by God's own design it was not an uncertain, haphazard affair but carefully structured. It was God's way of doing things to "put the Word of reconciliation" into the general priesthood's responsibility, and that the proclamation of the Gospel, divinely revealed, should sound forth through men."[6] Chemnitz then adds:

> All Christians are indeed priests (1 Peter 2:9; Rev. 1:6), because they offer spiritual sacrifices to God. Everyone also can and should teach the Word of God in his own house (Deut. 6:7; 1 Cor. 14:35). Nevertheless, not everyone ought to take and arrogate to himself the public ministry of Word and sacrament. For not all are apostles; not all are teachers (1 Cor. 12:29), but those who have been set apart for this ministry by God through a particular and legitimate call (Acts 13:2; Jer. 23:21; Rom. 10:15). This is done either immediately or mediately. Paul prescribes a legitimate manner of calling which is made through the voice of the church (1 Tim. 3:2-7; and Titus 1:5-9). Christ Himself indeed called certain men to this ministry immediately, in order to show that he approves the ministry of those who are chosen and called by the voice of the church according to the rule prescribed by the apostles.[7]

The opening question in Chemnitz' valuable *Enchiridion*, or *Handbook of Christian Doctrine*, asks: "What kind of office is the preaching (or pastoral) office?" His answer, in perfect accord with the above, is:

> It is not a secular rulership, for the purpose of supervising temporal or political matters, Lk. 22; 2 Tim. 2. It is also not a spiritual rulership with power of its own to govern arbitrarily over the churches, 2 Cor. 1; 1 Pet. 5. It is also not an industry or a business that exists for profit reasons, 1 Tim. 3 and 6; 1 Pet. 5. It is rather a spiritual office of service to the churches, established and ordained by God, 2 Cor. 14, in order that there would be and would continue to

be preachers as servants in Christ's Kingdom and stewards of God's mysteries, 1 Cor. 4; Col. 1. These have been charged and mandated by God through a regular call, to feed the congregation of God with the pure teaching of God's Word, Acts 6 and 20; Eph. 3 and 4; with the handling and administering of the sacraments, Matt. 28; 1 Cor. 11; with rightful use of the church's Keys to loose and to retain sins for people in general or individually, Matt. 16; John 20; and all of this in accord with the express will and command of the Chief Shepherd who gave such instruction in His Word, Matt. 28.[8]

True it is that all Christians have a common call and command to proclaim the Word of God, Rom. 10; to speak of it among themselves, Eph. 5; to admonish one another on the basis of God's Word, Heb. 5; to reprove, Eph. 5 and Matt. 18; to comfort, 1 Thess. 4; and especially in the governing of one's house to exhort and admonish, Eph. 6. But the public ministry of Word and Sacrament is not entrusted to all Christians in general, 1 Cor. 12; Eph. 4; since for that office there is need for a special call, Rom. 10.[9]

In his *Loci theologici* Gerhard takes note of the Romanist Bellarmine's taunting criticism of Luther and the Lutherans for giving every baptized person the right to administer the sacraments, without having noted that this right which is the common property of all believers is not to be exercised by them in arbitrary, selfwilled, willy-nilly manner. That would lead to disorder, a disorder that God Himself obviated through the institution of the regularly called parish pastor. "For this office they (baptized Christian believers, in contrast to unbelievers) are eligible and qualified when they have been regularly called," that is, through the congregations.[10] In treating of the pastoral office Gerhard states that it is necessary "to distinguish between the general mandate and call, which all the faithful have by virtue of their being ordained into the Christian fellowship, and the particular call through which qualified persons are chosen by the common consent of the churches for the office of administering Word and sacraments in the public assemblies of the Church."[11]

Johann Baier concurs completely with his predecessors, adding that the church, therefore, is like "a republic," in which "the ministers of the Word are, so to speak, the magistrates or conductors of public affairs, upon whom the care of the whole republic rests"; but "the power to appoint them is vested in the very nature of the case in the whole church," and it remains there fundamentally even when for the public exercise of the office it is transferred to a given individual.[12]

Walther edited the *Compendium* of Baier and utilized the slightly emended edition for his own classroom teaching. Sufficient for our purposes here is to note the exact parallelism between the positions of the theologians of post-Reformation Lutheran theology and that of Walther. Together they all recognized the ministry in general which God had entrusted to His royal priesthood of believers and the distinct office of the holy (because divinely instituted) pastoral ministry which God established in the midst of and through His church.

Luther's odyssey from the stranglehold of the Romanist priesthood, subjugated under the papal hierarchy, to the glorious freedom and station of the pastoral office under God and under God's people, the royal priests, was an arduous one. It was not the case of a rebel arbitrarily and thoughtlessly throwing off a burdensome yoke; it was rather the valiant struggle of a pious soul casting off the bonds of an oppressive human bondage and gladly taking upon his shoulders the servanthood of his Lord and Master Christ, who had given great gifts to His church, including not least the holy ministry. To the royal priesthood belonged the task of evangelizing the world (Matt. 28:19) and theirs was the responsibility under God of establishing in orderly manner the office of the public ministry, the parish pastorate, in their midst.

Already in the Old Testament the precedent was set. "Because of faith and the Word," what is otherwise ordinary and no greater accomplishment than that of the worldling, the task of a Christian champion, like Abraham (who also had gathered his laurels in battle), becomes a truly elevated one.[13] Luther bears in mind that as a man of God Abraham was "appointed bishop and teacher by God's voice," prophet, priest, and pastor in his house, "a distinguished servant of God, than whom the world has nothing more sublime."[14] Nor was Abimelech any less so when he turned to God and repented.

God gets His preachers ofttimes right out of the midst of the masses. "Today many say that they would embrace the Gospel if the kings themselves were to preach it, but that sensible people are repelled because most preachers are so wretched, poor, despised, and downright plebeian."[15] This is an obvious dodge, Luther avers. The godless unbeliever will reject even the noblest of men, even an angel from heaven. Take a case in point from current history, Luther suggests. "Did not our most illustrious prince of sacred memory, John, Elector of Saxony, teach the Gospel of Jesus Christ in the year 1530 through his frank confession at the Diet of Augsburg in the presence of Emperor Charles and all the imperial estates, and not he alone but with him and after him many others?"[16] Luther's point is that God's royal priesthood of believers has always contended and witnessed for the faith, even as "also John, Elector of Saxony, of sacred memory, confessed Christ with great courage before the entire world." This is often "the lot of those to whom God has entrusted the ministry of the Word."[17] But in them "He nevertheless has His little church," "for God is not without a people."[18]

Abraham's place as a prophet of God was unique. This Luther recognizes. But he also underscores the points of similarity between Abraham and every royal priest, or believer. To be sons or pupils of the prophets it is not necessary "that future events be revealed to us," Luther states. "For the office of a prophet it is enough that we understand Scripture and are able to teach others and also to help one another with prayers."[19] These are the earmarks of a "prophet" in the sense which applies to every believer. "Therefore the name 'prophet' belongs equally to all Christians," Luther contends, "and he who denies this also denies that he has been baptized and has been instructed through the Word."[20] I am not under some kind of delusion that makes me think that I am an Abraham, or an Elijah, is Luther's point; but I certainly am one of God's true spokesmen because I have His Word and because His Spirit dwells in me through that Word. Luther could hardly have described the general priesthood of believers any more vividly, nor its task of ministry any more realistically.

The Word of God is never an idle thing in a Christian's life like some bowl of soggy Rice Krispies that just lies there with no "snap, crackle, or pop." It not only has the power to bring you to faith, says Luther, but also "it will remind you to think about calling upon and praising God" with your life, and "it will make you a priest and prophet of God, one whose sacrifices will be most pleasing to God because His eyes have regard for faith."[21] Princes or peasants, the Word's transforming energy is there for each one, and thus Isaac and Abimelech were such in whom the Word had worked its miracle and made them men of God who "were baptized in the Holy Spirit."[22] Luther sees a remarkable convergence and confluence of God's purposes in bringing His Word into the lives of His people, according to which earthly and physical blessings or stations in life must serve the spiritual ends or blessings in their lives, be they parents, teachers, ministers, or whatever. "He has created the ministry of the whole creation," in order that His kingdom might come.[23]

What Luther has in mind is not just the general testimony of the natural realm concerning God's being and rule, but specifically the things that happen through His Word, His special revelation and means of grace. As a result "those things which the saints speak should be regarded as being spoken by God Himself."[24] True, "when we teach the Gospel, baptize, call men to the ministry of the Word, and ordain ministers, we ourselves do not preach, we do not baptize, we do not ordain, but God is speaking through us." In one breath and with sweeping stroke Luther herewith accounts for the ministry which all Christians have under God and then also the specific office of the public ministry or parish pastorate to which the preaching of the Word and administering of the sacraments are entrusted. "So it is called God's Word, God's sacrament, God's ministry, and it is rightly said: 'God is speaking, God is baptizing' when He does it through ministers, since indeed all things are attributed to God which holy men have spoken."[25]

Luther recognizes that "even though we were all called" by our faith and Baptism to confess God to those with whom we have to do, yet "we cannot all preach," for that office belongs to those whom the congregation appoints and "who are called in this way to proclaim the Word of God." So, while "in Baptism we all receive the chrism and the priestly garb," we leave the task of public preaching to others, who have been called for this special office by the royal priests, or congregation.[26]

Side by side with these truths is the parallel truth of "that common and spiritual priesthood by which we all sacrifice ourselves mystically" (Rom. 12:1) day by day in our Christian faith and life.[27] Only unbelief could cause a man to forfeit such great gifts, as Cain

did.[28]   A Christian is called to be faithful in his ministry as a child
of God who is ruled by His Word, for "God appoints me leader
against the gates of hell (Matt. 16:18), against the raging of the
whole world."[29]   It is on the basis of this verse that papal pretension
was wrongfully built; "but by this very statement Christ wants Peter
to be a confessor and minister of the Word," Luther shows, "not a
tyrant who would burden consciences with human traditions"; and
thus, though "they say that Abraham was a layman," he likewise was
one of God's ministers, because he had God's Word, believed it, and
taught it.[30]

It is in the nature of the Keys that faith should receive the
promised forgiveness which they extend, since Christ "moves every
Christian heart to faith so that when a man is absolved by the priest
he may be sure that he is absolved by God."[31]   Thus the Keys are
what God made them, not what the Church supposedly has made
them; and they are "the common property of all Christians," even the
lowliest.[32]   This is so because of the general calling to faith which
gives Christians their status before God.[33]   Of this fact the apostle
Paul reminds Timothy, causing him to remember that his undergirding for his special ministry as parish pastor at Ephesus or shepherd
in God's church was his "faith and the fruit of the Gospel" by which
he had laid hold on eternal life.[34]

It is not wrong to assert that every believer, man, woman,
child, has the prerogatives which faith brings, the treasures of the
Keys, to hold and to administer.   That fact leads Luther to aver that
also "a woman can baptize," and it is an uncontestable fact that the
person "who teaches and baptizes is a greater prophet than Jacob or
Moses," he adds.[35]   Yea, "even a child can absolve and can transfer
from the kingdom of the devil into the kingdom of God by no other
means than the Word."[36]

It is especially in his treatise "Concerning the Ministry" of
1523 that Luther presses this great truth home.   We are Christ's
brethren "only because of the new birth," not by tonsures, long
robes, and the like; not by the "episcopal ordinations" under the
aegis of the papal hierarchy; nor by any other externals.   The fact is
that true priests before God are those by "birth," that is, by regeneration, by Baptism.   This makes the ministry of the Word something
which "is common to all Christians," and this "highest office in the
church" thus "belongs to all who are Christians, not only by right but
by command."

Luther goes on to lay to rest the fictions of priestly powers belonging to the episcopally ordained clergy which made them into a kind of "miracle-working caste" in connection with the Mass, the Keys, Penance, prayers, and judges of doctrine. Luther does not minimize the fact and entity of the pastoral office itself, and "the right and command to commit such office to a minister by vote or consent of the congregation," but he contends eloquently for the Scriptural truth that those powers inhere first of all in the royal priesthood of believers whose duty it is under God to see to administering of Word and Sacrament, and to call qualified men into the preaching office. Dismiss from your minds, Luther reminds tender consciences, the care and concern of whether you can be a true church of God or not, because you lack, or seem to, the episcopal authority claimed by the papalists. Their claim is a thorough-going fiction, and he urges them rather to "take (their) stand as on a rock" on this matter of the general priesthood and its lofty God-given excellencies or prerogatives, duties and responsibilities.[37]

What belongs to all believers, is not to be done publicly by all, lest there be confusion in the churches. The public pastoral office is God's own design and purpose; it must not be omitted or made optional. "Christians are all priests," it is true, states Luther, (and) "all have a priesthood, but they do not all have the priestly function."[38] These comments are drawn from Luther's *scholia*, or commentary, on St. Paul's epistle to Titus (1527). It is with Titus' office in mind that Luther states: "Although all can teach and exhort, nevertheless one ought to do so, and the others ought to listen, so that they do not speak at the same time." The apostle is very carefully instructing Titus concerning the pastoral office, Luther notes, as he (Paul) states: "You have seen me ordain several elders in each city. Do the same thing. Moreover, I do not want you to ordain just anyone indiscriminately. Ordination was not performed as our bishops do it, but the elders gathered and performed it by the laying on of hands."[39]

In his commentary on the *First Epistle of Peter* (1522) Luther reinforces the same teaching, calling attention to the fact that "those who are now called priests would all be laymen like the others," should they lack the divine call into their office from the Christian congregation.[40] In the same context Luther underscores that while in other respects no distinctions are to be observed between Christians, whether male or female, young or old, in accord with Galatians 3:28, yet for the pastoral office "one person must be chosen," and that person a qualified man, not a woman, for "women should not speak in the congregation," as St. Paul teaches in 1 Corinthians 14:34. The only exception which Luther sees is "if only women were present and no men, as in nunneries," in which case "one of the women might be authorized to preach."[41]

So "the order must be preserved intact so that we do not teach in a confused manner," states Luther in his commentary on the prophet Isaiah; and, moreover, Luther is frank to retain his high esteem for the called pastor by stating: "I would rather hear him who has been sent, and I will hear him, than preach myself, unless I were sent myself."[42] He could hardly have stated his position on the office of the called pastor more forcefully and clearly! Such called pastors are certainly "reservoirs of the church" in whom "alone is kept the Word of God"; and the oral, preached Word of God is a mighty force against Satan's assaults.[43] Luther very firmly upholds the position in administering the Lord's Supper that this should be done by the called pastors, not by every housefather, for that would "in the long run do much harm, causing divisions and creating sects." He counters the plea that under tyrannical superiors it might then not be possible to receive the Sacrament, with the reminder that each man "can be saved through believing the Word," even if he cannot partake of Communion.[44]

Perhaps the classic passage above all others on the relationship between Christ and His church with a view toward the ministry which He has entrusted to it comes in Luther's *Commentary on Psalm 110* (1535). First of all, Luther notes that Christ, the Word, and the Angel of the Lord in the Old Testament, is the preacher par excellence.[45] He notes, however, how God "confers this honor," that is, of proclaiming His saving Word, "upon all Christians."[46] Now, of course, Christ is no longer on earth personally preaching His Word, but He has purposed to do so "through the apostles and their successors," an office which He bestowed upon pastors and preachers through His general priesthood of believers, all of whom are priests and holy by their Baptism, by faith in His Word. This makes the office then "the common property of all Christians." They select presbyters, or bishops, or pastors, from those who are qualified, "the best, the most mature men, well-tried, learned, fit, and experienced . . . for the sake of the office," much like qualified men are selected for other offices. Thus, for example, one does not become a citizen by being elected burgomaster or judge, but one is elected to the office because one already possesses citizenship and is a member of the citizenry" and is deemed especially qualified by one's fellow citizens.[47] "To take another illustration," Luther says, "a wife, the mistress of a house, does not become a woman by taking a husband. If she were not a woman already, the act of matrimony would never make a housewife out of her. No, she brings her female nature into matrimony, and then she receives the keys to the house."[48] "This is the way it is in Christendom, too," avers Luther, and then he goes on at length to say:

> Out of the multitude of Christians some must be selected who shall lead the others by virtue of the special gifts and aptitude which God gives them for the office. Thus St. Paul writes (Eph. 4:11.2): "And His gifts were that some should be apostles, some prophets, some evangelists, some pastors and teachers, for the equipment of the saints" (this means those who are already Christians and baptized priests), "for the work of the ministry for the building up of the body of Christ" (that is, the Christian congregation or church).

> For although we are all priests, this does not mean that all of us can preach, teach, and rule. Certain ones of the multitude must be selected and separated for such an office. And he who has such an office is not a priest because of his office but a servant of all the others, who are priests. When he is no longer able to preach and serve, or if he no longer wants to do so, he once more becomes a part of the common multitude of Christians. His office is conveyed to someone else, and he becomes a Christian like any other.

> This is the way to distinguish between the office of preaching, or the ministry, and the general priesthood of all baptized Christians. The preaching office is more than a public service which happens to be conferred upon someone by the entire congregation, all the members of which are priests.[49]

What Luther here details at some length is nicely summarized and illustrated in one of his letters. It was written to his friend George Spalatin, September 9, 1521, "from my wilderness," or "Isle of Patmos," or "land of the birds," as Luther dubbed his temporary hide-out on the Wartburg. He emphasizes the concept of the royal priesthood of believers, the rights and prerogatives of each individual royal priest, and the possibility of such priest, even though an unordained layman, to hold forth in a sermon, "in the old manner" of doing things in the church.

> I really wish Philip (i.e., Melanchthon) would also preach to the people somewhere in the city on festival days after dinner to provide a substitute for the drinking and gambling. This could become a custom which would introduce freedom and restore the form and manners of the early church. For if we have broken all laws of men and cast off their yokes, what difference would it make to us that Philip is not anointed or tonsured but married? Nevertheless, he is truly a priest and actually does the work of a priest, unless it is not the office of a priest to teach the Word of God. In that case Christ Himself would not be a priest.[50]

No demeaning of the pastoral office is intended, only a rightful setting of the office in relation to the priesthood of believers, when Luther, therefore, states that "this is the way to distinguish between the office of preaching, or the ministry, and the general priesthood of all baptized Christians."[51] The latter is primary and gives the needed platform on which the other, the parish pastorate, or *Pfarramt* rests. To Luther it is inconceivable that the latter should exist without the other; but where the priesthood of believers is, there it is necessary also for a suitable, qualified man to be selected by them for the public ministering of the Word and sacraments. Accordingly, Luther states: "The preaching office is no more than public service which happens to be conferred upon someone by the entire congregation, all the members of which are priests."[52] The ministry in the wide sense, and the ministry in the narrow and usual sense referring to the pastoral office, are thus both seen as vital in God's ordering of things for His Church.

NOTES

1   Walther, C. F. W., *Die Stimme unserer Kirche in der Frage von Kirche und Amt*. Zwickau, 1894 (4th edition).

2   Walther, *KA* 194. Cf. Hoenecke, Adolf, *Evangelical Lutheran Dogmatics*, IV, 175.   Hoenecke, contemporary of Walther and a leading theologian of the Wisconsin Evangelical Lutheran Synod, agreed with Walther's teaching concerning the pastoral office and the priesthood of all believers, to whom first of all the Office of the Keys (ministering Word and sacrament), is entrusted. Today, however, and for most of the past century, through the influence of theologians like John Koehler, John Schaller, and August Pieper, WELS theologians have argued that there is no Scriptural warrant for asserting that the public pastoral office exists by and under a distinct command or institution of God.   They hold that this can be said only of the ministry of the Word, an office which is given to the general priesthood of believers and is ordained by God for His church in the New Testament (Matt. 28:19).   Christian congregations, according to this thinking, in the freedom and wisdom provided by God, carry out the command of God for ministering the Word by calling a qualified man to execute this office publicly in their midst and in their behalf.   According to WELS thinking the New Testament lacks an express, specific command of God whereby the office of Pastor, or parish pastorate is instituted.   Thus they reject Luther's and Walther's contention that the pastoral office itself exists within the church *jure divino*, by divine right and mandate, an office of ministry distinct from and by the side of the general ministry of the Word which is given to all believers, or royal priests.   Luther and Walther taught that ministry in Scriptural terms has both a narrow, restricted sense, in other words, the public pastoral office, and also a wide and inclusive sense, in other words, the ministry of the Word in which all believers share and have a responsibility.   These are not competing ministries but two God-given poles around which, as in an ellipse, the ministry of the Word moves or rotates in God-given harmony for the sake of the Gospel and salvation of souls.

3   *LW* 40, 34f.; *WA* 12, 189f.

4   Ibid.   Cf. footnote #2 above.   WELS theologians understandably resonate to the translation "community" because it accords better with their notion that church in New Testament usage is not only "congregation" (as well as *una sancta*) but also larger groupings like synods or church bodies.

5   *LW* 40, 25; *WA* 12, 182f.

6   *Examination of the Council of Trent*, Part II, 678.

7   Ibid.

8   *Enchiridion,* 10. Poellot trans., 26.

9   *Enchiridion,* 14. Poellot, 29.

10 *Loci theologici, de sacr.,* 29. Quoted in Walther, *KA,* 188.

11 *Loc. theol., de min. eccl.,* 67 Quoted in Walther, *KA,* 191.

12 Baier, *Compendium,* III 689f. Trans in Schmid, *Doctrinal Theology,* 608.

13 *LW* 3, 322; *WA* 43, 106.

14 *LW* 3, 338; *WA* 43, 117.

15 *LW* 3, 340; *WA* 43, 119.

16 Ibid.

17 *LW* 3, 343; *WA* 43, 122.

18 *LW* 3, 345; *WA* 43, 123.

19 *LW* 3, 364; *WA* 43, 136.

20 Ibid.

21 *LW* 5, 5; *WA* 43, 432.

22 *LW* 5, 84; *WA* 43, 487.

23 *LW* 6, 258; *WA* 44, 191.

24 *LW* 6, 257; *WA* 44, 190.

25 Ibid. Luther identifies "public ministry" and "parish pastorate" as did C. F. W. Walther and theologians of the LC-MS; but WELS does not recognize them as signifying the same thing.

26 *LW* 22, 479; *WA* 47, 189.

27 *LW* 9, 124; *WA* 14, 645.

28 *LW* 1, 299; *WA* 42, 220.

29 *LW* 5, 130; *WA* 43, 517.

30 *LW* 4, 141; *WA* 43, 237.

31 *LW* 32, 42; *WA* 7, 366.

32 *LW* 32, 51f.; *WA* 7, 382.

33 *LW* 28, 46f.; *WA* 12, 132.

34 *LW* 28, 374; *WA* 26, 113.

35 *LW* 8, 309; *WA* 44, 806.

36 Ibid.

37 *LW* 40, 18-43 passim; *WA* 12, 178-196.

38 *LW* 29, 16; *WA* 25, 16.

39 *LW* 29, 17; *WA* 25, 17.

40 *LW* 30, 55; *WA* 12, 309.

41   Ibid. WELS theologians take exception here to Luther's reference to "congregation" rather than "church," because the latter allows them to speak of synods as churches." Such larger groups of believers are church on the same plane as individual congregations, or even higher, possessing similar prerogatives, including exercise of the Office of the Keys, in this thinking.

42   *LW* 17, 13; *WA* 31², 270.

43   *LW* 18, 401; *WA* 13, 686.

44   Currie, Margaret A., *The Letters of Martin Luther*. London, 1908, 336.

45   *LW* 13, 270; *WA* 41, 129.

46   *LW* 13, 294; *WA* 41, 153f.

47   *LW* 13, 331; *WA* 41, 208. WELS theologians see the ministry of the Word extending to various offices of service in the church besides that of the congregation's pastor (minister or preacher). The latter thus is but one species of a larger genus of office in the public ministry of the Word, including synodical officials, professors of religion, parochial school teachers, editors of church publications, etc. Walther in contrast held these to be auxiliary to the pastoral office which is by God's ordaining distinctly unique, and no mere species of the wider genus of ministry of the Word.

48   Ibid.

49   *LW* 13, 332; cf. also *LW* 39, 312ff.; 13, 65; *WA* 41, 209f.; 11, 413ff.; 31¹, 211.

50   *LW* 48, 308; *WA*, Br 2, 387ff. Melanchthon was a layman, but a very trusted and able theologian in his own right, so recognized by Luther.

51   *LW* 13, 332; *WA* 41, 210.

52   Ibid.

Chapter 2

By Whose Authority?

The ministry is no mere outgrowth of the congregations, for reasons of good order and efficiency. While these latter benefits might be true, the fact remains that the ministry itself is not the creation of the congregation or church but of God Himself. It came into being, and still does, by divine ordering, not human design. Not first-century wisdom, enlightened perhaps by the discretion of the early church leaders, not even the apostles, but God's own directive to His church called the pastoral ministry into existence.

Christ, the Head Shepherd of His church, directed that there would not only be apostles for the founding of the church in His name, but He also provided, through the apostles, that they would be followed by successors into the preaching office. There would be this difference: the apostles entered upon their office through the direct call of Christ, their Lord, Himself; their successors, or under-shepherds, or understudies, entered the preaching office through the call of the congregations they were to serve. The apostles in the beginning directed this procedure. Titus 1:5 is often cited in behalf of this conferred office which carries on the work of the apostles. Luther points out in connection with it that one must bear the context in mind, especially verse seven, as also 1 Timothy 3:2, Acts 6:3 and 6. These help one to understand that the action of the congregation was that of calling a qualified pastor, while the apostles and their understudies guided congregations and ordained the new incumbents of the pastoral office.

It would not be amiss to draw some parallels between the priestly office of the Old Testament and the pastoral office of the New Testament. In both offices the incumbents were there by the express will of God. But the differences are more striking than the similarities. The first office centered upon the sacrifices prescribed by God and the priest's mediating position between God and His people. The Levites predominated in this priestly service, particularly the house of Aaron.

In the New Testament things were quite different. Sacrificing was now at an end, since Christ had rendered the once-and-for-all perfect sacrifice of Himself in sinners' behalf (Heb. 9-10).

All believers now had the ministry of the Word, to proclaim the saving Gospel of Christ's atoning, vicarious sacrifice for all

men's sins to the world. (Matt. 28:19; Lk. 24:47.48; 2 Cor. 5:14-21)
But not all among them were to fill the office of pastor who would
publicly preach and administer the sacraments in behalf of the
congregation. For this office they, the people of God, the royal
priesthood, were to elect or choose a qualified man. This was God's
command. Thus they would not merely have God's unction for, or
blessing upon, something that was their own initiative. The initiative
and the order were God's; the Christian believers were His instruments for carrying out His will as they chose men who in effect and
reality were successors to the apostles, though in a way delimited by
God's own ordering, for the office of apostle was unique and not
repeated. (Tit. 1:5; Acts 14:23; Acts 1:2; 1 Pet. 5:1; Col. 1:7; John
21:15-17; Acts 20:28; 1 Cor. 3:5; 4:1; 12:28; Eph. 4:11; 1 Pet. 5:2;
2 Tim. 2:1; 1 Tim. 5:17; 1 Cor. 9:14; Heb. 13:17)

God had promised that He would be with His people, be
they as few as two or three gathered together in His name (Matt.
18:20). He promised that congregations would exist locally at given
places, wherever His Word would come to be believed, till the end
of the world. God's Word cannot be without God's church, Luther
repeated so many times. No power in heaven or earth, and surely
not the gates of hell, would prevail against His institution of the
churches or congregations. Now side by side with this promise is
the divine mandate which provides the church with the pastoral
office and qualified men to fill it. Thus congregation and ministry
are in correlative relationship, though the former always takes
precedence in time. That is so because it is conceivable that a
congregation may under certain circumstances continue to exist
lacking the public office of ministry for a time, as long as the Word
is still present there, while it is not conceivable in the same way that
the ministry would continue if it lacked the undergirding presence
of the Christian congregation. Of course, as little as congregations
can ever decide not to exist, so little can they decide to abolish the
pastoral office, change its nature or its duties, or the qualifications
which incumbents who fill the office ought to have in accord with
God's command.

There are two extremes which have appeared from time to
time as regards the pastoral office, the one the Romanizing view, the
other the "congregationalist" notion which has devalued and
denigrated the office into a mere "job." According to the first, the
office of the clergy, or priest, has been elevated entirely out of

proportion to what God intended. It was conceived to be a higher, self-perpetuating estate. It became a virtual means of grace, according to which the ministrations of the ordained priest were counted as essential to salvation, episcopal ordination itself being viewed as essential. According to this aberration an indelible character is conveyed or conferred through the ordination which makes the administrator of the means of grace efficacious as to his own person. A similar high-church notion has appeared in Lutheran theology time and again. Walther had to contend against it in the person of and by the stir caused by John Grabau in the 19th century. Concurrently Wilhelm Loehe also fostered a mistaken notion concerning the self-perpetuating nature of the pastoral office. He stated: "The Office transplants itself. Only he who has the Office can transfer it to another."[1]

The second faulty notion, however, is virtually as destructive of the Lord's intent concerning the office of the ministry. It views the office as a kind of free creation of the early church, having apostolic precedent and sanction, but not resting upon distinct divine command. It loosely describes the position of Johann Hoefling, a 19th century Erlangen theologian. As might be expected, this led to a downgrading of the office in the eyes of those who were served by it, as well as of the duties, responsibilities, and prerogatives pertaining to it. Gone, or at least subdued, was the direct link with divine authority, that God had expressly ordained its existence, and that God held those who filled the office accountable for certain prescribed duties. Gone, too, was a high sense of divine authority, under which the incumbent of the office viewed his calling as originating with God and the congregation viewed its task as a solemn mandate under God to call a worthy servant into the office and to accord him due respect in his office as God's emissary speaking His Word for their obedient hearing. The office had slipped into low esteem as a sort of contractual arrangement, a practical, business-like solution to a congregation's need.

When Christian congregations call pastors into their service they are not exercising an option which has desirable advantages for their work but they are proceeding in accord with God's express command. The necessity of the pastoral office, or the holy ministry, is a divine necessity tied to God's holy will for His church on earth. God spells out the credentials that incumbents of the office should possess and in a general way the procedure by which a congregation obtains such a servant of the Word. The electing, or choosing, is the responsibility of the priesthood of believers or of those to whom they commit or delegate this trust. (This will be treated at greater length in Chapter 4.)

The Confessions of the Lutheran Church very clearly and expressly support this Scriptural teaching, that the public pastoral office in the church is a creation of God, also that it exists and will so continue by His holy ordering. Previously, in connection with ministry in the wide or general sense, we have cited Article V of the *Augsburg Confession* as implicitly inclusive of the special and unique office of the parish pastor. Administration of Word and Sacraments publicly are in his hands.

Walther argues that the specific office of the parish minister must be seen as embraced within this article, because the Schwabach Articles (VII), composed by Luther in 1529 and usually referred to as a forerunner of the articles in the *Augsburg Confession* of 1530, clearly imply the office of pastor in the words, "God has instituted the ministry, or the oral Word," the Gospel which belongs to all Christians.

It is the basis for Walther's contention that Lutheran theologians of the past have consistently taught that the fifth article of the *Augsburg Confession* must be understood as including in it the divine institution of the pastoral office, or parish pastorate (*Pfarramt*).[2] In support, reference is usually made to *Augsburg's* article XIV on ecclesiastical order in the church and article XXVIII on the Office of the Keys administered by the bishops, i.e., pastors. According to *Augsburg* XXVIII, states Walther, the ordinary way in which the means of grace are administered in the churches is through the pastoral office.[3] This, in turn, comports well with a further affirmation of the *Augsburg Confession* (XXVIII, 21ff.) concerning the office and power of bishops (pastors) in the church:

> Again, according to the Gospel, or, as they say, by divine right, there belongs to the bishops as bishops, that is, to those to whom has been committed the ministry of the Word and the Sacraments, no jurisdiction except to forgive sins, to judge doctrine, to reject doctrines contrary to the Gospel, and to exclude from the communion of the Church wicked men, whose wickedness is known, and this without human force, simply by the Word. Herein the congregations

of necessity and by divine right must obey them, according to Luke 10:16: 'He that heareth you heareth Me.' But when they teach or ordain anything against the Gospel, then the congregations have a commandment of God prohibiting obedience. (Matt. 7:15; Gal. 1:8; 2 Cor. 13:8)

In order properly to emphasize the divine institution of the public pastoral ministry Melanchthon in the *Apology* indicates that the Lutheran party would not be unwilling to stretch, as it were, the use and meaning of "ordination" to be understood as having sacramental significance, as long as it would enhance the Scriptural teaching concerning this office as instituted and approved by God and would exclude the notions of the Romanists as bestowing certain indelible characteristics and powers beyond God's intention (XIII, 11ff.). "The authority to call, elect, and ordain ministers," wrote the framers of the Tractate to the *Smalcald Articles* (67), "is a gift which in reality is given to the Church," and as God's gift it is a possession "which no human power can wrest from the Church," not even the pope. It was an authority dependent "upon the Word of God," and the office of pastor, as well as the manner of its conferral, was to be perceived as "proceeding from the general call of the apostles" (Tractate 9).

When Luther asserts that the "church has the power to engage pastors," he does so because God's Word empowers it to do so.[4] In a sermon from his famous series on John's Gospel, based on chapter 3, verse 34, Luther expounds the manner in which men are called by Christ into His special service in the holy ministry:

> John is speaking here about calling or sending, particularly about the sending of Christ . . . There are two ways of sending. First, God sent His messengers, the prophets and apostles, like Moses and St. Paul, directly and without the help of an intermediary. These men were called by God's word of mouth and without human agency . . . This exalted method came to an end in the New Testament with the apostles, who were the last to be called directly by God.
>
> The other way of sending is indeed also one by God, but it is done through the instrumentality of man. It has been employed ever since God established the ministry with its

preaching and its exercise of the Office of the Keys. This ministry will endure and is not to be replaced by any other ... We were sent according to this method; according to it, we elect and send others, and we install them in their ministry to preach and to administer the Sacraments. This type of sending is also of God and commanded by God. Even though God resorts to our aid and to human agency, it is He Himself who sends laborers into His vineyard.[5]

The divine sanction and aegis under which the pastoral ministry originates and continues to exist until the end of time are taught with steady refrain in the writings of the theologians in the generation after Luther. Chemnitz, for example, stated in full agreement with the first Martin:

The church has a command about calling and appointing ministers. And the promise is added:

1. God approves the ministry of those who have been called and set apart for the ministry by the voice of the church ...

2. The promise is added that God will give grace and gifts by which those who have been legitimately called will be able rightly, faithfully, and profitably to do and perform the tasks which belong to the ministry ...

3. This promise is also added, that God is present with the ministry, that by His blessing He gives the increase to its planting and watering, and that He is truly efficacious through the ministry to call, enlighten, convert, give repentance, faith, regeneration, renewal, and, in short, to dispense through the ministry everything that pertains to our salvation.[6]

Chemnitz then goes on to explain that the service of ordination (or installation) was, and is, "the public testimony and the public attestation of the church" that the person being installed was qualified, that he had a genuine call from the congregation, and that the blessing of God would be upon him in his ministry.[7]

In a similar vein, in his *Enchiridion*, Chemnitz answers the question concerning the basis for valuing the pastoral office so highly, citing three reasons: 1) God wants it; 2) God supplies the needed gifts for it; 3) God gives His Spirit to supply the affirming power.[8] Christ, the Chief Shepherd, supplies the church with the needed under-shepherds, ordaining that the churches, or congregations, were to be His instruments for calling qualified workmen into His service in their midst, to nurture them with Word and sacraments.[9] Scripture teaches us that the apostles were called directly; the pastors who follow in their place and line perform the same tasks, but are not called directly as were the apostles, but indirectly through the congregation's voice, by God's will and command.[10]

God's command to proclaim His Word is given in general to all Christians, but it is given specifically to those whom God has called, through the medium or instrumentality of the congregation, into His service for the pastoral office. "All Christians are indeed priests," states Chemnitz, and each believer has the right and the duty to "teach the Word of God in his own house," but it does not follow that he may "take and arrogate to himself the public ministry of Word and sacrament." For that office "a particular and legitimate call" are required.[11]

While our Savior is now at the right hand of the Father, it is He who "still gave His church shepherds and teachers for the upbuilding of His mystical body," or church, affirms Gerhard.[12] The "sacred and public office" of pastor is entered into by "a legitimate call, to certain (qualified) men."[13] There is a "difference between the mediate and immediate call," but it has to do only with this that "the former is effected through ordinary means," while the latter comes directly "through God Himself, or through some representative."[14] It is "one and the same office" and the mediate call "is not less divine than the immediate."[15] Finally Gerhard stresses the fact that the necessity of the pastoral office, as also its significance, must be traced entirely and alone to "God's ordaining," for the fact remains that "God could without means and in extraordinary ways," even "without the instrumentality of the church's ministry" accomplish His purpose to save people, if He so purposed.[16]

Others of the orthodox Lutheran theologians can be shown to support the position of Luther and his immediate followers. "God's Word earnestly forbids that anyone should enter upon the office or service (of ministry) without a call or express command of

God," writes Heshusius.[17] Hutterus underscores that this office "has been established certainly not by man, but by God Himself."[18] "By the divine call," writes Hollaz, we understand "the appointment of a certain and suitable person," who then possesses "the right to teach in public, to administer the Sacraments, and exercise ecclesiastical discipline."[19] While God in times past chose such shepherds, like the apostles, directly, such "an immediate call is not to be expected in the church today," Hollaz counsels.[20] Thus the "less principal cause constituting the ministry (today) is the church," but this power of electing and ordaining is by no means without divine unction, for it is His Will so to do.[21]

It is evident that the primary cause behind the ministry, whether by immediate or mediate causation, is God Himself. The Lutheran theologians, to a man, concurred in this judgment on the basis of Scripture.

In his *Confession Concerning Christ's Supper*, 1528, also known as "Great Confession," Luther observed that there are three basic institutions established by God for mankind's sake. They correspond more or less to the natural orders by which the world is governed and structured. "The holy orders and true religious institutions established by God are these three: the office of priest, the estate of marriage, the civil government."[22] Luther terms them "religious," because they conform to God's holy will and intention for mankind. Particularly "holy, proper, good, and God-pleasing" are "all who are engaged in the clerical office or the ministry of the Word."[23] By the year 1528, of course, Luther was certainly not intending to place some sort of unction or halo around the priestly order as conceived by the papalists, who had made of it a self-- perpetuating, tyrannical canonical prelacy that burdened consciences. He explains what he has in mind concerning the "clerical office" in *A Sermon on Keeping Children in School*, a treatise addressed to the city of Nürnberg in 1530. At the time of writing Luther was on the Coburg and the Diet of Augsburg was in session. He indicates that the pastoral office is indeed "established and instituted by God"; but he adds: "I am not thinking of the spiritual estate in the monastic houses," or as Rome conceived it. "The estate I am thinking of is rather one which has the office of preaching and the service of the Word and sacraments, and which imparts the Spirit and salvation."[24]

God established the holy ministry. It was He who "anointed Abraham to fill this priestly office among his people," something which the popes lack and are unable rightly to claim for themselves.[25] "Abraham," as a matter of fact, Luther says, "deserves to be held up to the churches as an example" of how people ought "to receive the ministers of the Word as the Lord of heaven," because of the office they hold and the Word they preach.[26] They deserve honor because of that ministry which they perform.[27] God "has established the external ministry," because "he does not want to" teach and enlighten hearts in any other way.[28] "God could rule the church through the Holy Spirit without the ministry, but He does not want to do this directly."[29] The Keys are administered by and through this ministry, and "these great gifts of the Holy Spirit should be praised and proclaimed by all, and in them God, who has given such power to men." It is a power, Luther notes, by which I as pastor "take an infant, and by baptizing it, I redeem it from death, the devil, and sins."[30] "This a pastor of the church does," states Luther, but in the same context he then adds appropriately that this is so because of the powers in the hand of every royal priest, for "in an emergency any Christian does so."

The Christian remains a sinner and, even as Jacob needed to "wash his garments" (Gen. 49:11) and repent of his sin, so the believing sinner stands in need of daily repentance and faith in the abiding power of God's Word and his baptism, which Luther terms "a bath for the old man." But he has specific reference in his own life to the ministry into which God placed him, "out into His harvest," "at the wheel and at the grindstone."[31] "There must be ministers of the church to teach the Word. The ministry is necessary; one cannot do without it," even as municipalities, institutions, and trades of various kinds cannot do without needed workmen.[32] Sheep need shepherding; people need "spiritual shepherding."[33] Since God established the necessity, it is also God who "provides people whom He orders to preach" and "He will surely also supply and send listeners who will take this instruction to heart."[34]

Luther is willing to say that "it would be impossible to retain Baptism, the Sacrament, and the knowledge of Christ," "if it were not done by the exercise of the public ministry."[35] So important is this office, that even though its incumbents fill it "very imperfectly" at times, so that it is "distorted or even perverted," yet, "despite this, God has preserved His own and has always given some who preached against the false teaching."[36] This is due, of course, to God's intent to preserve His church, often in spite of the false teachers, the pope, the sects, or heretics like Arius. Let popes, monks, bishops, and so forth go, but "there must be pastors," and God will see to it, Luther says confidently in the remarkable treatise which he wrote from the Coburg, *Exhortation to All Clergy Assembled at Augsburg*, 1530.[37] Pastors are needed precisely because the "people (cannot) teach and admonish themselves."[38] They require steady and faithful tutoring in God's Word. It is not "that people ought to be driven to the sacrament at certain times and season"; that kind of coercion existed under the pope who "captured and coerced the consciences so that the people participated in it without joy and free will, without benefit and salvation" and "made of it not a sacrament of faith but a work of merit."[39]

Even as the apostle Paul exults in his call into the apostleship, we, too, as called pastors rejoice in our call into the ministry, states Luther in his commentary on Galatians. "The reason for our proud boasting is that we are in a divine calling and in God's own work, and that the people need to be assured of our calling."[40] When seen from the perspective of what the apostle is stressing, "this is not a vain pride," but "a holy pride against the devil and the world."[41] "Our calling is from God," Luther assures the evangelical preachers. "God calls in two ways, either by means or without means. Today He calls all of us into the ministry of the Word by a mediated call, that is, one that comes through means, namely, through man."[42] While this differs from the apostles' call, "nevertheless it is divine."[43] The apostles "all had been taught and called by God" directly, and Christian pastors to this day, though called indirectly through the people of the parish, are likewise called by God.[44]

A Christian Congregation Has a Right to Call is the title of Luther's treatise to the people of the town of Leisnig, troubled by doubts over this very question (1523). Luther assures them that a Christian congregation by virtue of having the Gospel "not only has the right and power but also the duty" to put off the yoke of self-styled prophets who "teach and rule contrary to God and His Word." "We must act according to Scripture and call and institute from among ourselves those who are found to be qualified and whom God has enlightened with reason and endowed with gifts to do so."[45]

Luther holds his readers to the doctrine of Scripture's divine inspiration and points to Titus 1:5-7 for the divine aegis under which pastors or bishops have their office, stating: "Whoever believes that here in Paul the Spirit of Christ is speaking and commanding will be sure to recognize this as a divine institution and ordinance, that in each city there should be several bishops, or at least one. It is also evident that Paul considers elders and bishops to be one and the same thing."[46]

"It is dreadful to live in such an evil and ungodly world," Luther states of the time of Noah, who likewise was a preacher of righteousness when the world was totally indifferent to God and His Word.[47] In contrast, Luther describes his own time in history as "a golden age," since "the sacraments are properly administered in our churches, and godly clergymen disseminate the Word in its purity," though not without persecution and suppression from the papal throne.[48] It is somewhat of an anomaly that just at the time when the heroes of faith, like Abraham, were alive, there should have been such wicked situations and centers like Sodom.[49] But a man of God like Adam, who had the promise of God for salvation which he was thereafter to share with those in his house, needed to remain steadfast in that promise, "convinced that he should not abandon the position into which God placed him."[50] In like manner, "though despised and all but trodden underfoot," pastors must remain content with their ministry because it is of God, lowly and scorned though they may be by their fellowmen, Luther counsels.[51] They must be sure that they "have been appointed in the church" because God wills it so and wishes that their services and ministry be honored and obeyed.[52] God could show His high esteem for the pastor's office in no more vivid way than to assure faithful pastors that "when we hear one of the brethren or ministers proclaiming the Word of God, we are hearing God Himself."[53] This is a remarkable thing. It was true of Abraham, and it is true for every faithful, godly pastor. "Certainly we should receive the spoken word of a human being," Luther says of such a man, "as the voice of God sounding from heaven."[54]

These faithful spokesmen are God's spokesmen. "Even it we heard angels preaching in their majesty, we would be affected no more than we are now when we hear a pastor or ministers. If we actually concluded that it is the Word of God that we are hearing, we would not snore this way."[55] Disrespect for God's spokesmen is disrespect for God and His Word. We are like brutes when we treat God's Word as mere human word. While Luther thus spanks the lazy listeners, he at the same time, of course, demonstrates the heavy responsibility that falls upon each pastor to narrate God's Word truly. A pastor needs to fall on his knees praying: "Lord God, Thou has appointed me prince, judge, head of the household, and pastor of the church. Therefore guide and teach me, give me counsel, wisdom, and strength to attend successfully to the office committed to me."[56] In the same context Luther expands the prayer, focusing on the need of the pastor, who recognizes his own unfitness for the office, to receive God's continuing help for his difficult office. Not least must he keep from "presumption and arrogance," lest he "destroy himself and others over whom he rules."[57] "In the church heresies, Epicurean contempt for the Word, desecration of the sacraments, etc., will arise" when such breakdown of prayerful reliance upon God insinuates itself, and the leader in the church, "the pastor, does not recognize GOD as the Author of all counsel and government" but assumes it to himself.[58] These are false leaders.

Forever and a day, faithful and godly preachers are to remember that God acts through them and that their words are to be His Word, so that the hearers know for a fact that "it is the Word not of a pastor, or Peter, or any minister but that it is the Word of the Divine Majesty."[59] "We should glory as follows," Luther states: "I am baptized. By whom? Was it not by a pastor? By no means but by the Holy Spirit. I have been absolved by the Holy Spirit, by God Himself. Why then should I be afraid?"[60] Luther has this confidence, for the time when he lived, for the times of the patriarchs, and for the times still to come: "When ambassadors and preachers were sent by God into the world, we must not think that their ministry passed away without fruit . . . God gathered a church in the world not only from the one family of the patriarchs but from all nations to which the Word made its way."[61]

A pastor is under an urgency to preach to the flock which God has given him, even as a father of a household senses God's mandate upon him to teach those that are his. To the question, "Why then do I preach?" Luther states, the pastor's answer must be: "Because God wanted this. He has appointed me a pastor, a teacher of the Word; and the people have need of instruction and doctrine."[62] God's ways are virtually too wonderful to behold, as He accomplishes His purposes through the mouths of men. "This proclamation of the Gospel He accomplished by the ministry of the apostles and their successors, for in them He spoke to the whole world."[63]   These spokesmen of God are like "cedars of Lebanon," "birds of heaven," "fountains in the valleys," "ascending mountains," is Luther's picturesque way of describing these instruments of God's saving work among men.[64] They are Christ's men, these "workmen of this Solomon,"[65] "feet of Christ,"[66] His "scepters."[67]

Luther conceives of the office which he and other pastors hold in very solemn terms: "They (God's people) must also come to Baptism and to Christ through our ministry and administration. For them we have been called; and it is for their sakes that we go on living, since our faith would be sufficient for our own persons, no matter at what hour we should die. And woe upon all woes, if we cast such a ministry and calling to the winds! God will require of us and hold us accountable for the souls of all."[68]   "Thus the process goes on," states Luther in reflection upon God's design for His church; "the Word is handed down to us through the agency of true bishops, pastors, and preachers, who received it from the apostles."[69]   Tied to the apostolic word, "in this way all sermons delivered in Christendom must proceed from this one Christ"; it is never a case of, this I say, or this you say, for "it is not we who are speaking; it is Christ and God Himself."[70]   Christ is the author behind the Scriptural Word and "thus the apostles and pastors are nothing but channels through which Christ leads and transmits His Gospel from the Father to us."[71] Wonder of wonders, through such ministry, "you may say without hesitation: 'Today I beheld God's Word and work. Yes, I saw and heard God Himself preaching and baptizing,"[72] to be sure through the hands and voices of human beings in His service, His ministry.

God blesses and keeps His church, His vineyard. True, "this vineyard is committed to the keepers' charge, but in such a way that God Himself keeps His eye on it. As the saying goes, God did not establish the earth and go away. He keeps His eye on it . . . For the Word of God cannot be taught without yielding fruit."[73]   The ministry belongs to God and it consequently bears His promise and blessing.[74] God might have transmitted His Word "inwardly," directly into men's hearts, "without preaching"; He has chosen not to, but by "teaching and the Spirit, which He Himself grants inwardly," and the preachers thus become His "assistants and fellow workers."[75] Faithful preachers do not divert from the Word of God, urging people "to do this or that," but they herald "the steadfast love of God."[76]

Luther includes a word of admonition to all Christians, but especially to preachers, concerning their vocation or calling in life. There is a unique pertinence for those who herald His Word in the churches, because their office is so signally central to God's purposes for His church. We need to learn from and adopt the attitude of patient, humble Abraham, Luther reasserts. But as things are now, "there are very few who live satisfied with their lot; the layman longs for the life of a cleric, the pupil wishes to be a teacher, the citizen wants to be a councilor, and each one of us loathes his own calling."[77] A pastor particularly needs to remember that his call into office is from God, and that God entrusts him with the Word that satisfies men's deepest need. So invested and commissioned, a man of God plods on like a loyal trooper; he entertains no prying questions, but learns to leave things that God has left unanswered, as to reasons why, in God's hands, as Abraham learned to do. He did not ask the rhyme and reason for the circumcision requirement which burdened his descendants; nor question God's intent concerning the salvation of the heathen who did not have this covenant sign, nor puzzle angrily or imperiously over the unanswered quandary, "What about the females? Will God not mark them too by some sign, just as He marked our males?" Abraham left these matters to God. Abraham "is intent on doing what he knows has been commanded him," Luther observes, for it was God's seal marking Israel as God's chosen people for the sake of the promise.[78]

With similar humility, patience under trial, fortitude, a Christian pastor faces up to his calling, stating, if God "wanted me to be a preacher (and) wanted me to bear the envy and the hatred of the world for the sake of the Word," so be it. "To others He assigns manual labor," but to me He has given the task of preaching His Word faithfully.[79] My calling, the pastor is to say to the end of his service among God's people, is from my Lord; therefore I will bear and do it gladly until my last breath, not laying my equipment down, until I myself lie down quietly by the side of the road, like a good soldier having given my all.

NOTES

1   *Abiding Word*, II, 489.

2   cf. Walther, *KA*, 195.

3   Walther, *KA*, 212f.

4   *LW* 22, 480; *WA* 47, 190.

5   *LW* 22, 482; *WA* 47, 191f.

6   *Examination of the Council of Trent*, II, 691f.

7   Ibid., 693.

8   *Enchiridion*, 15. cf. Poellot, 29.

9   Ibid., 16f. cf. Poellot, 30.

10   Ibid., 16ff. WELS theologians argue that the meaning of church should be broadened to include synods, not primarily or only the congregation.

11   *Examination of the Council of Trent*, 678f.; cf. *Enchiridion*, 14.

12   *Loc. theol., de ministerio ecclesiastico*, 49. Quoted in Walther, *KA*, 203.

13   *Loc. theol.*, XIII, 224. Trans. in Schmid, *Doctrinal Theology of the Lutheran Church*, 606f.

14   Ibid. 12, b, 75. Schmid, *op. cit.* 607.

15   Ibid. 81. Schmid 607f.

16   *Loc. theol., de min. eccl.*, par. 3. Quoted in Walther, *KA*, 218.

17   Walther, *KA*, 208.

18   *Loc. theol.*, 186. Schmid, *op. cit.*, 607.

19   *Examen Theologicum Acroamaticum*, 1332. Schmid, *op. cit.*, 607.

20   Ibid., 1333. Schmid, ibid.

21   Ibid., 1334. Schmid, op. cit., 608.

22   *LW* 37, 364; *WA* 26, 504.

23   Ibid.

24   *LW* 46, 219f.; *WA* 30^2, 526f.

25   *LW* 2, 287; *WA* 42, 467.

26   *LW* 3, 187; *WA* 43, 9.

27   *LW* 3, 218; *WA* 43, 31.

28   *LW* 3, 288; *WA* 43, 81.

29   *LW* 8, 94; *WA* 44, 648.

30   *LW* 8, 182; *WA* 44, 712.

31   *LW* 8, 269; *WA* 44, 776.

32	Ibid.
33	*LW* 12, 154; *WA* 51, 273.
34	*LW* 22, 5; *WA* 46, 538.
35	*LW* 24, 131; *WA* 45, 580.
36	Ibid.
37	*LW* 34, 44; *WA* 30², 331.
38	*LW* 38, 100; *WA* 30², 597.
39	*LW* 38, 101; *WA* 30², 598.
40	*LW* 26, 20f.; *WA* 40¹, 63f.
41	Ibid.
42	*LW* 26, 17; *WA* 40¹, 59.
43	Ibid.
44	*LW* 26, 102; *WA* 40¹, 186.
45	*LW* 39, 309; *WA* 11, 412.
46	*LW* 36, 155; *WA* 8, 500.
47	*LW* 2, 84; *WA* 42, 321.
48	Ibid.
49	*LW* 3, 232; *WA* 43, 41.
50	*LW* 1, 214; *WA* 42, 160.
51	*LW* 4, 66; *WA* 43, 182.
52	*LW* 4, 72; *WA* 43, 186.
53	*LW* 4, 295; *WA* 43, 347.
54	Ibid.
55	*LW* 5, 23; *WA* 43, 444.
56	*LW* 5, 122; *WA* 43, 512.
57	*LW* 5, 124; *WA* 43, 514.
58	Ibid.
59	*LW* 6, 225; *WA* 44, 166.
60	Ibid.
61	*LW* 6, 227; *WA* 44, 168.
62	*LW* 7, 182; *WA* 44, 434.
63	*LW* 11, 160; *WA* 4, 9.
64	*LW* 11, 336; *WA* 4, 186.
65	*LW* 11, 540; *WA* 4, 400.
66	*LW* 13, 24; *WA* 8, 24.

67 *LW* 13, 265; *WA* 41, 123.

68 *LW* 13, 192; *WA* 51, 237.

69 *LW* 24, 66; *WA* 45, 520.

70 Ibid.

71 *LW* 24, 67; *WA* 45, 521.

72 Ibid.

73 *LW* 15, 263; *WA* 31^2, 767.

74 *LW* 15, 327; *WA* 54, 79.

75 *LW* 20, 171; *WA* 23, 513.

76 *LW* 14, 255; *WA* 19, 593.

77 *LW* 3, 128; *WA* 42, 639.

78 *LW* 3, 129; *WA* 42, 639.

79 Ibid.

Chapter 3

Duties of the Pastoral Office

The pastoral office is a ministry of service to Christian believers, God's royal priests. We are speaking specifically of the parish pastorate. Its focus is on the care of souls, and the holder of the office is by God's design and command to be a caring *Seelsorger*, or curate of souls. The authority of his office devolves from this task; it is a spiritual authority that has God's precious Gospel as its fulcrum. By God's authority, in and through God's Word, and in behalf of the congregation which he serves, a pastor exercises the Office of the Keys. The ministering of the Keys is, as the *Small Catechism* (Luther) puts it, "a peculiar church power which Christ has given to His church on earth," thus an authority which belongs in the first instance and by its very nature to the congregation, to each and every royal priest. By his acceptance of a congregation's call a pastor assumes responsibility for the *public* exercise of the office, for the preaching and teaching of the Word, the administering of the sacraments, for exhortation to repentance and faith, for discipline, for consolation in time of trial and cross-bearing.

Gospel ministry is thus not unique to the pastor alone. All believers are priests before God by their faith and baptism. As members of the royal priesthood they possess all the treasures which Christ gives to His church. Between them and the called ministers of the Gospel there is no basic difference as to their persons; the only difference is one of office. Pastors are not priests by reason of their office. They are priests by faith and baptism, just like parishioners whom they serve. The latter, in turn, are not ministers or pastors (*Pfarrer* or bishops) by virtue of their priesthood. The office of public pastor and the universal priesthood are, therefore, not equatable or identical. The former has its roots in the latter. God Himself has ordained that the conferral of the pastoral office should be through the congregation. Accordingly, it is Scriptural to say that the ministry which has been conferred directly upon the royal priests by the Holy Spirit's call to faith through the Word, is conferred indirectly or mediately to pastors who are called for this office by the Christian people gathered at one place, or locality, in a congregation.

The Keys which are conferred upon the called pastor for public exercise in the congregation do not cease to be the inalienable rights and possessions of the priesthood of believers by virtue of such conferral. Were that so, it would no longer be possible for the royal priests to tell the Gospel, or under certain circumstances, validly administer the sacraments. There are, as there have been in the past, extremities which can only be met because the Keys are still in the possession of the royal priests. This prerogative, however, is never to be exploited in any way by self-ruling and self-styled prophets, nor is the public ministry to be short-circuited by "royal" priests grasping wrongfully for things that are not theirs to do. The called minister has the mandate, from God through them, to conduct the duties of the public ministry. And even though, unknown to his people, he be a hypocrite, or an apostate, the validity of the Word and the sacraments in his hands does not lose its God-given power. After all, the ultimate authority is always Christ's. It is He who prescribes the tasks of the Gospel ministry, especially that which pertains to the called servant. He gives the Word. The pastor is Christ's servant, and as the Lord's steward he strives to be found faithful by his Master (1 Cor. 4:1; Acts 20:28). However, at the same time, and with perfect convergence of task and responsibility, he is also the servant and steward of the congregation of royal priests, "to fulfill the word of God, whereof I am made a minister" (Col. 1:24.25; 2 Cor. 4:5).

It follows from the above that the office of pastor is not a separate or higher order or station among Christians. The church according to Christ's ordaining, does not have various orders, some more holy, more lofty, more prestigious, more privileged than others. In his office a pastor ministers (διακονέω) in behalf of all those things that are the common possession of all, the Keys. It is a position or an office of high trust. While "all things are yours," as the Apostle Paul writes to the Corinthians (1 Cor. 3:21ff.), that congregation, as well as every other, was exhorted to esteem highly its pastor for the sake of his office (1 Cor. 4:1; 1 Tim. 5:17). They, the pastors, have their call from the priests, the congregation, and for them they publicly administer the treasures of the Gospel which belong to all. When they preach, they are doing so for the congregation. When they administer the sacraments, they do so for the congregation. When they exhort to repentance and pronounce absolution, they are doing it for the sake of the congregation and for all within its ministration and outreach. This is a ministry given, mandated, and imposed by God.

When the apostles founded congregations, they referred to them not by the person of the pastor, or in his name, but as the church in that place, city, or home (Phil. 4:15). The Keys did not first come to exist when the pastoral office came into being. It is rather because the Keys were present in the midst of a people, like those on Crete, that the Apostle Paul exhorted Titus to proceed with the setting up of the pastorate in their midst (Tit. 1:5). The apostles and their successors guided the congregations in the process of electing qualified men as pastors, but the New Testament example points clearly in the direction of concurrence and consent of the congregation of royal priests. Thus even Paul and Barnabas go forth on their first missionary journey under the aegis, or with the call (commissioning), of the Antioch congregation (Acts 13:2ff.).

Luther speaks of a *Knechtsgestalt*, or servant posture, as the only proper one for a Christian in his attitude toward and respect for God's Holy Word, the Sacred Scriptures. This is so, of course, because of what God has constituted the Scriptures to be by His divine inspiration. There is a similar servant stance that a pastor bears in his relation to his congregation. He views his office properly when he understands it as a divine trust. In turn, this rules out any kind of servile, feudal, base, obsequious, menial notion concerning the office of parish pastor. He is not in a sort of hired-hand station, or job, to be hired or fired at the whim of a willful crowd that acts in arbitrary, tyrannical, godless manner toward him and his office. Theirs is not to be a mobocracy, of many over one; nor is his to be a tyranny, of one over many. Were he merely a hireling, and were he indeed to view and enter his office as such, then he would deserve to be dismissed, and in fact should be. The pastor, on the other hand, who has been duly called by a congregation, who faithfully carries out his pastoral functions, and who earns his people's respect by his godly example, deserves and will have the enduring esteem and love of the people whom he serves. His is but one task really, and that is ministering the Word of God in its fullness.

That will require of him keen, discreet discernment between the Law and the Gospel, between what Luther calls God's "alien Gospel" and God's "proper Gospel." Both Law and Gospel belong to God's Word. Both are to be proclaimed, each in all its fullness, each at the proper place and time. Neither one can be omitted. The Law will always precede in a preparatory way, fulfilling its accusatory role, as the Lutheran Confessions emphasize, or its smashing of all pretension of self-righteousness as Luther prefers to describe its main and continuing task; the Gospel will forever bring the "balm of Gilead," comfort the troubled sinner with God's forgiveness, lift up, quicken, convert, draw forth faith, and console. A person knows something by nature of and about his sin; but he knows nothing about the Gospel, and even after his conversion he inclines towards a return under the Law and a forgetting of what God has done for him in Christ. He tends to want to turn the Law into Gospel, and the Gospel into Law, thus making, or trying to make the one do what only the other can do.

Such confusion leads either to anti-gospelism or antinomianism, or both, with the eventual obliterating of the saving truth of God's grace in Christ. Those guilty of such confusion neither know how to preach justification nor sanctification; neither the Gospel of salvation by God's grace, by faith, for Christ's sake, nor the fruits of faith which are sanctification.

Luther, as most will agree, is the modern day master in this regard for his incisive insight into this important task of the ministry; of the discrete roles which Law and Gospel play in the pastor's task, in order that justification *sola gratia/fide* might be maintained unscathed and undiminished in the church, at the same time that sanctification of life, in accord with God's holy will (Law) be prompted and empowered by the Gospel. In one of his most influential works, *On the Councils and the Church*, 1539, Luther scored severely the antinomian spirits in the church, that is, the "freedom of the Gospel" distorters, for being what he called "fine Easter preachers, but poor Pentecost preachers."[1] This simply underscores the importance of the preacher's task as a minister of God's Word in all its fullness; the whole counsel of God's Word needs to be proclaimed through faithful preaching and teaching by the pastor in the midst of the royal priests.

Such preaching is with authority, and because it is, it deserves respect and obedience from the hearers. But the pastor is not a lord or master who domineers unjustly and unwisely over God's people in tyrannical, harsh, unloving, oppressive way (1 Pet. 5:1ff.). This would be to betray entirely his shepherd's role which his office has bestowed upon him. In necessary matters, necessary because God's Word clearly teaches and requires them, the congregation of Christians owes their pastor due respect and obedience, under God's sovereign Word; in matters that are indifferent, or free, the pastor with his people will seek for consensus, freely given, without binding of consciences in a wrongful, un-Scriptural way.

The end and aim of the pastoral office will always be the nurture and safe-guarding of the individual soul(s), the edifying, or upbuilding, of the church, and the cultivating and exhorting of Christian graces in those who have been touched by God's justifying grace through faith. Christ's giving of such pastors and teachers in the church was expressly and explicitly for the "perfecting of the saints" unto eternal life (Eph. 4:11f.). This is "the work of the ministry" and it redounds to "the edifying of the body of Christ."

Christian discipline is not a negative concept. It has to do with genuine concern of a pastor, in the name of a congregation and by the will of God, administering Law and Gospel for the salvation of souls. Daily contrition and repentance unto faith are stock-in-trade, central items, on the agenda of the pastor's work among his people. If this seems like a yoyo sort of business, it appears that way to the unbelieving outsider, or unbeliever, only. The Christian believer knows well enough his day-by-day need for the hammer blows of the Law, for repentance, for recourse to God's forgiveness through Christ, as it is sealed to him in his baptism. When a pastor, therefore, fulfills his task of preaching unto repentance and faith, he is carrying out God's own command for his office.

A pastor's concern for the individual soul whom he admonishes because of transgression and points to Christ's cross is in full accord with God's admonition and gracious concern. For the sake of the individual's spiritual health and everlasting salvation no effort is spared (Eph. 4:13-16; 1 Tim. 4:16). Even the extreme steps which lead to a man's excommunication are ultimately tied to the goal or hope of saving the man's soul. The apostle Paul had this concern when he placed the matter of the manifest, unrepentant sinner on the conscience of the Corinthian congregation. He was concerned for the spiritual health of the congregation, for the repentance of the manifest sinner, when he called for their concurring action in putting the transgressor from their midst. The steps were fully in line with what Christ Himself had ordained in the matter of Christian discipline (Matt. 18:15ff.).

The Lutheran Confessions underscore the same purpose and procedure for administering discipline. Should it come to the extreme step of exclusion, or excommunication, from the Christian congregation, it is to be the pastor's task finally to pronounce the drastic end point, but with concurring consent and consensus of the Christian congregation. Christ's words and the apostolic precedent establish both when it is to be done and how it is to be done, also the end purpose of rescuing, if possible, the unrepentant soul and snatching him out of Satan's hands.

Luther had often remarked—and the Confessions pick this up—that "God is superabundantly rich (and liberal) in His grace and goodness" in that He "not merely in one way" but in manifold ways extends His grace to sinners:

> 1) through the spoken Word by which the forgiveness of sins is preached in the whole world; which is the peculiar office of the Gospel; 2) Baptism; 3) the holy Sacrament of the Altar; 4) the power of the keys, and also through the mutual conversation and consolation of brethren, Matt. 18:20: "Where two or three are gathered together," etc. (SA III, iv)

The office of the Keys is a definite, carefully defined power which Christ has given to His church. The Keys, thus, are in the first instance not the church's nor the pastor's but God's; they are to be exercised in keeping with His will, for the care of precious souls. (AC XXVIII, 5-8)

The *Apology of the Augsburg Confession* points out that a proper, Scriptural understanding of repentance forms an integral core of Gospel preaching. Because "the writings of the adversaries," in other words the Romanists, were "full of errors and hypocrisy" on this matter, it followed that such teaching, writes Melanchthon, "obscures the benefit of Christ, the power of the keys, and the righteousness of faith." (*Apol.* XII [V], 10)

Proclamation of the Gospel is always, because of its very nature as a pronouncement of God's forgiveness, like a general absolution, according to Luther. Melanchthon gives the concurring word in the *Apology*: "The power of the keys administers and presents the Gospel through absolution, which (proclaims peace to me and) is the true voice of the Gospel." (*Apol.* XII [V], 39)

This office and power which Christ has given to His church, Luther states in the article on the Keys in the *Smalcald Articles*, "is not in our power, but belongs to God alone." (*SA* III, vii) It is followed immediately by the article "Of Confession," where Luther identifies the Power of the Keys with Absolution; and, since this is so, he exhorts that "Confession or Absolution ought by no means be abolished in the Church," since it is such a great "aid and consolation against sin and a bad conscience, ordained by Christ (Himself) in the Gospel." (*SA* III, viii)

No doubt the classic and most remembered statement on this subject concerning the Keys is Luther's brilliantly clear and succinct instruction in the *Small Catechism*. To the question, "What is Confession?" he answers:

> Confession embraces two parts: the one is, that we confess our sins; the other, that we receive absolution, or forgiveness, from the confessor, as from God Himself, and in no wise doubt, but firmly believe, that our sins are thereby forgiven before God in heaven. (*SC* V, 16)

This is followed by Luther's lucid explanation of how this is to be done, how we are to recognize our sins, and how the confessee and confessor are to proceed, so that all is done freely, without coercion, and with the greatest consolation to the penitent heart. (*SC* V, 17-29)

Because of the importance of these Keys and their rightful exercise in the church, it is good to note how often the urgency of their retention in the church is stated.

Augsburg Confession:

> Private absolution ought to be retained in the churches, although in confession an enumeration of all sins is not necessary. (*AC* XI)

> On account of the great benefit of absolution, and because it is otherwise useful to the conscience, Confession is retained among us. (*AC* XXV, 13)

Apology:

> (Melanchthon writing critically of Rome's denigrating and distorting of confession and absolution, states:) They doubt whether it is in attrition or in contrition that remission of sins occurs. And if it occurs on account of contrition, what need is there of absolution, what does the power of the keys effect, if sins have been already remitted? Here indeed, they also labor much more, and wickedly detract from the power of the keys. Some dream that by the power of the keys guilt is not remitted, but that eternal punishments are changed into temporal. Thus the most salutary power would be the ministry, not of life and the Spirit, but only of wrath and punishments. (*Apol.* XII [V], 6f.)

> It is the greatest importance that the true doctrine concerning . . . contrition and faith be preserved . . . For we also retain confession, especially on account of the absolution, as being the word of God which, by divine authority, the power of the keys pronounces upon individuals. (*Apol.* [V]), 1f.)

The *Formula of Concord* (XI, 38) refers back to Article XI of the *Augsburg Confession*, in full support, and states simply that "we also retain private absolution, and teach that it is God's command that we believe such absolution." Thus the issue of the church's or congregation's relationship to its pastor was very important and key in Reformation history. It still is to this day. The Tractate, written chiefly by Melanchthon with the assistance and consensus of the theologians assembled at Smalcald, 1537, is appended to Luther's *Smalcald Articles* and addresses this matter pointedly in various ways. (Tractate 13, 24, 31, 67, 69) As regards the duties of the called minister the Confessions tie these very closely to the Keys which Christ has given to His Church. Congregations are to heed and respect the ministry of their faithful pastors. Only "when they teach or ordain anything against the Gospel," do they "have a commandment of God prohibiting obedience." (*AC* XXVIII, 20ff.; cf. *Apol.* XXVIII, 13; Tractate 60)

In responding to the Romanist interpretation of the Greek term *leitourgia* as meaning "sacrifice," Melanchthon takes exception to tactics through which Rome turned the Mass into a sacrifice, stating that the "word does not properly signify a sacrifice, but rather the public ministry." (*Apol.* XXIV [XII], 79f.) Likewise he impresses the truth that priesthood in New Testament usage is not to be understood "as referring to sacrifice," as Rome had twisted it, but to "the ministry of the Word and administering the Sacraments to others." (*Apol.* XIII [VII], 7ff.) In Rome's thinking and teaching "other sacrifices" (for example the Mass) are thought necessary, thus implying that the "one sacrifice of Christ" was "not sufficient for our sins." (*Ibid.*) The fact is, of course, that the one propitiatory sacrifice of Christ availed for the world's sins.

The Lutherans did not object to speaking of "eucharistic sacrifices," such as "the preaching of the Gospel, faith, prayer, thanksgiving, confession, the afflictions of saints, yea, all good works of saints," but these "sacrifices" were not to be viewed as "satisfactions for those making them, or applicable on behalf of others," for they are fruits of faith and not ground for justification. (*Apol.* XXIV [XII], 22-33) To make "other mediators and propitiators out of the priests and sacrificers who daily seal their work in the churches," wrote Melanchthon with justifiable ire, "absolutely destroys the merit of Christ's passion and the righteousness of faith." (*Apol.* XXIV [XII], 57ff.) The only priest really needed in the New Testament era, once the Levitical priesthood has been superseded, was Christ. Any other claimants are apostates and counterfeiters; yet it must be remembered, especially for tender consciences, that "the fact that the Sacraments are administered by the unworthy (does not) detract from their efficacy." (*Apol.* VII. VIII, 28)

Melanchthon with keen insight notes that one of the reasons why both kinds in the Sacrament were not given to the laity was the simple fact that Rome had wrongfully set up a distinction of orders between the laity and the clergy, the one of lower standing, the other of higher. The intent very obviously was "that the dignity of the order may be the more highly exalted by a religious rite." But, even if we should "say nothing more severe, this is a human design," Melanchthon writes. (*Apol.* XXII [X], 9) Scripture's very clear injunction simply demands the use of both bread and wine in the Lord's Supper by clergy and laity alike.

Yet in none of this is there any intent on the part of the Reformers, nor, therefore, of the Lutheran confessors in general, to lower or diminish the high office of the called pastor. Luther, in his

treatment of the 4th Commandment in his *Large Catechism*, includes
pastors among those who deserve honor and obedience because of
the high office into which God has placed them. They are also
among those "called fathers in the Scripture." (*LC*, 1, 141)

> Thus we have two kinds of fathers presented in this com-
> mandment, fathers in blood and fathers in office, or those to
> whom belongs the care of the family, and those to whom
> belongs the care of the country. Besides these there are yet
> spiritual fathers; not like those in the Papacy, who have
> indeed had themselves called thus, but have performed no
> function of the paternal office. For those only are called
> spiritual fathers who govern and guide us by the Word of
> God . . . Since they are fathers they are entitled to their
> honor, even above all others. (*LC*, I, 158f.)

Johann Brenz was one of Luther's staunchest friends and
most loyal supporters from the time when he first heard the
Reformer present his notable twenty-eight theses before the August-
inians at Heidelberg in early spring, 1518. Brenz was present at the
Marburg Colloquy (1529), Augsburg Diet (1530), Smalcald meeting
of allied princes (1537), and he distinguished himself at other crucial
moments as a key figure in the Reformation, especially in Swabia
and Wuerttemberg. He was above all a practical, pastoral theologian. To the question whether the Office of the Keys was limited
to the apostles alone, in view of Christ's institution of it in their
presence (John 20:23), Brenz replied that "this office is not tied to
their persons but belongs to the whole church," that is, the priesthood of believers.[2] Each Christian believer exercises this right and
duty over against his brother who privately seeks the pronouncement
of God's pardon of forgiveness upon his confession of sin; but "it is
to the servants of the church," the pastors, says Brenz, that "the
public ministration of the Gospel and the means of grace have been
delegated (*uebertragen*)."[3]

Martin Chemnitz, superintendent in Braunschweig for many
years, performed admirably in his role as a pastor's pastor, as an
excellent administrator, and above all as theological leader and
teacher for what we may call a pilot program of in-service training
for the clergy. He well knew from Scriptural injunction the spiritual
focal point which the pastoral ministry had to retain. A faithful

pastor would have no time for plowing the fields, if he conscientiously tended the Lord's acre or vineyard of believers. "A preacher's office," he said, "is to study and read the Scriptures diligently (1 Tim. 4), work hard in Word and doctrine (1 Tim. 5), and nurture the flock and congregation of Christ thereby (1 Pet. 5; Acts 20); in this way he serves the church with God's Word and Sacraments."[4] It is an office, says Chemnitz, which indeed possesses "power, divinely bestowed (2 Cor. 10:4-6; 13:2-4), but circumscribed with certain duties and limitations, namely, to preach the Word of God, teach the erring, reprove those who sin, admonish the dilatory, comfort the troubled, strengthen the weak, resist those who speak against the truth, reproach and condemn false teaching, censure evil customs, dispense the divinely instituted sacraments, remit and retain sins, be an example to the flock, pray for the church privately and lead the church in public prayers, be in charge of care for the poor, publicly excommunicate the stubborn (unrepentant) and again receive those who repent and reconcile them with the church, appoint pastors to the church according to the instruction of Paul, with consent of the church institute rites that serve the ministry and do not militate against the Word of God nor burden consciences but serve good order, dignity, decorum, tranquility, edification, etc. For these are the things which belong to these two chief points, namely, to the power of order and the power of jurisdiction."[5]

Chemnitz never loses sight of the power of the Keys which inheres first of all in the priesthood of believers, and which, then, by God's command, is delegated to the pastor through the congregation's call. The fact that in emergency situations every believer, as a royal priest, may and, indeed, should exercise the Office of the Keys and, for example, pronounce the absolution upon a penitent sinner, is evidence, states Chemnitz, of where the power in the first place resides.[6]

This is also borne out by the fact that the congregation which calls always retains the power to set aside this call and remove a pastor who is guilty of false teaching or ungodly life. But this is not an arbitrary sort of power, states Chemnitz. "As long as God endures one of his servants who is faithful in teaching correctly and lives a godly life, a congregation has no right or power to dismiss him from office."[7] If neither of those two grounds exist, a congregation would offend against God's clear injunctions concerning the pastoral office, if it were to withdraw a pastor's call on ground that had no support in God's Word.

Johann Gerhard likewise attests the servant role which the pastor by his office has in ministering to the congregation of royal priests, to whom first of all the Keys belong.[8] A pastor's office necessarily focuses on at least seven duties states Gerhard: 1) proclamation of the Word of God; 2) administration of the sacraments; 3) prayers in behalf of the entrusted flock; 4) a godly life and conduct; 5) application of church discipline; 6) preservation of church rites; 7) support of the poor and visitation of the sick.[9] A pastor who is faithful in the performance of these duties is fulfilling his God-given assignment as a called shepherd, or steward of the Lord, and servant of the congregation.[10]

The basic authority resides with the congregation of believers, to whom God has given the Keys, says Gerhard, but carrying out the duties of the office is the function of the called pastors.[11] When pastors fulfill their tasks faithfully, as servants of God to the congregations, they are indeed worthy of honor, respect, love, and childlike obedience; but it also follows, states Gerhard, that such shepherds dare never become tyrants or despots who abuse the high trust that has been vested in them.[12] Also in matters of discipline, particularly the ban of excommunication, pastors do not act independently, but with their congregation's consent, as St. Paul teaches in his Second Letter to the Corinthians, states Gerhard.[13]

Abraham Calov concurs fully with Gerhard on the conduct of churchly discipline, noting that the congregation has not relinquished this right of judging in matters of doctrine and discipline, but shares the burden with its called pastor.[14] Thus at all times, states Calov, the power of the Keys remains tied to the general priesthood of believers; they can neither surrender it, nor be stripped of it.

Walther finds himself in full harmony with the orthodox teachers of the 16th and 17th centuries on the relationship of the pastors to the congregations, and their respective rights and duties. He fully supports the view that the office of pastor is a very high one, ordained of God, to be entered into only through the regular call of the Christian congregation. Under no circumstances should the rights and privileges of the royal priesthood be understood in such a way that the individual believer ventures to exercise the functions of pastor on his own, or because he feels himself called by inner motivation of the Spirit. Having laid down this demurrer, however, Walther goes to great length to show his support, by many quotations from the 16th and 17th century theologians, for the fundamental truth that the Keys belong in the first instance, and continue to belong, even after a pastor is called as servant to the congregation, to the general priesthood of all believers.[15]

To press his point home, Walther cites a number of authorities, particularly Johann Gallus and Tilemann Heshusius, both contemporaries of Luther, for the proposition that in times of emergency, where in actual fact the procurement of a regularly called and qualified pastor is impossible, an assembly of Christian believers might find it necessary to elect from their own midst one who would minister both Word and Sacraments for them, and they would be right in doing so. Such exceptions—and Walther cites the careful qualifications noted by Gallus and Heshusius—simply prove the generally prevailing rule which must be respected and adhered to, namely, that the called pastor is the one who administers the means of grace for the congregations. The exceptions highlight the truth, however, that the powers which they, the people, confer or delegate to the called pastor, are a possession or trust which by God's ordaining they continue to hold, preserve, and foster, albeit through the pastoral office.[16]

It was a truth which Walther and those whom he quotes had learned to know from Luther's brilliantly clear teaching on church and ministry, especially his notable emphasis on the priesthood of all believers in contradistinction to the Romanist view of a priestly hierarchy upon which, as supposed, God had bestowed certain powers in an indelible way for rule over the church.

Luther

Beginning with his *Genesis Commentary* Luther has a great deal to say concerning the role of the pastor as servant to his people, of his work, of his responsibilities. Citing Augustine's example, Luther states that one would hardly venture to describe Augustine's life as easy, a life "lived in idleness," when in fact the tasks of his office, as of every faithful pastor, were more arduous than that of any other, even the busiest magistrate.[17] The burdens upon the pastor's person as *Seelsorger* were heavier than the average person could imagine, says Luther; for "to work in the church means to preach, administer the Sacraments, contend with the enthusiasts, remove offenses, edify the godly, etc.," not to mention defending the flock against the "disturbers of the church" who seek to "overthrow completely the teaching of Christ."[18]

"Today no charge can be brought against our ministry," Luther contends concerning the faithful pastoral servant, because by the Word we call and exhort the masses "out of their smugness to the fear of God."[19] Enoch (Gen. 5:21-24) was a patriarch whose example ought serve for every minister of the Gospel, "that he may shine in his public ministry," because of the "unusual fulness of the Holy Spirit and outstanding courage" which Enoch showed against Satan and the Cainite church.[20] As a result, "that age was truly a golden one," in Luther's estimation, and "in comparison with it our age hardly deserves to be called an age of mud."[21] It was so in Adam's case, too, because here was a man who "went out from the face of the Lord." But Luther does not minimize the great blessings that are ours through Word and sacrament, and the pastoral ministry, for thereby we, too, like Adam have "those things by which God shows that He is with us."[22]

Luther sees the pastoral office as very comparable to that of the Old Testament patriarch or priest. It is twofold: "In the first place, to turn to God and pray for himself and for his people; in the second place, to turn from God to men by means of doctrine and the Word," to teach and minister unto the flock.[23] God is always a God close at hand through His chosen revelation of Himself; in the Old Testament this was often by unusual theophany, but in the New Testament it is through His Word and Baptism and the Lord's Supper.[24] These are God's chosen *larvae Dei*, or veils, by which He discloses Himself and "puts before us an image of Himself." Why? "Because He shows Himself to us in such a manner that we can grasp Him. In the New Testament we have Baptism, the Lord's Supper, absolution, and the ministry of the Word."[25]

In our sophistication we may wonder at times why this was necessary and why God chose these particular avenues or veils for making Himself known to sinful man. Here it is best to put the finger on the lips, Luther admonishes, and have great respect and reverence for God and for His amazing kindness, especially when we think or realize "that in so short a time the world deteriorated so much."[26] Surely we, the recipients of God's grace, should be the last to quibble about or over the manner of His delivery of that grace to us. "Thus God is present in Baptism, in the Lord's Supper, and in the use of the Keys because His own Word is present there." "Therefore," says Luther, "even though we do not see or hear Him but see and hear the minister, God Himself is nevertheless truly present, baptizes, and absolves. And in the Lord's Supper He is present in such an extraordinary way that the Son of God Himself gives us His body with the bread and His blood with the wine."[27] This is an extraordinarily fine statement by Luther in explication of his view on the *larvae Dei* and God's pronounced use of them in His church and in the New Testament.

When God is at work through His Word, He is at work through Law and Gospel, the upper and lower millstones. This is a familiar figure of speech with Luther, according to which "the upper millstone is the fear and judgment of God" and "the lower millstone supports, (or) signifies the hope and feeling of mercy."[28] Very properly he adds: "Thus the ministry should connect the Law and the Gospel, penitence and the remission of sins."[29] This is properly the goal of preaching the Law and the Gospel, that the proud might be "frightened by God's wrath" and that the humbled and terrified might "apprehend the comforts" of God's Word; for this reason "God has put the ministry of the Word into this world," to counteract antinomians on the one hand and purveyors of anti-gospelism on the other.[30] "This," Luther says, "is the work of the Holy Spirit to direct the hearts of men by means of the Word and confession," with the "thunderbolts" of the Law and the "comforting knowledge" of the Gospel.[31]

In this way the preacher's mouth and God's mouth fuse, "so that one can truthfully say that the mouth of a godly teacher is God's mouth and that the hand which you extend to alleviate the want of a brother is God's hand."[32] That is why Luther becomes so exercised when men would strip God's power from the outward means of Word and Sacrament, for they "divest God altogether of the ministry," for these are His chosen means of grace.[33] This especially is a neuralgic point in the church when the preachers themselves express doubts or misgivings about the instruments which God has placed into their hands, the Office of the Keys through the royal priesthood. "Therefore those who are chosen as teachers of the churches to rule over others," admonishes Luther in very fatherly, pastoral manner, "should offer special prayers that they be preserved from this affliction as from the greatest and most dangerous evil."[34]

As Luther treats of Joseph's reunion with his brethren, he notes that in a similar way "faithful and diligent care must be exercised by the ministers by pouring on oil and wine." The one has its caustic effect, "for sin is a very cruel disease," while on the other hand "conscience is a very delicate thing" and requires balm and "the healing which customarily takes place in the church through ministers" applying the Gospel.[35] This accords well with Luther's comments in connection with the great penitential Psalm 51: "The priesthood which he (God) approves is that in which not animals are offered but contrite and humbled hearts . . . (for) God is the kind of God who does nothing for any other purpose than to regard and love the contrite, vexed, and troubled."[36] He divides the Word of God well who knows the Law's sphere and is able to distinguish it from the Gospel's.[37] Already in his famous *Heidelberg Theses* (1518) Luther had explained that "the law humbles, grace exalts," and that "such preaching concerning sin," that is, the Law, "is a preparation for grace," and "yearning for grace wells up when recognition of sin has arisen."[38] In his very early (1518) *Explanations to the 95 Theses* Luther had already said much the same thing: "True evangelical preaching is to magnify the sins as much as possible in order that man may develop fear of God and proper repentance," thus expecting everything from the Gospel and nothing from indulgences![39]

Luther did not doubt that "preachers of repentance and grace remain even to our day," in spite of the many aberrations in the Romanist system of theology, as long as this truth stands, that "repentance proceeds from the law of God, but faith or grace from the promise."[40] This statement from his *Freedom of a Christian* (1520) verifies the fact that Luther's understanding of *theologia crucis* and the proper distinction between Law and Gospel was well set in cement by this date. To preach about Christ merely to move people to compassion and sympathy for Christ, is not to preach the Gospel, Luther states. "Rather ought Christ to be preached to the end that faith in him may be established that he may not only be Christ, but be Christ for you and me, and that what is said of him and is denoted in his name be effectual in us."[41] This is the liberty or freedom with which the Gospel makes us free indeed. "This kind of preaching," states Luther in his treatise *On War Against the Turk* (1529), "will hit home with Christians and find them out," for that is the nature of the Law and Gospel when properly applied.[42]

Faith and the promise, or Gospel, are in correlative relation, and it is as true as day following night that faith "does not exist where there is no divine promise," nor, by the same token, "do the works please Him" where there is no faith, or where faith is an invented fiction.[43] By faith we "shall be partners of the angels, guests and table companions in the kingdom of God."[44] This is the true glory of the means of grace, in the faith which they effect by the power of the Holy Spirit; "they are equal to—yes, they even surpass—all the appearances of all angels, in comparison with which Abraham had only droplets and crumbs."[45] For Abraham it was the external Word of the angel which brought him a glorious promise, which he did not doubt; for us it is the external Word of Holy Scripture which cements tight the promise of God and makes it sure for faith. This we must never doubt, says Luther.[46]

A faithful pastor knows that the tools of his trade are not earthly falderal, take-it-or-leave-it sort of things, but heavenly power, able to give spiritual rebirth, so that a man is "renewed for the future life and immortality."[47] Far be it, therefore, that a faithful pastor ever use them as a "simonist," or "become rich" from them or earn glory in this world. "Thus the benefit of Baptism," for example, "is that I am transferred from the bosom of my mother and out of the grave and am put back into paradise, out of death into life," says Luther in behalf of the power and value of God's stated means of grace.[48]

The pastor handles sacred things, spiritual instruments that provide nurture for eternal life. What he does in his ministry of the means of grace is, in fact, "something far greater than if Isaac blesses Jacob," Luther observes. "For it is just as if I were saying: 'I give you the kingdom of heaven, power over the devil.' Of course, we do not do this with our own strength; but we do it by virtue of the authority and command of God, who has given men the power to lead one another to eternal life through the priesthood of Christ."[49] Word and Sacrament are our High Priest's gifts for and unto life. The pastor's calling is this ministry of the Word.[50]

In effect, what a faithful pastor is saying through his ministry of Word and Sacraments is this: "Have confidence, my son; believe that you have been baptized, that you have been pastured and fed in the Lord's Supper and absolved by the laying on of hands, not mine, but God's who has said to you: 'I forgive you your sins; I promise you eternal life.'"[51] As faith believes, so it also has. And even though in the exercise of his office the pastor finds himself conducting "even the lowliest and most servile services," he may rest assured that his office "entrusted to him" by God does not cease.[52] As a matter of fact, says Luther, also the Gentiles respond to the Word, as was often the case "when the patriarchs were teaching" and "many of the heathen flocked to them (and) embraced their doctrine."[53] The curate of souls has a task which is often as difficult as that of dealing with Joseph's brethren, who were shattered by the knowledge of their sin against their father; at such a time to assure the troubled conscience that there is forgiveness for the repentant heart is the highest and most rewarding task of the Gospel ministry.[54]

Joseph, in his lofty position as powerful ruler in Egypt, remained nonetheless a humble man, a man who saw his servant role in behalf of humanity. This, says Luther, epitomizes the place and office of the pastor: "For what else is a teacher than a servant of his pupil?" And a pastor but a servant of his flock?[55] Not least among the duties of one who is placed into such a position of trust over others, like a pastor, is that he "keep watch earnestly over purity of doctrine and the true use of the sacraments, and to separate false and godless teachings from those that are true."[56] Such "watchfulness must increase in proportion to the greed with which rapacious wolves gape at the flock," to see how they might "lure the hearts of the godly into deception."[57]

Even in a strange land, Joseph did not fail to preach the saving Word and the "doctrine concerning God," "the true religion and the wisdom of God."[58] Not ceremonies and rites, like circumcision, were the burden of his message, but "he was careful to impress on them that they should believe in God, who had promised the Seed that was to come."[59] In comparing Joseph's lowly estate at first with that of ministers of the Lord, Luther asks: Who is this fellow? "Who has given us this certainty and consolation? The minister of the Word, the priest! What, I ask, does this man teach, this man who is altogether worthless, needy, poor, and a beggar with barely the wherewithal to pay for a cord? How could this man give the kingdom of heaven?"[60] Luther answers: the power lies in the means of grace which he dispenses, "because he has the power and the divine command, he can and should absolve and remit sins."[61] Thus all depends upon his office as servant of God's people in the ministry of the Word.

God's Word is, therefore, the control center in a pastor's ministry. Pastors are not to subject God's people to "their laws and to the works ordained by them," but to God's Word alone, and thus "be ruled by faith" in that Word of God.[62] Any other arrangement would be to "shear us and seek their own advantage and glory, namely, our wool and produce."[63] "From this it follows," says Luther, how completely foreign and even pestilential those teachers in the New Testament era are who trouble consciences with laws and works, when this prophecy concerning Christ totally wipes out and does away with that ministry."[64] Human traditions and laws dare never supplant God's Word in the pastoral ministry. "The Word is their possession and wealth," and it is there that their concentration must be "that they may inherit the Land of Promise, namely, the salvation of souls."[65]

An awl is an instrument for a specific use, for piercing through materials of various kinds; so the Word of God needs to be handled aright, distinguishing between Law which pierces and the Gospel which consoles and triumphs. Therefore, the preacher does "not take the awl into the mouth but into the hands, for the devil ridicules the preachers of the Word," and the awl of the Law must not be made to do what only the Gospel can do; the time comes, after the awl has done its work, when one takes the "sword in hand," the Sword of the Spirit, the Gospel, which triumphs and wins men's hearts.[66] Ideally ministers of the Gospel are such who "with the grace received from Thee (God) further administer it to others"[67] and who "by expounding the Scriptures labor to bring out the bread of the Word of God, as the farmer brings bread out of the earth by tilling the soil."[68]

Faithful preaching of the Word is more powerful than is often recognized. Commenting on Psalm 23, the familiar Good Shepherd psalm, Luther states:

> Here the prophet also touches upon the office of preaching. For through oral preaching of the Word, which enters the ears and touches the heart by faith, and through the holy Sacraments our Lord God accomplishes all these things in His Christendom, namely, that men are brought to faith, are strengthened in faith, are kept in pure doctrine, and in the end are enabled to withstand all the assaults of the devil and

the world. Without these means, Word and Sacrament, we obtain none of these things.[69]

It is precisely at this point, in ministering the means of grace, that it may be said "that every preacher is a harpist of God."[70] God of course provides the message, as Jesus promises, "for it is not you who speak, but the Spirit of our Father speaking through you" (Matt. 10:20). It follows, says Luther, that "where God does not provide the message, a sermon is useless."[71] But see what this makes of the local parish and its ministry, affirms Luther, "the gates of righteousness!" For the parish then is nothing other than "the ministry of the church—preaching, praising God, thanksgiving, singing, baptizing, distributing and receiving the Sacrament, admonishing, comforting, praying, and whatever else pertains to salvation."[72] Pastors who serve the parish in this way "sit (as) councilors of the spiritual kingdom of God."[73]

Though it appears to be a remnant, "for the sake of the remnant one must serve the whole mass," Luther exhorts, and be resolved to "stick to the definite work which has been assigned and commanded by God, and belongs to your calling, the office of preaching."[74] It is good to remember God's role in this ministry. "It does not depend on the person, regardless of how skillful he may be. In war the strong are often defeated by the weak, and great armies have often been vanquished by the smaller ones; this is because the outcome does not depend on strength . . . The Lord reigns in our very weakness; He will rule, He will perform it."[75] Commenting on Isaiah 8:20, "to the Law and to the testimony," Luther underscores that there is fruit in simply reading the Scriptures as there is fruit likewise in the hearing of the preached Word or testimony![76]

Luther never tires of repeating that preaching requires both Law and Gospel proclamation. In his *Galatian Commentary* he states:

> If we want to be preachers and teachers of others, we must take great care and hold to this distinction between the righteousness of the Law and that of Christ. This distinction is easy to speak of; but in experience and practice it is the most difficult of all, even if you exercise and practice it diligently."[77]

"The preacher's first message is to teach penitence, remove offenses, proclaim the Law, humiliate and terrify the sinners," and Luther insists that "no one can do this but a godly preacher."[78] But then "preachers are called clouds flying very swiftly and by their teachings sending down fruitful rain upon the people," because they are true proclaimers of the saving Gospel, and not "empty clouds" that signify nothing and bring no moisture.[79] In the same context (Is. 60:8), Luther refers to Scripture's additional allusion to preachers as "doves," because they fly quickly with the saving message. It was God's promise, "after the apostles," to "provide good preachers who will uphold the church and peace," "peace before God and men,"[80] forgiveness and righteousness.

This is a Gospel worth fighting and contending for; this is the ensign of God around which the faithful must rally, as the call for trooping the colors sounds forth, for "the Word is a fighting Word," as Isaiah (62:10) teaches.[81] God stretches out His "net over all the children of Israel by sending out the Gospel Word about Christ," but not all hear, nor "wish to be gathered into this sheepfold of Christ, and so they are not gathered."[82] God is faithful through the ministry of His prophets; but Israel turns a deaf ear, thwarting the "promises of God" preached by the prophets with "murmuring" and "stout, hard hearts."[83]

The work and ministry of the prophets paralleled closely that of the New Testament pastors. Habakkuk did his work faithfully, as had Jeremiah and the other prophets. Yet, what was the people's response to Habakkuk, asks Luther? They resented his preaching of the Law and his targeting of them under its threats, saying: "What did he preach? He surely preached at us. We are always the target of his threats." Even so the people in our day, Luther says, level their complaints against preachers who faithfully and fearlessly preach the severity of God's Law charging that "they make hell hot and paint the devil black for us."[84] Under the circumstances, preachers, like the prophets of old, incline towards "growing tired and weary of preaching," in order to avoid the people's "punishment."[85]

Drawing on a figure of speech from Zechariah, Luther states that standing firm in the preaching of the Word is like the "lampstand" that stands firmly in God's house; moreover, "the lampstand is single, that is, the preachers and teachers among the people of

God are of one heart and of one mind and teach one and the same thing. Their message is gold, that is, it is pure divine wisdom and not of clay or earth, which means that they do not have men's words," though indeed their gifts or talents may be various.[86] The pure Word is equipped "with wings," and flies quickly; God's Word "is a flying book," for not only is it written, as by Moses, but "it is a teaching that is spread through the office of preaching."[87]

It may seem a strange thing, but with His message of peace God is waging war against the godlessness of men, for "that is the way things go in the Spirit: when one preaches the Gospel, everything happens; one works and keeps peace and wages war as well; one builds and destroys as well; the warring and destroying are directed against the unbelievers and heretics; peace and building prevail among the believers."[88] The victory for the believers is twofold, as Luther correctly points out: "These, then, are the two blessed freedoms of which eternal life consists; and it is of these two freedoms or redemptions that Isaiah 40:2 speaks: 'Jerusalem has received double for all her sins. For her iniquity is pardoned, and so her warfare (that is, her servitude under the Law) is ended.'"[89] Luther has correctly interpreted the oft misinterpreted and misunderstood words of Isaiah 40:2 that Israel "hath received of the Lord's hand double for all her sins." Prophets and preachers thus are like "storm clouds": that, on the one hand have a lowering, threatening aspect, and, on the other hand, a nurturing, life-giving effect like "a spring rain."[90]

The church works with an entirely different tool than the state, where the sword is "a fisted sword, and a rod of wood to inflict physical punishment." "The preacher's rod," on the other hand, "smites only the consciences, which feel the impact of the Word, the oral sword."[91] "These two rods and swords must be kept apart and separate, so that the one does not infringe on the province of the other."[92] Christian believers, especially pastors, are to "take the touchstone of God's Word" into their hands as their "criterion for testing, trying, and judging all that the fathers have preached, written, and said, as well as all the precepts and human ordinances that have been promulgated."[93] Luther is convinced that, if the "polishing stone" of the Word of God, Holy Scripture, had been respected and applied in the past, many of the terrible errors and aberrations would have been kept out of the church. Much depends upon our knowing and believing "that God carries out His work and accomplishes great things through this humble form of Word and Sacraments." In fact, says Luther in his down-to-earth way: "He could pull a great whale from the ocean with a human hair—something we would be unable to do with many thousands of ropes. Therefore we should remember who this great Person is that deals with us in the Sacrament and addresses us through the office of the ministry. In six days He created heaven and earth. What sort of hands did He have for this task? Certainly not my fingers!"[94]

The task of calling sinners to repentance is never an easy one for God's prophets or preachers. Luther fronts the problem straight on:

> If you are in the ministry and see that you have rascals and knaves, fornicators, adulterers, and robbers in your parish, you must say: "Since this is my duty, I will point out sins to peasants, burghers, and noblemen, and rebuke them for these without paying attention to their complaints when they say: 'Look here, you are defaming me!'" For if I held back, I would make myself guilty of your sin. And why should I go to hell for you?[95]

Luther well recognizes that it is in man's nature to cry out in protest and say "lay off," "let us alone." But a faithful pastor cannot do this; "this burden has been imposed on the poor preachers," and they cannot "keep silence in the presence of sin" which is not repented of.[96]

In accomplishing this end the "written Word" is as powerful as the "oral Word" of God, for the Holy Spirit is at work in both, affirms Luther.[97] "Would to God," exclaims Luther, "that we could gradually train our hearts to believe that the preacher's words are God's Word" and its force, therefore, is more than that of "a hundred thousand angels"; indeed "the Divine Majesty Himself is preaching here."[98] This is Luther's attitude towards the Word of God in the mouths of faithful preachers of that Word.

There is a running commentary in Luther's writings in behalf of the Scriptural authority of the Word, "the rule or touch-stone or Lydian stone by which I can tell black from white and evil from good" and which "illumines everything just as the sun does."[99] Clearly he has the written Word of God in mind, Holy Scripture, which one can hear, read, and preach, which the weak human voice can tell, which "I see only (as) a poor letter of the alphabet in the book," but which is more powerful than the River Elbe in its washing, cleansing effect, and power.[100]

Luther singles out the preacher's task in connection with that Word by personalizing the matter graphically: "I, too, am still preaching of God's grace, and let him who rejects this grace have His wrath. I cannot and dare not preach differently."[101] What I thus do, Luther states in commentary on the first chapter of Romans, I do in my ministry "for the benefit of all," that they "submit themselves to faith."[102] God urges "every faithful pastor to seek out not what the sheep have, but the sheep themselves."[103] We have this excellent task assigned by God, to bring the Gospel to the Gentiles, and like the apostle Paul we who are pastors emphasize the call into the ministry which we have received "for without the call of God neither the ministry nor teaching succeeds."[104] Luther touches on the mission aspect of the holy ministry, of "preaching Christ where He is not known," of turning from those who despise the Gospel to those who hunger and thirst after righteousness.[105]

Proper rebuke by the loving pastor is always fatherly, intending not injury but repentance and healing by the Gospel.[106] "God supplies the Spirit" in such faithful preaching "and performs powerful deeds in the hearers" that lead to faith and the fruits of faith.[107] In this way the preacher begets spiritual sons and gives birth to them as a natural mother begets children; for "like a mother he carries them in a womb as undeveloped seed until the Spirit lends His aid and forms them into Christ."[108] "Paul is happy to boast of his ministry" on this account, "because it is his grace as a teacher to know for certain that he preaches the Word of God" by "which is conveyed the treasure of redemption."[109] To the reading of the Word, Luther says, the apostle Paul exhorts that sound teaching be added "to impress it, foster it, follow it up, lest it grow cold; (and) use proof texts and examples with which you admonish the conscience of your hearers."[110] The preacher is a man with a trowel in one hand, by which he builds the church through the Word; and the sword in the other hand, the same Word of God, by which he fends off the assaults of the devil, the world, and the flesh. He must "not put the Bible aside" but "immerse himself completely in Scripture" and "diligently study Holy Scripture," if he wants "to be the kind of man Paul has described here" in his letter to Titus.[111] "Even though you know Holy Scripture, nevertheless it must be read over and over again, because this Word has the power to stimulate you at all times."[112]

Luther is especially eloquent in his commentary on 1 Peter concerning the task of pastoral ministry. It has to do with "the precious inheritance" which is given to faith. "For this is the sequence," says Luther: "Faith follows from the Word, the new birth follows from faith, and from this birth we enter into the hope of looking forward to this blessing" of eternal life and salvation.[113] Even our sufferings and cross-bearing have purpose in this pilgrimage unto life eternal. "It is the purpose of the cross and adversities of all kinds to enable one to differentiate between the false and the true faith. God afflicts us in this way in order that our faith may be proved."[114] This is all taught us very clearly in Holy Writ, "and it is necessary to study Scripture well in order to become certain of faith," Luther admonishes.[115] Christ and His apostles handled the Holy Scriptures in this same way as they sought to convict and convince the Jews from their own Scriptures of who the Christ was.[116]   If there is one lesson here, it is to "see how St. Peter teaches us to outfit and equip ourselves with Scripture."[117] In greater detail Luther expounds this matter:

> But the spiritual girding—of which the apostle is speaking here—takes place as follows: Just as a virgin is physically pure and blameless, so the soul is spiritually blameless because of faith, through which it becomes the bride of Christ. But if it falls from faith into false doctrine, it must go to ruin. For this reason Scripture consistently calls idolatry and unbelief adultery and whoring, that is, if the soul clings to the teachings of men and thus surrenders faith and Christ. St. Peter forbids this here when he tells us to gird the loins of the mind. It is as if he were saying: You have now heard the Gospel and have come to faith. Therefore see to it that you remain in faith and not be moved by false doctrine, that you do not waver and run hither and thither with works.[118]

Luther sees little difference between the church of his day and that of St. John's, for in that day, too, "there were people who deceived themselves by using the name 'Christians,'" and "the preachers of the Word of God always had work to do and exhortation to deliver," just as now.[119]   The apostle John's writings are replete with exhortations to faithfulness, repentance, and standing firm in the faith.

In his treatise *On the Defense and Explanation of All the Articles* (1521) which had been condemned in the papal bull, Luther not only levels the offices in the church, pastor with bishop, etc., but he also emphasizes the truth that all pastoral work must serve and nurture faith.   God's Word of forgiveness "belongs equally to everybody" and it is papal pretension in its most blatant, repugnant form "to drink the best wine out of the very cask from which others can scarcely get water," says Luther in obvious disgust over the neglect of Gospel preaching.[120]   Through all Luther is constantly concerned that Law and Gospel be not mixed or confused. He puts it in a picturesque, graphic way, so that none can misunderstand: "Be sure that you do not make Christ into a Moses, as if Christ did nothing more than teach and provide examples as the other saints do, as if the Gospel were simply a textbook of teachings or laws."[121] Luther has thereby touched on the sorest ill in much of Protestant and Romanist theologizing, as well as synergistic or pietistic Lutheranism. "The chief article and foundation of the Gospel is that before you take Christ as an example, you accept and recognize him as a gift, as a present that God has given you and that is your own. This is what preaching the Christian faith means."[122]

That is also what the pastoral office is all about, proclaiming the saving Gospel. So Christ ordained "ministries," not "lordships" in the church, avers the Reformer in his famous *Babylonian Captivity* (1520).[123]   God's Word always goes with God's work; proclamation is the name of the game in God's church, Luther states in his notable "Great Confession" of 1528.[124]   In no way does this denigrate the Supper, and it would be wrong to state the question this way: "Since the Gospel and the remembrance of Christ can be had in all preaching, what then is the need of celebrating a Supper in addition?" By the same token one might ask: "What is the need for anyone to read the Scriptures for himself?"   Or, "what is the need for anyone to admonish and comfort another individually, since all this can happen in regular public preaching?" Luther squares off against such insolent thoughts and states: "Aren't these childish, blind thoughts in such important matters?   God means to fill the world and give himself to us in many different ways, to help and strengthen us by His Word and works; shall we be so complacent and bored that we hinder him, and tolerate nothing but the way that happens to please us?"[125]

Luther states that he writes his treatise on *Admonition Concerning the Sacrament* (1530), in order "to provide clergymen and preachers with the reasons to be used in admonishing their people and attracting them to the sacrament."[126] As he treats of the disputed matter of the *Private Mass and the Consecration of Priests*, Luther lays to rest the notion that there is either justification for or merit in priests celebrating "masses" privately, and he sets the record straight on their receiving Holy Communion with their congregations, not apart from them.[127]

Luther likewise settles the dispute concerning the so-called "moment" of the Real Presence, whether it is the consecrationist or the receptionist view that ought to be followed. Neither one, Luther answers, for it all goes back to "Christ's ordinance, command, and institution."[128] "So it is not our work or speaking but the command and ordinance of Christ which makes the bread the body and the wine the blood, beginning with the first Lord's Supper and continuing to the end of the world."[129] It is the same for Baptism. "We join the water to the Word, as He commands us to do; however, not this action of ours, but Christ's command and ordinance make it a baptism."[130]

In writing of *The Papacy in Rome* (1520) Luther sets aside the papal pretension of applying Christ's tender words, "feed my sheep," to the office of the Roman pope, and he asserts rather: "It is Christ's intention to instruct all preachers in the person of St. Peter as to what their mission should be."[131] In the same context Luther asserts: "I fight for only two things." The one is to keep men from establishing new articles of faith. The second is to uphold Scripture's authority and honor, for Luther cannot bear with anyone who "makes a liar out of the Holy Spirit and my Lord Christ, whom I preach."[132] The meaning of "feed my sheep," therefore, simply is "the great service of preaching the Gospel and faith" and in this way "build the church on the rock, Matthew 16" through the Word and baptism.[133] Every minister—Luther includes himself at Wittenberg—"must take to heart Christ's command, 'Feed my lambs.'"[134] In this work the shepherds do not seek their own advantage or gain, "as though they were selling and the Christians buying the Gospel from them," for "the treasure is too great" and "it cannot tolerate the buying and bargaining" which goes on in worldly affairs.[135] It may seem ironical but the "prophets' reward is to hazard and wager body, wife, child, good, and everything" for the sake of the Gospel and for Christ, the Lord.[136]

There is no higher calling and "whoever has the office of preaching imposed on him has the highest office in Christendom imposed on him."[137] In his treatise on *How Confession Should Be Made* (1520) Luther goes to considerable length, first of all, in explaining the great value of private confession and absolution in the sinner's life; and, secondly, the importance of the faithful pastor's ministering to such needy souls, not coercing them, or lording it over them, or drawing up long lists of grievous sins, or driving terror into hearts that are on the brink of despair, but of leading them gently to repentance and then to the "sweet promise" of God's forgiveness for Christ's sake by faith.[138] It is in this context that Luther expresses his agreement with John Gerson's viewpoint, "that a man should at times go to the altar or to the sacrament with a scruple of conscience, that is, without confessing, (so that) that man learns to trust God's mercy more than his own confession or effort."[139]

Christ's merits, not our works are the focal point of saving faith. This was Luther's *theologia crucis*, theology of the cross, as opposed to *theologia gloriae*, theology of glory, according to which man's efforts were highlighted, as in the Romanist system. Of this latter, monasticism was the most glaring, vivid example. Luther's *Instructions for the Visitors of Parish Pastors* (1528) formed a very practical guideline for pastors who were making the transition from the sterility of the Romanist church life to the evangelical thrust of Lutheran theology. Luther spells out some of the necessary steps: in treating doctrine, don't "preach about the faith," but "how one shall attain to this faith," namely, through "repentance and forgiveness of sins"; expound carefully the Ten Commandments; explain the purpose of cross-bearing in the Christian's life; emphasize the abiding power and efficacy of baptism, also for children; state the meaning of the Real Presence and the proper use of the Sacrament; remind the flock of the true nature of repentance, at the same time showing them that even in his good works a Christian still sins; show the value of good order in the worship service, even though it has become a matter of Christian liberty and not papal regulation; support the sanctity and goodness of marriage; and explain the duties of each in his station or vocation, and how they please God by their faithful performance of the same.[140]

There are many other practical applications to Christian living which Luther touches upon, including such things as military service and the support of the schools. In the same context, again with his balanced, evangelical mind, he gives this good advice, which sets things straight for our day, too. On the matter of attendance at the Lord's Supper, we ought to urge faithful, regular use of the Sacrament by the people; but he then adds that "the people are, however, to be instructed not to go to the sacrament merely on account of custom,"[141] or as Walther says, merely according to the almanac.

In his *Exposition of the Lord's Prayer*, which appeared already in 1519, Luther presses what "a great blessing" it is "whenever God permits Christ to be preached and taught." Nothing ought to characterize the pastoral ministry more than that "only Christ should everywhere be preached."[142] To show people their sins, "which all pastors should do," is necessary, first of all, in order that they "may long for the kingdom of God" and His righteousness.[143] Effective preaching of the Gospel is always preceded by effective preaching of the Law. In his highly respected and widely used *Personal Prayer Book* (1522) Luther voices this prayer: "Graciously grant that all pastors preach your word and Christ throughout the world in a way effective for salvation," with the hope also expressed that the hearers might thus come to know the Gospel, lead godly lives, and false doctrine be excluded.[144]

Preaching, therefore, can never be an idle or academic affair, for the hearing of God's Word preached "is the only ceremony or practice Christ has instituted for which Christians are to assemble."[145] Faithful preaching of the Word, Law and Gospel, leads to repentance and faith, to confession and absolution. This is central in a Christian congregation's life, as in each individual believer's life. But in Luther's day it was often abused within Romanist practice. Hence his exhortation that the evangelical core be carefully safeguarded, "for I have come to confession not to be trapped," Luther asserts, "but to be absolved."[146] Should the unsavory and unwelcome situation arise where priests or pastors of the parishes refused to absolve the penitent sinners—as was the case among many of the faithful who had turned to follow Luther's evangelical lead—then the Reformer advised: "Do without the sacrament, the altar, the priest, and the church, because the Word of God is far more than all the rest put together."[147]

In a parish where the Gospel prevails the pastor's one weapon or tool is the blessed Word of God. This shapes his ministry from beginning to end. Luther asks: "Does he not do all of this exclusively with the tongue or with words? And the congregation likewise brings no sword or spear to such a ministry but only its ears."[148] In a letter to John Lang, October 26, 1516, Luther speaks of tasks at the local city church (*Stadtkirche*) which parallel closely the form of the evangelical ministry which he later so beautifully exemplified in his own practice and teaching.[149] Writing to Archbishop Albrecht of Mainz in a letter accompanying his 95 Theses, October 31, 1517, Luther contends that "the first and only duty of the bishops is to see that the people learn the Gospel and the love of Christ" rather than indulgences, which are worthless.[150] While he languished in his unhappy "exile" on the Wartburg after the Diet of Worms, he wrote to John Agricola, May 12, 1521, that he hoped that all was well "with the preaching and who was entrusted with it" at Wittenberg, so that his heart and mind could be at ease for the Gospel's faithful proclamation.[151]

From the same perch, at the Wartburg, he assures Melanchthon of his readiness to go anywhere, at any risk, for the Gospel's sake, for "look how big a harvest there is everywhere, and how few are the harvesters."[152] In another letter, just a little later, September 9, 1521, to his colleague Nicholas von Amsdorf, Luther candidly states that in his opinion it would be better if Melanchthon did the preaching back at Wittenberg rather than Karlstadt, and he dismisses the notion that Melanchthon is only "a layman" and urges that he be permitted to preach the Gospel, on the grounds of the priesthood of all believers and because he was theologically qualified.[153] In a letter to Nicholas Hausmann, November 17, 1524, Luther underscores the evident point that pastors are shepherds over the flock, over the congregation.[154]

Pastors are empowered "through the power of the Word," and not with their own power, Luther states in another letter, March 5, 1525.[155] So important is their ministry, Luther states in a letter to Justus Jonas, November 10, 1527, that even in time of plague they ought not cease from the task of *Seelsorger*, curate of souls.[156] Fools for Christ they might seem to be, but they suffer this gladly.[157] In the second of his famous eight sermons at Wittenberg, after his return from the Wartburg, Luther uttered the memorable "I did nothing, the Word did everything," as he accounted for the success of the Reformation up to that point, March 1522.[158]   In his third sermon he exhorted: "Let the Word alone do the work, as I said before; the Word must first capture the hearts of men and enlighten them."[159]   In the last and eighth sermon he made a special appeal for the retention of private confession, on a voluntary basis, because of its great consolatory benefit for souls troubled by sin.[160]   The goals of Christian preaching, as Luther saw them, were to preach God's Word purely, receive it into the heart, pray, and stand confidently in your baptism.[161]   In the last sermon of his life, February 15, 1546, at Eisleben, he exhorted among other things that we must let God speak in the churches and in our lives: "Dear heavenly Father, speak thou, I am willing to be a fool and a child and be silent."[162]

Accept the Word, not the preacher, was Luther's rule of thumb as regards the respect that congregations should retain for each in their proper order. "For whoever does not accept the Word on its own account, is never inclined to accept it on account of any preacher, even if all the angels were preaching to him."[163]   So it must be faith in the Word, not in the person of the preacher, that holds us. We honor the pastor because of his office as preacher of the Word, and this holds true even though his person be of such a nature that we are not attracted to him. The Word is preeminent, not his person.[164]   "Preachers are to be only precursors and witnesses of this light to men, in order that all should believe in the light," which is Christ and His Word.[165]   Luther again stands by the position that the oral Word proclaimed was not a different Word from that which was written in the Scriptures. Of course, we as preachers are to "extract the living word," that is, the Gospel core, from those Scriptures. But the Scriptures remain authoritative, and we know no other Christ than the Christ of Scriptures; and God saw the need for inscripturating His Word, in order to preserve His truth.[166]

In his treatise on *The Order of Public Worship*, written to the people of Leisnig, 1523, and *Concerning Ordination of Ministers of the Word*, 1539, Luther sets forth a careful, balanced brief or rationale for regular, well-arranged worship services in the Christian congregations, for their instruction, edification, consolation, exhortation to godly life. He takes a stand against the abuses connected with the Romanist Mass and appeals for the placement of the preached Word into the center of the worship service in the churches. The need for the churches to be confessional churches, besides confessing or witnessing communities, is also on his heart.

He is equally concerned that Holy Communion be faithfully celebrated in the churches, even though the Mass as practiced under Rome had been repudiated.[167] Memorable especially is Luther's hymn on the Word, written in 1541: "Lord, Keep Us Steadfast in Thy Word."[168]

While Luther was responsible for placing the office of the ministry in proper perspective with the priesthood of believers, so that it was not elevated above it as a spiritual estate of special prerogative, he nonetheless persisted in upholding its place of honor and respect, even though filled by human, and thus fallible, beings as elders and pastors. He even exhorts: "Do not be offended if they act rashly" and "keep in mind that God, who wants the ungodly to be offended and provoked, has amazing ways with His saints."[169] Thus also Abraham, as "a man of prayer" and spiritual leader in his house "deserves also to be honored" as a minister of God. Moreover, this "prophet of God" was "the father of the promise."[170]

As Luther translates this down to his own time, he stresses how the Word of God teaches the support of the elders or pastors who labor among the people, "especially the ministers who are in need, because they are now married and no longer live in impure celibacy."[171] Luther at many places speaks in behalf of the minister's support by his people, but nowhere perhaps more plainly than in the context of Abraham's receiving a gift of land for the burial place of Sarah. "Here," he says, "the question arises whether a minister of the Word may demand or receive support for his office." "My answer is," says Luther "by all means."[172] If the power to forgive sins were only in my hands and "nobody could be absolved from sins unless he had paid me several guldens, I would rake together all the wealth of the world in a single day."[173] This is the stunt, says Luther, which the papacy had tried. But evangelical Christians do not think and operate that way; they freely have received, and they freely give, also to the elders who serve them. "Therefore when we (pastors) receive sustenance from the church, it is not a price equivalent to this gift, which is worth so much that the wealth of the whole world cannot pay for it. But because this stupendous and incalculable gift cannot be administered except by men who need food and clothing, it is necessary to nourish and support them. This, however, is not payment for the gift; it is payment for the service and the work."[174] In the same context Luther defends the right of a pastor to have and own private property, as a result of savings from the remuneration received; but it is not to be looked upon as "an ecclesiastical benefit," deserving of special consideration, but simply as a secular thing, which it is. Much of the abuse of that day, as well as ours, is at focus here in Luther's comments.

The rapport between pastor and people is pretty much that of obedient children listening attentively to their parents, says Luther.[175] Such honoring of and support for the ministry is God-pleasing, and "God wants us to help the ministry, to contribute for the purpose of supporting the studies of the pupils and of propagating the doctrine; then God is truly praised and glorified."[176] Such honoring of the office of pastor begins from the top down, and Luther is happy to be able to state: "Thanks to the kindness of God, we have a very good prince."[177] Luther has no qualms over the fact that some of "the spoils of Egypt which were gathered under the papacy" were now being used to support and build the parishes and schools after the Reformation.[178] Moreover, Luther is quite convinced that to the extent we neglect the parishes and the schools, in order to advance things like roads, bridges, and military armaments, we will later be paying the Devil's ransom, as it were.[179] The ministry, or office of pastor, is a despised thing in the eyes of the world, "but before God it is altogether pure and beautiful," says Luther in support of its divine institution and function in the church.[180] This is so, of course, because by God's will the pastor is handling "the ministry of the Word (and) offers and administers the sacraments."[181]

Luther's *Commentary on Deuteronomy* appeared in 1525 and already then, just a few short years into the Reformation, Luther deplored the lack of support for ministers in the parishes, some of whom "for want of bread are forced to leave the ministry and become farmers and ply trades."[182] To back up his remonstrance over this sorry state of affairs, Luther cites the apostle Paul's straightforward teaching on the support of the pastoral ministry in 1 Corinthians 9:7f.; 1 Timothy 5:17; Galatians 6:6.[183] Nor does Luther neglect citing the root passage from Deuteronomy (25:4), on the basis of which he then states, "That the mouth of the threshing ox is not to be bound we use as a metaphor to denote that subsistence is due the ministers of the Word for their ministry."[184]

The true glory of the office, of course, centers around the Word, not worldly goods.[185] But that it should be a salaried office, is surely not wrong; for it is not a case of buying Word and sacraments, but of supporting the person who fills the pastoral office, along with his family.[186] After all, says Luther, the pastor who faithfully proclaims God's Word is preaching not his own word but the Word of God and he is thus the voice of the Divine Majesty Himself.[187] "I blush with shame," Luther admits as he reads the apostle Paul's exhortations in behalf of support for the ministry in the Epistle to the Galatians (6:6) and then sees the gross neglect of the pastors by the people. He urges those "who are in the ministry" that they should "not have a bad conscience about accepting wages for their work," for the laborer is worthy of his hire.[188]

Luther's very influential *A Sermon on Keeping Children in School*, written from the Coburg, while the Augsburg Diet was going on in 1530, contains a number of sententious statements by the Reformer in behalf of the pastoral office. First of all, there is his bold affirming that it "is the highest and chief of all" offices, because of the Gospel which emanates from it.[189] Parents, therefore, could do no greater thing than give their sons into this service, for "there is no dearer treasure, no nobler thing on earth or in this life than a good and faithful pastor and preacher."[190] Can there be a greater service on earth than to have your son devote his life to this great work, to "snatch one soul from the devil or rescue one person from hell?"[191] Not even a king or prince could lend his son to the Lord for a greater cause! Perhaps not all of the boys devoted in this way to service in God's kingdom will become "highly learned doctors and masters of Holy Scripture," skilled in the languages, says Luther, but then the church also has great need for "ordinary pastors who will teach the Gospel and the catechism, baptize and administer the sacrament."[192] After all, "for a good building we need not only hewn facings but also backing stone."[193] God will as little tolerate despising and scoffing of His chosen servants as He will scoffing "at the Lord Himself."[194]

Luther is under no illusion when he views the rigors of the pastoral office. In fact, he is ready to say that the demands are more arduous, that a pastor puts forth more "work and sweat than a farmer does in an entire month."[195] We may excuse Luther for overstating the comparison of occupations and overweighting the amount of sweat on the side of the pastors, but we need not apologize for him for setting the record straight in the minds of many people, who like the world tend to despise the ministry as worthless,[196] as blamewor-

thy,[197] as apparently accomplishing little, if anything.[198] Though the
world thus despises the office,[199] the faithful pastor persists nonetheless and does not give up in despair.[200] He knows that he is the
devil's special target, "running the gauntlet," as it were, "of spears
which strike and stab from all sides."[201] The attack is not so much
against his person as it is "excessive contempt for the Gospel." Such
"loathing of the Word" he must simply learn to cope with and
expect.[202] When one remembers that by the Savior's injunction we
are to "convince the world of sin," it is to be expected that the
"world shows its hostility by crying out that this is offensive,
intolerable preaching,"[203] or that the preacher be rebuked for harping
on that which is "old hat."[204] "Oh, this man can preach about
nothing but Baptism, the Ten Commandments, the Lord's Prayer,
and the Creed, with which even the children are conversant. What's
the idea, that he constantly harangues us with the same message?
Who is not able to do that?"[205] This is the world's and Satan's old
refrain. *Caveat* Christian, let the Christian beware!

Under the circumstances, no one is likely to risk stating that
the pastor's office is a "lark." No wonder that even men like
Abraham and Paul were reticent about assuming the responsibility
for the office conferred upon them; yet they gave themselves
willingly to the assignment from God.[206] The prophets were
mistreated in times past, and Luther notes that, even though the
Reformation has come to pass and one might expect a changed
attitude, the same sort of thinking prevails still.[207] But though the
ministers in the church often must suffer, they go gamely on, and,
as Luther says, "we simply live from spoils" derived from what
might be an ofttimes miserable existence.[208] Because Satan and our
own heart often beat against our continuing fortitude, thus attacking
from without and within, nonetheless we must rest "assured that this
is in no sense man's work but God's work."[209]

"It takes toil and trouble to engender faith in people by the
God-ordained means of the preaching ministry, absolution, and the
Sacrament," Luther acknowledges,[210] but the faithful pastor persists,
and he does not become careless and indifferent over against license
and brazen evil in his parish.[211] Luther's treatise *On the Jews and
Their Lies* has often been misunderstood and maligned in our day,
but a careful reading will show that his primary concern, also here
in connection with the pastoral office, is because "they (the Jews)
publicly blaspheme and curse God the Father when they blaspheme

and curse this Jesus."[212] The Christian pastor will, because of his office, have to bear some of the same onus.

Luther takes it as no insignificant sign that, wherever the Gospel is faithfully proclaimed, there will also be disdain and persecution of the Gospel and those who proclaim it. "The office of preaching is an arduous office," Luther, therefore, repeats, "especially when it is like what Paul encountered here" (at Corinth). "I have often said that, if I could come down with a good conscience, I would rather be stretched upon a wheel or carry stones than preach one sermon. For anyone who is in this office will always be plagued; and therefore I have often said that the damned devil and not a good man should be a preacher. But we are stuck with it now."[213] Luther adopts this rather dismal picture of the ministry, because people challenge a man's qualifications, as they challenged the apostle Paul, or because wiseacres seek to self-qualify themselves and preach what they please, striving to supplant God's called servant. People often do not want to hear what God says in His Word, Luther laments; but then he adds this judgment: "It is impossible for a sectarian to preach the New Testament" because of their blind legalistic spirit.[214]

There are pluses and minuses as regards the pastoral office. Under the papacy the office was abused through the snatching of secular power as the princes neglected their duties, and as a result spiritual nurturing came to a virtual standstill. The same temptation is always present for those in the office of minister, Luther warns, and if they succumb "they will eventually arrive at pontifical honor by this road."[215] But that is a dubious honor. It is a threat to the church and its ministry in any day, that its clergy become so worldly that they are of little spiritual good. The extreme is reached, of course, when the church begins to "peddle its goods" for a price. Nothing could be more offensive. Luther describes the situation in his own inimitable way: "If a minister or pastor of a church were unwilling to give you instruction concerning the remission of sins and the blessings of the Gospel or refused you absolution unless you bought it from him for a hundred guldens, that would be simoniacal."[216]

Under no circumstances must Luther be understood as opposing secular authority. Throughout his life he retained a high regard for the ruler's task and authority, as long as the secular realm was carefully distinguished from the spiritual. But there was much

to gain from living under a government that did its work well and
kept the peace. "Political peace is a great thing," Luther states, "and
is of a great benefit for the spread of the Word."[217]   The apostles
were greatly helped by *pax Romana*, by the fact that the Roman
empire successfully maintained a generally good peace. "There is,"
after all, says Luther, "something great about a good ruler."[218]
Luther could hardly be counted among the nitpicking radicals of his
day who opposed all constituted authority.   We are aware of
Luther's support of military service at the call of the ruler, or prince.
Perhaps not so familiar is the support he gave for the office of
military chaplains.   It is reminiscent of some of George Wash-
ington's statements in behalf of the military chaplaincy in the
Continental Army, to hear Luther already stating:

> Especially do we call on the army chaplains to warn,
> correct, and threaten the soldiers, including the wild, tough,
> coarse mercenaries who are such experts in all sorts of
> profanity, swearing by God's passions, by the wounds of
> Christ, by the French sickness (venereal disease), by the
> plague . . . I call on the military chaplains to exhort, plead,
> and rebuke them to stop such blasphemy. Instead have the
> soldiers pray the Lord's Prayer and the Apostles' Creed.
> For they need to know that we are not fighting against flesh
> and blood, but against the devil and hell, and that cursing
> and swearing at the Turk won't defeat him.[219]

It is completely consistent with Luther's view of the state
and its powers, to uphold its authority in punishing evil doers
wherever they are found, in high or low places, in secular or
spiritual realms.   The so-called "spiritual estate" cannot claim
immunity from the ruler's sword for crimes committed. "Since the
temporal power is ordained of God to punish the wicked and protect
the good," states the Reformer, "it should be left free to perform its
office in the whole body of Christendom without restriction and
without respect to persons, whether it affects pope, bishops, priests,
monks, nuns, or anyone else."[220]   Luther's point of reference, of
course, is to civil statutes and law. That Luther did not denigrate or
minimize other vocations, when he tabbed the ministry as the
"highest" of all, is evident from this fine statement in his treatise *On
Temporal Authority*:

You ask: Why did not Christ and the apostles bear the sword? Answer: You tell me, why did Christ not take a wife, or become a cobbler or a tailor. If an office or vocation were to be regarded disreputable on the ground that Christ did not pursue it himself, what would become of all the offices and vocations other than the ministry, the one occupation he did follow? Christ pursued his own office and vocation, but he did not thereby reject any other . . . Now, it is not essential to His kingdom that He be a married man, a cobbler, tailor, farmer, prince, hangman, or constable; neither is the temporal sword of law essential to it, but only God's Word and Spirit. It is by these that His people are ruled inwardly.[221]

Problems in the ministry, we can be sure, there will always be, simply because "God regularly does everything through the ministry of human beings."[222] Thus, for example, the question often arises, "Is God able to save without Baptism?" Luther's answer is that "in the church we must judge and teach, in accordance with God's ordered power, that without that outward Baptism no one is saved."[223] But he sets this general rule alongside of the possible exceptions or circumstances which somehow prevent a person from being baptized, and he affirms: "God is able to save without Baptism, just as we believe that infants who, as sometimes happens through the neglect of their parents or through some other mishap, do not receive Baptism are not damned on this account."[224] If Luther seems to be ambivalent in his answer here, it is only apparently so; for he recognizes that Scriptures do not speak of the absolute necessity of Baptism, in the sense that without it no man could possibly be saved. So, not the absence of Baptism, but the despising of it is what Luther emphasizes as the fundamental error.

In a letter to Lazarus Spengler, August 15, 1528, Luther supports the local clergy who demur at celebrating the Lord's Supper every day, simply because that was the rule under the papacy, whether there are communicants or not. Luther sides with them and contends that the frequency of the celebration is a free matter and that we should "not compel anyone to come to or abstain from the sacrament," or arbitrarily legislate when and how often it must be celebrated.[225] By no means does Luther speak for a reduction in the people's opportunity to receive the sacrament; but he does underscore the fact that it is to be a congregational affair, and not a private matter, as it had been with the papistic private masses. Thus there ought be no legal requirement attached to the use of the Sacrament, nor should consciences be burdened as regards the frequency of use or the readiness for attendance; and preachers, too, should not be made to feel unfit to conduct the celebration of the Sacrament because they are sinful men with feet of clay.

A person's baptism should be a matter of certainty, Luther cautioned; "it is better now that Baptism be a matter of certainty, at least for the baptizers themselves, who afterwards could testify before the congregation."[226]   The question concerned a second baptism, if the first was uncertain for some reason; for example, if a midwife was involved who may not have administered it correctly. While Luther does not doubt the validity of the lay baptism, in this case where there was an element of doubt he is stating that the "second baptism" was not really a second Baptism, but the real, or first. This letter was written because of Anabaptistic accusations that the Lutherans themselves were practicing a second baptism, something Luther, of course, strongly repudiates.

In a letter to his prince, Elector John, Luther rejects the plea of a magistrate in the Saxon court who pleads that his "womanizing" is unavoidable and that he should, therefore, not be barred from the Sacrament.   Luther rejects completely such rationalization: "I informed him of my refusal to associate with him personally, and privately forbade him to come to the sacrament."[227] Pastoral practice and discipline remain the same today, with the same concern for unrepented sin.

Faithful church attendance was a lively concern for Luther with his pastoral heart. As he announced the series of sermons on the *Catechism* which he was preparing to preach during the Advent season, 1528, sermons incidentally which became the immediate precursors for the *Small* and *Large Catechisms*, he exhorted his hearers on the First Sunday in Advent, from the pulpit, to see to it that they would be in attendance for this weekday series of sermons which would run consecutively day after day. "I hold the office of pastor, and I will preach these sermons," he states, and "I admonish you to assemble at the designated time with your families."[228] This may sound strongly legalistic rather than evangelical, but if it does, it is only because Luther is seeking to twit their lackadaisical consciences and attitudes towards church attendance and the hearing and study of God's Word. It is the meaning of God's own injunction in the third commandment to "take heed that you do not despise the preaching and neglect the Word!"[229] As Luther treats the meaning and power of Baptism in the Christian's life, he says, among other things, that there is a changed attitude towards God's Word in the life of one who has been baptized, illustrated, for example, in this: "I do not compel you to come to the preaching. But God ought to move you to come."[230] We dare not be cold and indifferent towards His Word!

In his personal life the pastor ought to be a man of prayer as Abraham was,[231] content in his office because of God's call.[232] In many ways the pastor's role is comparable to that of parents in theirs.[233] As to motivation for his office the pastor ought to reflect as follows, says Luther: "I shall perform my duty diligently, not because I am expecting some reward from those whom I serve—for I am simply giving up all hope of gratitude—but I shall imitate the kindness of my heavenly Father."[234] Because the "dog is a faithful animal," I like to compare the office of preacher to them, says Luther; they warn against the intruder who seeks to break in and rob, who insinuates false doctrine, and who seeks to hurt people. Now then, what kind of preachers, indeed, will we be? True "watch dogs"? Or "pillow dogs" who are lazy and protect no one?[235]

Aside from problems of casuistry and difficult theological conundrums, there is the temptation to trust one's own fine thoughts or contemplations as a pastor and servant of God. Luther compares the folly of such self-elevation to the pathetic case of a nun who "thought she was dressed in a golden robe and adorned with a golden crown, like a bride at her marriage," only to discover to her chagrin and horror that instead of "a golden crown" it was "cow dung."[236]

It is a blessed work in which the pastor is engaged, but by no means does it imply that he himself no longer requires forgiveness.[237] Like a good shepherd, the faithful pastor remains steadfast no matter what the peril.[238] Perhaps the loveliest example of all, illustrating Luther's pastoral heart, is found in Luther's own letter of comfort to his mother, May 20, 1531, who was seriously ill and who died shortly thereafter. He points her to her Savior, Jesus Christ, "who suffered for us and for our sins," and in whom, therefore, we can cheerfully look forward to eternal life in heaven.[239] This is the final glorious role and privilege of the Christian pastor, pointing the weary pilgrims to their gracious heavenly Father who welcomes them to Himself in the heavenly home.

NOTES

1   *LW* 41, 114; *WA* 50, 599. Different from Luther, Chemnitz, Walther, Hoenecke, etc., and LC-MS theologians in general, WELS believes that this chapter ought to focus on the duties of the "public ministry" rather than the specific "pastoral office"—consistent with their denial that Scriptural warrant exists for the office *jure divino*

2   Commentary on John 20; quoted in Walther, *KA*, 327.

3   Ibid.

4   *Enchiridion*, 29. cf. Poellot, 38.

5   *Examination of the Council of Trent*, II 678f.

6   From Chemnitz' *Harmony of the Gospels*; cited in Walther, *KA*, 33.

7   *Loc. theol., de eccl.* III, 331; quoted in Walther, *KA*, 368.

8   *Loc. theol., de min. eccl.*, 14.15; cf. Walther, *KA*, 234.

9   *Loc. theol., de min. eccl.*, 265; cf. Walther, *KA*, 241.

10   *Loc. theol., de min. eccl.*, 87; *W*Alther, *KA*, 335.

11   *Loc. theol., de min. eccl.*, 87; Walther, *KA*, 339.

12   *Loc. theol., de min. eccl.*, 7; Walther, *KA*, 369f.

13   *Loc. theol., de min. eccl.*, 201; Walther, *KA*, 378.

14   *Syst. loq.*, VIII, 334; Walther, *KA*, 393.

15   cf. e.g. *KA*, 327-341.

16   Walther, *KA*, 328ff.

17   *LW* 1, 213; *WA* 42, 159.

18   Ibid.

19   *LW* 1, 272; *WA* 42, 201.

20   *LW* 1, 343f.; *WA* 42, 252.

21   *LW* 1, 342; *WA* 42, 252.

22   *LW* 1, 309; *WA* 42, 227.

23   *LW* 2, 19; *WA* 42, 275.

24   *LW* 2, 46; *WA* 42, 294.

25   Ibid.

26   *LW* 2, 382; *WA* 42, 536.

27   *LW* 3, 220; *WA* 43, 32.

28   *LW* 3, 327; *WA* 43, 44.

29   Ibid.

30   *LW* 3, 240f.; *WA* 43, 46ff.

31   Ibid.

32   *LW* 3, 272; *WA* 43, 70.

33   Ibid.

34   *LW* 3, 8f.; *WA* 42, 554.

35   *LW* 8, 54; *WA* 44, 618f.

36   *LW* 12, 403; *WA* 40^2, 458.

37   Ibid.

38   *LW* 31, 51; *WA* 1, 361.

39   *LW* 31, 241; *WA* 1, 622.

40   *LW* 31, 364; *WA* 7, 64.

41   *LW* 31, 357; *WA* 7, 59.

42   *LW* 46, 173; *WA* 30^2, 119.

43   *LW* 4, 124; *WA* 43, 224.

44   Ibid.

45   *LW* 4, 126; *WA* 43, 226.

46   *LW* 4, 128; *WA* 43, 227.

47   *LW* 4, 401; *WA* 43, 424.

48   Ibid.

49   *LW* 5, 142; *WA* 43, 525.

50   *LW* 5, 50; *WA* 43, 462.

51   *LW* 6, 132; *WA* 44, 98.

52   *LW* 6, 163; *WA* 44, 121.

53   *LW* 6, 227; *WA* 44, 168.

54   *LW* 6, 370f.; *WA* 44, 276f.

55   *LW* 7, 185; *WA* 44, 437.

56   *LW* 7, 205; *WA* 4, 451.

57   Ibid.

58   *LW* 8, 130; *WA* 44, 674.

59   Ibid.

60   *LW* 8, 184; *WA* 44, 714.

61   Ibid.

62   *LW* 9, 151; *WA* 44, 660.

63   Ibid.

64   *LW* 9, 179; *WA* 44, 677.

65   *LW* 9, 189; *WA* 14, 685.

66   *LW* 10, 189; *WA* 3, 228.

67   *LW* 11, 312; *WA* 4, 160.

68   *LW* 11, 334; *WA* 4, 184.

69   *LW* 12, 170; *WA* 51, 287.

70   *LW* 12, 258; *WA* 40^2, 554.

71   *LW* 13, 12; *WA* 8, 12.

72   *LW* 14, 91; *WA* 31^1, 162.

73   Ibid.

74   *LW* 15, 146.151; *WA* 20, 160.163.

75   *LW* 15, 151f.; *WA* 20, 163.

76   *LW* 16, 95; *WA* 31^2, 66.

77   *LW* 26, 10; *WA* 40^1, 49.

78   *LW* 17, 277; *WA* 31^2, 474.

79   *LW* 7, 316; *WA* 31^2, 504.

80   *LW* 17, 323; *WA* 31^2, 510.

81   *LW* 17, 350; *WA* 31^2, 532. Cf. *LW* 20, 103; *WA* 13, 634.

82   *LW* 18, 228; *WA* 13, 313.

83   *LW* 18, 415; *WA* 13, 699.

84   *LW* 19, 157; *WA* 19, 355.

85   *LW* 19, 159; *WA* 19, 356.

86   *LW* 20, 45.225; *WA* 13, 587.560.

87   *LW* 20, 60.233; *WA* 13, 601; 23, 567.

88   *LW* 20, 185; *WA* 23, 526.

89   *LW* 20, 292; *WA* 23, 618.

90   *LW* 20, 299; *WA* 23, 624.

91   *LW* 22, 225; *WA* 46, 735.

92   Ibid.

93   *LW* 22, 254; *WA* 46, 767.

94   *LW* 22, 308; *WA* 47, 37.

95   *LW* 22, 372; *WA* 47, 95.

96   Ibid.

97	*LW* 22, 473; *WA* 47, 184.
98	*LW* 22, 526; *WA* 47, 227.
99	*LW* 23, 174; *WA* 33, 276.
100	*LW* 23, 274; *WA* 33, 436.
101	*LW* 23, 341; *WA* 33, 549.
102	*LW* 25, 5; *WA* 56, 6.
103	*LW* 25, 7; *WA* 56, 8.
104	*LW* 25, 447; *WA* 56, 455.
105	*LW* 25, 521; *WA* 56, 525.
106	*LW* 26, 186ff.; *WA* 40[1], 309ff.
107	*LW* 26, 220; *WA* 40[1], 351.
108	*LW* 27, 308; *WA* 2, 548.
109	*LW* 28, 269; *WA* 26, 41.
110	*LW* 28, 330; *WA* 26, 82.
111	*LW* 29, 31; *WA* 25, 26.
112	Ibid.
113	*LW* 30, 14; *WA* 12, 270.
114	*LW* 30, 17; *WA* 12, 272.
115	*LW* 30, 18; *WA* 12, 274.
116	*LW* 30, 19ff.; *WA* 12, 274ff.
117	*LW* 30, 25; *WA* 12, 280.
118	*LW* 30, 26; *WA* 12, 281.
119	*LW* 30, 272; *WA* 20, 704.
120	*LW* 32, 75f.; *WA* 7, 421.
121	*LW* 35, 119; *WA* 10[1], 10f.
122	Ibid.
123	*LW* 36, 82; *WA* 6, 543.
124	*LW* 37, 92; *WA* 23, 189.
125	*LW* 37, 140f.; *WA* 23, 267f.
126	*LW* 38, 102; *WA* 30[2], 599.
127	*LW* 38, 153f.; *WA* 38, 200f.
128	*LW* 38, 199; *WA* 38, 240.
129	Ibid.
130	*LW* 38, 202; *WA* 38, 242.
131	*LW* 39, 99; *WA* 6, 320.

132   *LW* 39, 101ff.; *WA* 6, 321ff.

133   *LW* 41, 344ff.; *WA* 54, 273f.

134   *LW* 41, 350; *WA* 54, 278.

135   *LW* 41, 353; *WA* 54, 280.

136   *LW* 41, 354; *WA* 54, 281.

137   *LW* 39, 314; *WA* 11, 416. Quoted from *A Christian Congregation Has the Right to Call*, 1523.

138   *LW* 39, 28-44 passim; *WA* 6, 157-169.

139   LW 39, 40; *WA* 6, 166.

140   *LW* 40, 269-318 passim; *WA* 26, 195-240.

141   *LW* 40, 309; *WA* 26, 232.

142   *LW* 42, 57; *WA* 2, 112.

143   *LW* 42, 176; *WA* 6, 133.

144   *LW* 43, 35; *WA* 10^2, 402.

145   *LW* 44, 57; *WA* 6, 231. *Good Works Treatise.*

146   *LW* 44, 224; *WA* 7, 291. *An Instruction to Penitent*, 1521.

147   *LW* 44, 226; *WA* 7, 295.

148   *LW* 47, 297; *WA* 53, 545.

149   *LW* 48, 27f.; *WA*, BR 1, 72f.

150   *LW* 48, 47; *WA*, BR 1, 111.

151   *LW* 48, 221; *WA*, BR 2, 335.

152   *LW* 48, 262; *WA*, BR 2, 359.

153   *LW* 48, 311; *WA*, BR 2, 390.

154   *LW* 49, 87; *WA*, BR 3, 373.

155   *LW* 49, 101; *WA*, BR 4, 452.

156   *LW* 49, 175; *WA*, BR 4, 279f.

157   *LW* 51, 35; *WA* 1, 267.

158   *LW* 51, 77; *WA* 10^3, 18f.

159   *LW* 51, 83; *WA* 10^3, 29f.

160   *LW* 51, 99; *WA* 10^3, 62.

161   *LW* 51, 342f.; *WA* 49, 599f.; cf. *LW* 51, 354; *WA* 49, 613f.

162   *LW* 51, 388; *WA* 51, 191.

163   *LW* 52, 32; *WA* 10^1, 129.

164   Ibid.

165   *LW* 52, 72; *WA* 10^1, 223.

166   *LW* 52, 206; *WA* 10¹, 627f.

167   *LW* 53 passim; *WA* 12, 35ff. 205ff.; 18, 417ff.; 35 passim.

168   *LW* 53, 304; *WA* 35, 467.

169   *LW* 2, 170; *WA* 42, 381.

170   *LW* 3, 359.361; *WA* 43, 133.135.

171   *LW* 3, 182; *WA* 43, 5.

172   *LW* 4, 204; *WA* 43, 282f.

173   Ibid.

174   Ibid.

175   *LW* 5, 71; *WA* 43, 478.

176   *LW* 5, 264; *WA* 43, 610f.

177   *LW* 8, 63; *WA* 44, 626. John Frederick, the Magnanimous, whose reign began in 1532 in Saxony, was the territorial prince at the time of Luther's writing of *Genesis Commentary*.

178   *LW* 8, 125; *WA* 44, 671.

179   *LW* 8, 126; *WA* 44, 671.

180   *LW* 8, 270; *WA* 44, 777.

181   *LW* 8, 310; *WA* 44, 807f.

182   *LW* 9, 140; *WA* 14, 653.

183   cf. also *LW* 45, 166.320; *WA* 12, 11ff.; 15, 360ff.

184   *LW* 9, 250; *WA* 14, 719. cf. Luther's Commentary on 1 Tim., *LW* 28, 348f.; *WA* 26, 95f.

185   *LW* 20, 70; *WA* 13, 608.

186   *LW* 22, 220; *WA* 46, 728f. *Sermons on John's Gospel*.

187   *LW* 22, 526; *WA* 47, 227.

188   *LW* 27, 122.126; *WA* 40², 157.160f.

189   *LW* 46, 221; *WA* 30², 529.

190   *LW* 46, 223; *WA* 30², 532f.

191   *LW* 46, 225; *WA* 30², 535.

192   *LW* 46, 231; *WA* 30², 545f.

193   Ibid.

194   *LW* 51, 353; *WA* 49, 614.

195   *LW* 1, 212; *WA* 42, 158.

196   *LW* 2, 36; *WA* 42, 288.

197   *LW* 3, 342; *WA* 43, 121.

198   *LW* 16, 204; *WA* 31², 144.

199   *LW* 5, 16; *WA* 43, 439. cf. *LW* 16, 249; *WA* 31², 181.

200   *LW* 2, 56; *WA* 42, 301.

201   *LW* 28, 153; *WA* 36, 609.

202   *LW* 17, 343.249; *WA* 31², 526.453.

203   *LW* 24, 337; *WA* 46, 35.

204   *LW* 28, 66; *WA* 36, 490.

205   Ibid.

206   *LW* 3, 5; *WA* 42, 551.

207   *LW* 4, 210; *WA* 43, 287.

208   *LW* 6, 21; *WA* 44, 14f.

209   *LW* 13, 140; *WA* 40³, 593.

210   *LW* 22, 48; *WA* 46, 577.

211   *LW* 27, 297; *WA* 2, 541.

212   *LW* 47, 274ff.; *WA* 53, 527.

213   *LW* 51, 222; *WA* 34², 157.

214   *LW* 51, 226; *WA* 34², 163.

215   *LW* 4, 76; *WA* 43, 190.

216   *LW* 4, 202; *WA* 43, 281.

217   *LW* 16, 275; *WA* 31², 200.

218   Ibid.

219   *LW* 43, 228f.; *WA* 51, 602. *From Appeal for Prayer Against the Turks*, 1541. WELS reviewer deemed it misleading to compare office of military chaplain in Luther's day with contemporary U.S.A. chaplaincies. This objection must be seen in the light of WELS policy which opposes and does not allow its clergy to serve in the armed forces as chaplains.

220   *LW* 44, 130f.; *WA* 6, 409. *From Open Letter to Christian Nobility*, 1520.

221   *LW* 45, 100; *WA* 11, 258.

222   *LW* 3, 274; *WA* 43, 71.

223   Ibid.

224   Ibid.

225   *LW* 49, 204ff.; *WA*, BR 4, 534ff.

226   *LW* 50, 15; *WA*, BR 6, 96f.

227   *LW* 50, 24; *WA*, BR 6, 122.

228   *LW* 51, 135.

229   *LW* 51, 144; *WA* 30[1], 65.

230   *LW* 51, 191; *WA* 30[1], 120f.

231   *LW* 3, 8f.; *WA* 42, 554.

232   *LW* 3, 128; *WA* 42, 639.

233   *LW* 4, 224; *WA* 43, 296.

234   *LW* 7, 97; *WA* 44, 371.

235   *LW* 17, 265; *WA* 31[2], 465f.

236   *LW* 3, 277; *WA* 43, 73.

237   *LW* 27, 121; *WA* 40[2], 155.

238   *LW* 43, 121; *WA* 23, 340. *On Whether One May Flee From a Deadly Plague*, 1527.

239   *LW* 50, 17ff.; *WA*, BR 6, 103ff.

Chapter 4

The Call into Office

Previously we have seen that the nature of the ministry has to do with the means of grace, the marks of the church, the public preaching and witnessing of the Gospel. This responsibility and authority rest fundamentally and first of all with the Christian congregation, with the royal priesthood. The office of public ministry, or pastorate, which congregations establish in their midst is by divine command, and includes directives as regards the criteria by which such a servant or steward should be judged qualified for the office. The necessity of this office is not a mere utilitarian discovery, or ecclesiastical arrangement, but a divine institution. The Scriptures make it very plain that it is an office stemming from the apostolic office, its predecessor, as a distinct entity which is to be delegated through the royal priests upon chosen successors of the apostles. The latter were called directly by God for service in His kingdom; the former, or successors of the apostles, are chosen or elected mediately through the instrumentality of the priesthood of believers at a given locale, that is, a local congregation. Walther had stated in his fourth thesis on *Church and Ministry* that it is the "true church of believers to which Christ has given the keys of the kingdom of heaven," and that "therefore this Church is the real and sole holder and bearer of the spiritual, divine, and heavenly blessings, rights, powers, offices, etc., which Christ has gained and which are available in His Church."[1]

Theirs are the Keys, and to them, therefore, belong the authority and power of calling a qualified pastor into their service. It, the congregation, has not only received such power, but it also has received directives in God's Word that (and how) it should establish and maintain the office of pastor in its midst. The key doctrine here which Walther uncovered for himself and the synod which he served in his day was the priesthood of believers. In spite of considerable turmoil and the threat of hierarchical tyranny, he learned by assiduous study of Scripture and Luther how central this doctrine was to the proper understanding of the church and the ministry. At the same time he repudiated all populist extremism, that is, any uncontrolled sort of anarchy in the congregation's handling of its prerogatives. Closely following Scripture's injunctions and Luther's guidelines, Walther taught that the office of

Pfarrer, bishop or overseer, should be filled with a qualified public servant, who in the name of the congregation could preach and administer Word and Sacraments in accord with God's holy will. It was not to be the result of *ad hoc* notions and/or actions of this or that group of people.

If the key doctrine for Walther was the royal priesthood of believers, the key word in the relation of the called pastor and the calling congregation was *Uebertragung*, delegating. By the will of God the local congregation conferred, or delegated, the office of pastor upon a qualified man. It was a position of high trust. Luther finds a parallel in the arrangement whereby a public magistrate is entrusted with his office by the people. By delegating such authority and trust the conferring body by no means surrendered its rights or powers. What the pastor, thus, would do for the congregation, would be that which was fundamentally their, or its, responsibility, and it would be correct to say, therefore, that a pastor does no more, can do no more, than that which a congregation itself can and should do. By the same token, it was God's divine plan and mandate that that which thus belonged to all, the priesthood of believers, should not be administered publicly by all but by one whom the congregation called for that specific purpose and who was qualified for the high calling. This did not constitute him, or his office, into a kind of means of grace (virtually the Romanist view, also so-called "high church" Lutherans!), but a duly called servant of God. This latter fact, in turn, kept the office in highest esteem among the royal priests, for they could hardly demean or show mere patronizing or token respect for an office which God Himself had ordained. Their pastor was doing for them what God had earnestly entrusted to their conscientious care and concern. Nor did the fact that the pastor's office was indirectly conferred upon him through their call diminish in the slightest the divine nature of his office and task in connection with the marks of the church, Word and Sacrament. His burden of office was to teach the whole of God's truth faithfully, comfort the troubled, safeguard the Word from adulteration, exhort and admonish his flock in pursuit of godly life.

The New Testament very clearly supports the ecclesiastical order or relationship of the general priesthood with the office of the called pastor. It was an order established by God Himself. The apostles entered into their office by Christ's own direct call; the apostles in turn instructed and guided the congregations, the possessors of the Keys, to elect, call, and commission their successors as bishops, elders, shepherds, pastors. (Matt. 18:17ff.; 1 Cor. 3:21f.; 1 Pet. 2:9. Cf. 2 Tim. 2; Acts 18:24ff.; 1 Cor. 14:30; 1 Tim. 3:2ff.; Tit. 1:5ff.; Acts 14:23; 6:2f.; 13:1ff.; 1:15ff.) Theoretically, each (male) Christian, of mature and certified qualifications, had the potential thus of becoming the called servant of a Christian congregation. Luther points this out in his treatise, *A Christian Congregation Has the Right to Call*, 1523.[2] Of the important passage, 1 Corinthians 14:31,39-40, in which the apostle Paul instructs the Corinthians concerning who may speak in the churches, Luther states in the same treatise: "Let this passage be your sure foundation, because it gives such an overwhelming power to the Christian congregation to preach, to permit preaching and to call."[3]

At the same place Luther also notes that the apostles did not arrogantly assume to themselves a kind of tyrannical rule over the congregations, but enlisted their concurring approval and consent in the election or commissioning of those who would "rule" over them as pastors. The congregation's call was, therefore, of the essence and determinative. This ruled out self-styled preachers of the *Schwaermer* or Enthusiast type who claimed a direct or immediate call similar to the apostles'. In a sermon from the *Church Postils*, on Matthew 4:18-22, Luther notes that there are two types of calls distinguished by the New Testament writers: the direct call, like the apostles', and the indirect call through the congregations, like their successors'. Should any individual claim more than this, "we will first want to test your doctrine," says Luther, "whether it agrees with God's Word, for false prophets can also claim that they do signs, as Moses pointed out to the Hebrews."[4]

It was such testing and election which led to the choice of Matthias in Acts 1, to the commissioning of Paul and Barnabas by the Antioch congregation in Acts 14, and to the electing of the "brother" who was to accompany Paul in Macedonia, 2 Corinthians 8:18f. The solemn, divine call by the Christian congregation then, as now, was the God-willed method of procuring successors in the ministry for the churches after the time of the apostles. Whatever variations may have entered in under given circumstances or cases, the fundamental principle still abides: the Scriptures do not teach or know of any other method of filling the pastoral office than through the call of the Christian congregations.

What Luther has to say in the *Smalcald Articles* concerning ordination and the call conforms very closely to the above. With considerable elasticity, under the circumstances prevailing in the Reformation era, Luther grants that the Lutheran party would permit faithful bishops in the future to ordain and confirm in our churches, out of a spirit of love and forbearance, as long as they recognize that such authority is man-made only, and not by divine necessity or ordering. And if, as they now do, they refuse to ordain ministers for our churches, says the Reformer, then "we ourselves will and ought to ordain suitable persons to this office." (*SA* III, x, 3)

In the second part of the Tractate to the *Smalcald Articles*, "On the Power and Primacy of the Pope," the Lutheran Confessors at Smalcald spelled out a similar stance, "that the church retains the right to elect and ordain pastors," and when the ecclesiastical authorities, then governing, refused to do it, "the churches are in duty bound before God to ordain for themselves pastors and ministers." (Tractate 67-72, cf. also 11, 24.) A significant historical precedent was set in the church, very early, all the way back to the Council of Nicaea. To this practice the Tractate refers:

> Again the Council of Nicea determined that bishops should be elected by their own churches, in the presence of some neighboring bishop or several. The same was observed also in the West and in the Latin churches, as Cyprian and Augustine testify. For Cyprian says in his fourth letter to Cornelius: "Accordingly, as regards the divine observance and apostolic practice, you must diligently keep and practice what is also observed among us and in almost all the provinces, that for celebrating ordinations properly, whatever bishops of the same province live nearest should come together with the people for whom a pastor is being appointed, and the bishop should be chosen in the presence of the people, who must fully know the life of each one, which we also have seen done among us at the ordination of our colleague Sabinus, that by the suffrage of the entire brotherhood, and by the judgment of the bishops who had assembled in their presence, the episcopate was conferred and hands laid on him." Cyprian calls this custom "a divine tradition and an apostolic observance," and affirms that it is observed in almost all the provinces. (Tractate, 13f.)

After citing other ancient synods and early writers, like Jerome and Gregory I, the Lutheran Confessors ask: "How can the Pope be over the entire Church by divine right when the Church has the election (or the right to vote)?" (Tractate, 20)

It is evident from the above, since the Confessions have their roots in Luther's theological thought drawn from Scripture, that the office of pastor is 1) divinely ordained and instituted by God; 2) mediately or indirectly conferred through the call of the congregation(s); and 3) the royal priesthood of believers at a given locale (by synecdoche only the believers present constitute the true church in such external grouping!) retain the powers and prerogatives of the Office of the Keys, even as they delegate the public exercise of Word and Sacrament to a called, qualified man who should do the preaching and teaching among them.

Luther was called on very early to clarify the points stated. This he did in a number of treatises which were directly addressed to contemporary situations involving test cases, as in Swabia (1525), to the peasants in 1525, and also to the congregation at Leisnig, 1523. We shall have occasion later to look at these statements more closely. What he expressed in these specific instances, however, were not only *ad hoc* random judgments; they concurred completely and perfectly with his theological stance in connection with the important doctrines on the royal priesthood of believers and their relationship to the called pastor.

Chemnitz, Luther's theological heir, speaks at considerable length on the whole matter in his chapter "Concerning Holy Orders" in his *Examen Concilii Tridentini.* "The question here is by whose voice and vote this election and call ought to be made in order that it may be possible to declare that it is divine?"[5] Chemnitz proceeds to cite the examples of the apostles, Acts 1, as Matthias is elected; Acts 6, as the deacons are chosen to assist the apostles in auxiliary duties; Acts 14, as Paul and Barnabas procure elders for all the churches to which they had brought the Gospel. Then as to the procedure, Chemnitz notes: "However, they did not take the right and authority of choosing and calling to themselves alone," but did it with the vote and consent of the people.[6] As a result, "in their choosing and calling both presbyters and people are partners."[7] Chemnitz detects a happy, freely- given cooperation and consensus of purpose on the part of the enfranchised people, the members of the congregations, and the apostles who did the guiding in such election of qualified teachers in the church. He concludes his Biblical and historical survey of the early church practice in this matter with the reminder: "I undertook this report in order to show that our churches have restored the true and lawful manner of choosing and calling, which was in use in the apostolic, primitive, and ancient church."[8]

In his gem-like *Enchiridion*, or *Handbook on Christian Doctrine*, Chemnitz, at about the same time of the issuance of the *Examen*, stated that the power and right to call pastors inheres first of all in God's divine injunction, and then in the congregation to whom He gives this right to call qualified men.[9] Chemnitz notes that in given instances the magistracies or powers of the state have become involved in this appointment of pastors, through consistories and the like; but he also judges this usage to be an exception to the rule, and in any case fundamentally dependent upon the authority and rights which have been delegated to such powers-that-be by the people. In this connection he recognizes a fundamental principle, which Walther later identifies as the *Uebertragungslehre*, that congregations may, if circumstances so dictate, especially in very large congregations, delegate the responsibility of calling to a designated representative body, such as a voters' assembly, or a board of elders, and the like. Through all, however, it is the Lord's will being exercised through the elective process by the people.[10]

Johann Gerhard, in the generation following Chemnitz, similarly taught that 1) the fundamental right to call men into the ministry belongs to God; 2) God continues to exercise this right through the indirect, or mediate call of a pastor by a congregation; 3) the Keys first and always are the inherent possession of the priesthood of believers, in the Christian congregation; and 4) the life of the church revolves around three estates or levels, none of which is greater than the other, but all of which contribute to its well-being: people, pastors, governing officials.[11] The latter, of course, are selected not by divine edict but simple expediency, for the governing of things decently and in order; for this there was apostolic and early church precedent. Fundamentally, however, one thing never changes, and that is the rudimentary authority and power which inheres in the Christian people. "Those who possess the Keys to the Kingdom of heaven as a gift from Christ Himself, possess the fundamental right and duty of calling qualified men into the pastoral office."[12] It is Gerhard's position that they have the right and duty to distinguish faithful shepherds from the unfaithful and untrue, and this right flows simply from the prior right of calling pastors into their service.[13]

Quenstedt, too, asserts that the basic enabling authority behind the ministry is God; the secondary authority necessary for the establishment of the office of the public ministry is the congregation of believers.[14] "The authority to choose and call pastoral servants into the ministry is by divine right, not first of all that of the clergy or those in ecclesiastical office, nor of the magistracy or rulers, nor simply that of the people, but of the whole church (or congregation); and without their consent and approval the calling cannot be considered valid."[15] Baier says simply: "The church (congregation) has the right and power, after its organization, to call pastors into its service."[16]

Walther also quotes approvingly the comments of Veit Ludwig von Seckendorf, Lutheran statesman and scholar, who became the head of the University of Halle in the latter part of the 17th century. Seckendorf, too, grounds his comments on the doctrine of the priesthood of believers as fundamental to a proper understanding of the doctrines of the church and ministry. He then raises the question whether it would be necessary in some far off land first to send the candidates for the ministry to the homeland consistory for proper validation and ordination, or whether this could not in fact be done there where the congregations were being founded and formed. Did these congregations, who were calling, not have the right to ordain or install into office those whom they called? His answer is: "Such congregations have the full right to establish the ministry in their midst and ordain their pastors."[17]

Baier articulates the position to which Walther himself also eventually came and with which he concurred:

> To the Church, after it has been planted, belong the right and power to appoint ministers. For she has the keys of the kingdom of heaven, Matthew 16:19; 18:18, given her as a Bride, by Christ, her Husband; and, therefore, as it is her prerogative to open and close the kingdom of heaven, so is it also her prerogative to appoint ministers, through whom she may open and close (the same). And, if we consider that the Church is a republic, and that the ministers of the Word are, so to speak, the magistrates or conductors of

public affairs, upon whom the care of the whole republic
rests, it is easily understood that the power to appoint them
is vested, *per se* and in the very nature of the case, in the
whole Church; nor does it belong to any one part, *unless, by
the common consent of all, it be transferred to some one
part.*[18]

Neither Baier, nor certainly Walther, have a kind of
Groszkirche in mind here when the "whole Church" is designated as
the ultimate authority under God for the calling of pastors.   The
tertium comparationis is the Christian congregation, the gathering of
believers at one place, who under God have the authority and the
duty to call a pastor into the public ministry of Word and Sacrament
in their midst.   *They* in turn may delegate this task to a smaller
body, if it is expedient; or again to a larger body, like a synod, if
expedient; but the fundamental right and authority will forever
remain with that entity, the local congregation, where Word and
Sacrament are regularly administered.   This was Walther's stance.
It was well-founded upon the writings of the Reformer and upon the
Lutheran Confessions, as well as, first of all, the Holy Scriptures
themselves.
   Luther was convinced that God did not desire to suspend the
public ministry, since He went to such lengths in supplying a line of
successors after the apostles. Nor was this to be a haphazard affair,
after the manner of the *Schwaermer*, or Enthusiasts, who sit in a
corner, as it were, waiting for the Holy Spirit to plummet upon them
suddenly.   The order was to be through the congregations calling
qualified men into their service as pastors. In a sermon on Paul's
conversion, Acts 9:1-22, in 1534, Luther warns against the Enthusiasts' version of the "Spirit-initiated call" into the ministry, stating:
"In place of the lovely Dove they will find a black raven, the devil
himself."[19] In the Old Testament in very many instances God's call
came directly to His chosen prophets and spokesmen; in the New
Testament it was quite the reverse: God chose to get His men for
the ministry through the instrumentality of the fellowship of
believers. Thus in a sermon on Exodus 4:1ff., as Luther expounds
on Moses' call and relates it to his own time in the 16th century, he
comments that nowadays it is possible that a man come to a place
where there are no Christians, begin to witness for the Gospel "and

instruct them in Christianity; and if a group then came together, chose him, and called him as their bishop, he would have a call."[20]

The basic principle was still the same, Luther observes, "for *God* set up the ministry of the Word in this people, where the hearers may sit at His feet and hear His Word."[21] Christ is the High Priest par excellence in both the Old and New Covenant. But there is this difference: while in the Old Testament there was a special order of priests, in the New Testament "He has bestowed this name on us, too," by "the general status of being a Christian," by our status as "fellow heirs through Christ," "as children of this Priest," by our baptism, for "every Christian is a priest already in Baptism."[22] In this same context, however, Luther is quick to point out the difference between the priesthood which belongs to every believer and the office of pastor. "We must make a distinction between the office or service of bishops, pastors, and preachers, and the general status of being a Christian."[23] The latter results from spiritual birth as children of God through faith and baptism; the former owes its beginning to their call or appointment to office. Even though the task of the pastoral office is unique and uniquely the office of one, the ministry of the Word itself "belongs to them all," to the "whole church," and from the church it takes its origin.[24] In commenting on the meaning of John 20:21-23, Luther at many places reiterates the point that unique powers were not given to St. Peter alone, but to all the disciples, indeed to the priesthood of all believers. If this is not so, then what is said in Matthew 18, John 20, and Acts 1, concerning the powers given by Christ to the church would make Him "a liar and heretic."[25] The Keys belonged to the church, the believers, and not to Peter only!

No one need dispute that God called Abraham directly, as with the other patriarchs and prophets; "but when you are called to the ministry," Luther says to his contemporaries of New Testament days, "you should consider the voice of the community as the voice of God, and obey."[26] However when the pope usurps this authority for himself and "claims to be the lord of the Word," this man is not only a "rude egotist," but "is altogether in conflict with the Word of God."[27] Abraham's calling was direct from God and accompanied by confirming signs; "but you should not ask for a sign from God because Abraham did," admonishes Luther.[28] Times and circumstances were different then from now. But one thing remains the same, "The call is required," and though today it comes mediately through men, one can still ask, and must ask, "Where is the call?"[29] The difference between Jacob and Esau lay primarily in this, says Luther, "that Jacob was appointed bishop, lord, and governor of the church and his house by the Word of God through the blessing of his Father Isaac," while Esau was not.[30] In similar manner Joseph was set apart from his "rustic group of brothers" by Jacob's blessing,[31] following the footsteps of his father as spiritual head, or "bishop," in his home, thus fulfilling the vocation bestowed by God.[32]

In this context Luther elevates each man's vocation, whatever it be, commenting that "it becomes each one to serve the one God and Lord of all according to one's ability and vocation."[33] So much abuse had entered into the spiritual, ecclesiastical offices of the church in his day, that Luther is led to say "that a woman suckling an infant or a maid sweeping a threshing floor with a broom is just as pleasing to God as an idle nun or a lazy Carthusian."[34]

Shortly before Luther left for the Coburg, 1530, he wrote a commentary on Psalm 82. It contains a number of important statements concerning the pastoral office. For one thing, Luther is greatly disturbed by the self-styled preachers who grab pulpits in helter-skelter, rabble-rousing sort of ways, like Muentzer and Karlstadt, among others. "Every bishop or pastor has his definite parish," is Luther's stiff reminder. The rule ought to be "that no preacher, however pious or upright, take it upon himself either to preach to the people of a papistical or heretical pastor, or to teach them privately without the knowledge and consent of that pastor," or, in other words, without a call.[35] "It is true that all Christians are priests," he reasserts in behalf of his pet emphasis concerning the royal prerogative of all believers, "but not all are pastors."[36] "To be a pastor one must be not only a Christian and a priest but must have an office and a field of work committed to him. This call and command make pastors and preachers."[37]

This rule is to be inviolable, in Luther's book. Even in his own case. His high status as a doctor of theology and professor at Wittenberg does not entitle him to enter any pulpit as he chooses. It is true that "as a Doctor," he says, "I must truly confess to the end of my life," for this is my sworn obligation by that office conferred upon me, whether before emperor or pope.[38] But for his preaching at Wittenberg, in the *Stadtkirche*, Luther recognizes another principle at work, the call that he has as pastor, or associate pastor, in that parish. So he states: "Even if I were not a Doctor, I am, nevertheless, a regularly called preacher and may teach my own people with writings."[39] Then, if others want to have these writings, too, that is their right and privilege, if they desire.

The safeguarding of the congregation's rights and integrity was never better stated than when Luther penned his treatise in behalf of the Leisnig congregation, 1523. To the objection that it was the apostles that did the governing, not the congregations, in the early church, that it was Timothy and Titus whom Paul told to ordain elders in the churches, Luther answered: "They still could not and should not do so without the will, the election, and the call of the congregation."[40] He realizes that exceptions might occur, that circumstances might alter cases, as "where need made it necessary, just as everyone should hurry to the scene of a fire in town and not wait until asked to come," in order to help.[41] Luther cites Acts 6 as an example "that the apostles were not permitted to institute persons as deacons without the knowledge and consent of the congregation."[42] In the same context, he advises, because there is present need, that "one must call from among the congregation because now there are no responsible bishops as there were in the days of Titus and Timothy."

It is much the same advice and counsel which Luther shares with the Bohemian Christians who were facing a similar dilemma, procuring qualified pastors. He sets down very plainly the rights of the Christian congregation: "Since they are a people of God it is due them that no one be set over them without their election," in order that the pastors may have "a certain call."[43] At considerable length, at the conclusion of this treatise to the Bohemians, Luther repeats that it is the congregation's duty to call; expounds on the pastor's duties, title, tenure; insists that this practice is not an innovation first drummed up by the Lutherans; describes in detail the solemnity of the calling and ordaining ceremony; and finally reassures the people of the parish, that though they may be dubbed heretics and outcasts from the church, "they truly are a church of God," for "a church is not known by customs but by the Word."[44] *Against the Infiltrating and Clandestine Preachers*, 1532, Luther, therefore, advises that "there is a way of convicting them easily and effectively." Just ask them, if they have a call? Who sent you?[45] These sheep and parish stealers do not have the credentials "to

preach and teach, as a parish pastor has."[46]   That is why, says
Luther, "If we emphasize the matter of the call, we can worry the
devil," and keep them from destroying and bringing to naught the
parish system.[47]

The nature of the divine call and outfitting is totally
dependent upon God's doing, otherwise there is fear and anxiety.[48]
It was so for the prophets; it is still the same thing for pastors today,
says Luther.   The preacher must himself "hunger and thirst for
righteousness," otherwise he will soon "become tired and impatient
and be chased into a corner" and be of little help to other people.[49]
But "a pious preacher has snatched many souls out of the jaws of
the devil and brought them to heaven."[50]   Luther sees his own office
as twofold, namely, "as a preacher and a doctor," and he knows that
God will require an accounting from him on both counts.[51]   The
Christian pastor has a weighty task; for God calls him to fulfill his
office in such a way that he is a "salt,"[52] a "light" especially against
the gainsayers,[53] public proclaimers of the truth,[54] "preachers of the
Gospel" who stand squarely in the Scripture, like the heroes of faith
at Augsburg, who testified "that our confession is purely Scriptural
and does not conflict with any article of faith,"[55] who are prepared
to rebuke those who defy God and His Word, "whatever does not
square with true doctrine."[56]   It is in the nature of things that
despisers of the Gospel are also despisers of the ministry, and "they
trample the ministers and the preachers underfoot and treat them
more cruelly than the peasants treat their hogs."[57]

In his commentary on John's Gospel, Luther expounds
carefully how the church is gathered through the preaching of the
Word, through Baptism, and the Lord's Supper, and then adds:

> This church has the power to engage pastors. The church
> selects such as are able and competent, not for their own
> sakes but for the welfare of the church. And in an emergen-
> cy everyone must take care of his own needs. Yet not all
> are authorized to preach, but only one is to preach to the
> entire congregation. Thus the ministry is not mine; it
> belongs to all the others; it is a public office and confes-
> sion.[58]

This form of ministry, Luther states, is by God's own
design; "it will endure and is not to be replaced by any other." The

incumbents of the office will die, but the office goes on.[59]   We
cannot argue with God's method of doing things: "We are sent
according to this method; according to it, we elect and send others,
and we install them in their ministry."[60] In this way God provides
workers for His vineyard. It is all tied to God's Word, not to man's
inventive mind, novelties, or cleverness. The persons of those who
fill the office, whether John Bugenhagen, or Martin Luther, are not
important; the Word which they proclaim and with which they are
entrusted, this is the issue, and this they must proclaim; and for this
they must have God's call through the congregation. "If a fanatic
were to come and ask to preach here," avers Luther, "I would not
permit it, even if he were twenty-four times more learned than I."
The same rule applies for me, Luther continues. "If I myself were
twice as learned as I am, I would nonetheless not preach in Leipzig;
for the ministry in that city has not been entrusted to me."[61] As a
called minister, a difference enters in; then a man is no longer his
own man; he is God's man. "Now he is a different person; now he
is attired in new clothes; now he is clad in authority. One must
distinguish between a public and a private person," Luther admonishes in behalf of the called pastor.[62] It is an authority, however, which
no faithful pastor ventures to abuse, for it "exists for the benefit of
his charges," and it would be better for him to resign than in any
way to offend one of God's sheep or little lambs; it is this he has
"been dedicated to, initiated in, and sanctified for."[63]

It is the call into the office which distinguishes the pastor
from the other royal priests. Luther states:

> Here is an example. If a layman should perform all the
> outward functions of a priest, celebrating Mass, confirming,
> absolving, administering the sacraments, dedicating altars,
> churches, vestments, vessels, etc., it is certain that these
> actions in all respects would be similar to those of a true
> priest, in fact, they might be performed more reverently and
> properly than the real ones. But because he has not been
> consecrated and ordained and sanctified, he performs
> nothing at all, but is only playing church and deceiving
> himself and his followers.[64]

Behind every pastor's call into his office is a definite authority, first of all God Himself, and then the agency or agent through which the call is issued. "Since the time of the apostles this has been the usual method of calling" a pastor into his office, Luther avers.[65] It is not a matter for "one or two citizens" to decide on their own, since that would lead to chaos; there needs to be definite order. In the apostles' day God acted directly, as with the apostle Paul himself; since then He channels the call through the people, or, Luther admits, through a recognized head, like the magistrates or the prince, acting in behalf of the people.[66]

The people deserve to have a trustworthy pastor, with the designated qualifications, so that "they may know that (the) word is in fact the Word of God."[67] In Galatia, as the apostle Paul's letter to the congregation evidences, there was much confusion and false doctrine, because "false ministers, the devil's ministers, had sneaked (in) under false pretenses."[68] Yet, in spite of such "wolves and robbers," the church was still there, because the faithful believers had the Word and their baptism.[69] But great harm had been done, and still is done by such intruders, for they give the "appearance of holiness," greater in fact than the "sincere preachers of the Gospel" and purport to be "the very pupils of the apostles" themselves.[70] "But," says Luther of such upstarts, "the holier the heretics seem to be in external appearance, the more damage they cause."[71] Luther's warning applies to every century, every nook and cranny, of the church's life and history down through the ages.

It is not a matter of playing church to assume the office of pastor for a congregation. Timothy, Luther points out, had faithful hands laid upon him in blessing at his ordination, but the apostle Paul's exhortation to him centered with all seriousness on the "calling" which he had received and which, as a good soldier of the cross, he must fulfill.[72] In turn, the apostle Paul exhorted Timothy to exercise due caution and *deliberate* speed in entrusting the office of pastor to any aspirant.[73] In any case, the call is of the essence; for "he who has the Word of God does not immediately teach it unless he is called," thus stepping out from the midst of the general priesthood, to assume the functions of that priesthood which are laid upon him by his call.[74]

It is evident in apostolic parlance, says Luther, that a "bishop is the same as elder," or "the steward to whom the Lord has entrusted everything," namely, the Lord's treasured property, which is the Gospel.[75] The apostle Peter likewise lays heavy stress upon the pastoral call for those who are fellow elders with him.[76] It is quite evident, however, Luther says in his *Thirty-Two Articles Against the Louvainists*, 1545, that there is no such thing as grades among the clergy ordained of God, and certainly the ministry must not be viewed as a sacrament and a kind of means of grace.[77] Pastors, or priests as we call them, says Luther, are simply "ministers chosen from among us," who by their "ministry of the Word" and the call become ministers, and who would be false priests, or hirelings, "or dressed in sheep's clothing," if they did anything else than preach the pure Gospel.[78] Again, the laity and the clergy have "nothing to distinguish them except that the one has a different office."[79] In his "Great Confession" of 1528 Luther confides that it would be a great thing if the monasteries and other institutions which now have gone vacant could be utilized for the training of qualified men for the pastoral office.[80]

Luther is not averse to some of the pomp and ceremony that went with the conferral of the pastoral office, but "basically consecration should not and cannot be anything other than a call or a conferring of the office of the preaching" by the laying on of hands at the congregation's consent.[81] All the activity of the pastoral office has to do with the things that Christ has commanded for the church's nurture through the means of grace, and we can now be grateful that he has made "available to the church once again the call or true consecration and ordination to the office of the ministry, as (the church) possessed it from the beginning."[82]

In his *Letter to the Christian Nobility*, 1520, one of the things Luther was ready to concede to the people of the parish was the right to choose or elect their pastors, or bishops. "A priest," he contended, "is nothing else but an officeholder. As long as he holds office he takes precedence; where he is deposed, he is a peasant or a townsman like anybody else."[83] Thus he levelled the so-called "spiritual estate" that had been constructed into a higher level of status before God and men. In the same treatise Luther wrote: "We clearly learn from the apostle that it should be the custom for every town to choose from among the congregation a learned and pious citizen, entrust to him the office of the ministry, and support him at the expense of the congregation. He should be free to marry or not. He should have several priests or deacons, also free to marry, or not, as they choose, to help him minister to the congregation with Word and sacrament."[84]

This is the broad, underlying principle which Luther defended on the basis of the Scriptural doctrine of the royal priesthood. That he modified his views somewhat, to safeguard the office against self-willed "prophets," is evident from some of his statements that have preceded. But the principle remained intact nonetheless, namely, the right of "filling the pastoral office in our parish, including the calling, choosing, appointing, and dismissing of our pastor for the sole purpose of preaching God's Word."[85] This is "our Christian liberty solely in conformity with the precept and ordinance of the divine biblical Scriptures."[86] This was one of the concessions Luther granted to be right and legitimate among the grievances voiced by the peasants, that the basic authority was theirs.[87] At the same time Luther recognized the need, perhaps even desirability, for the constituted authority, hence the electoral prince in Saxony, to take the initiative in seeing to it that the parishes in his realm would be adequately staffed.[88] Luther, however, never yielded on the principle that the fundamental right belongs to the people, the priesthood of believers. This is nicely stated in *The Ordination of Ministers of the Word*, 1539, which comes at a very mature point in Luther's life. The story is still the same: "To exercise this priesthood publicly for the benefit of others, a man needed a call."[89]

Concerning his own call as preacher in Wittenberg Luther had no doubt; also he had no misgivings that it was God who wanted him in the office, though he confides that if "I had known beforehand," the trouble it would bring, "God would have had to take more pains to get me in."[90] But now that he is in, Luther is determined to do his utmost to fulfill his ministry faithfully. "When I regard him who called me, I would not take the whole world not to have begun it."[91] So while he has some disquietude over the burdens and unpleasantries of the pastoral office, he is resolved to do a proper job of it, quite different from the pope who fills the office in a sense, but as an unqualified person without proper call.[92] To preach the Gospel, Luther believes that he had a definite call; to render sacrifices, as under the old Romanist order, he has none.[93] But even then, Luther admits— and here he shows the feet of clay of which every mortal man who fills the high office is nonetheless made—that at times "I am so very tired of it" and "I would rather hear no other news than that I had been deposed from the preaching office."[94] In a day and age when so many are quitting the ministry for one reason or another, it is reassuring to read Luther's response to his own self-defeatism: "But the poor souls will not let me (stop preaching). Besides, there is a man, named Jesus Christ who says 'No' to my resignation. I rightly follow Him to whom I am even more indebted."[95]

Qualifications for Office

The office of pastor is a high one; the qualifications for the office are high. They may not seem so to the world, which generally despises the office, or at best tolerates it. But in the eyes of God things are different. He sets down the criteria by which a man qualifies for the office of minister in His church.

First and foremost, the men God wants are men of spiritual soundness, men of repentance, like Noah, for in a man like him "Holy Scripture is describing the thinking of those men who are in the ministry."[96] Luther marvels at the faith of Noah. "Surely, great was the faith of Noah that he was able to believe these words of God." In comparison to himself Luther humbly and in self-effacing manner admits: "I would certainly not have believed them."[97] Luther no doubt is overstating the case against himself, but, as he confides in his lecture notes on Romans, it is certainly true that "he who teaches must first know and be taught what he teaches others," not least being true repentance.[98]

It is one of the twisted anomalies of life that "perverse teachers are most ready to teach, and the common people are most eager to listen."[99] This is one of the banes of the ministry and of the church at large, leading to terrible confusion for the faithful. Melchizedek, the staunch figure of a truly God-fearing man, stands out as noteworthy exception, for here was a true priest of God, after the manner of God's own choosing, simply because he held to the Word of God.[100]

The pastor's task is made all the more difficult because of the high demands laid upon him personally, that "not only should his own life be blameless," but he must strive hard to elicit godliness in the lives of those whom he serves, including those of his own home first of all.[101] This was so of Abraham, and the apostle Paul exhorts Timothy to be above reproach and to require the same of all aspirants to the pastoral office. Of course, no man is perfect, also not the incumbents of the pastoral office. This we know very well, says Luther, that "before God no one is above reproach, but before men the bishop is to be so."[102] As stewards "to whom the Lord has entrusted everything," Luther writes in his *Commentary on Titus*, they who serve God in the pastoral office must conduct themselves in keeping with the high trust that is theirs in dispensing Word and Sacrament.[103] While their own personal life will never be without sin, the fact remains that our goal must be that "our ministry, or the Word, in no sense (be) impaired because of our sin."[104] That requires first of all that we, as pastors, rule our own houses well; that we "have chaste and quiet spouses, obedient and pious children; otherwise they may offend the Christians more through their home life than they can improve them with their preaching," Luther exhorts.[105]

It virtually goes without saying, moreover, that "a teacher in the church must be well informed and experienced in both respects (that is, be able to counter both the Epicurean as well as the antinomian spirits), in order that he may be able to refute and crush the gainsayers and to comfort again those who have been refuted and crushed, lest they be devoured."[106] Luther is concerned that in the preaching of the Law, for the conviction of sin in the sinner's heart, there be a point of stopping, lest the despairing sinner be driven over the brink and be lost. Therefore, its effect must be to bring men "to the point of despair," and that, Luther says, "is as far as the Law goes"; then the Gospel's balm and forgiveness must be proclaimed.[107] The handling of Law and Gospel correctly by the preacher was never more adequately and beautifully portrayed than in Luther's *Commentary on Galatians*. This became the base for C. F. W. Walther's classic on *The Proper Distinction Between Law and Gospel*. When a Christian pastor faithfully fulfills this assignment in connection with Law and Gospel preaching, he indeed is worthy of his congregation's respect and obedience.[108]

It is well known that Luther defended the right of the clergy to marry, and he castigated the evils of enforced celibacy. Thus it was a deep wish and hope which he held all his life that, because of the many evils attached to it, "celibacy may one day be removed from the establishments of the priests and bishops, and that they may be permitted or commanded to marry, just as the ministers of our churches live piously and honorably in matrimony."[109] The Lutheran track record in connection with marriage might disappoint Luther, were he alive today, but still more disappointing would be the pertinacity with which the Romanist hierarchy has persisted in its demand for celibacy on the part of the clergy, as well as the "religious" in general, men and women. In his *Commentary on 1 Corinthians* Luther charges his opponents with gross distortion on this very point, saying: "My friends, if you had only not meddled with this one little principle, that according to the example of the apostles and the teaching of Christ married men may become priests, and if you had not persisted in forbidding priests to marry, there would not have been so much trouble."[110] A wife, also in the parsonage, can and should be a source of great blessing and happiness, the Reformer is convinced, for "women who do such work are ten times better in their lives than if they lived in a convent and meanwhile were filled with evil thoughts and lusts because they were idle."[111]

That which makes the pastor is his call, as we have seen above, along with the proper qualifications, and not external trappings, whatever they might be. Thus old Isaac would have been wiser not to be deceived by the clothes Jacob wore, which reminded him of Esau.[112] Robes still do not constitute the makings of the priestly office today, Luther reminds us. Esau was proud and haughty, a man who smugly thrust everything to the wind and "sold and repudiated his birthright."[113] Luther terms the pious notions connected with monasticism "satanic illusions," and admits that "I myself had almost been taken in (by them) when I was still a monk," a situation which might well have gone on, "had I not been withdrawn through Staupitz, who drove me to the public profession of theology, when, at his advice and order, I had been declared to be a doctor of theology."[114] Thus Luther credits his beloved old prior with "rescuing" him from a base delusion.

What is required in a steward of the mysteries of God is that he be faithful, like Abraham, like David, says Luther. There are some things, some of the hidden mysteries of God, like the doctrine on divine election, which you will never fully understand in this life, Luther continues. God prefers to remain *Deus absconditus* at some points. Let it be that way; let God be God. As far as you are concerned, "remain in your calling and within the limits of the Word."[115] Luther's earnest prayer is that "God may grant us faithful laborers and pastors who are sincere and adhere to the Word."[116] It is bad enough when unconcern and insolent disregard affect the average man vis-a-vis God's Word, "but when this finds its way into the pulpit and the article of faith is assailed by those who are preachers," then the result is "murderous damage."[117]

It is also good for a pastor, reflecting on his high trust, that he forever realize and remember that "God does not need *my* service," as though I were some irreplaceable treasure of myself.[118] Luther illustrates this point with a reference to Joseph's attitude towards the high trust placed on him in Egypt. He remained a humble man, moved by faith in God. Blown-up heads, Luther says, result very often from the fact that certain individuals view their office in the ministry as though "this heavenly gift is provided by birth."[119] Nothing hurts the church quite so much as lazy preachers, who sit back and think: "I shall do nothing and shall not be concerned about my ministry."[120] Speaking of Jacob's high spiritual side as a man of God, Luther says here "was a high priest filled with the Holy Spirit"; and "he taught his church diligently and celebrated a festival for his household and neighbors or for strangers who wished to take part in the religious acts and at the same time to hear and to pray."[121] A staunch, firm man the preacher is to be, like Jacob in his later years, "an immovable rock which is not carried away by the assault either of winds or of waves," but while "the Elbe rushes along," he like "the rock remains firm."[122] "A teacher in the church should be like this. Certainty is necessary throughout life, but especially in the teachings of the church. He who does not want to be firm will finally lose the ministry and the certainty of the Word."[123]

The godless preacher or teacher in the church, on the other hand, is quite unlike the above. He is more like an ostrich, Luther says, stupidly covering its head from what is going on around it. "Thus a godless teacher seizes upon one particular saying of Scripture and thinks his notion is fine, not noticing that he is maintaining his position as one who is bare and unarmed on every side."[124] In other respects the godless teacher is like an owl which "does not see when there is light but sees by night." Or like the cuckoo which places its own eggs in the nest of the hedge sparrow after having eaten the sparrow's eggs, and when its young are hatched and grown they in turn devour the mother hedge sparrow. This is the way of the false teacher, Luther states, in that he "steals away the children of the church by which they had been nourished."[125] The faithful preacher contrariwise has more of the good qualities of the ox; for "to chew the cud is to take up the Word with delight and meditate with supreme diligence" upon it and absorb it to oneself.[126] As a key part of this devotion to the Word, Luther singles out the ability to sift Law and Gospel properly:

> Whoever, therefore, sets either the Gospel alone or the Law alone over the twofold man, namely, the inner and the outer man, does not part the hoof (that is, does not rightly carry out the business of teaching). For through the Gospel alone he teaches complete liberty, that is, liberty of the spirit and the flesh, so that at the same time the conscience rejoices and is freed from works and the body rests from the bondage of love. Again, through the Law alone he teaches complete captivity, that is, both of the spirit and the flesh, so that at the same time the conscience is troubled with anxieties and unrest, and the body with effort and work. Therefore let the heart become free through the Word of grace, and let the body become a servant through the law of love; then the hoof will be properly parted.[127]

In this way the ox may be thought of "as the symbol of the evangelists, teachers, preachers," Luther states.[128] With the knowledge of Scripture well in hand such preachers can hardly be characterized as "spiritual eunuchs," theologically unable to perform their God-given function.[129]

Luther was particularly expert in "rightly dividing the word of truth" (2 Tim. 2:15), though at another time and in another context he stated that it would take a 100 years of experience in the ministry really to learn the art well. One cannot mistake the principle involved though, as one reads a distinction between Law and Gospel like this: "To preach what has to do with the salvation of the spirit and the new man is to sound the silver trumpet, but to preach what has to do with the humiliation of the flesh and of the old man is to sound the horn."[130] "There are two kinds of preaching in the church," therefore, Luther states; one that has to do with rejoicing and joy in the Lord, and the other which has to do with "exhortation of grief and penitence in oneself."[131] The one is taught alone by God; the other we learn something about by merely looking at ourselves and the evil present there. "With the one we sing of the righteousness which is for us from God, with the other we sing of judgment" which is against us.[132]

Now then, the good preacher will be marked by faithful Law and Gospel preaching; he will meditate steadily "on the sacred books" of Holy Scriptures, strive for a godly life, extract spiritual understanding from God's Word as a bee gets its honey from the flower, freely preach even as he has been freely blessed with God's Word, speak boldly without fear or favor or fawning flattery, skillfully dispense the Word to the weak and the strong according to their capacity to receive instruction.[133] Preaching, Luther says, tends to be of "two kinds," either "cold and obscure," that is, disinterested with no word of explanation, or alive, because, after all, "I am teaching faith and Christ," and I should "impress it, foster it, follow it up, lest it grow cold."[134]

Luther always works or thinks with this principle engaged, like gears on an engine: "Where His (God's) congregation is, there you will find Him."[135] Since this is the case, this wish is much in place: "Would God that only faithful men had this office and administered it faithfully and purely," and that the pulpits were filled by loyal servants, not knaves.[136] The two sins which Luther finds particularly repugnant in men of the cloth are unfaithfulness, which of course comes in many shapes, and backbiting, which in every instance exacerbates the evil already there.[137] Partisanship, siding with one party against the other, whether peasants or princes, is likewise distasteful to Luther's way of thinking when the pastor's office is involved. "The thing to do is to chop up both parties in one bowl and make one dish out of the two of them," is Luther's inimitable way of handling or confronting the situation; "for a preacher is neither a courtier nor a hired hand; he is God's servant and slave, and his commission is over lords and slaves; he is to do what is right and proper, not with a view to favor or disfavor, but according to God's Word, which knows no distinction or respect of persons."[138] He calls a spade a spade, and thus, for example, in Germany where he must deal with "Mr. Guzzle" and his "thirsty and parched" throat, the faithful pastor according to Luther, will have his hands full exhorting to godly temperance and sobriety.[139]

The pastor's office is "the ministry of the Word" and in reality this "is the only office the bishops really have," and yet it "is the office they neglect the most."[140] This was the situation as Luther found it under the Romanist aegis; with the advent of evangelical preaching it ought to have changed and Christ ought to be preached "in the purest manner," Luther believes. The last thing preachers ought to be are drones, who more than anything else prove a hindrance to the Gospel,[141] or who are unfaithful and whose heart is not in it.[142] What is needed are men who "will not desert their office through discouragement at the difficulties and ingratitude of men."[143] Commenting on the Song of Solomon, chapter 4, verse 3, "your lips are like scarlet thread," Luther is led to make a typological theological application related to Law and Gospel: "Rosy lips are wonderfully fitting in a girl. The lips further signify the office of teaching. They are paired, just as the character of doctrine is also twofold: Law and Gospel."[144]

Luther's *Commentary on Isaiah* is replete with descriptive marks of the Christian pastor as one who rejoices in Gospel proclamation; preaching Christ only; strong and unswerving in assertions that have to do with God's Word, because they are true; clinging earnestly to Christ and His promises as the chief things, no matter what the opposition; able to cope with the threat of self-glory; persevering straight on, no matter what doubts may come and assault, and what the boredom that seeks to overwhelm one; persuaded that it is high trust to bear the vessels of God in Word and Sacrament.[145] Drawing from some of the minor prophets, in similar vein, there is, says Luther, the appeal to stand firm, to fend off the temptation of pride in oneself, to be ready to be criticized and condemned by the world, and to remember that, in the final analysis, for the work we are doing as pastors, we are privileged to come as "angels of God" to sinners in need.[146] The difference between "jewels" and "non-jewels" is the difference between true and false teachers or preachers,[147] "and with all Christian faithfulness I therefore ask and admonish everyone," says Luther in comment on the prophet Zechariah, "not to despise those who can expound the Scriptures and ably interpret and teach the difficult books."[148] This is a talent or skill to be prized. True it is that "one can very well be a Christian and be saved without this cleverness," but really good teachers are not easy to find. "Such teachers are rare birds."[149]

Singleness of heart is a mark of a true teacher, and "we must not bother ourselves about whether we are pleasing people or not," but leave the verdict upon our work "for God to decide."[150] Luther is especially eloquent as he comments on Matthew 7:15, in his delineation of the evil insinuated by the false preacher. What is so damaging is that "they have a valid office, and in addition they give such a beautiful impression and appearance that no one can say anything except that they are true, pious preachers, interested in everyone's salvation," while, of course, the very opposite is the case.[151] It is incumbent, therefore, upon every individual who loves God and His Word truly to "take it seriously" and "be concerned about really having it and keeping it." In this the loyal, faithful preacher will lead as his "greatest work."[152] The false leaders and preachers, after all, "are mere parasites and hirelings; slaves, not sons; aliens, not heirs; they turn themselves into idols, whom God is to love and praise and for whom He is to do the very things they ought to do for Him."[153] Therefore, not cowl, or the clergy "uniform," is of the essence in this whole matter, but hearts that are true.[154]

The church needs preachers, but it certainly does not need "those who preach against the Word of God and Christ."[155] "I, too, am a pastor and a doctor," Luther affirms; "the ministry and the mysteries of God have been entrusted to me; but if I were to preach at variance with Christ's command, one would justly say to me: 'You are the devil or Judas with the red beard.' Whoever preaches against Christ is the devil."[156] "Everyone wants to have the reputation of preaching God's Word," of course, says Luther, but the true test is whether his preaching "is supported and buttressed" by the Word of God or by his own fine thoughts. "After all, his words and all his ideas perish with him," but "God's Word endures into all eternity."[157]

The proper attitude for the pious preacher is to stand before God and say: "Dear Lord Christ, I want to be Thy pupil, and I believe Thy Word. I will close my eyes and surrender to Thy Word." In this way, says Luther, "He makes me a free nobleman, yes, a fine doctor and teacher, who is captive to the Word of God and is able to judge the errors of the faith."[158] Being a pastor, after all, is in itself no ticket to heaven; the important thing rather is the ability "to distinguish between the righteousness of works and the righteousness of faith."[159] Then I might rightly claim, not by and in myself, but in and through Christ's teaching, that "I am a true teacher," and a light to those whom I teach.[160] Again Luther confided that he might find his office as pastor wearisome, because of the "danger, contempt, ignominy, reviling, and all sorts of grief and torment from the devil and the world" that goes with it, were it not that the love for Christ drives him on.[161]

There is a wrong kind of softness in carrying out one's ministry, which would "allow the things that belong to God to be trampled underfoot," and, on the other hand, there is the wrong kind of "grimness" or harshness which "frightens people" and instead of making one's ministry "as fruitful as possible for others" ends with making "it as frightful as possible."[162] These are extremes to be avoided.   Contentment issues forth from the knowledge and conviction that God has called one into the ministry, "for without the call of God neither the ministry nor teaching succeeds."[163] Feet of clay, the preacher knows he has, and not even sins of lust will leave him alone, but may in fact conjure up the illusion that "I was dancing in a chorus with girls," says Luther.[164] But probably hardest of all will be the job of keeping his own reason in tow, for he will always be tempted to resolve things "in accordance with what is and what is not consonant with his reason"; but, then, if that were not the jeopardy accompanying his office, says Luther, "he would not need faith or the Holy Spirit."[165]

Academic pride has a way of affecting one's whole perspective. It was so in Luther's day; it is so in ours. The thinking is: "Whoever has not been to the university knows nothing, but he who has been there and studies knows everything." Luther puts the perfect squelch to that notion when he states: "One must first crown the donkey; then he goes forth and rules."[166] It remains a fact, then as now, that many a man has received too much education for his intelligence, or his humble service in God's kingdom.   Fortunately there will usually be enough criticism to level a man; and Luther's only concern is that he be ready to endure the criticism directed against his person, as long as the office, which is an office of mercy, proclaiming the saving Gospel, retains its respect and honor among the hearers of the Word.[167]

In his exhortation to Timothy, Luther notes that the apostle Paul, strongly urges that a mature and tested man be chosen for the office of shepherd or elder, a man who is well able to control himself, as well as the sheep entrusted to his care.[168] He is a true shepherd, not a hireling, able to care for the sheep, resolved to preach the Word with power, ready, if need be, to die for the brethren, or the sheep.[169] The false shepherds have no such valor, but merely aim at setting snares for the sheep.[170] In his inimitable way Luther describes what it means to be faithful to one's assigned task:

> Here is an illustration. Suppose a housefather had a wife, a daughter, a son, a maid, and a hired man. Now he speaks to the hired man and orders him to hitch up the horses and bring in a load of wood, or drive over to the field, or do some other job. And suppose he tells the maid to milk the cows, churn some butter, and so on. And suppose he tells his wife to take care of the kitchen and his daughter to do some spinning and make the beds. All this would be the words of one master, one housefather. Suppose now the maid decided she wanted to drive the horses and fetch the wood, the hired man sat down and began milking the cows, the daughter wanted to drive the wagon or plow the field, the wife took a notion to make the beds or spin and so forgot all about the kitchen; and then they all said, "The master has commanded this, these are the housefather's orders!" Then what? Then the housefather would grab a club and knock them all in a heap, and say, "Although it is my command, yet I have not commanded it *of you*; I gave each of you your instruction, you should have stuck to them."[171]

The pastor is called to a specific office, and it is that call which empowers him, not some special ceremony which is determinative. "For the person who was supposed to become a pastor, or a preacher," says Luther, "it was not enough that he had been consecrated and had received the chrism, but he had to be called or appointed anew and let himself be invested and inducted in order to receive and accept such a pastoral office."[172] Luther follows the rehearsal of the basic principle governing the pastoral office with the reminder that those who "float around" as it were making much of their chrism, or anointing, or consecration, or ordination, or whatever, and who do not have a call that ties them to the office, parade around with a fiction and likely serve their own bellies.[173]

As is well known, Luther makes a very strong plea for a strong educational system, especially for the retention of the Biblical languages in the training of the clergy. *To the Councilmen of*

Germany, 1524, Luther writes: The average preacher can get along without great expertise in Greek and Hebrew, "but when it comes to interpreting Scripture, and working with it on your own, and disputing with those who cite it incorrectly, he is unequal to the task; that cannot be done without languages."[174] The church will always require scholars who know the Scriptures as given in the original languages. Moreover, it is also true that such competence in the original will help to keep preaching from going "flat and tame" and will give it "freshness and vigor."[175]

Luther's own pastoral heart is shown in a down-to-earth way in a letter addressed to Katie, his wife, February 27, 1532, in behalf of a young student, John Rischmann, who had lived with them and served Luther faithfully in a number of tasks. Luther urges Katie to "reach into your wallet and let nothing be lacking for this fine fellow."[176] It typified Luther's solicitude for those who devoted themselves to the study of theology and preparation for the ministry.

Concerning the woman's place as regards the ministry, Luther leaves nothing in doubt. He has recourse to the created order of things under God and states simply: "A woman must be a woman and cannot be a man." She, therefore, does not qualify for the ministry. It is as simple as that and it also settles the question. There is, of course, nothing demeaning about anyone's station, male or female; and Luther affirms that "he who scoffs at a station scoffs at the Lord Himself."[177] The Lord God made them all and all are to be honored and esteemed accordingly.

In his notable *Table Talk* Luther often is quoted on the subject of the pastoral office. To the young preacher, filled with some trepidation over the awesome responsibility that was his as he mounted the pulpit, Luther advises:

> When you are to preach, speak with God and say, "Dear Lord God, I wish to preach in thine honor. I wish to speak about thee, glorify thee, praise thy name. Although I can't do this well of myself, I pray that thou mayest make it good." When you preach, don't look at Philip (Melanchthon) or Pomeranus (Bugenhagen) or me or any other learned man, but think of yourself as the most learned man when you are speaking from the pulpit. (As an aside, Luther added:)

I have never been troubled by my inability to preach well, but I have often been alarmed and frightened to think that I was obliged to speak thus in God's presence about his mighty majesty and divine nature. So be of good courage and pray.[178]

He was not particularly fond of long sermons, a tendency which Bugenhagen apparently had, and Luther with wry touch of humor once stated that Bugenhagen "sacrificed his hearers with his long sermons, for we are his victims; and today he sacrificed us in a singular manner."[179] Luther advised variety in preaching style and method; the good preacher, like a good carpenter, varies his approach even though he works with the same material, in this case, the Word of God.[180] Getting tied too tightly to one's notes may detract from good preaching, Luther advises, noting that "it has often happened to me that my best outline came undone" and that "when I was least prepared my words flowed during the sermons."[181] It is doubtful, of course, that Luther would set that bit of advice down fast and firm as a paradigm for good preaching, since he was a stickler for thorough preparation in and with the Word of God. A master of Scripture like Luther, living literally out of its content, which he knew virtually by heart, could well launch out and away from his notes without any hurt, either to the hearer or to God's Word.

The target of his sermons, he states, was never the wise and learned, but the "little ones," the "sucklings," who needed to be nurtured.[182] Though Luther himself was at times "guilty" of long-winded sermons, his general advice is for sermons of reasonable length, which would hold the average person's attention. In a light mood he once answered Conrad Cordatus, who had asked him to explain good preaching technique, as follows: "First, you must learn to go up to the pulpit. Second, you must know that you should stay there for a time. Third, you must learn to get down again."[183] More on line, and more seriously stated, Luther commented to the individual who stated that he had exhausted the text's content and had "emptied my bag of all that was in it" as follows: "Then it was time to stop, for I have learned this art: When I have nothing more to say I stop."[184]

Not least in Luther's *Table Talk* are the responses he gave to questions of casuistry. Sound pastoral advice and counsel are often enlisted for matters which the Scriptures do not directly address. Here guidelines must be sought from the abiding principles implicit in given doctrines. We cannot possibly cite the many bits of advice which Luther offered in the course of his life. These would constitute a separate study in themselves. Nor would we probably find ourselves in complete agreement with Luther on all matters of casuistry to which he responded. Generally, however, his vast knowledge of Biblical teaching equipped him to give answers which have abiding import to this day. An example of this would be his reply to a question raised concerning the propriety of receiving the Sacrament from someone who denied the Real Presence. They may argue, Luther says, that Christ is present spiritually and everywhere, as with His grace, and for that reason say, Yes, it would be all right to receive the Sacrament. But Luther's answer was No, "on the ground that in this instance it is not the worthiness of the person but the thing itself that would cease."[185]

This judgment conforms well with other similar statements by the Reformer as regards altar fellowship. He rightly viewed participation at the Sacrament of the Altar as one of the highest manifestations of oneness in faith. Good pastoral practice, for the sake of the truth taught by Scriptures concerning the true body and blood of Christ in the Sacrament, demanded that the truth be served, ahead of concerns for show of love and fellowship based on shallow sentimentalism.

It may be claimed without fear of contradiction that Luther's great pastoral heart, which burned with a passion for the souls of his fellowmen, burned with even greater intensity for the truth of God's Word given in Holy Writ. Luther lived out of its content and he taught by its precept.

NOTES

1   *Kirche und Amt*, 29; *Church and Ministry*, 58.

2   *LW* 39, 305ff.; *WA* 11, 408ff.

3   *LW* 39, 311; *WA* 11, 413.

4   *St. L* 11, 1910; *WA* 11, 2547.

5   *Examination of the Council of Trent*, II 707.

6   Op. cit., 708.

7   Op. cit., 709.

8   Op. cit., 713.

9   *Enchiridion*, 16ff. cf. Poellot, 30f.

10   *Enchiridion*, pp. 16-25 passim. cf. Poellot, 30-38.

11   Cf. Walther, *Kirche und Amt*, 260f.

12   Op. cit., 266.

13   Ibid.

14   Op. cit., 277.

15   Op. cit., 278.

16   Op. cit., 280.

17   Op. cit., 275.

18   Quoted in Schmid, H., *Doctrinal Theology of the Lutheran Church*, 608. WELS conceives of the agency of calling individuals into ministry of the Word as extending to other groups of believers—a view dangerously close to *ecclesiola* (little churches) existing within the *ecclesia* or local congregation (church).

19   *WA* 52, 615; translation in Plass, E. *What Luther Says*, p. 6.

20   *WA* 16, 35; cf. Plass, p. 47.

21   *LW* 9, 304; *WA* 14, 740.

22   *LW* 13, 329; *WA* 41, 202f.

23   Ibid.

24   *LW* 14, 303; *WA* 5, 40.

25   *LW* 41, 321; *WA* 54, 250f. *Against the Roman Papacy*, 45.

26   *LW* 2, 272; *WA* 42, 456.

27   *LW* 2, 275; *WA* 42, 457.

28   *LW* 3, 30; *WA* 42, 569.

29   *LW* 4, 346; *WA* 43, 385.

30   *LW* 5, 238; *WA* 43, 592.

31   *LW* 6, 325; *WA* 44, 242.

32   *LW* 6, 347f.; *WA* 44, 259f.

33   Ibid.

34   Ibid.

35   *LW* 13, 64f.; *WA* 31[1], 211f.

36   Ibid.

37   Ibid.

38   *LW* 13, 66; *WA* 31¹, 212.

39   Ibid. cf. *LW* 41, 350. "I am a preacher of the church at Wittenberg."

40   *LW* 39, 312; *WA* 11, 414.

41   Ibid.

42   Ibid.

43   *LW* 40, 11; *WA* 12, 172.

44   *LW* 40, 34-43 passim: *WA* 12, 189-196.

45   *LW* 40, 383f.; *WA* 30³, 518f.

46   Ibid.

47   Ibid.

48   *LW* 20, 34ff.; *WA* 13, 577ff.

49   *LW* 21, 27; *WA* 32, 320.

50   Ibid.

51   *LW* 21, 44; *WA* 32, 334.

52   *LW* 21, 54; *WA* 32, 343.

53   *LW* 21, 61ff.; *WA* 32, 349f.

54   Ibid.

55   *LW* 32, 71; *WA* 32, 358.

56   *LW* 21, 124; 212f.; *WA* 32, 402.

57   *LW* 21, 226; *WA* 32, 486.

58   *LW* 22, 480; *WA* 47, 190. Cf. *LW* 54, 80; *WA*, TR 1, 211.

59   *LW* 22, 482ff.; *WA* 47, 193ff.

60   Ibid.

61   *LW* 23, 322f.; *WA* 33, 517f.

62   *LW* 23, 343; *WA* 33, 553.

63   *LW* 25, 140ff.; *WA* 56, 162ff.

64   *LW* 25, 234f.; *WA* 56, 284f. From *Commentary on Romans*, 1515-1516. Luther's comparison turns on the point that even as a man is saved by faith and not by the works of the law, so an individual requires the call into the pastoral office before he assumes the functions of that office.

65   *LW* 26, 18f.; *WA* 40¹, 59f.

66   Ibid.

67   Ibid.

68   *LW* 26, 23f.; *WA* 40¹, 66ff.

69   Ibid.

70   *LW* 26, 52f.; *WA* 40¹, 110ff.

71   Ibid.

72   *LW* 28, 250ff.; *WA* 26, 28ff.

73   *LW* 28, 354; *WA* 26, 99.

74   *LW* 29, 5.16ff.; *WA* 25, 7.16.

75   *LW* 29, 22f.; *WA* 25, 21f.

76   *LW* 30, 132f.; *WA* 12, 387f.

77   *LW* 34, 357; *WA* 54, 428.

78   *LW* 36, 113ff.; *WA* 6, 564. *Babylonian Captivity*, 1520.

79   *LW* 36, 158f.; *WA* 8, 502. *Misuse of the Mass*, 1521.

80   *LW* 37, 364; *WA* 26, 504.

81   *LW* 38, 186; *WA* 38, 228. *Private Mass and the Consecration of Priests*, 1533.

82   *LW* 38, 198-212 passim; *WA* 38, 240-256.

83   *LW* 44, 128ff.; *WA* 6, 407ff.

84   *LW* 44, 175; *WA* 6, 440.

85   *LW* 45, 177; *WA* 12, 16.

86   Ibid.

87   *LW* 46, 10.12.37.38; *WA* 18, 325f.; cf. *LW* 49, 31; *WA* Br   3,23.

88   *LW* 49, 138; *WA* BR, 3, 628.

89   *LW* 53, 122; cf. 122-126 passim; *WA* 38, 423-431.

90   *LW* 54, 12; *WA*, TR 1, 42.

91   Ibid.

92   *LW* 54, 47; *WA*, TR 1, 138.

93   *LW* 54, 100; *WA*, TR 1, 262.

94   *LW**LW*34, 50; *WA* 30^2, 340f. *Exhortation to All the Clergy Assembled at Augsburg*, 1530.

95   Ibid.

96   *LW* 2, 44; *WA* 42, 293.

97   *LW* 2, 87; *WA* 42, 323.

98   *LW* 25, 189; *WA* 56, 204.

99   *LW* 2, 243; *WA* 42, 435.

100   *LW* 2, 384; *WA* 42, 537.

101   *LW* 3, 98; *WA* 42, 618.

102   *LW* 28, 284; *WA* 26, 51.

103   *LW* 29, 18ff.; *WA* 25, 18ff.

104   *LW* 13, 80; *WA* 40^3, 487.

105   *LW* 13, 169; *WA* 51, 218.

106   *LW* 4, 51; *WA* 43, 172.

107   *LW* 26, 313; *WA* 40^1, 485.

108   *LW* 4, 285; *WA* 43, 340.

109   *LW* 5, 192; *WA* 43, 561.

110   *LW* 28, 22f.; *WA* 12, 110f.

111   *LW* 29, 56; *WA* 25, 46.

112   *LW* 5, 136; *WA* 43, 522.

113   *LW* 5, 167; *WA* 43, 543.

114   *LW* 5, 346; *WA* 43, 667.

115   *LW* 6, 30.105; *WA* 44, 22.78.

116   *LW* 28, 62; *WA* 36, 485.

117   Ibid.

118   *LW* 7, 146f.; *WA* 44, 407.

119   *LW* 7, 164; *WA* 44, 421.

120   *LW* 7, 221; *WA* 44, 463.

121   *LW* 8, 76; *WA* 44, 635.

122   *LW* 8, 212; *WA* 44, 733f.

123   Ibid.

124   *LW* 9, 135; *WA* 14, 650.

125   Ibid.

126   *LW* 9, 136; *WA* 14, 650.

127   Ibid.

128   *LW* 10, 321; *WA* 3, 381.

129   *LW* 9, 235; *WA* 14, 711.

130   *LW* 11, 273; *WA* 4, 12.

131   Ibid.

132   Ibid.

133   *LW* 11, 331; *WA* 4, 182f.

134   *LW* 28, 330; *WA* 26, 82.

135   *LW* 13, 49; *WA* 31^1, 196.

136   Ibid.

137   Ibid.

138   *LW* 13, 216; *WA* 31^1, 198.

139   *LW* 13, 216; *WA* 51, 257.

140 *LW* 14, 331; *WA* 5, 60f.

141 *LW* 15, 65f.; *WA* 20, 77.

142 *LW* 15, 92; *WA* 20, 107.

143 *LW* 15, 237; *WA* 31^2, 704.

144 *LW* 15, 229; *WA* 31^2, 681.

145 *LW* 17, 4.14.92.116.172.174.180.213f.; *WA* 31^2,261.270.334.252. 396.397.402.427.

146 *LW* 18, 256.263.363.377; *WA* 13, 256.334.508.538.

147 *LW* 20, 105; *WA* 13, 635.

148 *LW* 20, 156f.; *WA* 23, 486.

149 Ibid.

150 *LW* 21, 136; *WA* 32, 412.

151 *LW* 21, 251ff.; *WA* 32, 507ff.

152 Ibid.

153 *LW* 21, 312; *WA* 7, 559.

154 *LW* 22, 452; *WA* 47, 166.

155 *LW* 23, 193; *WA* 33, 306.

156 Ibid.

157 *LW* 23, 225; *WA* 33, 354f.

158 *LW* 23, 230; *WA* 33, 365.

159 *LW* 23, 247; *WA* 33, 393.

160 *LW* 23, 331; *WA* 33, 531.

161 *LW* 24, 133; *WA* 45, 582.

162 *LW* 25, 139; *WA* 16, 161.

163 *LW* 25, 447; *WA* 56, 454.

164 *LW* 27, 69; *WA* 40^2, 86.

165 *LW* 28, 69; *WA* 36, 492.

166 *LW* 36, 224; *WA* 8, 558.

167 *LW* 28, 89; *WA* 36, 517.

168 *LW* 28, 286-291 passim; *WA* 26, 52-56 passim.

169 *LW* 30, 135f.163, 277f.; *WA* 12, 389f.; 14, 27f.; 20, 711ff.

170 *LW* 31, 374; *WA* 7, 71.

171 *LW* 35, 172; *WA* 16, 388f.

172 *LW* 38, 176; *WA* 38, 220.

173 Ibid.

174 *LW* 45, 363; *WA* 15, 40.

175   *LW* 45, 365; *WA* 15, 42.

176   *LW* 50, 49; *WA*, BR 6, 270f.

177   *LW* 51, 352; *WA* 49, 611.

178   *LW* 54, 157f.; *WA* TR 2, 144.

179   *LW* 54, 179; *WA*, TR 3, 60. Cf. *LW* 54, 428; *WA*, TR 5, 4.

180   *LW* 54, 31; *WA*, TR 1, 98f.

181   *LW* 54, 213; *WA*, TR 3, 357.

182   *LW* 54, 236; *WA*, TR 3, 419; cf. *LW* 54, 383f.; *WA*, TR 4, 634.

183   *LW* 54, 393; *WA*, TR 4, 692.

184   *LW* 54, 292; *WA*, TR 4, 4.

185   *LW* 54, 471; *WA*, TR 5, 303.

Chapter 5

Rite of Ordination

With the Reformation came the rejection of the Romanist doctrine which claimed that ordination imparted an indelible character, power, authority, and particularly sacramental grace upon the ordinand for the celebration of the Mass. Luther held that ordination, while well-grounded in apostolic example, was not commanded or required by God, particularly not as the act by which the ministry itself was conferred or bestowed. God effected this through the call of the Christian congregation, Luther held. Scriptures are silent on ordination deriving from an express command of God. The "laying on of hands," however, at moments of solemn importance, like the commissioning or electing of men for pastoral service, Luther never doubted was firmly set in apostolic example or precedent (Acts 6:6; 1 Tim. 4:14; 5:22; 2 Tim. 1:6).

There can be no question, therefore, that in early ecclesiastical usage this rite continued in vogue, following closely upon apostolic practice. Ordination attested publicly and solemnly the call into the office of a pastor by his congregation, as when Paul and Barnabas were commissioned and sent on the first missionary journey by the Antioch congregation. It also served the good, blessed purpose of expressing the earnest prayers of the people in behalf of the man called, beseeching God's guidance, protection, and good fruit upon his ministry.

These, and other gifts of the Holy Spirit, were prayerfully petitioned in this way, and there was no doubt in the believers' mind that God would fulfill His promised help, in accord with Jesus' words in Matthew 18:19 and Matthew 28:20. The ordination rite, or laying on of hands, thus served to ratify publicly the bond or union between the pastor and the people of the congregation, the royal priests summoning him by their call into this God-pleasing ministry.

It was Luther's position, as it is the position of Lutheran theology to this day, that such public attestation of the bestowal of the pastoral office did not impress an indelible character or status upon the person ordained. If he should cease to preach and exercise the office of the ministry, or fulfill his call, he would again take his place as an average Christian in the ranks of the royal priests and relinquish his office. We need to repeat here, therefore, that it is the call of the congregation, as stated above, not ordination, which makes the pastor.

This stance on the significance of ordination, as taught by Luther, and affirmed by Scripture first of all, was the position espoused by C. F. W. Walther. First, however, he had to divest himself of the hierarchical notions imbibed from Martin Stephan. Walther soon found himself clashing with some of his contemporaries, who, though conservative in theology as he was, nonetheless retained "Romanizing" views on the significance of the pastoral office, especially ordination. Thus Wilhelm Loehe, a leading church figure both in Europe and also in America—Loehe prepared and sent many workers into the mission fields of the new frontier—maintained the position that the pastoral office is transmitted from pastor to pastor, and that only he who has the office can transfer it to another.[1] John Grabau, feisty opponent of Walther in the "Buffalo Synod" of the Lutheran Church, held firmly to a similar view, that ordination, like the ministry itself, was established and commanded by God.

The last and least thing that either Walther, or Luther before him, wished to imply was that ordination was an empty ceremony or rite. That would not have been in keeping with the facts. If Scripture had not supported it, Luther would have discarded it entirely. Because Rome had made a "holy order" out of it, as with confirmation and marriage, did not now mean for Luther that it should be totally abjured and relegated to the ecclesiastical rubbish heap. Luther was no iconoclast, also not as far as ceremonies and rites in the church were concerned. He simply set these externals into their proper Scriptural perspective. He found nothing in Scripture to support the Romanist notions, that sacramental grace, indelible character, supernatural power (as with the Mass), etc., were conferred by the bishop upon the ordinand, also nothing that supported the special prerogative of bishops so to do. Luther detected that it was part of the sacerdotalistic pyramid that had been built up within the church without divine command or sanction, and for that reason he repudiated it, particularly from the time (1519) of the Leipzig debate with Dr. Eck onward.

We know that the ordination ceremony was conscientiously retained and used in Wittenberg during Luther's lifetime, but with the meaning and significance which Scripture pressed and taught. Luther rejected the notion of the episcopal succession, requiring the consecration by a bishop for a valid ordination, as though there was an unbroken chain from the office of St. Peter in Rome to his day. After all, the Reformer pointed out, it was simple presbyters and elders who "laid on hands" in the case of Timothy (1 Tim. 4:14). This was as valid as the hands of the apostles, Luther argued. He made his case very plainly when he himself consecrated his friend, Nicholas von Amsdorf, as bishop at Naumburg. Luther, who never presumed to be anything more than a pastor and a doctor of theology, did the ordaining. It was a solemn induction or installation into office, based upon the call of the people in Naumburg, not upon pretended hierarchical power and right.

The Lutheran Confessions use the word "ordination" in a twofold sense, either to mean or be equivalent to "call into the office of ministry," or in the sense of laying on of hands in order to implore God's blessing upon the ordinand. In the *Apology* (XIV, 24) Melanchthon notes that the adversaries (Romanists) refuse to honor the Lutheran position on "rightly called" (*AC* XIV), unless it be understood in the sense of "canonical ordination." Melanchthon states that the Lutheran party by no means intended radical upheaval in church polity and in the various "grades" of the ministry, for they understood that such ecclesiastical usage had a long and cherished place in the church. But Melanchthon entered a demurrer at, or on, the point of divine institution, charging that such notions or regulations had entered into the church "by human authority." Ecclesiastical government, such as structured under the Roman papacy, we can live with, Melanchthon says in effect, as long as it is not demanded by divine right and as long as our position that orders like ordination are by human design is recognized and allowed to stand. This, of course, the Romanists refused to grant.

Virtually the identical answer is given by Luther in the *Smalcald Articles* of 1537. In Part III, Article X, "Of Ordination and the Call," Luther states that the Reformation party could live with the Romanist episcopal system, "for the sake of love and unity," and even allow them to ordain our clergy, "but not from necessity." In other words, if they insist on this as a divine right or rule, and if because of our refusal to recognize this pretentious claim they refuse to "ordain and confirm us and our preachers," then we will remedy the lack of pastors and "we ourselves will and ought to ordain suitable persons to this office." It is evident from Luther's title to this article that the meaning of ordination which he has in mind is closer to the concept of "rightful call" into the pastoral office than to the laying on of hands.

In the Tractate on the Power and Jurisdiction of Bishops, which the theologians adopted at Smalcald, testimony is given, not only that the grades among the clergy are of human origin, but also that, contrary to what Rome claimed, "ordination administered by a pastor in his own church is valid by divine law" (65). Also the right is claimed for the churches to ordain qualified pastors for themselves, if the established church (Rome) refused to grant them pastors: "Therefore it is necessary for the Church to retain the authority to call, elect, and ordain ministers" and this is an authority "which in reality is given to the Church, which no human power can wrest from it" (67). The Confessors cite how "Augustine narrates the story of two Christians in a ship, one of whom baptized the catechumen, who after Baptism then absolved the baptizer." The point was that the Office of the Keys was bestowed by God upon His church, the priesthood of believers, and they never surrender these keys, even when in line with God's command they call a pastor to administer the means of grace for them publicly (69; cf. also par. 24).

Previously we have also referred to Melanchthon's willingness to speak of ordination as a sacrament in Article XIII of the *Apology*, "On the Number and Use of the Sacraments." The Romanist opponents wanted to emphasize the sacrificial role of the priests. This Melanchthon is ready to grant only if "the one sacrifice of Christ" were recognized as totally "sufficient for our sins," but not if the mediatorial role of the priests became part of the package. So he states: "But if ordination be understood as applying to the ministry of the Word, we are not unwilling to call ordination a sacrament" (11). If, however, the priests in any way whatsoever are thought of as rendering sacrifices, such as the Mass, for the salvation of sinners, then, says Melanchthon, we reject it absolutely. On the other hand, we are not at all against "adorning the ministry of the Word" with every praiseworthy usage or term, such as designating the "laying on of hands" as sacramental, if thereby God's Word is enhanced. As time went on, however, and as it became evident that the Romanist position was set in cement and reinforced with steel, the Lutheran party steadfastly refused to add confusion in the church by ambivalent use of the term ordination as a sacrament, lest the people be disturbed by ambiguous doubletalk.

One of the three "walls" levelled by Luther in his *Open Letter to the Christian Nobility*, 1520, was the Roman church's claim that "the pope, bishop, priests, and monks" constitute a "spiritual estate" separate and above everyone else.[2] This was pure fiction, as Luther showed on the basis chiefly of 1 Peter 2:9, which so plainly teaches the priesthood of all believers, to whom also belong the Keys. In another treatise of the same year, the *Babylonian Captivity*, Luther launched a frontal attack on Rome's sacramental system, which he saw as a studied intent by the Roman church to control the souls of the faithful from the cradle to the grave. It was totally without Scriptural foundation. Yet, Rome claimed to be the only rightful dispenser of the sacraments, the channels of "grace" without which none could be saved. As a result of Luther's shattering blow to this pretension, not only the fabricated sacramental system, but also the fabricated sacerdotal system, came tumbling down, or at least took a serious blow in its theological solar plexus.

Ordination was among the invented doctrines of Rome, at least to the claimed extent that it was God-commanded and bestowed an indelible character, with unique authority and power in a sacrificial, mediatorial way. Here, Luther held, were the roots of the detestable tyranny of the clergy over the laity. All baptized believers are priests, Luther showed, through their regeneration by faith and baptism. The supposed "holiness" of the order of priests, ordained in the episcopal succession of Rome, was clearly an invention of the church, lacking Scriptural (also historical) grounds. It is by the ministry of the Word that we become "priests," not, as was supposed, by the unction or chrism or consecration of an ordaining bishop. "Therefore this 'sacrament' of ordination, if it is anything at all, is nothing else than a certain rite whereby one is called to the ministry of the church."[3]

Lutheran theologians have consistently followed Luther in their repudiation of the sevenfold sacramental system as fabrication by the Roman church. Notably ordination as a "sacrament" formed the fulcrum of this critique. Under no circumstances, however, do any of these theologians set the ordination ceremony itself aside as being of no value in the church's life and practice. Quite to the contrary, there is very positive support for the continuation of the "laying on of hands," to testify publicly of the bestowal of the pastoral office upon a chosen and qualified man, and to beseech God's blessings upon him in the presence of the calling congregation. The right to call is grounded in Matthew 18, Melanchthon notes. In the same context of his *Loci communes*, Melanchthon affirms that "it is customary and praiseworthy" when pastors are being installed into their office for "several other Christian pastors to be present, to hear the pledge of doctrinal loyalty, and in testimony thereof to lay their hands upon the ordinand."[4] Similarly, Chemnitz states very much to the point: "Although ordination does not constitute the call, yet if someone has been rightly called it is a custom which publicly attests that the call is a rightful one."[5]

In his *Examen* Chemnitz devotes a separate chapter to the so-called sacrament of ordination as taught by the Romanists.[6] He notes, as we have above, that the Lutheran Confessions (*Apol.* XIII) are willing in a closely restricted way to let it be termed a sacrament. But under no circumstances can it be admitted that a certain indelible character is bestowed by the ordaining bishop upon the ordinand, along with given authority and powers, since that would, virtually make ordination a means of grace. This has led to all manner of aberrations, in the Roman church, as well as in other churches where episcopal and hierarchical authority is defended as resulting from ordination. Chemnitz notes how extremists in the Romanist camp have viewed it as more excellent than Baptism. He can rightly assert: "I undertook this report in order to show that our churches have restored the true and lawful manner of choosing and calling, which was in use in the apostolic, primitive, and ancient church."[7]

Chemnitz previously had examined in detail the various Scriptural references which bore upon the manner of calling, or electing, of pastors or shepherds for the congregations in apostolic times. Like Luther, Chemnitz recognizes the leadership role which the apostles exercised in this process, but also the important role of the congregations in exercising the franchise in the selection of qualified men for the public ministry among them. So, Chemnitz is affirming that in the Lutheran churches ordination continues in usage, "that it might be signified by this visible rite that God approves the calling which is done by the voice of the church, for just as God chooses ministers by the voice of the church, so He also approves the calling by the attestation of the church."[8] Moreover, like Luther, Chemnitz believes that "this earnest prayer at the ordination of ministers is not without effect, because it rests upon a divine command and promise."[9] The reference is to 1 Timothy 4:14. When comparing ordination, however, to the sacraments of Baptism and Lord's Supper, Chemnitz states:

> The difference is plain. Baptism and the Lord's Supper are means or instruments through which God applies and seals the promise of reconciliation or forgiveness to individual believers. Ordination is not such a means or instrument.
>
> Now the ministry of the Word and the sacraments has divine promises, and the prayer at ordination rests on these, but these promises are not to be tied to the rite of the imposition of hands, about which there is neither a command of Christ nor such a promise as there is about Baptism and the Lord's Supper. This reminder must be added, because the papalists contend that ordination is truly and properly a sacrament of the New Testament, just as are Baptism and the Lord's Supper.[10]

On a more popular level Chemnitz repeats the same distinctions in his *Enchiridion*, explaining how the Scriptures so plainly state the qualifications for the pastoral office and how these men are called into the public ministry through the voice of the congregations. Concurrently therewith came the rite of ordination, or laying on of hands, in public attestation of the call and to implore the Lord's blessing.[11] Very nicely and helpfully he traces the practice and rite of the laying on of hands at moments of solemn significance to the ordaining of pastors in the New Testament. They are pledged to faithful preaching of the Word and administering of the sacraments in public ceremony before the calling congregation which thereby prayerfully and solemnly inducts them into its service, fellow pastors (elders or presbyters or bishops) being present for the laying on of hands.[12]

Gerhard chimes in that ordination is not "necessary as a divine command," nor "is the nature of the preaching office itself constituted thereby," nor "an indelible character impressed through it"; but nonetheless it is a useful and desirable rite in the church which goes back to apostolic example and, therefore, should be retained.[13] Ordination cannot be deemed a sacrament, Gerhard held, but he did recognize that the gifts of the Holy Spirit are thereby invoked and bestowed since God has promised to hear our prayers.[14] In succinct summary Gerhard capsules the nature and meaning, therefore, of ordination in the church:

> Ordination is a public and solemn declaration or attestation, through which the ministry of the Church is committed to a suitable person, called thereto by the Church, to which he is consecrated by prayer and the laying on of hands, rendered more certain of his lawful call, and publicly, in the sight of the entire Church, solemnly and seriously admonished concerning his duty.[15]

Walther indicates that the other 17th century theologians expressed themselves similarly, rejecting the absolute necessity of ordination, as a divine command, or a sacrament, and asserting the desired continuance of a solemn rite which had regularly been employed in the church since the days of the apostles and whose roots, in fact, reached back into the Old Testament. This placed it into a different perspective than that of a mere adiaphoron.[16] Luther scholars like Koestlin of the 19th century and Althaus of the 20th bear out the correctness of this judgment, based on their study of Luther's writings.[17]

Luther's position on ordination was not confined by any means to his polemical, public treatises like the *Babylonian Captivity* and the *Open Letter to the Christian Nobility*. The stance taken, however, in these early writings (1520) was one he retained throughout his life. Ordination is a respected church usage or rite, which Luther by no means wished to see discarded. The petitioning of God's blessing upon given individuals, especially those entering an office of high trust, like the prophets and kings of old, was very dear to Luther's heart. He stood opposed, therefore, merely to the embellishments which Rome had added to the rite, by which it had attained sacramental place and become a virtual means of grace. Such fabrication, Luther saw, militated against Scripture's central article on justification, confused Law and Gospel, and typified Rome's deadly insinuating of *theologia gloriae* in place of *theologia crucis* into Christian theology's heart. By so doing it had returned Christianity to the level of natural theology, Luther contended. This was a serious charge. The ballooning of ordination into such unwanted and unjustified prominence contradicted the Gospel itself.

Yet, as stated, Luther wished dearly that the rite and practice of ordination continue. His writings, early to late, demonstrate this concern. In his *Genesis Commentary*, which was not completed until 1545, Luther describes Melchizedek's encounter with Abraham after the latter's remarkable victory over the four kings "in the vale of Siddim, which is the salt sea" (Gen. 14:3). Melchizedek, like Abraham, was a God-fearing man, and when they meet, says Luther, "this was a very beautiful gathering of the church from all nations." "Melchizedek, the priest and king, delivers an excellent sermon, in which he first bestows high praise on the kindness of God, who had blessed Abraham" in his signal victory. So, first of all it is a thanksgiving service, led by Melchizedek. But then also, says Luther, Melchizedek "adds a prayer and blessed Abraham."[18] The significance of Melchizedek's act and words, in Luther's mind, takes the form of a declaration, as in the ordination rite, "that only with him, in his house and family, are the church, the kingdom of heaven, salvation, forgiveness of sins, and the divine blessing."[19] Abraham would not only be the genealogical line of descent for the Savior but the bearer of the glad tidings of the Gospel to the world around him.

Luther compares Jacob's wonderful encounter with God at Bethel with God's avenues of grace and mercy to us in the New Testament through Word and sacrament. "Therefore," says Luther, "one must learn contrary to the view of the flesh that it is not a simple word and only an empty sound, but that it is the Word of the Creator of heaven and earth."[20] It is significant that into this very same context, immediately following, Luther places the office of the called pastor of the Word. He states: "Thus the imposition of hands is not a tradition of men, but God makes and ordains ministers. Nor is it the pastor who absolves you, but the mouth and hand of the minister are the mouth and hand of God." One could hardly justify the kind of elevation the Romanists gave to ordination on the basis of this statement; but it does evidence Luther's high regard for the pastoral office, as well as the "laying on of hands" which regularly accompanied the entrance of a man into the office.

We have previously noted Luther's citing of Joseph, as a man of outstanding humility, willing to serve in high office, but not grasping at or conniving to get the office.[21] In that same context Luther expands on God's manner of blessing His people in other moments of sacred importance. He mentions the marriage ceremony and ordination rite as two such examples. "It is not for nothing, therefore, that special rites are employed in the church to unite men and women in matrimony, likewise for ordaining ministers of the Word."[22] At the marriage ceremony "we bless the bridegroom and the bride," and petition God to "protect this estate" which He Himself has founded. Similarly, in the ordination ceremony, "we lay hands on the ministers and at the same time pour forth prayers to God."[23] In either case, states Luther, the meaning is simply that we thereby testify concerning God's own ordinance in connection with these important functions, stations, or offices. The one applies to the household; the other to the church; and, says Luther, we might just as properly include God's ordinances as regards the state. "In the papacy this doctrine was altogether unknown and buried; for men invented the idea that the church is nothing else than a gathering of pontiffs, cardinals, bishops, etc.," says the Reformer.[24] All of God's ordinances which have to do with home, church, and state, were grossly distorted in Romanist thinking, with great harm to the precious Gospel itself, "the light of the Word of God."[25]

In order to become the pastor of a congregation, it was Luther's position, as we have already shown, a man "must have an office and a field of work committed to him" by a proper call, from a congregation, parish, or diocese. He does not merely grasp for himself such station or office. "This call (by the congregation or parish) makes pastors and preachers."[26] This is the basis for Luther's right to preach at Wittenberg; for his right to defend God's Word against the Romanist plague, he appeals to his position as a sworn doctor of theology. His very familiar reticence at assuming the latter is known to most readers: "I was forced and driven into this position in the first place, when I had to become Doctor of Holy Scripture against my will."[27] He is referring to his obedient compliance to Staupitz's prodding, as an Augustinian monk carrying out his prior's wish.

The divine call through the parish is of the essence here, as far as holding the preaching office in the local congregation at Wittenberg. This is tantamount to being commanded, called, ordained of God, is Luther's considered judgment and theological position drawn from Scripture.

It astounds Luther that the simple, though important, laying on of hands should have led "men to make a sacrament of confirmation."[28] It was the same story with ordination, of which "sacrament" "the church of Christ knows nothing; it is an invention of the church of the pope," states Luther. "Not only is there nowhere any promise of grace attached to it, but there is not a single word" which can be cited to prove it "to have been instituted by God."[29] Luther, in fairness to the long history behind ordination, recognized that it has a centuries-old, honored place in the church; but to claim that it is divinely instituted is "the invention of human fictions."[30] We would become "a laughing-stock to our opponents," were we to grant this notion. It is rather a classic instance of the clash between Scripture's authority and the Roman church's power. The question of which came first, the chicken or the egg, is no problem to Luther who recognized the Creator's creative might in creating all living things. The same holds true here: "The Word of God is incomparably superior to the church." Therefore, how can the creature, which is the church, create something which the Word has not first of all ordained? Since when is it true that a man "begets his own parent?"[31] How utterly false, therefore, to accept ordination as divinely instituted, when the Word of God does not so ordain, but only the church in its arbitrary use of authority!

The proper standing of ordination in the church, according to Luther, is to recognize that it is "a certain churchly rite, such as the consecration of vessels, houses, etc."[32] Perhaps in later years Luther might be shown to have lifted his sights a little in making a comparison like this with "vessels, houses, bells," etc.; but he would have remained adamant on the point that it not be viewed as a sacrament, "since no promise is attached" to it, as little as to these other things.[33] For any rite to be a sacrament we need Christ's instituting word and attached promise of forgiveness and grace. Ordination does not fit these requirements, and as a result "incredible injury of the grace of baptism and the gospel" have resulted from this confusion. Moreover, "here are the roots of that detestable tyranny of the clergy over the laity." This in itself is bad enough, says Luther, but worse still is this: "Trusting in the external anointing by which their hands are consecrated, in the tonsure and in vestments, they not only exalt themselves above the rest of the lay Christians, who are only anointed with the Holy Spirit, but regard them almost as dogs and unworthy to be included with themselves in the church"; and, as a result, "Christian brotherhood has perished, shepherds have been turned into wolves, servants into tyrants,

churchmen into worse than worldlings."[34] Again, Luther reiterates
that the true and real ordination of a pastor into his office is his call
through the people, the royal priests, and his ensuing proclamation
of the Word. "Does ordaining such babbling priests make one a
bishop?" Luther parries. His answer: "Certainly not. Any deacon
or layman could do as much. It is the ministry of the Word that
makes the priest and the bishop."[35]

As regards the office of the ministry, therefore, we must not
be misled by ecclesiastical dissembling, whatever quarter it comes
from, states Luther at the close of his treatise on *The Private Mass
and the Consecration of Priests*, 1533.[36] His conclusion is still the
same: "Our consecration shall be called ordination, or a call to the
office." He has said it earlier and he repeats it in this treatise:
"Basically consecration should not and cannot be anything other, if
it is carried out rightly, than a call or a conferring of the office of
the ministry or of the office of preaching."[37] This conforms to the
apostolic pattern and significance of the "laying on of hands."

Not rites, ceremonies, customs, however solemn and pious,
constitute ordination, therefore, but the congregation's call. "Since
they are a people of God, it is due them that no one be set over
them without their election," is the recurring theme that runs as
leitmotif through all of Luther's writing and teaching. This
particular statement is found in his treatise *Concerning the Ministry*,
1523, and it underscores Luther's stance on ordination as flowing
from "the example and decrees of the Apostle," for the purpose of
establishing the office of the ministry of the Word at a given place,
by the concurring consent of the people.[38] It is an office that is
grounded upon the priesthood of believers, Luther thunders, and "it
is obvious that these pseudo-ordainers—the bishops—blaspheme and
err in holding that their anointing and Ordinations are so necessary
that without them no one can be a priest."[39] This "masquerade of
episcopal ordination" should yield before "the ministry of the Word"
which "is common to all Christians."[40]

The rite of ordination which Luther composed in 1539, *The
Ordination of Ministers of the Word*, conforms completely with the
principles articulated by the Reformer above. Because he stood
opposed to the Romanist elevation of the rite to a position unwelcome to the Scriptures, Luther sought to place the ceremony into
proper evangelical perspective. The first step in this order of things
included the ascertaining of the theological readiness or qualification

for the pastoral office through examination.[41] The order of service which Luther then composed conforms pretty well to the order which still obtains in Lutheran churches to this day. Included are the exhortations found in the pastoral epistles and elsewhere in the New Testament, for example, Acts 20:28ff., and then the declaration of the call by the church (churches) into service of the ministry of the Word. The ordinand is asked to declare his readiness to assume the stated responsibility, as the assembled clergy lay their hands upon the head of the new pastor(s) praying God to bestow His richest blessings upon him. Finally there is the charge to the ordinand to take charge of the flock to which he has been sent, being careful to feed them diligently with the Word of God. The ordinator then speaks the benediction upon the ordinand, and the congregation sings an appropriate hymn, like "Now Let Us Pray to the Holy Ghost." Apparently celebration of the Lord's Supper very often followed this order in the service.[42]

Men are ordained in the church, not in order to make or produce something which is not there, is Luther's constant emphasis, but to administer what they find in the church already, Word and sacrament. These certainly they do not produce, bring with them, or invent, but faithfully give and administer those things which God commands His church to do.[43] Thus it is Luther's confirmed opinion that he was ordained originally for the wrong reason, namely, to perform sacrifices for the people, as in the Mass, whereas the true office and function of the pastor was that of minister (*diakonos*) of the Word and servant (*doulos* of God's people.[44] It is that office of the Word which Luther has in focus when he advises the Bohemian Christians as follows:

> When you have so prayed, have no doubt that He to whom you have prayed is faithful and will give what you ask . . . Proceed in the name of the Lord to elect one or more whom you desire, and who appear to be worthy and able. Then let those who are leaders among you lay hands upon them, and certify and commend them to the people and the church or community (*Gemeinde*). In this way let them become your bishops, ministers, or pastors.[45]

NOTES

1   Cf. Foelber, *Abiding Word*, vol. 2, 489.
2   *LW* 44, 127; *WA* 6, 407.
3   *LW* 36, 116; *WA* 6, 6.
4   Quoted in Walther, *Kirche und Amt*, 302.
5   *Loci theol.*, de eccl., 126. Quoted in Walther, *KA*, 302f.
6   *Examination of the Council of Trent*, II 677-714 passim.
7   Op. cit., 713.
8   Op. cit., 694.
9   Ibid.
10   Op. cit., 694f.
11   *Enchiridion*, 25f.; cf. Poellot, 36.
12   Op. cit., 26f.; cf. Poellot, 36f.
13   Quoted in Walter, *Kirche und Amt*, 306.
14   *Loci theol.*, XII, 168. Quoted in H. Schmid, *Doctrinal Theology of the Lutheran Church*, 611.
15   Op. cit., 145. Translation in Schmid, op. cit., 611.
16   *Kirche und Amt*, 305; cf. 304-314 passim.
17   cf. J. Koestlin, *Theology of Luther*, vol. 1, 373.406; vol. 2, 544; P. Althaus, *Theology of Luther*, 327-332.
18   *LW* 2, 381; *WA* 42, 535.
19   *LW* 2, 391; *WA* 42, 543.
20   *LW* 5, 249; *WA* 43, 600.
21   cf. p. 261. of this manuscript.
22   *LW* 7, 146f.; *WA* 44, 407.
23   Ibid.
24   Ibid.
25   Ibid.
26   *LW* 13, 65f.; *WA* 31, 211f.
27   Ibid.
28   *LW* 36, 91; *WA* 6, 549. *Babylonian Captivity of the Church.*
29   *LW* 36, 107; *WA* 6, 560f.
30   Ibid.
31   Ibid.
32   *LW* 36, 108; *WA* 6, 1.
33   Ibid.
34   *LW* 36, 112; *WA* 6, 4.
35   *LW* 36, 115; *WA* 6, 6.

36   *LW* 38, 214; *WA* 38, 255.

37   *LW* 38, 186; *WA* 38, 228.

38   *LW* 40, 11; *WA* 12, 172f.

39   *LW* 40, 19f.; *WA* 12, 179.

40   *LW* 40, 20f.; *WA* 12, 179f.

41   We have reference to one of these examinations in Luther's *Table Talk*, as recorded by Anthony Lauterbach for June 16, 1539. The proposition for debate and discussion was: "Faith justified; faith is a work; therefore works justify." Luther chaired the debate and discussion. *LW* 54, 359; *WA*, TR 4, 420.

42   *LW* 53, 122-126; *WA* 38, 423ff.

43   Cf. *LW* 54, 119; *WA*, TR 1, 309.

44   *LW* 54, 100f.; *WA*, TR 1, 262f.

45   *LW* 40, 40; *WA* 12, 193.

Chapter 6

Auxiliary Offices

When C. F. W. Walther stated in Thesis VIII of his *Kirche und Amt* that the ministry "is the highest office in the Church," his one purpose was to underscore that the office of the called pastor is the distinctive office God has instituted for the sake of the church's continuance in the world. Of course, the church's existence is grounded solely and entirely on the Word, he emphasized, not on the pastoral office. But that office is mandated by God for the sake of the Word in the church. It is He who dictates its need in the life of the church on earth, and the individual congregations cannot, therefore, do without it or make it optional.

It naturally follows from this that other offices constituted within and by the church may, indeed, have a God-pleasing purpose and function, but they would in each case derive in some way from the one divinely ordained office, and thus be auxiliary to or derive from it. They devolve from a felt existential need, and are created in Christian liberty to be of assistance to the pastoral office. So, for example, even the apostles saw the necessity for deacons to assist them in their multiple duties in the growing church, Acts 6:1-15; Philippians 1:1; 1 Timothy 5:17.

Walther had this in mind, when in the second part of the same thesis he added that these helping, or auxiliary, offices issued forth from the pastoral office "as from the stem." It would not be wrong, therefore, to say of them, in view of their deriving from the one divinely instituted office, that they coinhere in that office, since the duties performed are in each case and in the first place incumbent upon the pastoral office. With the concurring consent of the church, or congregation, or grouping of congregations like a synod, these offices are fulfilling or performing certain functions which assist the ministry of the Word and the work of the church. Their status in relationship to the pastoral office is readily seen when one asks the question concerning their premanency under God. Must they exist, as the pastoral office must exist? A church cannot abrogate the public pastoral office. But can it exist without the assistant pastor, vicar, parochial school teacher, elders, deacons, professors at synodical institutions, district and synodical presidents, and other officers? Theoretically at least, a church or church body could dispense with some or all of these offices without harming the church itself. But that could not be said for the pastoral office, which Christ through His apostles mandated in the church for its upbuilding, nurture, growth, and spiritual life. It may not be abrogated.

The *functions*, therefore, of these auxiliary offices are divinely ordained or instituted functions. They belong to the pastoral office. But the particular *form*, structure, or polity under which the congregation or group of congregations employs or structures them is a matter of Christian liberty. That liberty, under no circumstances extends to the pastoral office itself. It remains the focal center of the total work of the ministry in a given place, or in a synodical confederation of like-minded congregations united in one faith. As a bearing point governs for the navigator on a plane or ship, the pastoral office sets the direction for all the auxiliary offices. They may have segmented functions, very important in their own right, but in some way they flow from the pastoral office itself. This was the picture or image which the Lutheran forefathers, like Walther and his colleagues, envisioned for the pastoral office in its relationship to the other offices established within the congregation, or within the synod. As from one main stream at its delta, the tributaries flowed in the direction called for by the pastoral office and its God-given functions. If the figure or image of the tree be used, the pastoral office itself is understood to be the trunk, from which the auxiliaries branch off according to need.

Even the ranks established in the government or polity of an organization like a synod must be understood as of human origin and agreement, thus not binding by divine command, but by human consent, for the good of the covenanted body of congregations, joined in common action and programs. Mission enterprise, efficient educational training schools for pastors and teachers, stewardship and growth programs, and the like were all seen as more effectively accomplished through joint, concerted effort than through each congregation acting on its own. Yet the congregations each remain autonomous in their own life and retain their God-given prerogatives, the Keys, and so also guardianship of the ministry in their midst. A body like a synod thus holds an advisory station over against its member congregations. However, they, in turn, do not act in arbitrary way or with wilful, unloving spirit of independentism.

Fraternal concern for each other dictates rather a spirit of mutual support and encouragement of each other for the work which they jointly, as members of the same synod, pledge to do together, joined in one united faith under one Lord. This followed the precedent of the apostolic era. It evidences respect for the common faith and loyal confessional stance in the partner congregations, and they pledged continuing support of the programs jointly launched with their sister congregations. The centralization of executive powers thus vested in the synodical body is effectively counter-balanced by the root authority grounded in the member congregations, to whom the synod remains answerable.

The picture, which we have just described for a body like a synod, is first of all also true for each congregation itself and the multiple offices for which it may find need in its support of the public, pastoral office. This office is filled by a duly called pastor or pastors. It is supported and sustained in the carrying out of the various functions through the auxiliary offices, none of which would really exist were it not that the divinely called pastor is at work in the midst of the congregation. A. L. Graebner, reflecting upon the assistants which the early church mustered for the sake of the apostles, clearly delineates the lines or limits along which and within which the pastoral office with its auxiliary offices moves:

> These deacons were subsidiary or assistant officers in the churches. Their office was not properly a second ministry with different duties and functions, as the functions of a secretary differ from those of a treasurer. The duties assigned to these assistants had previously been performed by the Apostles as pastors of the congregations, until these pastoral labors exceeded their united energies and the church began to suffer in consequence, Acts 6:1ff.[1]

"To meet this *want, chreia,*" Graebner goes on, "certain functions of the ministry were delegated to a sufficient number of men who were qualified for the performance of these particular duties."[2] The point is, as the early history of the church showed and later history has also borne out, the church always responded with the proper measures to meet and support the needs of the ministry in its midst. Thus also deaconesses are spoken of in the very early church, like Phebe, who carried Paul's epistle to the congregation at

Rome and in other ways distinguished herself in support of the apostle Paul's ministry (Rom. 16:1f.). However, from the ministry of the Word proper, the office of elder, or bishop, or pastor—women were excluded (1 Cor. 14:34; 1 Tim. 2:12). Their supportive ministry in many other functions devolving from the pastoral office was then, and also now in today's church life, highly significant and valued.

When Walther terms these supportive offices "merely a part of the office of the ministry," he in no way denigrates them, nor speaks lightly of them. This could hardly be his intent, for he closes his comments with the asseveration that they "are all to be regarded as sacred offices of the Church," simply by virtue of their rootage.

Article XV of the *Apology*, "Of Human Traditions in the Church," clarifies the Lutheran position that, while rites and ceremonies in the church are to be respected, they must be seen as of human origin, useful very often but in no way of themselves conducive to or effective for the delivery of God's grace—except when they embrace the Word. They dare never compete with the solely meritorious work and sacrifice of Christ, as indeed they often came to do within the Romanist system. In this context, then, Melanchthon explains that, while such traditions of themselves might be harmless and indifferent matters, the church has a prior responsibility of keeping the God-mandated functions very clear and in primary place. These have to do with the Word and sacraments of Baptism and the Lord's Supper, also with Christian discipline. It is with these that the public ministry, the pastoral office, is to occupy itself. It is also because of these God-given treasures, with which the pastor has to do in his office, that "the ministry is the highest office in the Church" (42). Under no circumstances can this function of Gospel ministry be omitted, since "the chief service of God is to teach the Gospel," which, as Melanchthon explains, incorporates all the other articles of faith taught by God's Word (43f.).

It is evident that the office of pastor is "highest," because it is the office commanded by God for each congregation and because of the duties or functions it embraces for the salvation of souls. Luther has the same thing in mind when he states in the *Smalcald Articles* that all will be well in the Church when Christ is recognized as the sole Head and Lord, "and all the bishops (as) equal in office, although they be unequal in gifts," and that the church "be diligently joined in unity of doctrine, faith, Sacraments, prayer, and works of love, etc." (II, iv, 9). This was the prevailing situation in the church already at the time of the apostles, down through the days of Jerome, until papal pretension distorted the relationship of the bishops with vaunted, but unjustified, claims of God-given superiority, Luther points out. There was room for the office of deacon and deaconess in this arrangement or structure, which had as its only God-ordained center the office of the called pastor, elder, presbyter, bishop, or shepherd.

Already at Augsburg the Confessors had testified that the power of the Keys is, by God's commandment, bestowed upon His Church, and that "this power is exercised only by teaching or preaching the Gospel and administering the Sacraments" by the churches through the ministry in their midst, "according to their calling, either to many or to individuals" (AC XXVIII, 5f.). Each believer has the burden of this ministry, but he does not presume to take to himself the office of the public ministry unless he be called thereto. The proclamation of the forgiveness of sins is the chief task of that office (AC XXVIII, 21). This distinguishes it from every other office. A bishop, or pastor, dare not alter in any way what has been given and commanded by God. Other things in the church, such as rites and ceremonies, belong in the area of Christian liberty, and the Confessors "disputed whether bishops or pastors have the right to introduce ceremonies in the church, and to make laws concerning meats, holy-days and grades, that is, orders of ministers, etc." (AC XXVIII, 30).

Implicit in this statement, of course, is the recognition of the fact that such grades or ranks are of human origin, jure humano, only, and that, while the church may establish them for whatever use and advantage they might bring, they nonetheless must be recognized as man-made and not ordained of God. Obviously, there was ample room in this thinking for the auxiliary offices which are spoken of in the New Testament, as in Acts 6:1ff. The abiding principle in things of this nature was "that things be done orderly in the Church," and, while this is primarily spoken of in connection with rites, it would apply as well to other ordinances, such as supportive assistants to the pastors, in the churches (AC XXVIII, 53f.). Underlying all is recognition of the fundamental truth that "the power of the Church" by God's ordaining revolves around the "commission to teach the Gospel and to administer the Sacraments"

(*AC* XXVIII, 12). This sets it quite apart from civil authority which has to do with laws governing the commonwealth (*AC* XXVIII, 13f.).

When Melanchthon dealt with "Ecclesiastical Order" in Article XIV of the *Apology*, he reinforced the ironclad nature of the pastoral office as an office entered into by rightful call, and not by "canonical ordination." At the same time he reassured his opponents that the Lutheran party maintained due respect for the orders and polity existing within the church of that time, as long as these regulations were seen as resulting from human arrangement and agreement, and not by divine ordinance, as Rome claimed (*Apol.* XIV, 24). Implicit once again in this article is the recognized flexibility with which the Lutherans were prepared to look upon various other things voluntarily arranged by the church, or churches, for the common good, such as rites, special days, auxiliary offices, and the like. Their only proviso, or reservation, was that these things be understood to be what in fact they were, structures of human origin and, therefore, not binding upon consciences.

The Tractate which was adopted by the theologians at Smalcald, 1537, reiterated these same basic truths. The pastoral office, or the "office of the ministry proceeds from the general call of the apostles," and not from a special call to St. Peter alone (10). Scriptural evidence for this "makes ministers equal, and teaches that the Church is above the ministers" (11). The reminder is included therewith that as regards traditions in the church, we must not "let any avail more than the Word of God." Notice is thereby given, however, that the Lutherans were perfectly ready to honor traditions, rites, ceremonies, and, we might add, auxiliary offices, as long as these were not seen as binding. Later, and at considerable length, the Confessors repeat in the Tractate that the called pastor, by whatever name, has his office *jure divino*, by divine mandate, through the congregation of believers. Grades or ranks among the clergy, however, are of human authority, and such distinctions, while useful, may be altered as the church sees fit.

Again, implicit in this section of the Tractate is recognition of the fact that, while the church or congregation has no option as regards the pastoral office itself, it may in Christian liberty adopt numerous other regulations, rites, or subservient offices, as long as these serve the advancement of the ministry of the Word and are not demanded as necessary by divine order. If distinctions are recognized between "the grades of bishop and elder or pastor," these must be seen, as Jerome already taught, as deriving from "human authority" only (60-67). Self-evidently, however, congregations have considerable liberty or freedom in this regard, even as it is their authority in the first instance by divine right "to call, elect and ordain ministers" (67). The latter is not a negotiable right; the former is, since it involves things of human arrangement and agreement only.

Article X of the *Formula of Concord* was written primarily to reinforce the principle that in time of persecution, *in statu confessionis*, even adiaphora, like rites and ceremonies, cease to be indifferent matters, because when the church and its teaching are being attacked on these matters the Gospel itself is the focal point of assault. At such time of persecution it is necessary for "the entire congregation of God, yea, every Christian, but especially the ministers of the Word, as the leaders of the congregation of God, to confess freely and openly the godly doctrine, and what belongs to the whole of pure religion, not only in words, but also in works and with deeds" (10).

Walther notes that the Latin version of this text places special emphasis on the responsibility of the called ministers of the Word at such time of testing. His point is to emphasize what in the first place he has singled out in his eighth thesis on the ministry, that the office of the called pastor is "the highest office in the church." As previously stated, the studied, deliberate purpose of Walther is merely to emphasize that this office is the one divinely instituted office given to the church. Walther immediately adds, however, to this thesis that there may indeed be other offices in the church, but these flow from the one divinely ordained office as auxiliary, or derivative, since they carry out functions that belong fundamentally to the God-ordained pastoral office. Their existence is readily acknowledged and honored. Their legitimacy is recognized as having divine sanction and blessing. They originated, however, in the exercise of Christian liberty from human wisdom, advantage, and expediency only.

In his opposition to the canonical ordinations and the episcopal control over the pastoral office in the church, Luther never lost sight of the fact that the Gospel ministry was the highest and greatest of all offices in the world, for it had to do with the saving Gospel. Moreover, it was an office especially commanded by God and conferred by the congregation's call. This is what he stressed in his response to the Bohemian query, 1523. Though it be bestowed by the people, by the general priesthood of believers, the pastoral office was truly apostolic. Moreover, it was the foundation for all other offices in the church. Thus is was set into the center, and belonged there. In comparison the offices of the hierarchical bishops, or the pope, were an ecclesiastical fiction when claimed as divinely ordained, said Luther. The fundamental rule must be this: "If the office of teaching (preaching) be entrusted to anyone, then everything accomplished by the Word in the church is entrusted."[3] That would mean preaching, teaching, baptizing, judging doctrine, defending the truth from false doctrine, etc. By its very nature this office "of preaching the Gospel is the greatest of all and certainly apostolic."[4] Moreover, "it becomes the foundation for all other functions, which are built upon it," as the church may deem necessary and of which the apostle Paul speaks in part in 1 Corinthians 12.[5] Luther notes on the basis of John 4:2 and 1 Corinthians 1:17 that it was because of the fundamental importance of preaching the saving Word that the Lord Jesus Himself, as well as his apostle Paul, concentrated on such proclamation and left matters like baptism in the hands of their disciples or assistants.

By saying this Luther in no way minimized the significance of one function in relation to the other, nor of the one office over the other; but he underscored once again heavily the fact that God had set up one office in the church, the office of the pastoral ministry. It had various functions. This he did not deny. How these were carried out, with what other assistants, was a matter of indifference, as long as it was recognized that they devolved from the one divinely ordained office of pastor. In a busy and large parish it might be necessary, Luther stated in a 1525 sermon, to divide it into four or five geographical parts, with various helpers assigned to assist the pastor in ministering to the soul and bodily needs of the parishioners. The primary responsibility, especially for the spiritual care, would reside in the called pastor; but we know from New Testament example, said Luther, that other helpers may be necessary, so that no one in the parish is neglected, body or soul. Such individuals could rightly bear the name deacon or deaconess, more deservingly as a matter of fact, than the so-called deacons presently consecrated by the Romanist bishops, Luther states. The only trouble is that we do not have enough of such well-trained

people, male and female, to fill these auxiliary posts.[6]   Luther
repeats essentially the same thoughts in his *Church Postils* on the
Epistles for 1525.[7]

Already in his *Babylonian Captivity*, 1520, Luther had stated
that "the diaconate is the ministry, not of reading the Gospel or the
Epistle, as is the present practice, but of distributing the church's aid
to the poor, so that the priests may be relieved of the burden of
temporal matters and may give themselves more freely to prayer and
the Word."[8] Luther cites the example of the apostles in Acts as they
choose deacons to aid them in similar tasks.   But the clergy
themselves have their work cut out for them in preaching the
Gospel. Now, says Luther of the tragic situation in his day, they
don't even know the Gospel, and the average priest, as well as
bishop, "is a kind of pest to the church, who under the false title of
priest or bishop, or dressed in sheep's clothing, actually does
violence to the Gospel and plays the wolf (Matt. 7:15) in the
church."[9]

On the basis of New Testament teaching and examples,
Martin Chemnitz subscribes fully to the position which Luther has
articulated concerning the pastoral ministry as the highest and
fundamental office ordained by God, and the auxiliary offices as
arising from the need in the church for additional help. "In the
beginning the apostles took care of the ministry of the Word and the
sacraments and at the same time also of the distribution and
dispensation of alms."[10] But as their duties multiplied, the apostles
chose helpers "whom they called deacons," that these might take
care of the physical, temporal needs of the people, while they
(apostles) devoted themselves to preaching and teaching of the
Word. So, the basic principle at work here, says Chemnitz, is this:
"Because many duties belong to the ministry of the church which
cannot all conveniently be performed by one person or by a few,
when the believers are very numerous—in order, therefore, that all
things may be done in an orderly way, decently, and for edification—these duties of the ministry began, as the assembly of the
church grew great, to be distributed among certain ranks of ministers
which they afterward called *taxeis* (ranks) or *tagmata* (orders), so
that each might have, as it were, a certain designated station in
which he might serve the church in certain duties of the ministry."[11]
When such auxiliary offices were constituted, says Chemnitz, it is
clear from the New Testament that it was done "for the welfare of

the assembly of the church."[12] Moreover, we see that the apostles
also viewed this arrangement as a kind of testing period or trial
vocation for these "deacons," "so that afterward heavier duties may
more safely and profitably be entrusted to them," Chemnitz observes.[13] This held true for Stephen and Philip, for example.

In assessing the Romanists' claims for the co-called "holy
orders," Chemnitz stressed three points: 1) We have no command
of God which sets such offices, or various ranks, like bishops, etc.,
in the church, but only the one office, the public pastoral ministry;
2) there is absolutely no basis in the Word of God, nor from the
apostolic example, to support the institution of a hierarchical form
of ranking or government within the church; and 3) the apostles at
first embraced within their persons and office all the duties pertaining to the care and nurture of their flocks, and only as their
congregations grew and it became humanly impossible for them to
fulfill all the needs of their parishes did they, for the sake of the
congregation's welfare, parcel out some of the functions which were
auxiliary to their ministry to others, carefully chosen individuals who
qualified as servants of God and enjoyed the esteem of their fellow
believers.[14]

Gerhard chimes in with Chemnitz that ranks or orders
among the clergy do not rest on the authority of God's Word, nor on
apostolic precedent. When they do appear, it is evident that no
claim is being made for divine ordaining of the arrangement, but that
the only consideration is the welfare of the church, in other words,
what best serves good order, decorum, and edification within the
congregations. Gerhard notes that the congregations are never shut
out from the process of procuring qualified pastors, elders, or
bishops for service in their midst; their vote or consent is always in
the picture. By the same token it is evident, according to Gerhard,
that for the laying on of hands in the public manifesting of the call
and installing of the called pastor, the presbyters or elders, or as
Luther says to the Bohemian Christians, "those who are leaders
among you," were the ones involved in the "ordination."[15]

The scholarly lay theologian, Veit Ludwig von Seckendorf,
reinforced the same position expressed by the theologians. God's
Word in no way supports the kind of distinction which the Roman
church has fabricated to distinguish bishops from the clergy and
other offices. Bishops and priests (or pastors) are on the same level
in the New Testament. Each parish pastor has all the duties of his

office as a called servant of the Word, no less or more than the
"bishops," or superintendents, or church officials, who govern in a
given area of the church. Such offices may indeed be legitimate but
they were of human origin. For the ministry the focus always zeroes
in on the preaching of the Word, the administering of the sacraments, and all that pertains to the pastoral care of souls, exhorting,
comforting, admonishing, disciplining, etc.[16]

The church, or congregation, may rightly follow the
apostolic example, as Walther notes, to supplement or assist the
work being done by the called pastor(s) by establishing auxiliary
offices. These continue and function within given limits as long as
there is demonstrated need for them and their services. They do not
become, nor are they, the pastors as such, as they perform prescribed
functions. This only happens, as Chemnitz explained, after their
service under the apostles, or their equivalents, gave evidence of
their qualifications for being called into the pastoral office itself.
The divinely sanctioned uniqueness of the pastoral office remained
singularly by itself, as God ordained.

Luther's recognition of the people's role in church life and
the fabricated claim of the ecclesiastical, or sacerdotal hierarchy,
came early in his life. He never altered his fundamental thoughts on
the principle involved. It turned or pivoted upon the high station
which God has accorded the royal priesthood of believers (1 Pet.
2:9). As time went on he recognized also, however, that "those who
are leaders among you," as he wrote to the Bohemian Christians,
would often need to take the initiative in matters that concerned the
local parishes. Thus we find him regularly calling on the magistrates of cities, princes, and rulers to take the leading role in the
interests of the common people and particularly the church in their
midst. He does not, however, change his basic position as he leans
on these individuals for competent leadership and initiative. The
power of the Keys is still vested in the *Gemeinde*, the congregation
of believers at a given locale.

To the end of his life Luther defended the fundamental right,
numbered among the twelve *gravamina*, or grievances, of the
peasants, prior to their uprising in 1525, namely, "the right to hear
the Gospel and choose their pastors."[17] Accordingly, though he
found armed insurrection by the peasants repugnant, Luther's
point-blank answer to the princes was: "You cannot reject this
request with any show of right," even though in other things the

peasants may be reaching further than they ought with "some selfish demands."[18] In fact, Luther took a forthright stand in behalf of religious freedom, stating that "no ruler ought to prevent anyone from teaching or believing what he pleases, whether it is the Gospel or lies."[19] Such liberty or freedom however, must not be stretched into license, whereby another man's rights are infringed; thus Luther had sharp words for *Infiltrating and Clandestine Preachers*, 1532, who ventured to sneak into another man's parish without proper credentials or call.[20] Basically his concern was still in behalf of the common man who tended to be exploited through such *Schwaermer* or Enthusiast machinations.

Closely coupled with Luther's teaching on the office of the holy ministry as devolving upon a qualified man through the call of the Christian congregation is his recognition of the fact that other offices in the church likewise belong in the realm of the congregation's freedom to act. This applied, on the one hand, to auxiliary offices designed to assist the parish pastor, and, on the other hand, to various governing offices which the church, or groupings of churches, found expedient for the church's well-being or joint efforts. In each case, however, neither of these could be shown to be of divine origin as was the office of the called pastoral servant of the congregation. The truth was rather this, that they found their rootage and source in that office, which in turn devolved from the congregation's possession of the Keys by God's ordaining. We have Scripture on our side, Luther asserts, when we say that "a Christian congregation (makes) a preacher by its call alone."[21] In addition, such congregation also had the right to create supplemental offices to accomplish its work. But the pastoral office always remains "the highest office, on which all others depend and from which they follow."[22] Should the pastoral office cease, or "where there is no office of preaching, none of the others can follow."[23]

That was Luther's answer for the so-called lower offices under the ministry, as well as and especially for the sacerdotal monolith under the papacy. "Present-day bishops are spiritual idols" as a result of the pretentious usurpation of power under the papacy.[24] Yet in his rejection of the system, Luther was rejecting only the faulty theology on which it was based, not the right of congregations and church bodies to adopt a polity or governing consistory, or the like, to advance the cause of the Word. In some of his early lectures on the Psalms Luther speaks of the church as "the hen, just as Christ is, whose pinions are the bishops and leaders and protectors of the chicks."[25] But such guardians of the faith and the truth are to be "faithful pastors, bishops, and teachers against these wolves who come in sheep's clothing (Matt. 7:15)."[26]

In its ministering of the Word the church is like a fortress, with many battlements and towers for defense against false doctrine, states Luther in his *Commentary on the Song of Solomon*, and these may refer "properly to the variety of ministries which are needed in the church."[27] Admittedly in these lectures (*scholia*) of 1530-1531 Luther's concern is for orthodox teaching, and it is his considered opinion that "where these two things are present—right teaching and defence against wolves—there of necessity follow peace and tranquillity."[28] This same conviction coursed through C. F. W. Walther's veins, as we know, during the troubled days of the 19th century when evangelical theology was sorely tried on all sides, especially in the heartland of the Reformation. Little wonder that *Lehre und Wehre* became Walther's watchword and the masthead for his theological journal by the same name.

God established no ranks as regards offices in the church, beyond the ordaining of the one office, the pastoral ministry. The ranks and grades, therefore, which the church establishes for itself, in order that things might be done in good order, are in each case man-made. The same applies to other externals in church life, like the vestments the clergy wear, whether "red, brown, black, or grey," says Luther. After all, "what knowledge or revelation from the Holy Spirit is necessary to prescribe that a cardinal must sit above a bishop, a bishop above a prince, etc.?" Luther queries. In things like this God has given us Christian liberty, to choose to do one way or another, and He has endowed man with reason, so that he is competent to judge and decide what is useful and expedient. But any heathen or non-Christian can do that too, Luther reminds his hearers in his sermon series on John's Gospel.[29] Thus it is possible, even though the foundation for their respective offices differs considerably, that "a faithful sexton is no less pleasing to God with his gift than is a preacher of the Word, for he serves God in the same faith and spirit."[30] Luther personally has no problem with ranks or supervisory offices which the church of the Reformation saw fit to create. Thus when he writes to Nicholas Amsdorf, his old colleague, whom he himself ordained as bishop of the church at

Naumburg, he addresses Amsdorf as his "esteemed superior" and "my superior venerably to be esteemed in the Lord."[31]

Luther also is not troubled by the apparent ranks which were distinguishable in the early, apostolic days. The apostles after all were chosen by Christ directly and deserved a certain distinction; yet they did not place themselves autocratically above their co-workers, but spoke of them as fellow elders and the like. Timothy obviously honored and showed deference to his mentor, the apostle Paul, who was his "spiritual father" in the ministry of the Word. Each was in that ministry, Luther notes, because of his call.[32] The real problem then, as now, Luther states, was the presence of "many fickle, big-talking false teachers who kept rushing about in all directions, saying that they were driven by the Spirit, by wisdom, and by their talent."[33] Of this kind of worker the church has no need. They are upstarts, without standing.

Even the papacy of Rome must come in for the same testing. Luther has no quarrel with the fact that God's providence has allowed the papacy to come into existence, but he demurs on two points: 1) The church cannot accept new doctrines concocted by the Romanists; and 2) everything the pope does or says must first pass muster before or under the Holy Scriptures.[34] Were the papacy ever to vaunt itself and its authority over the Holy Scriptures, "I would freely say that he is the true Antichrist, of which all Scripture speaks."[35] It was shortly thereafter, 1520, that Luther was convinced that all the evidence was present for that conclusion. The ground for his charge lay in usurpation of authority over Scripture and the distortion of Scripture's central article on justification *sola gratia/fide*, not on the fact that Rome had created an ostentatious episcopal system, or certainly not because various auxiliary offices had been added to and above the parish priest's post.

Nothing transcends the pastoral ministry in Luther's estimation. He underscores what the apostle Paul has to say about "one aspiring to the office of a bishop" (pastor) as being a good thing and "a noble task." And Luther deplores the prevailing situation, as he sees it in 1545, in his last blast *Against the Roman Papacy, An Institution of the Devil*, that parents are not giving their sons for the ministry, because they want them to work at something that will bring them a bigger income and a softer life. With that kind of attitude, says Luther, they deserve what they get and "may God grant you that you become a pope, cardinal, or member of the

Roman See, thus getting what you deserve."[36] Christ will see to the advancement of His Church, nonetheless. "It still has no other Gospel and Scripture, no other baptism and Communion, no other faith and Spirit, no other Christ and God, no other Lord's Prayer and prayer, no other hope and eternal life, than we have in our church in Wittenberg."[37] Gifts may differ in the church, but "everything belonging to the Church is equal," whereby Luther wants to reemphasize the fact that there is but one office of public pastor, the names, "bishop, elder, pastor, preacher," being used inter-change-ably.[38]

Luther is especially vocal and outspoken on the subject of getting good workers for the church in his *A Sermon on Keeping Children in School*, 1530. If we do not train competent men, we will get what we had before, "ignorant louts."[39] First and foremost he has the office of pastor, or preacher, in mind; but implicit throughout this "sermon" is his concern for all auxiliary offices, teacher, deacon, and the like. He faults the parents severely for refusing to let their children advance academically in preparation for service in the church and the state.[40] "Think, too, how many parishes, pulpits, schools, and sacristanships there are," opportunities in other words for worthwhile service in the churches and communities. These must be filled, states Luther, and there is a continuing attrition through death, illness, and retirement. Luther gives some statistics, as these were available to him: "When I was a young student I heard it said that in Saxony there were (if I remember rightly) about eighteen hundred parishes. If that is true, and every parish required at least two persons, a pastor and a sacristan (except that in the cities there are preachers, chaplains, assistants, schoolmasters, and helpers), then in this one principality about four thousand educated persons are needed, of whom about one-third die off every ten years."[41] Luther is, moreover, convinced that their sons "can easily get as good a living from the preaching office as from a trade."[42] No doubt he would include the auxiliary offices referred to earlier as well.

NOTES

1	*Theological Quarterly*, 1903, 22.
2	Ibid.
3	*LW* 40, 36; *WA* 12, 191.
4	Ibid.
5	Ibid.
6	*WA* 11, 2754f.; *St. L* 11, 2065. *Church Postils* (Gospel), 1525.
7	Cf. *WA* 12, 455ff.; *St. L* 12, 338f.
8	*LW* 36, 116; *WA* 6, 567.
9	Ibid.
10	*Examination of the Council of Trent*, II, 683.
11	Op. cit., 682f.
12	Op. cit., 683.
13	Ibid.
14	Op. cit., 685.
15	*Loci theol.*, de ministerio eccl., 238 Quoted in Walther, *KA*, 354ff.
16	Cf. Walther, op. cit., 349.
17	*LW* 46, 22; *WA* 18, 298. *Admonition to Peace*, 1525.
18	Ibid.
19	Ibid.
20	*LW* 40, 383-394; *WA* 30^3 518-527.
21	*LW* 39, 313; *WA* 11, 415. *That a Christian Congregation Has a Right to Call*, addressed to the Leisnig magistracy, 1523.
22	Op. cit., 314.
23	Ibid.
24	Ibid.
25	*LW* 11, 214; *WA* 4, 68.
26	Ibid.
27	*LW* 15, 260; *WA* 31^2, 763f.
28	Ibid.
29	*LW* 24, 175; *WA* 45, 620.
30	*LW* 27, 103; *WA* 40^2, 132.
31	*LW* 50, 262-265; *WA*, Br 11, 115.
32	*LW* 28, 281; *WA* 26, 49.

33   Ibid.

34   *LW* 39, 101; *WA* 6, 321f. *On the Papacy at Rome*, 1520.

35   Op. cit., 102.

36   *LW* 41, 355; *WA* 54, 282.

37   *LW* 41, 358; *WA* 54, 284.

38   Ibid.

39   *LW* 46, 218; *WA* 30², 524.

40   *LW* 46, 222ff.; *WA* 30², 531ff.

41   *LW* 46, 234; *WA* 30², 549.

42   *LW* 46, 236; *WA* 30², 553.

Chapter 7

Right of Judging Doctrine

From Luther's day forward the doctrine of the royal priesthood of believers was a treasured possession of the Lutheran church. Scripture taught so plainly that the Keys were the possession, not of popes and bishops, nor of the so-called clergy estate, but of the believers. They formed the Christian congregation. To them as a whole, as well as each individual Christian first of all, belonged all the rights and privileges of the priesthood which Christ had won for them by His vicarious atonement. They would witness for the faith before men (Matt. 10:32f.; 1 Pet. 3:15); they as an assembly of Christians at one place would exercise their rights not by each opting for the public pastoral office, but by calling a qualified man to lead them, to preach the whole counsel of God's Word, and administer the sacraments for them. In their own families they would bring up their children in the fear and nurture of the Lord by inculcating His Word. They would minister to the spiritual and physical needs of their neighbor, whoever he might be, but especially those of the household of faith. (Gal. 6:10; 1 Thess. 5:11-15; Col. 3:16; Heb. 10:24.25) They would pray for all men, for all that pertained to their well-being, also for those in authority (1 Tim. 2:1-4). They, as children of God themselves ruled by His Word, would also be spiritually equipped through their study of Christian doctrine to sift carefully between what was true and false, between faithful and false teachers of the Word. All these, and more, were among the rights and privileges bestowed by God through His calling of believers to faith into the royal priesthood.

Purity of doctrinal teaching thus is not only a proper and rightful concern of laymen; it is their responsibility as well. Through the years, from the days of the apostles onward, as can be seen from the apostle Paul's greetings in his Letter to the Romans, chapter 16, laymen have had an honored place and a needed role in the church's life. Luther was quite convinced that the Scriptures were written with such clarity that, if the average man had the tools of language and grammar, he could not only safely read and learn for himself, but he could also judge those who claimed to be interpreters of Holy Writ with special prestige and authority.

Against Erasmus, in his very influential *Bondage of the Will*, Luther asserted Scripture's clarity and its inherent God-given attribute and ability to make its meaning evident to the attentive and believing reader.[1] Against scholars and theologians who opposed Scripture's truth, Luther would write with learned argument and erudite literary terminology. But ordinarily it was his deliberate purpose and intention to preach, speak, and write in such a way that the average intelligent lay person could understand. He knew it was a fiction that only popes, bishops, and clergy were intended by God to know and understand His Word. Therefore, many of his appeals for correction of abuse and reform in theology were addressed to pastors and laymen alike, usually therefore in German, rather than Latin, the language of academe.

It was the ground swell of the laity rising in protest against the papal excesses on both counts, abuses and doctrinal aberration, which to a large extent spelled success for the Reformation movement. Since then the church has again and again witnessed the phenomenon of laymen keeping the ship of the church on even keel by their protest against the intrusion of a foreign "gospel" into its ranks. When the pulpits became sterile through the inroads of Liberalism and various kinds of "Ego-theologies," the people in the pew were often the solid phalanx of resistance that kept the Word of God alive and well in the circle of believers. Scripture not only makes the average Christian competent to judge in doctrinal matters, but requires it of him. (Matt. 7:15; Rom. 16:17; Col. 4:17; John 8:31f.; 1 Pet. 4:11) The norm for judgment, of course, is not within themselves, their insights or wisdom, but solely within and by the Word of God, Holy Writ.

We have previously noted that the power of the Keys, the means of grace, Word and Sacrament, is fundamentally the possessions of all believers. Thus, the right to baptize, or to absolve from sin, belongs to them, as well as to the called pastor. While they by their calling of the pastor empower him to act publicly in their stead, the fact remains that they have not surrendered or given up the power which they thus invest upon the called pastor. Luther is quick to point out that herein is the reason why absolution, or baptism, or teaching of the Word is as valid and certain when done by a layman, under given circumstances, as by the pastor. Accordingly, the very fact that in cases of need a layman or woman may dispense the mercies of God is indication enough that the power of the Keys still resides first of all with the believers themselves.

When God through the mouth of his apostle Peter exhorts that Christians must "be ready always to give an answer to every man," it is evident that this is said to laymen. "St. Peter spoke these words to all Christians, pastors, laymen, men, women, young and old, and of whatever state they may be," states Luther in commentary.[2] "It follows from this that every Christian should account for his faith and be able to give a reason and an answer when necessary."[3] It had been Satan's trick up till now, states Luther, to cause the people to believe the lie that the Bible was a forbidden book for them, reserved only for the church and the clergy. Luther has his finger on a sore spot in Romanist theology when he explains how Satan's reasoning went: "If I can keep the laity from reading Scripture, then I shall bring the priests from the Bible into Aristotle,"[4] and the people will content themselves with the babbling and chatter of the priests, whatever they preach or teach. That could lead a man straight to hell, if he in the process came to believe just the opposite of the saving Gospel, Luther says in horror. "Therefore, we must know what we believe, namely, what God's Word says, not what the pope or the saintly fathers believe or say. For you must not rely on a person. No, you must rely on the Word of God alone."[5]

From Luther's day onward this has been the stance of the evangelical Lutheran church. The Confessors at Augsburg, at Smalcald. at Bergen Cloister, where the *Formula of Concord* was drawn up, all stood on that same platform. It was C. F. W. Walther's stance, with his colleagues, when the Missouri Synod was founded in 1847. Doctrine is given of God. The right and duty of knowing and testifying for it belong to pastors and people alike. Thus in the congregations the laity are expected to know and judge in matters doctrinal, and not only the clergy, though the latter may have greater theological training. As Luther pointed out, false *prophets* are not in the pew, but in the pulpit, and it is the hearers who are exhorted by God in His Word to judge between the false and the true prophets on the basis of His Word. Thus from the very first, in congregations, as well as in the synod they soon formed, the pastors and laymen shared alike in the judging of doctrinal matters, not as though these first of all had to be formed or shaped, but rather faithfully discerned from Holy Scripture, God's clear fountain of truth, and faithfully taught.

It is a fact of no little significance that the Lutheran Confessions were as much the fruit of concerned laymen acting in behalf of the truth, as first of all of theologians involved in their production. Thus, for example, the *Augsburg Confession* was not only presented at the Diet in the name of the lay signators, the various territorial princes, but also the venerable Saxon statesman and doctor of laws, Chancellor Gregorius Brueck, actually composed the introduction and the conclusion of the Confession, Melanchthon's being discarded as too long and involved. Again at Smalcald it was the laymen, in this case the leading princes of the Lutheran territories, who played a large role in the proceedings, especially in seeing to it that Luther's *Smalcald Articles* were generally and wholeheartedly approved, even though Melanchthon had succeeded, during Luther's grave illness there, to keep them from being publicly read at that time. In addition, it was the laymen who again pressured Melanchthon and the rest of the theologians present to produce what has become generally known as the appendix to the *Smalcald Articles*, the Tractate on the Power and Jurisdiction of Bishops. In actual sequence it was publicly read and approved after the re-reading of the *Augsburg Confession* and *Apology* at the Smalcald conclave of lay leaders and theologians, in 1537. Again, in the production of the *Formula of Concord*, laymen like Prince August played no small role in pressing it through to completion, even though the actual composition was in the competent hands of men like Chemnitz and Andreae.

A most significant role was played by Lutheran laymen across the Lutheran territories when it came time to issue the *Book of Concord*, June 25, 1580. True, once again the facile pen of the astute theologian, Andreae, was called into service for the drafting of the beautiful preface to the *Book of Concord*. Very plainly, so that there could be no possible misunderstanding, this document spoke of God's gracious favor in giving unto men His precious Word through the Sacred Scriptures. All the articles of faith taught in Holy Scripture constituted the confessional platform, a fact demonstrated by the various Confessions and their articles. The story is told completely, yet succinctly, of how through various assaults from the Romanist opponents and bitter controversies within the Lutheran church itself, the church had finally come to this memorable moment in history when with great unity and unanimity of mind, heart, and faith the signators by the thousands, many of them the leading princes and magistrates of commonwealths placed their signatures under the document in the name and behalf of the regions they represented. This point was reached only after careful study of the Confessions and the firm conviction that they were a true and correct exposition of Scriptural truth. Because (*quia*) they were, the Confessors were ready to say: "Therefore we also have determined not to depart even a finger's breadth either from the subjects themselves, or from the phrases which are found in them, but, the Spirit of the Lord aiding us, to persevere constantly, with the greatest harmony, in this godly agreement" (Preface to the *Book of Concord, Triglot*, 23).

There was no question whatsoever that laymen, besides theologians and pastors in general, were able and were expected to judge in matters doctrinal, or theological. This is a basic assumption throughout the period when the Confessions were coming into existence, pressed out of the church by the need for witnessing to the truth and fending off error. Already by the time of the Augsburg Diet, 1530, it simply was implicit in Lutheran thinking and church life, because of the fundamental and key role which the doctrine of the priesthood of believers filled in the evangelical cause of the Reformation.

It is, moreover, explicit in each of the Confessions that laymen, too, are to be instructed in the truths of God's Word and, thus, "to try the spirits whether they are of God." Luther's *Small* and *Large Catechisms* of 1529 accentuate this in many different ways, particularly as he lays the burden on parents and pastors to inculcate the articles of Christian doctrine in the hearts and minds of the children and all entrusted to their care. Each of the chief parts—six in the *Small Catechism*, five in the *Large*—is written in such a way that the average man could know and fully understand the Scriptural truth expounded. This presupposition is especially explicit in the prefaces to the catechisms, as well as in the Table of Duties. Luther burns with deep concern that people should know and, having come to know, also believe and trust what God had taught for their sakes on the Commandments, the Creed, prayer, baptism, confession and absolution, and the Lord's Supper. The *Catechism* was to be like a small Scriptures, "a compend and brief summary of all the Holy Scriptures" (*LC*, Preface 18). If a person knows these chief parts, Luther is quite convinced, then every man or woman or child would have what pertained to life and salvation (*LC*, Preface 17). In turn, when the prefaces to the *Formula of Concord* and to the *Epitome* are drawn up by Andreae, Chemnitz, and their four co-workers, they likewise express this confidence, that the *Small* and *Large Catechisms* of Luther most adequately dealt with and summarized the essential Biblical truths. The Epitome states:

> And because such matters concern also the laity and the salvation of their souls, we also confess the *Small* and *Large Catechisms* of Dr. Luther, as they are included in Luther's works, as the Bible of the laity, wherein everything is comprised which is treated at greater length in Holy Scripture, and is necessary for a Christian man to know for his salvation (*Epit.*, Preface 5).

This is not mere heroic, hyperbolic sort of language concerning the esteemed teacher and leader of the Reformation and his theological gems, the catechisms, but deliberate, considered opinion and stance on the theological content and value of these key works of Luther. The *Formula of Concord* itself expresses much the same opinion, stating that "the Christian doctrine from God's Word is comprised in them in the most correct and simple way," so that the average person may easily grasp and understand it (*FC*, Comp. Summary 8). By its help Christian people, young and old, learned and simple, are enabled to "distinguish between pure and false doctrine" (Ibid.). Such Christians are exhorted by Melanchthon in the *Apology*, Articles VII and VIII on the Church, to discern the false teachers who do not faithfully present God's Word, but their own, and to desert or avoid them (*Apol.* VII and VIII, 48). In the *Smalcald Articles* Luther pleads for much the same stance against the intrusion of error into doctrine, stating: "The rule is: the Word of God shall establish articles of faith, and no one else, not even an angel" (*SA* II, ii, 15). In the Tractate drawn up by the theologians at Smalcald there appear similar appeals to the average Christian, not just to the theologians, to discern the false teachings brought on by the Pope and the kingdom of Antichrist, and, despite the threat of persecution and death, to reject them (Tractate 41, 49f.).

The lay leaders, with their people, were deeply concerned Christians. They took their faith and Christian doctrine seriously. For it they were ready to risk all, their very necks and all they possessed. This doctrine was publicly presented in the various confessional documents. These presentations had been shown to be in full and perfect accord with the Scriptures. They did not intend to surrender any part of their faith. With the six men who first signed the *Formula of Concord*—Chemnitz, Andreae, Selnecker, Chytraeus, Koerner, Musculus—they were fully prepared to state: "We will neither privately nor publicly speak or write anything contrary to it, but, by the help of God's grace, intend to abide thereby; therefore, after mature deliberation, we have, in God's fear and with the invocation of His name, attached our signatures with our own hands" (*FC* XII, 40).

This is an oft repeated pledge, made not only by pastors who bind themselves with *quia* subscription to the Confessions at the time of their ordination or call into office—that is, subscribing them without equivocation *because* they are a true exposition of Scriptural teaching—but also by many laymen, articulate and learned in the Confessions as well, who wish to indicate their agreement in every way with the stated position of the Confessions.

The die was cast for Lutheran theology by Luther's unequivocal espousal of the doctrine on the priesthood of believers under Christ, and by his forthright application of this teaching to cases in point, or situations as they applied in the parishes. Sacerdotalism in its severest form had prevailed in the Roman church till now, but a whole new direction was set when Luther declared that by this doctrine "Christ takes both the right and the power to judge teaching from the bishops, scholars, and councils and gives them to everyone and to all Christians equally."[6]

Luther's followers did not depart from this fundamental principle, though there may have been local or regional adaptations to suit specific needs or circumstances. Martin Chemnitz wrote his *Enchiridion* expressly for the purpose that it might be a handbook on doctrine, whereby the clergy themselves would be helped and have a handy doctrinal reference, but also in order to supply the laity with a plumbline of doctrine by which they might test the doctrinal fitness of those who were called to serve in the high office of pastor. It was Chemnitz' hope and prayer that this little book would aid and abet Christian unity and concord throughout the Braunschweig territory. God's Word is pure and our teaching, the pastors' and the people's, should likewise be pure and orthodox, Chemnitz held. God has chosen to use the instrumentality of the congregations for calling pastors into their office. This requires that the people themselves be informed on doctrinal matters.[7]

The papalist authorities were in error when they excluded the people, especially the leaders among them, from the process of choosing qualified pastors and leaders in the church. Especially the leading laymen, Chemnitz acknowledges, are by their background, education, and experience able to exercise salutary judgment and discretion in this matter of procuring qualified pastors for the local churches.[8] But implicit in this choice is the will of the people, and it should always be understood as a matter of expediency and wisdom when the magistrates act as representatives of the people or congregation at large.[9]

By the same token it often would be impossible and unwise to try to submit the calling of the pastor to an assembly made up of every last member of the parish. Chemnitz, however, never loses sight of the fact that that is where the authority lies in the final analysis, though he definitely wishes to eschew the kind of mobocracy prevalent among the Anabaptistic groups of that day. From apostolic times the apostles and their co-workers took a leading role in the procurement of worthy shepherds and bishops or elders for the churches, but they never did this without the understood consent of the congregations, with whom the final authority lay.[10]

Chemnitz' own conduct in office as superintendent of the churches in the Braunschweig territory was a fine example of how this worked in practice, especially in the relationship of the clergy with their people in the congregations. His was not an autocratic sort of control of the clergy or the churches. On a voluntary basis he enlisted the clergy in what might be called in terms of our day an "in-service study program." And when the individual parish confronted a problem as regards the ministry in its midst, he had the matter laid directly before the congregation for its adjudication in line with the Word of God.[11]

Gerhard especially took note of the place and the part played by so-called "lay theologians." The term *theology* is appropriate in a wide use of the term for all believers, he states, "for the Christian faith and religion is found in all believers, the learned as well as the unlearned, and in this sense all who know and accept the articles of faith," or "who teach and profess these articles" are called theologians and may judge in matters theological according to God's Word.[12] Franz Pieper notes that the knowledge of doctrine on the part of many laymen is often outstanding, and that, therefore, from the very first years of the Missouri Synod's history, in accord with Lutheran practice, laymen, too, were allowed to participate in synodical meetings, even as they already did in congregational affairs, and to pass judgment on doctrine, whether true or false, by the touchstone of the Word of God and the Lutheran Confessions.[13] We do not intend, says Gerhard, to "make shepherds of the sheep," but by the same token, "we do not want them to be brute sheep, which neither can nor should distinguish between shepherds and wolves."[14]

From Luther onwards the theologians to a man recognized the expediency of a congregation acting through a representative body or group in the execution of its ministry or work. Pieper capsules this nicely: "The Church is free to take care of some things through representatives chosen by it for this purpose. Thus the elders or the church council can represent a congregation, and conferences, synods, councils, etc., can represent other Christians and small or large groups of congregations."[15] But the ultimate authority or power is always seen as residing in the congregation of believers, the royal priests, whence such representative power is granted. Leonhard Hutter, a contemporary of Chemnitz, acknowledged that the structure within a congregation or church body often appears to be what he termed "aristocratic," that is, in the hands of specially trained and able leaders. But in the final analysis this was only apparent, for in reality the ultimate power lay with the electorate, which could be described more as having "something in common with a democracy."[16] It is interesting that he should already have used the term, democracy, and that he actually was quoting from Flacius Illyricus, Luther's strong-willed, assertive colleague.

The pattern was well established. "In councils, the teachers and *delegates of the Church* are assembled," states David Hollaz.[17] Johann Baier also recognized that laymen who were "experienced and skillful in sacred affairs, godly, and peace-loving," and who enjoyed the support and confidence of the people in general, could and should participate in councils and synodical meetings, just as the early Christians had done at the time of the apostles, Acts 15.[18]

Quenstedt rules the same way, namely, that while "a promiscuous multitude does not judge," a representative body of able laymen indeed participate in assemblies of the congregation or the church at large.[19] Thus "also believing Christians, familiar with the Scriptures, both laymen and clerics, sent by the congregations to the council," according to Quenstedt, should share in the matter of judging in doctrinal matters. Hollaz underscores this right and prerogative over and over again, as does Gerhard, in order to forestall any hierarchical take-over similar to what happened under Romanist rule.[20] But all such judging or arbitration is always seen as happening under evident authority of the Word of God, Holy Scripture.

The role that the laymen play, therefore, along with the clergy in the matters that pertain to the ministry of the Word in the congregation and in larger groupings of the congregations, like synods, is never a domineering role which forms or fabricates doctrine, but which dutifully subscribes to what God has plainly taught in His Word. Since that Word is clear, as Luther contended, it is incumbent on all the "priests," not only the few from a so-called priestly caste, to know and to be arbiters of the truth. Franz Pieper has stated the case well: "If the question at issue pertains to matters taught and decided in God's Word, the Christian position is that no man and no assembly of men, no matter how learned and renowned they may be, can decide for a Christian what is Scriptural doctrine. This matter every single Christian must decide for himself on the basis of the clear, infallible Word of God."[21] There is no room here for wild subjectivism, since the judgment is simply to resonate forth from "the clear, infallible Word of God." Therefore, voting and balloting in Christian congregations and synods, according to Pieper, "has a different significance when it concerns Christian doctrine than when it concerns indifferent matters." On the latter a simple majority vote decides the question. But with doctrine it is a different ball game. "The only purpose of voting in matters of doctrine is to see whether all now understand the teaching of the divine Word and agree to it" and "not to decide the correctness of a doctrine by majority vote or even by unanimous vote."[22] This is frequently misunderstood. But for peace, unity, and concord there is need for all, laity and clergy, to bow before the Word of God, drive down personal views or private opinions, and assent freely and believingly to God's truth. The prayer of C. F. W. Walther is still very much in place, for both clergy and laity:

Lord, our God, most graciously didst Thou give us Thy Holy, unerring Word to be a lamp unto our feet and a light upon our path. Preserve us from making our blind reason or the opinion of the wicked world our guide. Grant us grace that by the aid of Thy Holy Spirit we may follow Thy Word alone, departing from it neither to the right nor to the left, until, having escaped all the dangers that threaten our souls, we shall have arrived at the end of our pilgrimage and have come into blissful communion with Thee in heaven. Grant our prayer for the sake of Jesus Christ, Thy dear Son, our Lord and Savior. Amen.[23]

Augustine's dictum still obtains: *In ecclesia non valet: hoc ego dico, hoc tu dicis, hoc ille dicit, sed: Haec dicit Dominus*, "that which prevails in the church is not, this I say, this you say, this that man says, but, thus saith the Lord." That is the true power of the ministry which has been given to the royal priests, and through them to the shepherds of the congregations.

As stated, Scripture's teaching concerning the royal priesthood of believers was Luther's keystone on the doctrine of church and ministry. It was his firm conviction that "because we have been baptized, we are children of God and fellow citizens of the saints in the kingdom of God." We have this certainty from even the lowliest of the servants of the Word, the Christian pastor of the Word, because in his hands are the Keys, "the power and the divine command" to forgive and absolve from sin.[24] Under the old dispensation the keys belonged to the God-ordained priestly class, the house of Aaron, "but now the whole world had them, the Word and the great deeds of God," and "in time of necessity the ministry of the Word is entrusted to any brother," even the lowliest Christian.[25] No believer does this on his own. "When I teach," Luther states, "I am not the one who teaches and gives comfort; it is Christ" who dwells in me. He "baptizes, comforts, and offers the sacraments through me, as He has promised."[26] In this faith we live and die, and neither Satan, nor the world, can separate me from Christ who died and rose again for me.[27]

Ungodly preachers do not belong to Christ, nor do they have the Keys; hence they need not be obeyed, for they are not preachers of the Word of Christ. Christ "knows only the just, not the unjust; that is, He does not approve of them."[28] The Church has often known the times when unbelief and unbelieving teachers so overran the external institution itself, that orthodoxy and faithful believers had to depend on the preaching of the Word among themselves, in their families and homes. Luther speaks of this dire situation, knowing full well that he lived in such an era: "It may happen that the world will become so utterly epicurean that we shall have no public ministry in all the world and the preaching will be solely epicurean outrage and that the Gospel will be preserved only in the homes by the fathers."[29]

It is the privilege, indeed the sacred duty, of a believer, as a royal priest, to judge teachings and teachers who run contrary to God's will. "In the New Testament," the apostles exhort us to remember, says Luther, that "all superiors are to be heard in such a way that everyone of the lowest degree may be free to judge the thought of the superior in matters of faith, much more so than the prophets could resist the important people in Israel without regard for the command of God," not on their own authority, of course, but according to the criterion of the given Word of God.[30] When the apostle Peter exhorts believers of all stations to exercise this fundamental God-given right, he does so very carefully, holding them within the limits of God's Word and the "clear statements of Scripture." They are "to stand firmly on this ground."[31]

It is by and because of the Word that the lowliest baptized child is over even the pope, states Luther. Hereby he asserts his great regard for baptism, on the one hand, and for the lofty station of a believer as God's child and royal priest, higher even than the proudest pope, on the other hand. "That is why every baptized child is not only a judge over the pope, but also over his god, the devil."[32] St. Paul, states Luther, "delegates to Christians the power to judge and condemn even an angel of heaven, if he should preach another gospel."[33] God's Word is the highest authority, a thing which the pope does not acknowledge because he does not know God's Word, a tragic fact by which he even excludes himself from the Christian church, in the Reformer's opinion.

It is a serious distortion of things, especially of the Word of God, to claim and decree "that only bishops, scholars, and councils should be allowed to judge doctrine," and that "the ordinary Christian is supposed to await their judgment and obey it," Luther writes to the Leisnig congregation, which is troubled with the question of whether they did indeed have within themselves the right and authority to call a qualified pastor to serve them.[34] The facts are that "Christ institutes the very opposite and gives them," that is, the powers and responsibilities to judge doctrine, "to everyone and to all Christians equally."[35] The bishops and pastors "have the power to teach" by virtue of the congregation's call, "but it is the sheep who are to judge whether they teach the voice, that is, the word of Christ or the voice of strangers."[36] Christ warns believers against false prophets, Matt. 7:15. Luther cites this verse and then states: "You see, here Christ does not give the judgment to prophets and teachers but to pupils or sheep." In his insightful and inimitable way Luther then adds: "Thus there cannot be a false prophet among the listeners, only among the teachers."[37]

This comports exactly with the apostle Paul's warning to the Thessalonians in his first epistle (5:21), that they "test everything by holding fast to that which is good," a thing which sets Christians apart from the world, which does not know nor honor God's Word.[38] The conclusion, therefore, is: "Wherever there is a Christian congregation in possession of the Gospel, it not only has the right and power but also the duty" to put off the yoke of self-styled prophets and rulers, who "clearly teach and rule contrary to God and His Word."[39] Luther bases this strong appeal on the royal priesthood, quoting 1 Peter 2:9, and stating: "No one can deny that every Christian possesses the Word of God and is taught and anointed by God to be priest" and that "it is their duty to confess, to teach, and to spread His Word."[40]

Everything hinges on the authority of God's Word. When the Judaizers are making inroads among the Galatian Christians, Paul warns the latter against the intrusion of another gospel. "We are presented here," says Luther, "with an example that enables us to know for a certainty that it is an accursed lie that the pope is the arbiter of Scripture or that the church has authority over Scripture."[41] Anyone can make audacious claims, even over Scripture, but that does not prove that he or anyone else is rightly above the Scriptures. "To refute this wicked and blasphemous doctrine of theirs," says Luther, the apostle Paul lets loose with a veritable "thunderbolt," as he "subordinates himself, an angel from heaven, teachers on earth, and any other masters at all to Sacred Scriptures." *Haec regina debet dominari!* "This queen must rule, and everyone must obey, and be subject to her; the Pope, Luther, Augustine, Paul, an angel from heaven."[42]   No wonder that a seven-year-old child, if equipped with the Word of God, is above all these and shall judge them.[43]

False doctrine is like the leaven, be it ever so small, that leavens the whole lump, as the apostle Paul warns in Galatians 5:9. Paul's point is clear. Just a little false doctrine will turn the whole of doctrine sour, or distort the lump. "On this score," therefore, says Luther, the apostle is saying: "We cannot yield even a hairbreadth. For doctrine is like a mathematical point; it cannot be divided, that is, it cannot stand either subtraction or addition."[44] In life there can be, and often is, error. But doctrine is of God; in it there is perfection, purity, wholeness; there can be no error, since it is given by Him. "Therefore doctrine must be one eternal and round golden circle, in which there is no crack; if even the tiniest crack appears, the circle is no longer perfect."[45]

That being true, says Luther, then "a curse on a love that is observed at the expense of the doctrine of faith, to which everything must yield—love, an apostle, an angel from heaven, etc!"[46] "It belongs to love to bear everything and to yield to everyone. On the other hand, it belongs to faith to bear nothing whatever and to yield to no one."[47] Luther has people as well as pastors in mind, for as he notes, "Paul warns both preachers and hearers with this statement not to think that the doctrine of faith is little or nothing and that we can play around with it as we please." That, of course, is not so. "I have said this at some length," therefore, Luther explains, "to encourage our own people and to instruct others, who are perhaps offended by our firmness and who do not think that we have definite and serious reasons for this firmness."[48]

It is the laymen's task, as well as the pastor's, to uphold the articles of faith as taught by God, no more, no less. It is a serious matter. "Take away assertions and you take away Christianity," Luther says with scorching ferocity against the namby-pamby Erasmus, who criticizes Luther for being so tied to Scriptural authority, whereas he (Erasmus) would prefer to "adopt a skeptical attitude here."[49] It is Luther's deepest conviction that "all the articles of faith held by Christians ought to be such that they are not only most certain to Christians themselves, but also fortified against the attacks of others by such manifest and clear Scriptures that they shut all men's mouths and prevent their saying anything against them."[50]

It is common knowledge that Philip Melanchthon, Luther's valued colleague, was not an ordained clergyman. This did not lessen Luther's esteem for him nor his estimate of Melanchthon's knowledge of Holy Scripture. Little wonder that Luther should have expressed the view in a brace of letters written from his "exile" on the Wartburg on the same day, September 9, 1521, one to Spalatin, the Elector's secretary, and the other to Amsdorf, Luther's colleague on the Wittenberg faculty, that it was his considered opinion and wish "that Philip would also preach to the people," for he is not only qualified, but this would also be a way of restoring "the form and manners of the early church."[51] Luther is not interested in upsetting the apple cart as regards ordination and call into the ministry. But he is interested in stating the truth of the royal priesthood. He in fact does this in so many words: "He is truly a priest and actually does the work of a priest, unless it is not the office of a priest to teach the Word of God," in which case "Christ Himself would not be a priest."[52] Luther's point is simply that Melanchthon is eminently qualified by his profound knowledge of the Word of God, to which he is totally committed and which he knows better than most priests and bishops. But Luther keeps his balance, as regards the congregation and its right to call and place a man in the pulpit. Accordingly, Luther states: "If the congregation demands and requests it, he ought not and cannot say no," especially since "the people are thirsty and in need."[53]

The Word finally takes precedence over all. Thus even Abraham had his Sarah, and when she appealed "to God as Judge against him," then it was God's Word which finally was the ruling answer. So it is still in the church. This queen must rule, the Word, not the church nor any other human agency or individual. Moreover, it is as powerful and binding in the hands of the laity as it is in the hands of the clergy, as much for sheep as for shepherd!

NOTES

1   *LW* 33, 24-27, 89-99; *WA* 18, 606-609, 625-659.

2   *LW* 30, 105; *WA* 12, 359f.

3   Ibid. In his Christmas *Postil* of 1521 (written at the Wartburg) Luther's sermon for Second Christmas Day includes the counsel that "their (the clergy) teaching should be subject to the congregation of believers," i.e.,

they have the right and duty to judge its conformity with God's Word given in Scripture.

4   Ibid.

5   Ibid.

6   *LW* 39, 306; *WA* 11, 409; cf. *LW* 20, 333 (*Lectures on Zechariah*).

7   *Enchiridion*, 20. Cf. Poellet, 32f.

8   Op. cit., 21.

9   Op. cit., 22.

10   Op. cit., 23.

11   Cf. Walther, *Kirche und Amt*, 410.

12   Quoted in Pieper, *Christian Dogmatics*, I, 43, fn. 69.

13   Cf. op. cit., I, 43f., 351ff; III, 428-334 passim.

14   *Loci theol.*, *De Ministerio Eccles.*, par. 88; quoted in Pieper, op. cit., I, 351, fn. 156.

15   Op. cit., III, 428.

16   Cf. Schmid, *Doctrinal Theology of the Lutheran Church*, 601f.

17   Op. cit., 602.

18   Ibid.

19   Ibid.

20   Op. cit., 603f.

21   *Christian Dogmatics*, III, 428.

22   Op. cit., 430.

23   Quoted in Theo. Engelder, *Reason or Revelation*, 176.

24   *LW* 8, 185; *WA* 44, 713f.

25   *LW* 8, 186; *WA* 44, 715.

26   *LW* 8, 187; *WA* 44, 715.

27   *LW* 8, 189; *WA* 4, 717.

28   *LW* 14, 309; *WA* 5, 45.

29   *St. L* 6, 938; *WA* 6, 1486; quoted in Pieper, op. cit., III, 449.

30   *LW* 14, 341; *WA* 5, 68.

31   *LW* 30, 105f.; *WA* 12, 360f.

32   *LW* 41, 359; *WA* 54, 285.

33   *LW* 41, 370; *WA* 54, 294.

34   *LW* 39, 306; *WA* 11, 409.

35   Ibid.

36   *LW* 39, 307; *WA* 11, 410.

37   Ibid.

38   Ibid.

39   *LW* 39, 308; *WA* 11, 411.

40   *LW* 39, 309; *WA* 11, 411.

41   *LW* 26, 57; *WA* 40¹, 119.

42   Op. cit., 57f.

43   Cf. *SA* III, XII.

44   *LW* 27, 37ff.; *WA* 40², 45ff.

45   Ibid.

46   Ibid.

47   Ibid.

48   Ibid.

49   *LW* 33, 21f.; *WA* 18, 604.

50   *LW* 33, 95; *WA* 18, 656.

51   *LW* 48, 308ff.; *WA*, Br. 2, 387ff.

52   Ibid.

53   Ibid.

PART III

Chapter 1

European Dialogues

A sabbatical leave during the autumn, 1978, provided me an opportunity to share discussion of Luther's teaching on church and ministry with some of Europe's leading theologians and Luther scholars. Most of them were known to me through previous, personal meeting, especially at Luther congresses; all had achieved more or less international notice through their work and writings.

The itinerary allowed for visits with individuals in Norway, Finland, West Germany, East Germany, and Switzerland. The contacts were representative, not exhaustive, either as to number or length of discussion. In order that the colloquia might have a common focus, a set of theses on church and ministry were sent ahead of my visit, in order to give the dialogue participants time for prior consideration. Since Luther was to be the take-off point, the theses were fleshed out with pertinent citations from the Reformer. This procedure served to keep the dialogues focused on a definite axis or center. In addition, in order to assure a more accurate record of the interchange, tape recordings were also made.[1]

Almost all of the theologians visited were also professional teachers of theology at some institute or university, or had been so engaged before retirement.[2] The large majority claimed the Lutheran church as their theological base; a few were of Calvinist or Roman Catholic communions; all shared a common interest in Luther studies.

In describing the results of these person-to-person dialogues on church and ministry in Luther, a number of pitfalls needed to be avoided. First, a mere rehearsal of events would be little more than a travelogue, of value perhaps to the principals as a diary of places and faces seen, but of lesser significance for the third party, the reader. Secondly, slavish sort of reiterating of the taped material would likewise be of questionable value, since by virtue of the *modus operandi* adopted for the interviews, it would necessarily have been repetitive. Therefore, the tack chosen here will be to accent given insights which added substance, significant viewpoints, or color to the topics of church and ministry in our day, particularly as shaped by Luther.

A remarkable consensus emerged through the dialogues on the theses as presented. This hardly could be claimed as resulting from the manner in which they were phrased or formulated. Rather it testified to the clarity of Luther's thought, as also the consistency of his position on church and ministry. Luther scholars today are in general agreement on this point, that on all the articles of the Christian faith Luther early on drove a steady, unwavering course. More and more the conviction grows that early and late, throughout his professional career, Luther was a steady drummer. Once he was thrown into the public arena, to fight for his theological life, as it were, Luther does not waver from Holy Scripture's norm. By the time he has addressed the Augustinian friars at Heidelberg, 1518, and debated Eck at Leipzig, July 1519—celebrating in a sense his July 4th!—Luther is on fixed theological beam with the Scriptures, out of which he so totally lived and to which he so totally subjected his thinking. Gordon Rupp, in fact, refers to Karl Holl's judgment that Luther's doctrine on the church is already evident and fairly well set in his 1515-1516 Psalm lectures.[3]

The preceding chapters have attempted to show from wide-ranging references in Luther's writings, early and late, the consistent pattern of the Reformer's thought on church and ministry. It is this which we have attempted to set into thetical statement in the formulations that follow. As already indicated, a rather remarkable consensus in support of this attempted delineation of Luther's teaching on church and ministry came to the surface in the discussions with almost three dozen European Luther scholars. In order that the reader might have the advantage of the same starting point as the conferees, the theses are reprinted here. Thereafter a summary of the conversations will be given.

Theses on the Church

1. PROPERLY SPEAKING THE CHURCH, AS LUTHER STATES IN THE *SMALCALD ARTICLES* (III, xii), "IS HOLY BELIEVERS AND LAMBS WHO HEAR THE VOICE OF THEIR SHEPHERD"; TO THIS CHURCH NO UNBELIEVER OR HYPOCRITE BELONGS. (Eph.

1:22.23; 5:23-27; 1 Cor. 3:16.17; John 11:51.52; Rom. 8:9;
1 John 2:19; John 15:6.)

Luther:

"The creed clearly indicates what the church is, viz., a
communion of saints, i.e., a crowd (*Haufe*) or assembly of
people who are Christians . . . with a special call and are
therefore called not just *ecclesia*, "church," or "people," but
sancta catholica Christiana, i.e., "a Christian holy people"
who believe in Christ." (*On the Councils and the Church*,
LW 41, 143; *WA* 50, 624f. Cf. *Large Catechism*, Creed
47-51.)

"He who does not believe and is not holy and righteous,
does not belong to the Holy Christian Church." (*Commentary on Psalm 118. LW* 14, 92; *WA* 31, 164.)

2.   SINCE GOD ALONE KNOWS THE TRUE BELIEVERS,
       THE CHURCH CANNOT BE SEEN BY MAN (HENCE
       INVISIBLE), BUT BY GOD ONLY. (Luke 17:20.21;
       1 Pet. 2:5; 2 Tim. 2:19.)

Luther:

The church is a high, deep, hidden thing which one may
neither perceive nor see, but must grasp only by faith,
through baptism, sacrament, and word. (*Against Hanswurst*,
LW 41, 211; *WA* 51, 507.)

3.   CHRIST HAS GIVEN THE KEYS OF THE KINGDOM
       OF HEAVEN TO THIS TRUE CHURCH OF BELIEVERS
       AND IT POSSESSES ALL THE GIFTS, POWERS,
       PRIVILEGES GAINED BY CHRIST FOR THE CHURCH,
       WHICH IS HIS BRIDE. (Matt. 16:15-19; 18:18; John
       20:22.23; 3:28.29; 1 Cor. 3:21-23; Gal. 4:26; 1 Pet. 2:9.)

Luther:

"The keys belong not to the pope (as he lies) but to the church. . . . They belong to the people of Christ and are called 'the church's keys' not '"the pope's keys."'" (*On the Councils and the Church, LW* 41, 154; *WA* 50, 632.)

4.   THE PRESENCE OF THE TRUE CHURCH MAY BE DISCERNED BY ITS MARKS, THE *NOTAE PURAE*, THE PURE PREACHING OF THE WORD AND THE ADMINISTERING OF THE SACRAMENTS IN ACCORD WITH CHRIST'S INSTITUTION. (Mark 4:26.27; Matt. 13:38; Is. 55:10.11; Matt. 28:18-20; 1 Cor. 10:17; 1 Cor. 12:13.)

Luther:

"God's church is where God's Word resounds (whether it is in the middle of Turkey, in the papacy, or in hell). For it is God's word which establishes the church. He is the Lord over all places. Wherever that Word is heard, where Baptism, the Sacrament of the Altar, and absolution are administered, there you must determine and conclude with certainty: 'This is surely God's house; here heaven has been opened.'" (*Genesis Commentary, LW* 5, 244; *WA* 43, 596.)

5.   INDIVIDUAL, OR LOCAL, GATHERINGS OR CONGRE- GATIONS ARE IN A SYNECDOCHICAL SENSE CALLED "CHURCHES" BECAUSE OF THE TRUE BELIEVERS FOUND THERE, SANCTIFIED BY THE HOLY SPIRIT THROUGH THE WORD. (Matt. 13:47.48; 25:1.2; 22:2.11; 18:17; Gal. 1:2; 1 Cor. 1:2.)

Luther:

"Jerome raises an important question here: Why does Paul call 'churches' those that were not churches? For Paul, he says, is writing to the Galatians, who had been led astray and turned away from Christ and from grace to Moses and the Law. I reply: When Paul calls them the 'churches of Galatia,' he is employing synecdoche, a very common practice in the Scriptures. . . . Even if the church is 'in the midst of a crooked and perverse generation,' as Paul says to the Philippians (2:15), and even if it is surrounded by wolves and robbers, that is, spiritual tyrants, it is still there." (*Galatians Commentary, LW* 26, 24; *WA* 40, 68f.)

6.   ERRING, HERETICAL CHURCHES ARE RIGHTLY CALLED CHURCH, AS LONG AS FUNDAMENTAL CHRISTIAN BELIEFS ARE STILL PRESENT; CHRISTIAN BELIEVERS, HOWEVER, ARE EXHORTED BY GOD'S WORD TO FLEE FALSE TEACHING, AVOID FELLOWSHIP THAT COMPROMISES THEIR FAITH, AND SEEK FELLOWSHIP WHERE GOD'S WORD IS PURELY TAUGHT AND THE SACRAMENTS RIGHTLY ADMINISTERED. (Gal. 1:2; Deut. 13:1-3; Matt. 7:15; 23.24; Acts 20:30.31; Rom. 16:17.18; 1 Cor. 10:18.21; 2 Cor. 6:14-18; Gal. 5:9; Tit. 3:10.11; Matt. 10:32.33; Luke 9:26; Rom. 10:9.10; 1 Cor. 1:10-13; Eph. 4:3-6; 1 John 2:19; Acts 2:42-47.)

Luther:

"There is one holy Christian Church on earth, i.e., the community or number or assembly of all Christians in all the world, the one bride of Christ, and his spiritual body of which he is the only head. . . . This Christian Church exists not only in the realm of the Roman Church or pope, but in all the world, as the prophets foretold that the gospel of Christ would spread throughout the world, Psalm 2 (8), Psalm 19 (4). Thus this Christian Church is physically dispersed among pope, Turks, Persians, Tartars, but spiritually gathered in one gospel and faith, under one head, i.e., Jesus Christ." (*Confession Concerning Christ's Supper. LW* 37, 367; *WA* 26, 506.)

"Therefore when they minimize this issue in such a dishonest way, they give ample evidence of how highly they regard the majesty of the Word. . . . Therefore let us leave the praise of harmony and of Christian love to them. We, on the other hand, praise faith and the majesty of the Word.

Love can sometimes be neglected without danger, but the Word and faith cannot. It belongs to love to bear everything and to yield to everyone. On the other hand, it belongs to faith to bear nothing whatever and to yield to no one. . . . In the issue of salvation, when fanatics teach lies and errors under the guise of truth and make an impression on many, there love is certainly not to be exercised, and error is not to be approved."

". . . I have said this at some length to encourage our own people and to instruct others, who are perhaps offended by our firmness and who do not think that we have definite and serious reasons for this firmness. Therefore let us not be moved when they make such a boast of their zeal for love and harmony; for he who does not love God and His Word does not count for anything, regardless of what or how much else he may love." (*Galatians Commentary*, *LW* 27, 38f; *WA* 40^2, 47f.)

Theses on the Ministry

1. THE HOLY MINISTRY, OR PASTORAL OFFICE, IS TO BE DISTINGUISHED FROM THE UNIVERSAL PRIESTHOOD WHICH BELONGS TO ALL BELIEVERS. (1 Pet. 2:9; Rev. 1:6; 1 Cor. 12:29; Rom. 10:15; James 3:1.)

Luther:

"No one individual can arise by his own authority and arrogate to himself alone what belongs to all. . . . One, or as many as the community (*Gemeinde*) chooses, shall be chosen or approved who, in the name of all with these rights, shall perform these functions publicly." (*Concerning the Ministry*, *LW* 40, 34; *WA* 12, 189.)

"For although we are all priests, this does not mean that all of us can preach, teach, and rule. Certain ones of the multitude must be selected and separated for such an office. And he who has such an office is not a priest because of his office but a servant of all the others, who are priests. When he is no longer able to preach and serve, or if he no longer wants to do so, he once more becomes a part of a common multitude of Christians. His office is conveyed to someone else, and he becomes a Christian like any other.

"This is the way to distinguish between the office of preaching, or the ministry, and the general priesthood of all baptized Christians. The preaching office is no more than a public service which happens to be conferred upon someone by the entire congregation, all the members of which are priests." (*Commentary on Psalm 110, LW* 13, 332; *WA* 41, 210.)

2. THE PASTORAL OFFICE IS A DIVINE, NOT A HU-MAN, ORDINANCE. (Matt. 10:1-42; John 20:21-23; Acts 20:28; 1 Cor. 12:28.29; Eph. 4:11; 1 Pet. 5:1; 1 Cor. 4:1.)

Luther:

"I hope, indeed, that believers, those who want to be called Christians, know very well that the spiritual estate has been established and instituted by God. . . . I am not thinking of the spiritual estate in the monastic houses . . . The estate I am thinking of is rather one which has the office of preaching and the service of the word and sacraments and which imparts the Spirit and salvation." (*Sermon on Keeping Children in School, LW* 46, 219f.; *WA* 30² 526f.)

"The holy orders and true religious institutions established by God are these three: the office of priest, the estate of marriage, the civil government." (*Confession Concerning Christ's Supper, LW* 37, 364; *WA* 26, 504.)

"For a bishop, as God's steward, must be blameless, etc. (Tit. 1:5-7). Whoever believes that here in Paul the Spirit of Christ is speaking and commanding will be sure to recognize this as a divine institution and ordinance, that in each city there should be several bishops, or at least one. It is also evident that Paul considers elders and bishops to be one and the same thing." (*The Misuse of the Mass, LW* 36, 155; *WA* 8, 500.)

3. THE PASTORAL OFFICE IS A MINISTRY OF SERVICE, NOT A HIGHER ORDER; ITS AUTHORITY IS A SPIRITUAL ONE, TO EXERCISE THE OFFICE OF THE KEYS PUBLICLY FOR THE CONGREGATION, i.e., PREACHING THE GOSPEL AND ADMINISTERING THE SACRAMENTS. (Matt. 23:8-12; 1 Cor. 3:5; 2 Cor. 4:5; Col. 1:24.25; John 21:15.16; 1 Cor. 4:1.)

Luther:

"Thus there is only an external difference because of the office to which one is called by the congregation. (*Sermons on 1 Peter, LW* 30, 55; *WA* 12, 309.)

"Therefore we are all priests, as many of us as are Christians. But the priests, as we call them, are ministers chosen from among us. All that they do is done in our name; the priesthood is nothing but a ministry. This we learn from 1 Corinthians 4:1." (*Babylonian Captivity of the Church, LW* 36, 113; *WA* 6, 564.)

"Since a Christian congregation neither should nor could exist without God's Word, it clearly follows . . . that it must have teachers and preachers who administer the Word . . . We must act according to Scripture and call and institute from among ourselves those who are found to be qualified and whom God has enlightened with reason and endowed with gifts to do so." (*A Christian Assembly Has a Right to Call, LW* 39, 309; *WA* 11, 411.)

"The church is recognized externally by the fact that it consecrates or calls ministers . . . who publicly and privately give, administer, and use the aforementioned four things (preaching of the Gospel, baptism, Lord's Supper, Office of the Keys) or holy possessions in behalf of and in the name of the church, or rather by reason of their institution by

Christ." (*On the Councils and the Church*, LW 41, 154; WA 50, 632f.)

4. THROUGH THE CONGREGATION, TO WHOM THE KEYS HAVE BEEN ENTRUSTED, GOD CALLS A QUALIFIED MAN INTO THE PASTORAL OFFICE. (Matt. 18:15-20; Acts 1:15-26; 6:1-6.)

Luther:

"The congregation which has the Gospel may and should elect and call from among its members someone to teach the Word in its place." (*A Christian Assembly Has a Right to Judge*, LW 39, 311; WA 11, 413.)

5. THE SCRIPTURES ARE SILENT ON ORDINATION DERIVING FROM AN EXPRESS COMMAND OF GOD; BUT IT HAS ITS PRECEDENT IN APOSTOLIC PRAC-TICE.

Luther:

"When you have so prayed, have no doubt that he to whom you have prayed is faithful and will give what you ask . . . Proceed in the name of the Lord to elect one or more whom you desire, and who appear to be worthy and able. Then let those who are leaders among you lay hands upon them, and certify and commend them to the people and the church or community (*Gemeinde*). In this way let them become your bishops, ministers, or pastors." (*Concerning the Ministry*, LW 40, 40; WA 12, 193.)

"It is not for nothing, therefore, that special rites are employed in the church to unite men and women in matri-mony, likewise for ordaining ministers of the Word. For we bless the bridegroom and the bride; we recite the words of the divine ordinance; we call upon God to be pleased to protect this estate. We lay hands on the ministers and at the same time pour forth prayers to God, for the sole reason that we may testify that there is a divine ordinance both in these and in all other estates of the church, of the state, and of the household." (*Commentary on Genesis, LW* 7, 146f.; *WA* 44, 407f.)

"For basically consecration should not and cannot be anything other (if it is carried out rightly) than a call or a conferring of the office of the ministry or of the office of preaching." (*The Private Mass and the Consecration of Priests, LW* 38, 186; *WA* 38, 228.)

6.   THE PASTORAL MINISTRY IS THE ONLY DIVINELY INSTITUTED OFFICE IN THE CHURCH; OTHER OFFICES COINHERE IN AND DERIVE FROM IT. (1 Tim. 3:1.5.7; 5:17; 1 Cor. 4:1; Tit. 1:7; Heb. 13:17; Acts 6:1-6.)

Luther:

"Inasmuch as the office of preaching the gospel is the greatest of all and certainly is apostolic, it becomes the foundation for all other functions (or) offices." (*Concerning the Ministry, LW* 40, 36; *WA* 12, 191.)

"Whoever has the office of preaching imposed on him has the highest office in Christendom imposed on him. . . . He may leave other lower offices to others." (*A Christian Assembly Has the Right to Call. LW* 39, 314; *WA* 11, 415f.)

7.   CHRISTIAN LAITY MAY ALSO JUDGE DOCTRINAL MATTERS ACCORDING TO THE WORD OF GOD. (1 Cor. 10:15.16; 1 John 4; 1 Thess. 5:21; Matt. 7:15.16; Acts 17:11.)

Luther:

"(Christ) takes both the right and the power to judge teaching from the bishops, scholars, and councils and gives them to everyone and to all Christians equally." (*A Christian Assembly Has the Right to Call, LW* 39, 306; *WA* 11, 409.)

Theses Prepared by E. F. Klug
August 15, 1978

These were the theses that preceded colloquies with various theologians. In presenting summaries of the discussions a chronological order will be followed for the most part. No attempt will be made to weave the results of the dialogues together at this point, but simply to let the comments of the named individual appear, along with the date of the conversation, and place of residence. The comments will be a digest, unless otherwise   indicated as direct quotation from the speaker.

Prof. Dr. Leiv Aalen - Oslo, Norway, September 22, 1978, formerly professor at the Menighetsfakultet (independent, theological school), Lutheran Confessions scholar, now deceased.[4]

-- In general Dr. Aalen expressed agreement with the theses, observing, however, that in his opinion Walther's position on the church, as well as Pieper's became a "low church view" as a result of reaction against Stephanism.

-- As regards the doctrine of the church, and marking its location, it is true that the church does have its signs, or marks, Word and sacraments.

-- The ministry derives from the main, or general, ministry of the church, but the laity in Norway do not understand what is meant by this, ever since the time of Hauge and Hallesby; the common conception can best be described as a kind of populist movement with these accents:

1) Teaching, preaching, administering the sacraments, belong to each Christian, and are each believer's right;

2) Only for the sake of decency and order in the church is there need of clergy;

3) Women in the ministry follow naturally, if point No. 1 is granted.

-- Aalen's response to this thinking:

1) If they had known the Lutheran Confessions they would not have gotten into this;

2)   They fail to see that the ministry as a public pastoral office was ordained by God Himself, as the
Scriptures teach.

a)   But now the Menighetsfakultet itself is
divided on this.[5]

b)   Their argument is that women in the ministry is a time-bound arrangement, limited to
the apostle Paul's injunctions to the Corinthians (1 Cor. 14) and to Timothy (1 Tim.
2);

c)   Scripture thus has become a waxen nose to
be shaped according to contemporary requirements;

d)   The teachers of the Menighetsfakultet
pretend to be conservative, but the situation, as a result, has become more dangerous than the frank espousal of liberalism.[6]

Prof. Dr. Inge Lønning - Oslo, Norway, September 21, 1978,
professor of systematic theology at the University of Oslo.[7]

-- In the main Prof. Lønning supported the theses as presented. At
the Luther Congress, in Erfurt, 1983, Prof. Lønning stated in similar
way that Luther never doubted the reality of the true church, as the
gathering of all believers, at the same time that he emphasized the
concrete, visible assembling of Christian congregations around the
preached Word. By virtue of the fact that the true church is a
spiritual entity it illustrates the same paradoxical verity like that of
God's revelation of Himself through Christ on the cross, very real
and existential, yet transcending governments and laws of this world.

Prof. Dr. Carl Wisløff - Oslo, Norway, September 22, 1978,
professor now retired.[8]

-- The theses on church and ministry were of special interest for
Dr. Wisløff, since he had just finished a similar study. The pastor
functions within the realm of the general ministry, he conceded, in
an office specifically ordained by God. Dr. Wisløff noted the degree
of unanimity on this matter between Lutheran and Catholic scholars.

-- The bottom line of what is involved in contemporary theology
is the authority question. We must ask: what is it that is given in
Scripture and because it is given, why a certain thing, or reported

miracle, like the raising of the widow of Nain's son, is true? The reason why women preachers are flooding into the church is simply because the Scripture's authority is being flouted and dismissed as time-bound or the like. Teachers are being told, in Norway, and so also in Sweden, "you must be objective," which is just another way of dismissing things that are plainly taught in Scripture, on the pretext of not being close-minded but "objective." There is need to be obedient to the Word of God, not to the prevailing mood of the day. To claim that there is nothing in the New Testament which makes it impossible to ordain women is to ignore deliberately the Word of God and its authority.

-- As regards ordination, Dr. Wisløff agreed that fundamentally the call of the pastor into office is his ordination, as Luther put it. This in principle is the foundation on which ordination stands. With 1535, the practice of ordination of the eligible candidates began at Wittenberg, in order to declare the certification of the men for parish work; before this time they were simply introduced into the congregations issuing the call. In Norway the custom has been to perform the ordination ceremony in the big cathedral; but now it often happens that the bishop does the ordaining in the candidate's home congregation; this is a new development. It appears to run closely parallel to the practice obtaining in the United States, perhaps for sentimental reasons, Dr. Wisløff observed. Basically, however, he held that there is need to go back to the underlying principle expressed above, the close tie between the call into the office itself and the public manifesting of the qualified candidate for the ministry who is about to assume his duties.

Rev. Dr. Jan Aarts -- Helsinki, Finland, September 25, 1978, pastor of St. Henrikus Roman Catholic Church and author.[9]

-- In Dr. Aarts' view the church has two sides: the priesthood of believers; then also the ministry and the sacraments. Whenever one assesses Luther, it is important to see that all his statements are linked to the Gospel, according to Dr. Aarts. It is the Gospel which makes the church spiritual, not worldly. The Gospel is like a treasure in a box; take it away and nothing is left. The ministry, as such, is men, and of no importance; but linked with the Gospel it is spiritual. The royal priesthood of believers and the ministry are two different things. A minister is not a minister by himself, but by the consent of the congregation. In speaking of the church, it is preferable to use the term *ecclesia spiritualis* rather than *invisibilis*, and *ecclesia carnalis* instead of *visibilis*; one cannot simply equate the *ecclesia carnalis* with the *ecclesia spiritualis*.

-- Luther's teaching on the doctrine of the church and ministry was very well set by 1525, as Peter Manns (Roman Catholic scholar of Mainz) has shown. It is closely linked to the Gospel as the source of everything in the church. There is evidence that by 1517 Luther already has the true meaning of the Gospel: "You can't win God's love for you. It is God's free gift in Christ." The Gospel and salvation are central for Luther.

-- A priest is the servant, *doulos*, of God, and the servant, *diakonos*, of the people. Something is taken away from him, factory work or whatever, and by his ordination he is marked, though not more holy. Luther said the minister is not the *sacerdos*, priest, or mediator, but Christ is. Everybody is free to enter before God, as a priest; for Christ is the Mediator for the priesthood of believers. But Luther failed, according to Dr. Aarts in that he did not recognize "the Peter office" as ordained by Christ Himself, *de jure divino*, by divine right, though the papacy itself exists *de jure humano*, by human right; often, in fact, the pope has been a better hunter and fighter than a pope.

Aarts' view on subjects like papal infallibility, women in the priesthood, celibacy, and canon law in general were close to those of Hans Kueng, and therefore, opposed to the Vatican.[10]

Prof. Dr. Uuras Saarnivaara -- Ryttala, Finland, September 25, 1978, professor and dean of the Mission School of the Finnish Lutheran Mission (independent).[11]

-- In discussing the doctrine of the church Dr. Saarnivaara urged careful distinction of:

1)   the nature of the church, in other words, the question, what constitutes the church;

2)   the congregation of believers at a given place;

3)   the visible church of professing believers on earth.

As early as 1515, in his Psalm lectures, Luther had correctly defined the church as the communion of saints, that is, true believers in Christ. In his Romans lectures, even before 1517, Luther had likewise identified the church with the priesthood of all believers. Thus this was not a new concept for him, or one developed only later in his thinking. Luther speaks very plainly of the church's marks in his treatise *On the Councils and the Church*, 1539. It is here that he lists seven things that mark the presence of the church: Word, Baptism, Lord's Supper, confession and absolution, as the main, underlying marks, and then adding the calling of a pastor, worship (and prayer), and finally cross-bearing as further tokens of the church's existence at a given location.

--   "Invisible church" is really not a good and proper term, according to Saarnivaara, because believers know each other by faith. It can only be called "invisible" in the sense that its boundaries cannot be known; but believers know one another by faith, though not 100%. Thus it is a concrete reality, which, while unknown to unbelievers, is nonetheless known by believers. By our baptism we commit ourselves to Christ's way or will, and He becomes our Lord, not only our Savior, requiring obedience of us, the obedience of faith. Dr. Saarnivaara characterized his Finnish followers as being not revivalistic or fundamentalistic, but a Bible-believing and evangelistic movement, with a stress on pietism as an evidence of the faith within and obedience to Christ as Lord. In keeping with this emphasis the Third Use of the Law is a very vital part of the Christian life which begins at one's baptism, for the Ten Commandments are the Law of Christ. Church life in the Lutheran Church of Finland is very lax according to Dr. Saarnivaara; hence the emphasis on living faith and piety.[12]

-- Christ gave the church pastors, elders, bishops. These were all the same office; the New Testament does not distinguish or rank them. The office did not merely grow out of the church's concern for good order; it stems from Christ's own action. When the early Christians elected qualified men for the office of ministry, or commissioned the apostle Paul and Barnabas for mission work, they were following God's ordering of things, for there must be a willingness or consent of the people supportive of the pastor's position or office.

-- The entire *Book of Concord* is the confessional base for the entire Lutheran Church of Finland, Dr. Saarnivaara noted, but there is hardly any discipline or *de facto* support of the Confessions as binding documents for the teaching of theology in the churches, schools, and the university theological departments.

-- A Mission Society was formed in 1968 in order to revitalize the outreach in foreign fields. Dr. Saarnivaara emphasized the point that only believing men are accepted who demonstrate that they have personal faith, though no special test of faith is required.

Prof. Dr. Lennart Pinomaa -- Helsinki, Finland, September 26, 1978, for many years "professor extraordinary" of theology at the University of Helsinki, now retired.[13]

-- In his book, *Die Heiligen bei Luther*, Dr. Pinomaa deals with the question, Who are saints? In our conversation together he reaffirmed that the distinction between visible and invisible church is regularly found in Luther's writings. One must recognize that believers are indeed visible, but one cannot select or point them out; they are known really only by God. (Note variance with Saarnivaara!) Indeed, because of the believers present in the local congregation it is properly called a true church; the unbelievers, or hypocrites, are not part of the church in reality. This is a difficult thing, of course. A pastor must bring comfort to the dying, comfort which will help a man be truly certain of his salvation and by which he can say, "I have nothing in or by myself, but I want to embrace that which God gives." When a man comes to zero point, then he has to have that which truly counts: Christ, not a *Schrank*, or empty cupboard! Even his faith does not *merit* forgiveness, and the best situation is when a person is "naked," with trust only in Christ.

-- Luther's definition of Church as the communion of saints was present already in his thinking and writing before 1519, though then it became especially evident in the Leipzig Debate. Luther never doubted the presence of believers in the Roman Catholic Church and that it could, therefore, be termed church. Similarly, on the doctrine on the ministry: the Keys belong to all; but the office of parish pastor is given to the one called.

-- On the question of women in the ministry, Dr. Pinomaa stated that the Lutheran Church of Finland does not permit them to hold the pastoral office, as in Sweden and Norway. He himself had no absolute opinion for or against it. In his view things had changed since Paul's day, and today more women are theologically equipped and apt in theological matters. Women serve in what is called the *Lectorsamt*; they may preach, serve as instructors preparing children for confirmation, and minister among the women as deaconesses. There is divided opinion within the church whether they should be allowed to become full-fledged pastors, perform confirmation, consecrate the elements, and be ordained. In fact, there is a prior

question, according to Pinomaa: Should ordination be reserved for
the pastoral office alone, or may it include other offices?

Hamburg, Germany -- September 29, 1978

Prof. Dr. Bernhard Lohse, professor of church history for more than
twenty years at the University of Hamburg.[14]

Prof. Dr. O. Hermann Pesch, a former Dominican, now released
from his vows, and professor likewise at the University of Hamburg
in systematic theology.[15]

The dialogue with Professors Lohse and Pesch was a joint, three--
way meeting in Lohse's study.[16]
-- According to Lohse: One could look at Luther's theology either
in a systematic or historical way as regards its development. Luther
presupposes or assumes certain things as fundamental:

  1)   the Gospel is the critical plumbline and plays the
         central role;
  2)   the church is the necessary fruit that flows from the
         Gospel's proclamation and is established by Christ;
  3)   the bishop's or pastor's office is likewise ordained
         by God.

-- Pesch: The theses lay too heavy an emphasis upon invisible
church; for Luther the emphasis was upon the *Ortsgemeinde*, the
local congregation, to which the believer belongs. Those who are
baptized are the church. Pesch's concern was, How does *ecclesia
invisibilis* relate to the church which has to do with Word and
Sacrament and a bishop? Luther, he felt, never resolved this in a
purely systematic way, only in a historical way.
-- Lohse: Luther did distinguish in a systematic way *ecclesia
carnalis* and *spiritualis*, that is, the total number of confessing or
professing Christians, and the sum total of true believers known to
God. Luther never denied that the Christian Church could be found
also within the Roman Catholic Church. Luther also held that the
church is a living, visible entity; indeed he emphasized the actual
existence of the church, accenting the corporeal nature. But he
considered it presumptive on the part of the Roman papacy to claim
that the pope's voice is the voice of Christ. Many popes and many
of the ruling ecclesiastical bishops or lords were, in Luther's

opinion, hardly spiritual. Moreover, one cannot say that Luther would have agitated for reform of the church if he had not recognized the validity of the existing church as church; but in failing to preach the Gospel, the Roman church had ceased to be a true church and the pope had surrendered the right of lordship.

-- Pesch: It is important to see a difference between Trent and Vatican II on the doctrine of justification, especially as regards man's merit playing a role in his salvation.

-- Lohse: There is need to speak a *plaedoyer* (plead a case) for the Roman Catholics here. In his opinion the *Formula of Concord* treatment was no longer entirely applicable to Romanist theology today.

-- Pesch: The fact that the Spanish Dominicans, in tune with Trent, speak quite differently from Hans Kueng and Karl Rahner on the doctrine of justification is not unusual, since a similar phenomenon, or disharmony, happens in Protestant evangelical circles as well.

-- Lohse: The Lutheran Confessions still have an ongoing significance, but situations alter cases. Today the question is, Who speaks for the Lutheran churches? Surely not the Missouri Synod! Leuenberg was a good effort (as Lutherans and Reformed theologians attempted a resolution of past disagreements), but finally it was deficient for our time.

-- Pesch: In his early years Luther finds himself opposed to the structured organization of Rome as the church; this sharpens as the years go by, because of the church's departure from Word and Sacraments, as Luther sees it. Many of the bishops in Luther's day were a sorry excuse as spiritual leaders; worldly lords, yes; but the bishop of Strasbourg, for example, had not celebrated mass for thirty-five years!

-- Lohse: As regards ordination the question arises, does it belong to the church's government, or is it only the outward public ceremony confirming the congregation's call? Present-day theologians, among them Joachim Heubach and Helmut Lieberg, hold that ordination is not only apostolic example but doctrine. In Lohse's opinion there is undeniable apostolic nature connected with ordination. He referred to renewed discussion in England first, then Germany, and most recently France. There seems to be support, in his opinion, for the position that it ought to be viewed as belonging to the church's government, as Heubach and Lieberg hold.

Prof. Dr. Karl F. Rengstorf -- Muenster, Germany, October 5, 1978, distinguished professor of New Testament Biblical studies, then retired, now deceased.[17]

-- The "holy and righteous" in Thesis No. 1 constitute the *una sancta* in Luther's thinking. The question is are they holy and righteous because of a happening *in* the believer, or *for* the believer? The pietists stress the former, as do also the Reformed and the Roman Catholics, all of whom obscure the distinction. But Luther stresses the latter, according to Rengstorf. Christ's imputed righteousness unto faith alone avails *coram Deo*, before God.

-- There is need to underscore *recte et pure*, as does *Augsburg Confession* Article VII in connection with "holy and righteous" persons constituting the church. What is necessary is not only pure doctrine but also pure proclamation; a binding obligation is thus placed upon preaching in the church for faith or trust. The church must not dilute and surely not deny the Word. The great difficulty in modern times is unanimity as to the meaning of the Gospel, its nature and substance. The churches preach. But what do they preach? What is the *Evangelium* which *must* be preached, *docendum*? The confusion we see in Lutheran-Reformed dialogues today is traceable to nineteenth century liberalism. The Gospel was obliterated with gnostic notions and so-called *Heilsgeschichte* "gospel," much of which was not truly Christ-centered. *Was ist die Kirche*? What is the church? is a question closely tied to the other question, *Was ist Evangelium*? What is Gospel? With Barth, Brunner, Bultmann, and others, a great deal of confusion entered into theology; traditional forms and structures were tied to the new ecumenical "gospel." It is oriented more towards improvement of society and realized eschatology than preaching for or towards eternity. There is no real comfort in that message for the church. The identity of the church, finally, is not determined by doing the best you can but with or by confessional loyalty. Of this fundamental truth a great part of the Lutheran world, and certainly all of the Reformed, know very little, and care even less. The Missouri Synod is often characterized as traditionalized orthodoxy, because of its confessional concern, but that is a caricature only, according to Rengstorf.

Prof. Dr. Kurt Aland -- Muenster, Germany, October 6, 1978, professor at the University of Muenster and noted New Testament and Reformation scholar.[18]

-- Prof. Aland found little to criticize in the theses as presented, nor did he have particular suggestions to make. He agreed that, as Luther viewed his position as professor at the University of Wittenberg and as pastor in the *Stadtkirche* of Wittenberg, the Reformer insisted that he had specific "calls" or authority under which he acted for each of these two realms in his life. In other words, the one did not provide an adit or ingress for the other; because he was a doctor of theology, it did not follow that he could mount the pulpit anywhere without proper call or credentials.

Prof. Dr. Joerg Baur -- Goettingen, Germany, October 8, 1978, professor of systematic theology at the University of Goettingen.[19]

-- Dr. Baur expressed strong agreement with the theses, both on church and also on ministry, especially as these relate to Luther's work. As regard the nature of the church, he was reminded of the *Smalcald Articles* statement by Luther which speaks of the church, Christ's kingdom, as a magnet which draws believers into it. This concept of the church is by no means *impersonal*, but involves a very strong *personal* connection, the one to the other, each through and to Christ.

-- Luther did indeed acknowledge that even in the church under the pope Word and Sacrament could be, and were, present; but the false teaching which accompanied the means of grace he absolutely repudiated. Hence in Thomas Aquinas Luther said that he could not find Christ.

-- A human, arbitrary union in Christendom, as exhibited by twentieth century ecumenism, supersedes that which is given of God, unto and by faith. As a result, the church, as God knows and builds it, may indeed be quite another entity from any ecumenical structure or organization. Truth after all takes precedence over love. How does faith proceed differently from love? That is evident in this basic principle: Harmony based merely on the love-principle seldom becomes anything more than fanaticism.

-- Thesis No. 1 on the ministry is very fundamental: the pastoral office or holy ministry must be carefully distinguished from the general priesthood and ministry which belongs to all believers.

Moreover, according to Dr. Baur, ordination ought to be strength-
ened rather than weakened in its significance.

-- When a man opposes all hierarchical or organizational structure
in the church, he is in danger of adopting a spiritualistic, pietistic,
personalistic view of the church. His polemic then against the
heretical church(es) tends towards a view which suggests a kind of
spiritualized, not real, conception of the nature of the church, a kind
of Platonic idea. People who make much of their "reborn experience," or intensified Christian happening, tend to hold such "person-
alized" view of the nature of the church; and their view of the
ministry corresponds therewith, ending with a leveling out of the
office of pastor as ordained by Christ.

Ratzeburg, Germany -- October 13, 1978

Prof. Dr. Bengt Hägglund, professor of Systematic Theology,
University of Lund, Sweden;[20]

Landesbishof Dr. Joachim Heubach, bishop of the Lutheran
territorial church of Bueckeburg;[21]

Prof. Dr. Albrecht Peters, professor of Systematic Theology,
Heidelberg University.[22]

(Dialogue with this group occurred during the time when the
Luther-Akademie convened in Ratzeburg, October 11 to 15, 1978.)
-- Peters: One must be careful with the terms visible and invisible
in speaking of the church. God sees from above who belongs, and
these are very real. In Germany it is no doubt to be preferred to
speak of the church as *sichtlich* and *unsichtlich*, that is, manifest or
evident and not manifest, or evident, rather than *sichtbar* and
unsichtbar, visible and invisible; for the latter terminology seems to
suggest unreality to the reader, while, in fact, the church is very real.
Moreover, in connection with the marks of the church, it is good to
note that Luther uses a wide and a narrow sense. In the wide sense,
of course, he speaks (as in the *Babylonian Captivity* already) of the
twofold means, Word and Sacraments (Baptism and the Lord's
Supper), as marking where the church can be found. In the narrow
sense, he will speak of the "one sacrament," which is Christ, who
gathers His own to Himself. Luther's understanding of church in its
primary meaning, as *una sancta*, is not tied to some location;

Christ's church transcends time and place. In his early writings one can say of Luther that he underscores *Gemeinde*, the congregation, when he speaks of the church which is gathered around the Word. In his later writings one finds him emphasizing more the *Amt*, the ministry. The chief thing is that the Gospel be proclaimed, and the priesthood of believers yields to the practical need for support in obtaining qualified pastors; hence Luther looks to the magistrates of cities and the territorial princes.

-- Hägglund: The theses in his opinion were very good, correctly and faithfully articulating Luther's thought. In connection with Thesis No. 2 on the church, he suggested that instead of invisible one speak of the church as hidden, that is, under suffering and cross-bearing, even though this happens openly. This does not make it unreal; but men cannot know who its members are.

-- Heubach: In line with European Lutheranism Heubach held that to the question, Who constitutes the church? the answer is, All who are baptized. One must retain a positive understanding of the pastoral ministry, both in terms of witnessing and also specifically of the office itself. The ordained man serves as long as he is able by the grace of God.

Also at Ratzeburg:

Pastor Dr. Hans-Lutz Poetsch, director of the Lutheran Hour in Germany and a pastor in SELK (Independent Evangelical Lutheran Church), in fellowship with the LCMS.[23]

Pastor Dr. Einar Huglen, a conservative pastor of the Norwegian Lutheran State Church.[24]

-- Poetsch: Rome's position is that unless we belong to the institution, or ecclesiastical organization, under the papacy, we cannot participate in salvation. This at least is its official teaching. Luther, on the other hand, identified the holy Christian people, or church, with the *communio sanctorum*, or communion of saints. (This Latin term cannot refer to the sacraments, as some have thought, for then it would read *communio in sacris*, communion in sacred things.) Luther's definition of the church never excludes, omits, or stands contrary to the means of grace. In Germany there are many who think and teach in the following manner: even if you do not believe but are baptized into the Christian church (you may be a dead man spiritually actually!), you are a member of the Christian church. This needs to be contested.

-- Huglen: Such thinking is Roman Catholic teaching.

-- Poetsch: Since Luther's time there has been opposition to the term invisible in describing the nature of the *una sancta*. So the question is, Can we use the word invisible or not? Elert, for example, thinks that we ought not. Pastor Poetsch stated that when he taught his confirmation class, the question What is the church? was closely followed by Where is the church? It is there where the *notae ecclesiae*, or marks of the church, are in use. But one can never define the church according to the marks. To define the church it is necessary to link the definition with *theologia crucis*, for this is integral to its existence. Believers gathered around the Savior from sin constitute the church. Thus "theology of the cross" does not first of all have to do with each one taking up his cross and following after Christ. That may indeed follow, but the church stands on the meritorious sacrifice of Christ for sinners; that is faith's focal point.

Moreover, *ecclesia*, or church, is not only congregation in the singular, but also *ecclesia concordita*; by that is meant the grouping of individual churches or congregations as church, or fellowship of churches as in a synod. The Missouri Synod, in Poetsch's view, has been in danger at times of emphasizing church only in the sense of congregation and not also as *ecclesia concordita*. The latter describes the bond of churches or congregations tied together in convenanted relationship and oneness of faith. This is not a commanded organization, but it does accord with God's will and New Testament example.

-- Comment (Klug): Thus Walther never ended up with extreme congregationalism or independentism, nor on the other hand with a kind of super-church. Scriptures do not speak concerning the organizing of a synod, only of believers gathering in congregations. Synods are not mandated, nor are certain kinds of administrations, bishops, etc. Scripture indicates that congregations seek 1) consensus, and 2) fellowship in reaching out and witnessing to the world together. In a group like the Ratzeburg meeting now taking place, there are many serious-minded Lutherans present who have a concern for the integrity of the Lutheran Confessions and for Holy Scripture; but they do not press the matter of what constitutes a proper basis for fellowship.

-- Poetsch: That is correct. What they are saying, is: You must accept us as we are and find ways to tolerate our existence, even though we continue to be part of the unionistic territorial churches. They skirt always the question of fellowship on a proper basis of full agreement on doctrine, and thus have no real desire to pursue it. One of the persisting problems for them is, what does fundamental doctrinal agreement mean? The Reformed settle that matter by saying: fundamental doctrines are those on which we agree; non-fundamental doctrines are those on which we do not agree. Some Lutherans have reduced things in recent times to the formula which says that what pertains to salvation, that is important. They have never answered the question really, Can faith be described as a quality *and* also a quantity? that is, as *fides qua* AND *fides quae*? Much of the sorry state in theology today can be traced to the influence of philosophy and science in determining what will be accepted theologically. There was a time in the olden days when preachers in general used to be called theologians, but not now anymore; there has been a sad decline; the field is left to the professional theologians at the universities, and now so-called "scientific theology" is the order of the day, much to the hurt of Christ's church.

Prof. Dr. Edmund Schlink -- Heidelberg, Germany, October 16, 1978, distinguished professor of Systematic Theology, at Heidelberg University, renowned for his work on the Lutheran Confessions, now deceased (May 1984).[25]

-- Concerning the Confessions: They are not dogmas constructed by the church but *Hauptstuecke Gottes*, the chief things of God's Word. When the church teaches in faithful adherence thereto, it does so in obedience to God.

-- Concerning the Church: The "holy and righteous," true believers in Christ as Luther says, do indeed constitute the church, the communion of saints. *Stricte dicta*, strictly speaking, the church is *invisibilis*; *late dicta*, broadly speaking, the church is a *corpus mixtum*, a mixed body. God alone knows the difference between believers and hypocrites, but the church at large does not. However, we cannot acquiesce to the Romanists' charge that we only believe in an invisible church; the church after all can be located wherever the means of grace are in use, though its members cannot actually be identified by men, but only by God. We can even admit, as

Luther did, that because the Romanists have baptism and the Lord's Supper, the church still is present there. In the *ecclesia visibilis* the *ecclesia invisibilis* becomes apparent or discernible. What you have to say in Thesis No. 5 concerning the local churches, or congregations, being rightly called "church" because of the believers present there, hence in synecdochical sense, is indeed true. Luther held that position.

In Thesis No. 6, should one not distinguish between schismatic churches besides heretical? There are divisions where there are no real doctrinal differences, and hence those churches are really one. Heresies involve a deep difference. Though Luther would not have know about lodges, like the Masons, he would have said that they were heretics, because they are Christ-deniers. Yet, if given preachers deny the virgin birth of Christ and meanwhile do not preach against it but still use the creed, there still is no ground for division, according to Schlink.

-- Concerning the ministry: Thesis No. 1 in the document is very important. Luther has often been misunderstood. The holy ministry, or pastoral office, must be distinguished from the royal priesthood and the ministry which is given to all under the Keys. (Schlink expressed high regard for Jan Aarts' book on Luther's teaching on the ministry.) Dr. Schlink also endorsed fully Thesis No. 2, that the pastoral ministry is ordained by God and is not a human ordinance or innovation. The same holds true for Thesis No. 3, that the pastoral ministry is a delegated office, by God's mandate, according to which the pastor exercises the Keys publicly for the Christian congregation which has called him. Some have held, mistakenly, that in Luther's early writing it can be shown that he at first held that the office of pastor evolved from the general priesthood of believers. The congregation does not create the *Amt*, or office, but possesses it as gift from God, delegating it by Christ's command to its called pastor.

Prof. Dr. Peter Brunner -- Heidelberg, Germany, October 16, 1978, longtime professor of New Testament and noted author, Heidelberg University, now deceased (1981).[26]

-- Concerning the church: It is important that we do not imply that the church is a kind of Platonic idea and that we do not say that the church is in no way visible. After all there are at least five signs by which we know its existence and reality; Christ gives the mandate:

to go (Matt. 28:19); to proclaim and preach His Gospel; to baptize; to absolve from sins; to administer the Lord's Supper.

With baptism there must be faith; God alone sees the hearts; this was clearly Luther's position. Luther must be recognized as a truly ecumenical man: he recognized that the circle of believers goes wider than the professing Christian church.

Dr. Brunner expressed pleasure with the theses, suggesting a twofold distinction:

1)   Concerning faith—it is not seen, because it is within; it is individual; known to God;

2)   Concerning works—these follow faith, give evidence of it, but in no way constitute it.

In treating of and teaching the Christian faith it is imperative, especially today, that we accent the doctrine of the Trinity; Father, Son, and Holy Spirit belong together and cannot be parted. This doctrine continues to be needed in sound dogmatics; it is the heart and core of Christian faith and the visible church. The German churches do not know anymore what the pure Gospel is; it has become a social gospel; it is linked with a denial of the Word; the Confessions already touched upon this and they are faithful to the Word. The Confessions are a measuring standard for true orthodoxy. Along with the Word, there is also the Lord's Supper; it too speaks, not only in what is here verbalized, but in what God promises in this sacrament. Without question, of course, the Word and its proclamation stand central.

As regards Thesis No. 6, on the church, we might note that as long as the possibility existed to root out the heresy, the apostle Paul continued to recognize the Galatian churches as churches. Within a congregation, or group of Christian people, it may even happen that worship ceases, and yet there may be Christians there. Christ's body, the church, is a spiritual body, of course, and it cannot actually be grasped or apprehended by human hands.[27]

-- Concerning the Ministry: The apostolic office is a specific office, with specific duties and powers, to preach, baptize, absolve, administer the Lord's Supper. Along with *Seelsorge*, or care of souls, goes also *paranesis*, exhortation to godliness. This belongs to the pastor's office; he is called to administer the Keys, by the will of God, in the footsteps of the apostles. With ordination a certain *charisma* is bestowed, which includes the permission and charge to fill and carry out the office. Luther used the word *Weihe*, consecration or ordination, because something is given from above, through the general priesthood. With reference to Thesis No. 1, under ministry, Brunner indicated disagreement with Luther's point that a preacher without the office, or call, returns to what he was before.

Prof. Dr. Wm. M. Oesch -- Oberursel, Germany, October 18, 1978, longtime professor (deceased, January 1982) at the Lutheran Seminary, Oberursel, and theological giant of SELK, the Lutheran Free Church, editor for years of the highly respected *Lutherischer Rundblick*.[28]

-- Professor Oesch was known for his straightforward manner: The Missouri Synod "flipflopped" theologically during the 50's and 60's. Its leaders during the years immediately after World War II were naive in thinking that as a result of the war there would now be real Lutherans in chastened Germany. The conferences at Bad Boll (1948 and 1949), for whatever their worth, "took Missouri in" by and large, and the *Volkskirche* theologians of the territorial churches paraded as authentic Lutherans—a total impossibility! Missourians were naive and too stubborn to listen to us and our warnings. There was a grand *detente*. A man like Lorry Meyer (Dr. Lawrence B. Meyer) was a great organizer, and much credit must go to him for helping to get the seminary at Oberursel started; but he was also the precipitator in the main of the fiasco of the Bad Boll Conferences. German theology has not actually advanced one bit towards conservative, confessional theology in the aftermath of the war.

-- Concerning the relation of churches and synod: A synod is a voluntary organization and is not an absolute fixture; Walther knew and said this. Yet it acts in the name of the *una sancta* when it deals with the *notae ecclesiae*, or marks of the church, Word and Sacrament. Congregations do not create a church when they form a synod. It is a church as to its Confession, not according to its structure. Congregations can, of course, withdraw from the synod, but they ought to maintain fellowship, which is wholesome. Synod is rightly called *ecclesia representativa*; it can do what the congregations grant to it; and thus it must be totally dependent upon the congregations. What Walther accomplished in the USA could never have happened in Germany because of the state-church complex or syndrome, the power of the consistories, and the influence of the universities. At Walther's time Vehse agitated for a democracy in the church; Marbach, the lawyer, also stood against the high churchism that had come in with Stephan and did a lot of reading in Luther. As a result Walther, too, was forced to read Luther himself and the great thing happened: he saw that the hierarchy of Stephan, etc., was entirely wrong; it led to an extreme form of clericalism. Walther steered a careful course between that extreme and the other, Vehse's, which would have splintered the church with independentism. The Wisconsin Synod would not have gotten the thing straight without Missouri's help and leadership.[29] Church, in other words, is not to be recognized by "state-church" sort of authority, but by the *notae*. The *notae* (marks) do not constitute the church, but they spot or locate the church; for where the Word is, there true believers will be gathered, by God's promise. You can check the Word of God and what God intends for His church, because you have the Scriptures. German theology was shot through with rationalism, and, on the other extreme, with pietism; it was in a hopeless state, and still is. What happens when there is some reaction against this trend is that another rival movement begins which usually ends up by going in pietistic direction, e.g., the Peter Beyerhaus group at Tuebingen. It is conservative when compared with the prevailing rationalistic spirit in German theology, but it is not genuine Lutheran theology.

-- Concerning the ministry: Hoefling, and so also the Wisconsin Synod, held that the pastor's office evolved out of the general priesthood, according to Matthew 28. In a certain way, of course, this is true, since a pastor's call originates from the congregation; but it is true in a restricted way and with a great difference; for those who succeed to the office of ministry after the apostles enter their office by God's express will and ordaining through the instrumentality of the congregation. Here in Germany the congregation really had ceased to exist; they were *Volkskirchen*, "people's churches," not congregations, but populations! There were only two options, either to go the way of pastors ruling over the people, or the populist way with total democracy and the people ruling the clergy. Both extremes were wrong. German Lutherans knew nothing really about a live, active congregation; this only the Methodists and Baptists had; the "people's churches" among the Lutherans did not.

-- Schlink and Brunner both held the "high" notion concerning the ministry. It's nonsense that a man who leaves his office as pastor still has a *charisma*, or power, as a pastor. I don't, moreover, like the idea current in the Missouri Synod of a "chief pastor," with reference to the synodical president; a man is a pastor insofar as he is pastor of a congregation. He is responsible to the congregation, but he is also responsible to Christ directly because his office is in fact an office which was created as an extract from the apostolic office by his calling through the congregation. These things must be kept in mind, otherwise it ends up as a mere democratic office, or professional post. The apostles, of course, had a unique, distinct authority above that of any of their successors.

For Peter Brunner the chief objection to women in the ministry is that they don't belong at the altar administering the Lord's Supper; but for us it is because the apostle Paul expressly forbids it on the basis of the natural orders, and with apostolic authority.

-- Other matters:

An *addendum* to the *Formula of Concord* in our day seems imperative, especially on the doctrines of the church, ministry, fellowship. To do this Missouri would have to regain, or reassert, the articles of its own Constitution as a first step. It needs, too, to address the authority question anew, the formal principle of theology, the *principium cognoscendi*. Without this it cannot proceed very far. The Australian Lutherans are too weak. We, too, here in Germany, in SELK (The Independent Evangelical Lutheran Church), are not entirely united. The initiative might come from us here but it ought to be an international thing; it is as serious as that. We thought we were united in the SELK organization, ten years ago; but that is not so. There is division both here and also among the Lutheran Free churches of East Germany. Now we've got ourselves a life-time bishop to boot. That was a foolish thing; now we have to keep him under control; that's not always easy when someone has been given authority and power.

Besides the doctrine of the church, there is need also for serious work on the Scripture and its authority as the Word of God. An in-depth critique of the historical-critical methodology has to be produced. A qualified person should be freed of his work load (teaching ten lecture hours a week makes such an assignment impossible!), in order for him to do all the spade work. He should also study the situation in Germany, in England, besides in America, in order to be fully aware of all implications. You can't win the battle unless something forthright and aggressive like this is done.

Concerning fellowship with the ALC: Missouri should terminate this because, in the first place, it compromises the orthodox position, and, secondly, because there really has never been *de facto* fellowship.[30] People can't talk one way and act another; the ALC can't be changed; it's in fellowship with the LCA and everyone else![31]

Yes, there is a possibility that, if Missouri did take a firm stand, it might be possible to call out the loyal Lutherans from the other synods. As far as the Wisconsin Synod goes, that is a different question. Much of Wisconsin's present attitude is traceable to Koehler (onetime professor and president of the Thiensville Seminary); he was a strong leader, who thought much of himself and opposed Missouri, even though on the doctrine of the church he was wrong and Missouri right.

Further association with the LCUSA organization ought to be terminated, except to pay for services given.

We ought not forget our brethren among the German-Russians of the Crimea, nor those in Chile, nor in China. Can the Missouri Synod completely neglect them? many of them victims of the last war and other world events in our century?

Prof. Dr. Hans Kirsten -- Oberursel, Germany, October 18, 1978, one of the surviving leaders of the Lutheran Free Church, former professor and rector at the Oberursel seminary, now retired.[32] (Present at this meeting was Prof. Dr. Gottfried Hoffmann, son-inlaw of Dr. Kirsten and professor of Systematic Theology at Oberursel.) -- As Dr. Kirsten described conditions in German theology after WW II, he spoke of the need for a documentation of these happenings, particularly in connection with the Bad Boll conferences between the American theologians, chiefly at first the Missouri Synod, later also representatives of other Lutheran synods (National Lutheran Council) from the U.S.A. He sustained the criticisms voiced above by Prof. Oesch. "The idea of the meetings was good, but church politics was at work too." The German Lutheran participants, virtually to a man (e.g., Hans Asmussen, Peter Brunner, von Campenhausen, Werner Elert, Helmut Thielecke, Edmund Schlink, Ernst Sommerlath, *et al.*), were held by, or committed to, the "*Volkskirchen*" sort of Lutheranism. Thus, while many of them were personally quite conservative, they were not willing to throw off the compromising yoke which bound them to the state-church syndrome. The Missouri Synod representatives never really met with our Lutheran Free Church men—for more than a century this church had maintained confessional Lutheran integrity and fellowship—in order to orient themselves properly in this mixed company of diverse theological tendencies. Naively the Missourians assumed that the *Landeskirchen* (territorial church) men would treat them as the Missouri Synod, and they, in turn, would want to become "Missourian," now that they were chastened by the trauma of WW II. There is no doubt that the Missouri Synod leaders did the *Landeskirchen* a lot of good; but as they curried their favor and acceptance they at the same time hurt the cause of the Lutheran Free Church which had remained confessional. Meanwhile the *Landeskirchen* theologians did not budge from their position, especially not as regards the important question of what actually constitutes a valid basis for church fellowship, agreement in doctrine (and practice). Hermann Sasse was deeply disturbed by these meetings because he could see that the Missouri Synod leaders did not understand really the theological situation of the Lutheran church in Germany, that they were unduly awed by the learning and reputation of the German conferees, and that they had no true grasp of the unionistic practice to which the German churches were committed and from which they would not budge. Nonetheless, in fairness it must be reiterated that the overtures and the assistance brought by the Lutheran Church-- Missouri Synod (food, money, theological books, etc.), not only made a deep impression but also no doubt was effective to some extent in twitting the consciences of all participants, if they in fact were at all serious in being true to the intent and meaning of the Lutheran Confessions in our day. These lessons of the past ought not be lost on our churches, the Missouri Synod and the Lutheran Free Church (SELK) today.

Leipzig, East Germany -- October 23, 1978

Prof. Dr. Helmar Junghans, professor of theology, Karl Marx University, (now University of Leipzig), and editor of the prestigious *Luther-Jahrbuch.*

Prof. Dr. Max Steinmetz, professor of history, Karl Marx University, Luther scholar and a key ideologist in the Communist party. (Now deceased.)

Prof. Dr. Gottfried Wachler, professor of theology and rector of the small Lutheran Free Church Theological Seminary, Leipzig, (East Germany), in fellowship with the Lutheran Church-Missouri Synod.

Prof. Dr. Gottfried Hoffmann -- Oberursel, Germany (West)

-- The meeting with these four Luther scholars and theologians took place at the Hotel Astoria in the center of Leipzig, East Germany. Each participant had again been supplied in advance with a copy of the theses on church and ministry. No tape could be run under the circumstances. Nonetheless a brief summary of the discussion can be given in a general way at least. For one thing, it should be stated that since the focus was entirely on Luther and his views on church and ministry, there was not only a congenial atmosphere but a remarkable sort of concurrence. Thus the theses as presented were not debated but supported with considerable approval as representing Luther fairly, not only by Professor Wachler and Hoffmann, but also by Professors Junghans and Steinmetz. There was little opportunity to probe into the questions of application of the theses in actual church life in Communist East Germany. The abiding influence of Luther and his writings was evidenced, however, in the meeting of the minds of what Luther had said and taught concerning church and ministry. Whether this was actually each man's personal conviction concerning faith and life, as it was for Luther, was impossible to determine in the short span of a couple hours. It was so for Wachler and Hoffmann, also for Junghans, a committed Lutheran under a Communist regime. Undoubtedly the *Volkskirche* sort of thinking and theology would be the ultimate point to which things would have gone, if there had been more opportunity to explore or probe. Steinmetz quite obviously conceived of Luther's greatest contribution not in terms of what Luther had meant for the German church through his rediscovery of the Gospel, but as the people's man who had meant much for the workers' movement, until, of course, and unfortunately (according to Steinmetz), he had failed to sustain his support of the peasants in 1524 and 1525. Perhaps the importance, therefore, of this little meeting was not so much in substantive accomplishment, but in effecting for the first time a minimal rapprochement between parties who otherwise might never have shared time around a conference table in East Germany.

Marburg, Germany -- October 24, 1978

Prof. Dr. Theo. Mahlmann, professor of Systematic Theology, Marburg, University.

Prof. Dr. Heinrich Leipold, professor of Systematic Theology, Marburg, University.

-- Mahlmann: Because faith evidences itself, Mahlmann favored not using the term *ecclesia invisibilis* at all, but *visibilis* only. He agreed with Melanchthon that the *ecclesia invisibilis* is, if anything, a *Kreis*, or circle, within the visible church. With Word and Sacrament, the *notae*, believers are gathered into the church visible. He described the theses as "old" dogmatics formulations. The *ecclesia universalis*, or church universal, has no existence in reality except only in the eyes of God. The existing church is the *ecclesia particularis*, the church at a given place and time. One must ask, How does the church which exists in the eyes of God exist in reality? By the preaching of the Gospel it can be seen and it can be organized. There is no congregation of people, or group, which is without some structure. The content of the Gospel is love to the enemy. Thus the church, as Dr. Mahlmann saw the problem of what or where the church is, stands revealed in this truth that the church is *Christus existierend*, that is, the existing, or becoming, Christ. The Gospel is freedom-making power that works horizontally through the world. Christ, the Head of the Body, is no more the Lord, but the eldest brother among brethren.[33] The view of the church expressed in your theses is difficult to translate to modern man. In fact, one may ask whether the concept of the church as taught in Romans, 1 Corinthians, Ephesians, and Colossians is not a quite disparate one. (Mahlmann expressed an obviously existentialistic type of ecclesiology.)

-- Leipold: In general he expressed agreement with the theses, especially as regards the definition of the church's nature. Of course, the Roman Catholics see the church as *Christus existierend*,

Christ existing, in the structure of the church as organized under the papacy. When one uses the definition of church as Thesis No. 1 gives it with students, they are likely to deny knowing such a church. In comparison, the church with which people have to do is real, in the Gospel proclamation which Christ gives; and this Gospel is very fundamental, if we are to make the church relevant. The charismatic movement seems to emphasize the quest for the renewal of the true church and the real church; but the greatest weakness of this movement is that it tends to detach itself from the *notae ecclesiae*.

Prof. Dr. Gerhard Mueller -- Erlangen, Germany, October 25, 1978, professor of Theology and Luther Studies at Erlangen University, editor of the massive, *Theologische Realencyklopädie*.
-- The term "invisible" is really a predicate rather than attribute of the church; it is not a description of the church but an *Urteil ueber die Kirche*, a judgment, or statement, about the church itself. With Luther, it is true, the external aspects of the church, as it exists in society, are secondary, though important too. That they are important Luther indicates when he lists seven characteristics of the church in the world; this occurs in his treatise *On the Councils and the Church*, as you have indicated. One could put it another way: *Lehre* (teaching and doctrine), *Leben* (life, godliness), *Leiden* (suffering or cross-bearing) attest the church's actual existence; a Christian's suffering hangs on *theologia crucis*, that is, it follows upon his believing Christ's atoning sacrifice in his behalf.

With the Peasants' War Luther saw that the congregations were not ready for governing themselves, but he never changed his fundamental teaching and belief that the congregation has the ultimate responsibility for the Keys in its midst and for guarding against false teaching. As regards the relation of church and ministry, we in Germany, too, have a dual movement, involving two extremes, each clamoring for attention; the one is the Romanizing tendency which elevates the office of the pastor beyond what the Scriptures allow and Luther taught; the other is the populist view, or people's movement, which tends towards laicism and a lowering or leveling of the pastoral office.

It is good to stress both the general priesthood and the special office of the pastor. Wilhelm Maurer, Dr. Mueller's distinguished predecessor, emphasized that in Luther's theology one finds not one but two thoughts as he drives home Biblical truth; for example, *Gott der Richter*, God the Judge, and *Gott der Barmherziger*, God the Compassionate. So, also here the general priesthood has the ministry of the Word; but the general ministry is set into tandem relationship with the special ministry in the narrow sense, the pastoral office. Luther did indeed respect the congregation's call, to preach or teach in the church, as in Wittenberg in his own case, or through the rulers or magistrates acting in behalf of the people. It is especially interesting and important to note that Amsdorf was ordained as bishop at Naumburg by Luther; thus Luther sharply differentiated between the Roman Catholic and Lutheran view of the pastoral office and how it is conferred; for Luther it is through the congregation.

Dr. Mueller advocated restricting the present study to the research of Luther's, Chemnitz's, and other Lutheran theologians' writing on the subject of church and ministry; the Scriptural foundation, which of course is fundamental, is after all covered faithfully in these men's writings. It will be most valuable according to Dr. Mueller, to know how the story has gone on as regards church and ministry from Luther to Walther, also for theology in present-day Germany.

A question presently unsettled, but much discussed, here in Germany is whether a Catholic priest who defected to the Lutheran Church would need to be ordained again or not. Dr. Mueller's personal view is that he should, in order to indicate his certification for ministry within the Lutheran church.

Neuendettelsau, Germany -- October 25, 1978

Founded by Wilhelm Loehe in the mid-nineteenth century the haven of mercy at this hamlet near Nuernberg continues its ministry to the sick, aged, handicapped, orphaned, and needy. The deaconess order which in many ways was the key to this ministry has experienced considerable decline, but the social welfare focus has not been lost; workers are still being trained for service in Germany and foreign fields. Loehe was also a key figure in the founding of what later became Concordia Theological Seminary in Fort Wayne, Indiana. In cooperation with men like Wilhelm Sihler, F. K. D. Wyneken, C. F. W. Walther, Loehe provided the initial funding and recruitment of workers for the American mission field and the founding of the seminary at Fort Wayne, Indiana, in 1846. The seminary was turned over to the Missouri Synod in 1847, at the time of the synod's founding in that year. Loehe never shared the views on church and ministry which Walther and his confessionally loyal followers came to espouse after the Stephan debacle. Loehe's views on church and ministry were essentially the same as those of Stephan in that he viewed the church body itself as possessing God-given authority over the congregations (similar to the consistorial system of Germany), and the pastors as possessing unique authority and power as a result of their ordination into the ministry. Present-day thinking at Neuendettelsau remains much the same, with what might be termed a "high" view of the church, as well as of the ministry.

Prof. Dr. Hermann Haering -- Tuebingen, Germany. October 27, 1978, professor and associate of Prof. Hans Kueng at the Ecumenical Institute, Tuebingen University. He is a lay professor for Roman Catholic Theology and director of the Institute during Kueng's frequent absences.

-- "I find the theses good." In connection with Thesis No. 1, it is true that *sanctitas*, or holiness and righteousness, is connected with *Ethos* and *Leben*, morality and life, in the Catholic church, while Lutherans think of the righteousness *coram Deo*, i.e., in relation to God, through Christ's atoning sacrifice. Likewise ecumenicity in the Roman Catholic thinking has to do with structure, whereas for Luther it had to do with universal grace.

Concerning Thesis No. 2, is not the term *Unsichtbarkeit*, state of being invisible, a polemical term? If Word and Sacrament are integrally connected with the church, is it not a visible entity? very real? something men see? Yet we would acknowledge that what a person sees concerning the church is not its true nature.

Thesis No. 3 emphasizes the Office of the Keys, and the binding and loosing of sinners. The Gospel is central here, and it would seem that the church must become quite transparent then. Vatican II would assent to much of what is stated here. Roman Catholic theology ties together Word and tradition, faith and works, God's power and man's action in the church. Evangelical theology helps us when it shows that God's Word underlies everything, and that when a dogma and Scripture conflict, Scripture has priority.

-- When Thesis No. 4 addresses the matter of pure doctrine or teaching, who is it that determines what is pure? How is the authority question to be answered? On the basis of Scripture and its ability to interpret itself as God's inspired Word? That's very right! Much depends on how Scripture is viewed. Ecumenical theology must deal forthrightly with this question, but there are many hermeneutical problems; yet one cannot quibble with Scripture's authority. Prof. Kueng has taken a stance for such authority of the Word, explained Dr. Haering, when he argued that the so-called infallibility question in the Catholic church had to be judged by Scripture and not only by the teaching authority of the church. But in what way is the Scripture infallible? There is truth in the whole of Scripture and in the church, in spite of incidental errors in each. Thus Prof. Kueng accepts some of Bultmann's demythologizing, yet in a critical sort of way; he may doubt "born of the Virgin Mary" as a fact, but the truth of the *kerygma* he upheld. The same holds true for Christ's resurrection: Jesus lives, and lives in God; but the physical resurrection accounts as recorded in the Bible are open to demythologizing as to their details. So, Scripture is indeed true, but much legend is there too. For Prof. Kueng these problems must be addressed pragmatically: what is it that existentially meets the needs of man in justification, faith, salvation? This is the main question.

As regards Theses Nos. 5 and 6, concerning the physical side of the church in contrast to the spiritual, the Roman Catholic church holds that the church's entity works itself out in the office of Peter, around or under which the church is structured.

-- Concerning the ministry: In Luther, according to Dr. Haering, there is no single consistent view of the office of ministry, though he recognized that ordination has its source in the call. In Roman Catholicism ordination is both a divine and a human ordinance for the bestowal of unique powers that belong alone to the priest. The practice and place of ordination among Evangelicals, in Dr. Haering's view, is presently being lowered or minimized; and these people are citing many Luther texts. At the same time, on the other hand, there are those who incline toward a very high elevating of ordination, and the office has virtually taken on sacramental significance. For Rome this is basic for ecumenical discussions, to retain ordination as a vital element; less important is the distinction between priest and bishop.

Prof. Dr. Heiko Oberman -- Tuebingen, Germany, October 27, 1978, professor of Historical Theology and author of numerous works on the Reformation.[34]

-- There have been many criticisms of these terms, *invisibilis* and *visibilis*, and for various reasons; but the fact is that we always return to the distinction because the terms are so pertinent and far-reaching. It would separate us from our Creed, if we do not make the distinction; and for the church to be truly *una, sancta, apostolica*, these terms are necessary. For Luther, over against Augustine, Calvin, Aquinas, and others, the term *invisibilis* is not just a mark of the church, but its very nature; faith relates to things not known to us, but which for faith are sure. So, for Luther, this is the ruling definition of the church. At the moment Dr. Oberman was editing a second volume of Luther on the Psalms, where it is evident how the Old Testament and God's dealing with His chosen people, the Jews, helped Luther to clarify the true nature of the church. In Dr. Oberman's opinion there was every reason to oppose Aland's thinking that there is considerable development between the early Luther and the late Luther.

-- Dr. Oberman expressed increasing respect for the material which we have in Luther's *Letters* and *Table Talk*. In a letter to the bishop of Meissen, 1537, Luther's stance remains consistent with what he held much earlier, 1520 for instance, when he in essence wrote to another correspondent, We do not want to get into your diocese without your permission. As long as the Gospel is proclaimed, there is no excuse to interfere. To Luther this is true apostolic succession in the right sense.

-- At Augsburg, 1530, Dr. Oberman felt that Rome and the Reformation were closer than at any other time. "You see, that is why your topic is so exciting, because you really have to do a whole theology of Luther." It is important not to become too dogmatic but remain historical in your treatment. Dr. Oberman doubted whether for Luther the hiddenness of the church was the same as the *ecclesia invisibilis*. The latter is something that has gone on before, for faith; while the hiddenness of the church has to do with the smallness of the church, suffering, etc., and with the contemporary reality of the church. The devil comes to a person and shows him what sin he has committed and tries to convince him that he is not a child of God. Against that kind of argument he must stand on his baptism. Exactly the same thing happens to the church. It is to be holy, one, apostolic, etc.   Against that is now also the *Verborgenheit*, the church's hiddenness. But there is the *petra*, the Rock, the faith, on which the church is built, says Christ. The advantage of the hidden and revealed church is that it helps us to see first the relation of the individual faithful ones and then the faithful church. The claims of faith are indicative, not imperative; if one tries to smooth out the contradiction of Christian faith, then the great danger is that he smooths out the real guts of Christianity. Dr. Oberman opined that the World Council was guilty of this in its theologizing.

-- Concerning the ministry: In the seeming contradiction between the priesthood of believers and the priestly office Luther clearly shows that there is need for the office of pastor. Each father in the home does not become priest in the church. The congregation's call is the ordination of the man to his office; that is Luther's teaching. In Dr. Oberman's opinion Luther along with Amsdorf believed that he could appoint men for the congregations, but apparently not without the congregation's consent. One needs to be careful not to find rigid principles in decisions Luther makes for certain situations; yet there are always principles upon which he is confronting the situation.

As indicated, Oberman generally pooh-poohed the idea that there are great differences between a young Luther and old: "Why in 1512, Luther is already 29 years old and has his doctorate! Most people don't have a new idea after they are 30!" Oberman jokingly referred to his own work and writings, stating that he finds that he tends to go over old territory covered earlier. His final comment was directed toward Chemnitz: "I'm a great fan of Chemnitz."

Prof. Dr. Eberhard Juengel -- Tuebingen, Germany, October 28, 1978, professor of Systematic Theology, Tuebingen.[35]

-- Dr. Juengel felt that Rome very obviously took the *notae ecclesiae*, marks or attributes of the church, like *una*, *sancta*, etc., and applied them to itself as a church. As a result the Reformers stressed that these attributes were present rather among them and their followers, that the true nature of the church was *invisibilis*, and that this church works among them through Word and Sacraments. Luther preferred the term *ecclesia abscondita*, it seems; he held that the Gospel is central in the church's being and creation.

Ministry is an office of service, *diakonia*. Luther preached because he had a call from the congregation (Wittenberg). The question is, Is a man called because he is qualified? Or is he qualified, if he is called? To the suggestion that it might be both, Juengel replied that he had problems with that. "We have colloquies, too, by which men may qualify; but the call is preeminent," he stated.

-- Concerning Thesis No. 7, Juengel expressed misgivings about the laity's right to judge in doctrinal matters, also that they might with proper qualifications be eligible to serve in the ministerial office.

Prof. Dr. Peter Beyerhaus -- Tuebingen, Germany, October 28, 1978, professor and director of the evangelical, conservative ecumenical institute at Tuebingen.[36]
-- Prof. Beyerhaus has gathered a following of about 100 students and represents a reaction against the higher-critical, ecumenically-minded rival institute at which Kueng, Haering, Moltmann, Juengel, Kaspar, *et al.* are the leading theologians. Beyerhaus lectures on the history of missions and ecumenical theology particularly as the latter is at work in the World Council of Churches. Critical of the historical-critical judgments against Scripture, he nonetheless looks for a reasoned defense or apology in behalf of Christian faith; he sees himself somewhat in the pattern of Carl F. Henry in America. Evangelical theology should take seriously the findings of science; yet at the same time it ought show the shallowness on which some of science's reasoning and judgments are based, specifically as regards undocumented and unproved theories. He evinced a strong desire to convene an international conference, involving evangelical scholars from various disciplines, for the sake of such in-depth study and discussion, with the added purpose of shaping a strong answer for the so-called cultured despisers of God's Word.

Prof. Dr. Gerhard Ebeling -- Zurich, Switzerland, October 30, 1978, professor of Systematic Theology and Luther scholar, University of Zurich. Also one of the editors of the Weimar Ausgabe of Luther's works.[37]

(Prof. Ebeling had just completed his manuscript for a new three-volume dogmatics, arranged according to the three articles of the Creed.)

-- Ebeling explained that his approach to the doctrines of church and ministry was exegetical- dogmatic, although he saw merit in the historical-doctrinal approach expressed in the theses of this study.

-- He acknowledged the theses to be a good summary statement of Luther's theology. Lacking perhaps is the handling of problems or questions concerning the *ecclesiola* and *ecclesia*, the gap between "occasional" churches, *ecclesiola*, and the *Volkskirchen*, people's churches, as in Luther's *Deutsche Messe*, or German Mass; and this appears to be necessary especially in *Kirchenzucht*, or discipline. Luther's *Kirchenbegriff*, or understanding of the nature of the church, remained consistent throughout his life; there are modifications that occur in his maturer years from the earliest period in his life, but these are minor and have to do with particular situations or problems. Indeed, the concept of *ecclesia invisibilis* is always basic in Luther's thinking throughout; it is always present. The concept of the hidden church, *ecclesia abscondita*, has to do with the visible church where believers are and where persecutions, cross-bearing, etc., are also present for the church's patient bearing. The remarkable thing in Luther is that in his concept of the church there is room always for the Romanists and the *Schwaermer*, or Enthusiasts. How the church comes to be is always a basic, fundamental concern for Luther. The body, or the church, is not constituted, or built, in any other way than through the constituting Word. Believers, Luther states, will always be present where the Word is. The emphasis is on faith, which Christ alone considers. The other figures for the church, like bride, sheepfold, etc., all underscore this same truth. Above all, it should be noted that Luther submitted the traditional sociological structure of the church in his day, which divided society into two distinct classes, the religious (clergy, monks, nuns) and the secular (the rest of the populace), "to a radical revision."[38] To Luther this was a "specious device" by which the first class exploited the other, the second.

This concluded the European dialogues. Summation and evaluation will follow in the last chapter.

NOTES

1   With but few exceptions the confreres readily accepted this arrangement. Since it was agreed that the tapes were to be for my own record as

notes on the discussions, they here serve only to guide me in general comments concerning the viewpoints expressed by the dialoguers, rather than as exact reproductions. Were the tapes to be released, the approval of each participant would be required. The tapes are in the custody of the library of Concordia Theological Seminary, Fort Wayne, Indiana, available as records of the colloquia.

2   Among those already retired: Leif Aalen, Carl Wisløff, Lenaart Pinomaa, Karl Rengstorf, Hans Kirsten, Wilhelm Oesch, Edmund Schlink, Peter Brunner. Of these Profs. Aalen, Oesch, Schlink, and Peter Brunner are now deceased; also Albrecht Peters, Steinmetz, and Rengstorf are deceased.

3   cf. *LW* 41, xi.

4   Leif Aalen, "Vestigia terrent," in *Von der Wahren Einheit der Kirche*, Ulrich Asendorf and F. W. Kuenneth, eds. Verlag Die Spur, Duesseldorf, 1973. Also *Dogmatisk grunnriss*. Universitetsforlaget Oslo, 1965.

5   Note: this faculty was originally formed as a conservative bloc against the theological faculty of the University of Oslo; it was to be a conservative theological school for training parish pastors; at the present time there seems to be little distance between this faculty theologically and Oslo University's theology faculty, since both have converged on points which earlier drove them into separate existence.

6   Prof. Aalen noted that, therefore, the distinction between the two faculties, one as conservative, the other as liberal, has more or less disappeared; also that a man like Prof. Inge Lønning of the University of Oslo faculty is not liberal in the usual German sense of the term; his dissertation on the "freedom of the Gospel" had demonstrated that this must be tied to the Lutheran Confessions.

7   Inge Lønning, "Das Blinde Wort und die Verborgene Wirklichkeit," essay presented to the Luther Congress, Erfurt, 1983.

8   Carl Wisløff, *Abendmahl und Messe, die Kritik Luthers am Messopfer*. Berlin: Lutherisches Verlagshaus, 1969.

9   Jan Aarts, *Die Lehre M. Luthers' Ueber das Amt in der Kirche*. Helsinki: Haemeenlinna, 1972, a dissertation written under the Finnish Luther scholar, Lennart Pinomaa.

10   Aarts showed the freedom of thought current in the Dutch Roman Catholic arena. Dutch himself by birth, he is one of ten Roman Catholic priests in the whole of Finland, seven others of whom are also Dutch. I would judge his theological stance and penetrating familiarity with Luther's writings to have been greatly influenced by recent Romanist leaders like Joseph Lortz, et al., and, above all, by his own personal study of Luther's writings.

11   Uuras Saarnivaara, *Luther Discovers the Gospel*. St. Louis: Concordia Publishing House, 1951.

12 Prof. Saarnivaara and his followers put a heavy emphasis on pietism along with their conservative, Biblical commitment.

13 Prof. Pinomaa is the author of several books on Luther's theology, the most familiar: *Faith Victorious. An Introduction to Luther's Theology.* W. J. Kukkonen, trans. Philadelphia: Fortress Press, 1963. See also: *Die Heiligen bei Luther.* Helsinki: Saarijaervi, 1977.

14 Bernhard Lohse, *Martin Luther.* Eine Einfuehrung in sein Leben u. Werk. Munich: Beck, 1981.

15 O. Hermann Pesch, *Luther Heute* (with Wolfgang Seibel). Butzon u. Bercker, 1969. Also: *Gerechtfertigt aus Glauben: Luther's Frage an die Kirche.* Freiburg: Herder, 1982.

16 An interesting sidelight: before 1905 the pastors of Hamburg, one of the so-called "free-cities" of Germany, served as a kind of theological faculty; then the university was founded, with the various faculties or departments, including theology.

17 Prof. Rengstorf is a member of SELK, the independent Lutheran church in fellowship with the Missouri Synod. He is the author of numerous books, notably: *Apostolate and Ministry.* Paul D. Pahl, trans. St. Louis: Concordia Publishing House, 1969. Also: *Die Auferstehung Jesu: Form, Art, und Sinn der urchristlichen Osterbotschaft.* Witten: Luther-Verlag, 1960.

18 Kurt Aland, *Kirche und Staat.* Edited with W. Schneemelcher. Berlin: De Gruyter, 1967. Also *Hilfsbuch zum Lutherstudium.* Witten: Luther-Verlag, 1970. And *Der Weg zur Reformation.* Munich: Kaiser, 1965.

19 Joerg Baur, *Die Vernunft zwischen Ontologie und Evangelium: eine Untersuchung zur Theologie Johann Quenstedts.* Guetersloh: Mohn, 1962.

20 Bengt Hägglund, *History of Theology.* Gene J. Lund, trans. St. Louis: Concordia Publishing House, 1968.

21 Joachim Heubach, *Die Ordination zum Amt der Kirche.* Berlin: Lutherisches Verlagshaus, 1956.

22 Albrecht Peters and Edmund Schlink, *Zur Auferbauung des Leibes Christi.* Festgabe fuer Peter Brunner. Kassel: Stauda, 1965.

23 Hans-Lutz Poetsch, *Wesen und Funktion der Theologie.* Bremen: Stelton, 1969.

24 Einar Huglen and Reidar Hvalvik, *Anden og Kirken.* Oslo: Luther Forlag, 1979.

25 Edmund Schlink, *Theology of the Lutheran Confessions.* P. F. Koehneke and H. J. A. Bouman, trans. Philadephia: Fortress Press, 1961.

26 Peter Brunner and Bernard Holm, *Luther in the Twentieth Century.* Decorah: Luther Press, 1961. Peter Brunner, *Vom Amt des Bischofs.*

Berlin: Lutherisches Verlagshaus, 1955. *The Ministry and the Ministry of Women*. St. Louis: Concordia Publishing House, 1971.

27   Brunner stated that as regards the church he distinguished between the Old and the New Covenant; the latter is highly eschatological, the former connected with the promise. When asked, "But wasn't Abraham and weren't all of the patriarchs also in the church because of their faith in the promise concerning the Messiah?" Brunner replied: "Yes, that is so. But I'll have to think that over some more." Brunner demurred to say whether the church was built or existed in the Old Testament or not.

28   Born and theologically trained in America, he spent virtually his whole ministry, more than fifty years, in Germany, except for a short period before WW II when he served in England. His last work was translated into English: *An Unexpected Plea. Since 1977: Addenda to the Formula of Concord*. Fort Wayne: Concordia Theological Seminary Press, 1983. J. Valentinus Andreae, trans.

29   For additional commentary on the WELS' teaching on church and ministry see Part I, chapter 5, footnote 1; also Part II, chapter 1, footnotes 2, 4, 25, 41, and 47.

30   Oesch's wish came about in 1981 when Missouri terminated fellowship with the ALC at its St. Louis convention.

31   Meanwhile the ALC (American Lutheran Church) has joined with the LCA (Lutheran Church in America) and other synods to form the ELCA (Evangelical Lutheran Church of America), 1988.

32   Recent book by Dr. Kirsten: *Einigkeit im Glauben und in der Lehre* (1981), detailing events after WW II as the Lutherans from America met with German theologians and pastors.

33   Theo. Mahlmann, *Das neue Dogma der lutherischen Christologie*. Guetersloh: Mohn, 1969.

34   Heiko Oberman, *The Harvest of Medieval Thought*. Cambridge: Harvard University Press, 1963.

35   Prof. Juengel explained that his release from the east zone of Germany as "an enemy of the state" came as an unexpected boon; he had taught in Madgeburg and Berlin. Among his writings: *The Doctrine of the Trinity*. Grand Rapids: Wm. Eerdmans Publishing Company, 1976.

36   A former missionary, Prof. Beyerhaus has written: *Missions: Which Way?* Margaret Clarkson, trans. Grand Rapids: Zondervan, 1971.

37   Gerhard Ebeling, *Luther. An Introduction to His Thought*. Philadelphia: Fortress Press, 1970.

38   Ebeling, op. cit., 180.

Chapter 2

Other Interpreters

Luther's definition of the church as "holy believers and lambs who hear the voice of their Shepherd" proved to be a model of ingenuous simplicity and beauty. It has won acceptance widely in many hearts. People usually show ill-conceived glee over his not-so-subtle jibe that even "a seven-year-old child knows" this definition, albeit they may never have met a seven-year-old that can come up with the answer. The fact is nevertheless that Luther's theology on the church's nature has stood the test of time. As demonstrated above there was little contention as regards the theses constructed on the basis of Luther's thought. Luther may have overstated the prowess of seven-year-olds, but he was dead-serious in saying it: "Thank God, a seven-year-old knows that the church is holy believers and lambs who hear the Shepherd's voice."

On the broad scale, therefore, on the subject of church there is general agreement among Luther's interpreters. Most recognize, as Bernhard Lohse points out, that in ecclesiology Luther may adjust what he says to the situation, but he never departs very far from what he finds the Scriptures very clearly articulating.[1] Thus, while Luther with one emphasis will speak of the church as one, as the communion of saints, he can also shift to speak of "*Die Zwo Kirchen*," the two churches. He does this, in order to stress "the relationship between what the church is and what is called church," states Carl Aurelius, that is, between what he designates as "spiritual, internal Christendom" and the second which is called "physical, external Christendom."[2] Luther makes the matter very clear in his early treatise *On the Papacy in Rome* (1520):

> Therefore for the sake of better understanding and brevity, we shall call the churches by two distinct names. The first, which is natural, basic, essential, and true, we shall call "spiritual, internal Christendom." The second, which is man-made and external, we shall call "physical, external Christendom." This Christendom is ruled by canon law and by prelates, (and includes) all those who are regarded as Christians, according to externals, no matter whether they

346

are true and real Christians, or not. For although such a community does not make a true Christian, it never exists without some people who are also true Christians. But those who are in the second community without faith and outside the first community, are dead before God.[3]

A great amount of effort has been expended on the question of whether Luther used the distinction between the invisible and visible church, a distinction very often attributed to St. Augustine first of all. In spite of the fact that Luther himself saw no clash in speaking of "*Die Zwo Kirchen*" and upholding at the same time the unity and integrity of the *una sancta catholica Christiana*, there has been considerable debate over the source and justification for doing so. Some Lutherans counsel that the usage should be jettisoned in view of the fact that it is taken from Calvinism. So Theo. Graebner apparently claimed, according to Richard R. Caemmerer and Erwin L. Lueker in their book, *Church and Ministry in Transition*.[4] Yet the same authors note that C. F. W. Walther, who was heavily dependent upon Luther, did employ the distinction, though it is missing in so many words in the Lutheran Confessions.[5]

Perhaps use of the distinction can lead to misunderstanding. On the other hand, it also serves a useful purpose as Luther demonstrates above, and need not confuse. Werner Elert acknowledges that Luther speaks of the true church as invisible and that "he demands again and again," that it must be believed "in exactly the same sense as all the other constituents of faith," which likewise are invisible.[6] As a matter of fact, says Elert, in Luther "the three concepts 'invisible,' 'spiritual,' and 'hidden' (*abscondita*) are obviously used synonymously," and "only a physical, visible, and external sign of them is given to us," that is, through the marks of the church, Word and Sacrament.[7] Elert may be correct in saying that Luther will often identify, or equate, "invisible" with "hidden," but it is also true, as Heiko Oberman and Gerhard Ebeling contend, that just as often Luther reserves the term "hidden" (*abscondita*) to describe the true church existentially, under suffering, cross-bearing, and persecution in this world.

Luther's references to the *true* church are often made in order to distinguish it from the false, the "church of Cain," in distinction from the "church of Abel." As Paul Avis rightly points out, "the most sustained exposition of it is to be found in Luther's lectures on Genesis," where through many allusions, like his reference to Cain, Luther sets the true church apart from enemies like the pope and the Turk.[8] Anyone may claim the name "church," as Luther frequently observes, but it is the marks, Word and Sacrament, which locate its presence, even though their use at any given place does not, and cannot, serve to identify the individual "lambs" or "sheep" in Christ's fold. Gordon Rupp has pointed out that Luther was "not concerned with defining the circumference of the Church, but with proclaiming its Christological center."[9] God has simply promised and His promises have never failed, that the preaching of the Word, the Gospel, will never be in vain, for it energizes and is the very heart of the so-called marks.[10] In line with this observation Paul Althaus chimes in to say that for Luther "no earthly power can draw the boundaries of the Church and decide who belongs to it and who does not," and that by the same token "the Christian existence of the individual is beyond the reach of every ecclesiastical organization."[11] The reality, yet the invisibility, of the church was never more accurately stated, nor more in line with Luther's original thought.

Sensitive readers of Luther are often offended at the coarseness of his vituperative denunciations of the Roman church and particularly the papacy.   The Catholic scholar Remigius Baeumer argues that as Luther grew older, the worse things got on this score. Scott Hendrix takes issue with this view, arguing that Luther's polemic against the Roman church "did not undergo radical shifts but progressed through finely differentiated stages until he became absolutely convinced that the papacy would not fulfill its pastoral duty."[12] This position was fixed already by the time of the Leipzig debate, 1519, and it did not alter for the rest of Luther's life. Luther excoriated the papacy on theological malfeasance, the failure of the papacy to perform the pastoral role. Luther was right, states Hendrix, in his charge, that "the pope should submit to the gospel if he wants the church to be filled with Christians served by pastors instead of with pagans served by tyrants."[13] "Luther does not replace theological arguments with irresponsible polemic," as some of his critics have claimed, contends Hendrix.[14] "Disappointment and anger at that perversion of the pastoral office spurred Luther to exercise 'the duty of a good pastor' to the end of his life."[15] None can ever accuse Luther of lacking a large, pastoral heart. It was this which drove him to denounce the papacy as the citadel of Satan.

Mark Edwards, in a notable recent study, concurs with Hendrix on this insight into Luther. However, he also inclines towards the view that as Luther grew older he was guilty of having "bestialized" his opponents.[16] Yet Edwards feels compelled to soften his criticism of Luther's treatment of his foes, because "the issues he discussed, indeed the very tenor of the disputes were frequently set by others before he ever picked up his pen."[17] Edwards also seems to question Luther's motives in the word battles, asserting that he was "vulgar and abusive when he wished to be, moderate and calmly persuasive when it suited his purpose."[18] Such judging of motives in Luther does not fit the portrait history draws of the Reformer. Edwards is closer to the truth as he concludes his study: "Luther could never just attack. He always had to profess and confess as well."[19]

As noted earlier, Roman Catholic evaluations of Luther have become increasingly more objective and accurate in recent years. Nor is this so merely among the so-called avant-garde circle of scholars who find themselves at odds with the papacy on various grounds, like the international gadfly, Hans Kueng, who scorches the Vatican for its infallibility doctrine. It is true that Kueng will frequently state things concerning the church's nature which harmonize with Luther's asseverations. John XXIII, says Kueng, like no pope of living memory, "succeeded in gaining a hearing once more for the gospel of Jesus Christ," and opened things up in the church to the world with "an exercise of service in the spirit of the New Testament," instead of "a primacy of jurisdiction."[20] But Kueng has trampled recklessly over the very articles of faith that Luther found in Scripture, as well as Scripture itself.

More in tune with Luther and more accurate than his teacher, Joseph Lortz, is the work of Daniel Olivier, a French Luther scholar who has read deeply into the Reformer's writings. Were it not for these writings, states Olivier, "we would perhaps have to admit that Luther had been the disturbing person that polemics has made of him."[21] The man who is equipped and gripped by the invaluable treasure of these writings will be led to admit, says Olivier, that "the tragedy is not that he (Luther) was condemned by a hasty procedure but that the magisterium of the Church found nothing positive to draw from a teaching which still profoundly touches the man of faith, whatever his background."[22] The ongoing tragedy is that "Rome has never seen fit to admit that the situation of the Church at the beginning of the sixteenth century called for a Luther, that is, for an advocate of the Gospel."[23] Olivier might have added, though it certainly is implicit in what he says, that this is the tragedy of ecumenical Christianity today across the board. Luther was right in calling the church back to its mooring point in the Gospel. There is no other foundation, nor can the church be built in any other way. Luther's "definition of the Church as the community of believers signifies that the pope," or any other authority or governing principle for that matter, "is not the criterion of the true Church," for it is Gospel alone, the genuine article on the sinner's justification *sola gratia/fide*, which alone builds the true church.[24] With penetrating accuracy Olivier states: "The cause of the Gospel in the Church is today more pressing than ever, for the Gospel is in jeopardy not in the world but first of all in Christian circles."[25]

It was Luther who first saw the intertwining nature of church and ministry. We have attempted to show that generally there is little debate over the doctrine of the church in Luther's writings. However, sides are drawn on the ministry, particularly over the way in which Luther ties the priesthood of believers to the pastoral office. Yet this happens more as a result of how Luther is received than through any inherent unclarity in his teaching. Werner Elert points out that there can be no doubt that for Luther the divine ordering of the congregation around the ministry of the Word is directly interconnected with the divine instituting of the holy ministry of the pastoral office through the instrumentality of the calling people, or congregation of "priests." "Luther," states Elert, "was unwilling to retract any part of the statement that the office is entrusted to the whole congregation and that for this reason it is delegated to the individual only by the congregation," a thing that is done through the call, and "Luther uses the concepts 'to ordain' and 'to call' synonymously."[26]

One of the most valuable studies as regards Luther's teaching on the office of the holy ministry in recent years is that of Wilhelm Brunotte, *Das geistliche Amt bei Luther*, which unfortunately is not available in English. Brunotte examines Luther's thought throughout his life, early to late, and demonstrates that from 1519 onward Luther is not only a very consistent thinker on the subject but also does not waver from the position which he presented publicly at Leipzig against Eck. There are a few contemporary writers who contest this judgment, but they are in the minority. James Pragman, for example, repeats the old notion that "Luther was no systematician," and that, therefore, "it cannot be said that complete clarity dominates Luther's teaching on the ministry."[27] Pragman sees it as a "problem" for Luther, how "to relate the universal priesthood to the church's pastoral ministry," and how to find "a rationale for a public ordained clergy."[28] To say that "Luther was aware of the problem," is probably to say more of a person's own problem than it is or was for Luther.

Lowell Green takes a similar tack. He contends that Luther's early view of the ministry deriving from the priesthood of believers went through radical revision after the holocaust of the Peasants' Revolt of 1525. Because this demonstrated to Luther the inability of the congregations of Christian believers to govern themselves and to take over the responsibility of calling a qualified pastor in a responsible sort of way, the later Luther, says Green, leaned more and more on the magistrates and princes, less and less upon the general priesthood. This may be historical, but the facts remain that whatever adaptation to circumstances Luther accommodated himself to, the fundamental principles did not change.[29]

Responding in friendly debate, Robert Fischer does not pursue the question of change in Luther's thinking. Rather he puts the weight on what he sees as a reciprocal relationship between the ministry of the Word which belongs to the church, the congregation of believers, and the special pastoral office which is divinely ordained and duly delegated from the congregation to the called pastor. It does not appear that he adds much more than has already been stated by Brunotte and Hellmut Lieberg, among others.[30] The fact remains that up to the present no definitive work, involving all of Luther's vast writings, has appeared in English. It is our hope, at least in part, to fill this vacuum.

The value of Brunotte's work, as stated, is that he does not confine his scrutiny of Luther's writings to merely one period, nor try to set a disjunction arbitrarily into the Reformer's teaching on the ministry. In addition Brunotte surveys the studies on Luther's theology of the ministry which had appeared up till his time of writing, 1959. The concentration is on the previous hundred years when interest in Luther's thought on the ministerial office began to take a new course, particularly as attention was focused on its connection with the royal priesthood of all believers.

Julius Stahl was a professor of church law in the mid--
nineteenth century. He stood for what up till then was the classical
way of viewing the pastoral office in ecclesiastical circles, that the
office of pastor must not be understood as related to the general
priesthood at all, but as an office instituted by God, to be *under* and
to be governed *by* ecclesiastical authority, namely, the institutional
church with its consistories.[31]

Johann W. F. Hoefling, on the other hand, taught that the
pastoral office derived directly out of the general priesthood of
believers, to whom first of all the office belonged and who then
exercised freely their authority in Christian wisdom, for the sake of
good order in the church, to call a pastor. Hoefling denied that there
was a direct divine mandate to establish the office. A pastor carried
out the ministerial functions delegated to him by the congregation.[32]

Brunotte cites G. C. Adolf von Harless, C. F. W. Walther,
and Theodore Harnack as representatives of the effort to synthesize
the opposing views of Stahl and Hoefling. Harless and Walther
particularly emphasized that the two doctrines, the priesthood of all
believers and the office of the holy ministry as divinely ordained,
need to be understood and taught as closely interconnected. God's
mandate for establishing the office is to be executed by His will
through the instrumentality of the royal priesthood of believers, to
whom first of all the ministry of the Word belongs.[33]

Other authors delineated by Brunotte are G. Rietschel,
Werner Elert, Martin Doerne, Ernst Wolf, Peter Brunner, Karl
Rengstorf, and Goesta Hoek. The latter's article on the ministry
appeared in English in the *Scottish Journal of Theology*, March
1954. Hoek demonstrated that Luther distinguished between a wide
and a narrow sense of ministry. According to the first, the ministry
of the Word is understood as entrusted to all Christians by virtue of
their priesthood received by baptism. In the narrow—and the usual,
proper—sense, ministry as taught by Luther refers to the God--
ordained office for the public administering of Word and Sacrament,
received through the congregation's call. For it is God's will that
the called pastor serve in this way, and that not all assume to
themselves that right, even though the Keys are vested in them.[34]

The dilemma which each of the writers seeks to address is
the matter of primacy: does the congregation stand higher, over the
office of the ministry, by virtue of its authority to delegate it to the
called pastor? Or does the office of pastor proceed to transfer itself

forward from one who is ordained by duly given ecclesiastical authority to another qualified individual, who by his ordination then continues to be a minister over his congregation? Brunotte's observation is that Luther simply lets the two things stand side by side, opting neither for the latter, or a hierarchical, primacy of the clergy, nor for the former, a congregationalist sort of primacy. It is by God's ordaining that the ministry of the Word is entrusted to the congregation of believers, the church. Likewise it is by God's ordaining that the special entity of the pastoral office is to exist and be conferred upon a qualified man through the congregation's call. Luther saw no problem here. He maintained a high view of both, the royal priesthood of believers *and* the pastoral office. There could be no insoluble tension, or unwelcome competition for primacy or authority between them, because God was primary and above all.

Brunotte is especially critical of Peter Brunner[35] because he sharply differentiates between what he terms the *sacerdotium*, the sacrificial offices given to the general priesthood, and the *ministerium*, which is that special office bestowed upon those who are commissioned by the church and placed into their office by ordination.[36] Such a distinction is foreign to Luther's thinking, who understands the priesthood of believers as possessing fully the treasures which then the called pastor administers in their name and stead publicly, because of his office, which is instituted by God.

The "high" view of ordination expressed by Brunner is widely shared by a great number of scholars, particularly on the European scene, where a strong influence of consistorial authority still governed ecclesiology in the state-church mentality and which pervaded thinking in the church for several centuries. Even Brunotte, though criticizing Brunner for the distinction between the "ministry" which the people have over against the pastor, also shares this thinking on ordination. Joachim Heubach simply subsumes it as integral to the pastoral office, that a particular "charisma" is thereby vested upon the called *and* ordained pastor.[37] Bernhard Lohse shares a view widely held by German scholars that the older Luther moved away from "congregationalism" as regards the pastoral office and ordination towards the "high" view.[38]

Hellmut Lieberg, too, sees eye-to-eye with Heubach on ordination, holding that it must be seen as a theological matter, a matter of doctrine.[39] It belongs essentially to the very nature of the pastoral office and the Gospel, and certainly must not be understood as an adiaphoron, or optional. The latter, of course, Luther never said or held, though he very plainly taught that if a man leaves, or is removed from, the pastoral office, he would perforce return to what he was before, no longer having the congregation's call. Luther rejected the idea that a kind of indelible character or charisma went with ordination. He viewed it as very important, manifesting publicly the call into service of the Christian congregation, by God's will, and beseeching God's blessing most earnestly upon the one so called. But he resisted the notion that thereby, rather than by the call, the office was conferred.

Lieberg recognizes that Luther moves freely and easily with the two poles in the ellipse, between the general priesthood and the public pastoral office. They exist in a God-given tension, not opposing each other, but complementing instead. Luther, he notes, seemed to emphasize the one over the other depending upon the circumstances or situation. Against the *Schwaermer* he stressed that no one should preach or mount the pulpit without proper aegis, that is, a proper call. That underlies the preacher's credentials for office. No free-wheeling individual or self-styled preacher claiming the Spirit's unction should be allowed in the pulpit. Thus the importance of the pastoral office under ecclesiastical authority or control! On the other hand, against his Romanist opponents Luther emphasized the ministry which was given first of all to the priesthood of believers, from whom the pastor's office stems, because it was to them God entrusted His Keys. Fundamental, therefore, in viewing these two poles, says Lieberg, is the ministry of the Word which underlies them both and which is given by God.[40]

Gert Haendler[41] concurs with Lieberg that for Luther the congregation as possessor of all rights and powers, including the bestowal of the office of the ministry, was fundamental to his concept of the general priesthood doctrine.[42] However, Haendler faults Lieberg for failing to work in what he terms a historical way, that is, "substantiating his investigations with Luther quotations taken from the most diverse chronological periods." Thus he finds a weak spot in Lieberg at the very point of his strength. Lieberg ranges widely through Luther's writings, to find that the Reformer was a very consistent thinker who did not alter his position, specifically as regards the ministry, from situation to situation.

In spite of the criticism voiced earlier about Brunotte's "high" view of ordination relative to the ministry, the fact remains that his study remains one of the most valuable among recent secondary sources on Luther as regards the ministry. Concluding his work Brunotte appends a useful summary, which we capsule here:

-- Luther's teaching on the doctrine of the ministry and the general priesthood harmonizes closely with the rest of his theology.

-- The holy office of the ministry rests on the express will and institution of God; it is not a mere development out of Christian freedom on the part of the priesthood of believers.

-- Luther rejects the idea that the laity and clergy are to be distinguished and divided into two distinct classes of differing spiritual qualifications.

-- At the same time Luther carefully distinguishes between the powers and authority given by God to the general priesthood of believers and the office of the pastor and the powers which He has given to it;

-- In private setting, or where the public pastoral office does not yet exist, God expects the individual Christian to proclaim the Word, thus exercising the Office of the Keys which he possesses by virtue of his Christian faith and baptism.

-- The called pastor exercises publicly, in behalf and in the name of the congregation which has called him, the means of grace, preaching the Word and administering the sacraments.

-- In order to carry out the functions of his office, the pastor requires the call of the congregation, which he is to regard as God's express will and call, since the congregation acts in keeping with God's mandate to establish the pastoral office in their midst.

-- Even as the congregation's call of a specific person establishes the pastoral office in its midst, so for given reasons (incapacitating illness, doctrinal malfeasance, moral failure), the call may be withdrawn, thus returning the individual again to what he was before he became a pastor.

--   The pastor by virtue of his office, as a called servant of the Word, is both God's servant and also the servant of God's people.

--   The church possesses the authority to set into office such auxiliary helpers as are needed for the pastoral office, though that office remains singularly one and intact as the one office ordained by God.

--   Luther sees that the Scripture includes various activities or actions in the calling process, such as choosing or electing, testing or certifying, commissioning and publicly manifesting or approving; all of these co-inhere and belong to the "calling."

--   Luther recognizes the significance of the apostolic practice of "laying on of hands," or ordination, but he rejects the idea that by this act the office itself is conveyed, though it manifests publicly that the office is bestowed upon a given individual who has been duly called, and petitions God's blessings upon him.

--   The individual Christian's faith and baptism are the necessary ground or precondition underlying his priesthood and thus the public ministry, though the public pastoral office is not bestowed thereby.

--   It follows on the basis of 1 Corinthians 14:34f. (as also Gen. 3:16) that women are not qualified for the public pastoral office.

Brunotte, finally, sees the need to repeat that there is the closest possible link between the general priesthood and the special office of the pastor, in line with God's own mandating. Luther placed heavy emphasis on a man's qualifications for that office, along with the congregation's call. Brunotte also repeats Luther's caution that no man should presume to take over a given pulpit and the pastoral functions unless he has been specifically invited. What Brunotte has in mind—and this accords with Luther's emphasis—is that even a retired pastor who functions as a supply pastor, or substitute, does so not because of an indelible character through ordination, or because he once was a called pastor somewhere, but because of the express will and invitation of the given congregation which requests his services to fill a given need in their midst. Brunotte, however, retains what we have called a "high" view of ordination nonetheless. It should also be noted that he leaves the door open for possible changes in the rule against women in the pastoral office, stating that Luther's objections may some day have to yield in the face of a new exegesis which interprets the key passages differently.

Except for the latter, Werner Elert concurs with Brunotte's assessment of Luther on the ministry. Elert acknowledges that Luther views the election and installation of a pastor into his office as an activity of "the whole congregation."[43] At the same time, however, he also notes in a practical sort of way that this cannot ordinarily involve every member of the local parish, or congregation, in the decision, but those who are especially able to "act in the name of the congregation." This leaves the matter of the governing body somewhat elastic, so that, for example, a voters' assembly, or board of elders, might be the decision-making body. Beyond this, it is evident that Luther also was willing, states Elert, to entrust things like the preparation and examination of candidates for the ministry, as well as the visitation of the parishes, to "the larger circle who are specially qualified in theology," because these "are functions of the larger church entity."[44] What Elert envisions is a composite entity like a synod.

Yet Elert always returns to what is fundamental to Luther's thinking, something which he emphasizes untiringly, namely, that the prerogative of calling and judging belongs finally "to the sum total of all Christians." It is "the right to which they are entitled on the basis of the priesthood of all believers," says Elert.[45] With good insight of what Luther always stressed concerning those who are the "believers and sheep who hear the Shepherd's voice," Elert underscores this salient fact concerning congregations in whose midst there may be hypocrites: "But this right does not inhere in their membership in the local congregation," that is, merely by an outward tie through profession of faith, as to some external organization or club or fellowship. "It inheres in the church of Christ in general," that is, the company of the faithful, or believers, for whom the church at a given place rightly bears the name "church." To be remembered and distinguished carefully and finally, says Elert, is that "the fact that they live with one another in local congregations is incident to their life on earth."[46] Of prior and primary significance is their relationship with the Savior, Jesus Christ.

This survey of contemporary secondary sources on Luther's view of church and ministry demonstrates a general, close harmony with the viewpoints uncovered through the personal visits and dialogues described in the preceding chapter.

NOTES

1   Bernhard Lohse, op. cit., 188.

2   Carl A. Aurelius, *Verborgene Kirche*. Luther's Kirchenverstaendnis in Streitschriften und Exegese 1519-1521. Hannover: Lutherisches Verlagshaus, 1983.

3   *LW* 39, 10; *WA* 6, 650f.

4   St. Louis: Concordia Publishing House, 1964, p. 51.

5   Cf. op. cit., 40.48.

6   Werner Elert, *The Structure of Lutheranism*. Vol. 1. Walter A. Hansen, trans. St. Louis: Concordia Publishing House, 1962, 261.

7   Ibid.

8   Paul D. Avis, *The Church in the Theology of the Reformers*. Atlanta: Knox, 1981, p. 1.

9   Quoted in Avis, op. cit., 3.

10   Cf. Philip Watson, *Let God Be God. An Interpretation of the Theology of Luther*. Philadelphia: Muhlenberg, 1949, p. 169.

11   Paul Althaus, *The Theology of Martin Luther*. Robert C. Schultz, trans. Philadelphia: Fortress, 1966, 292.

12   Scott Hendrix, *Luther and the Papacy*. Philadephia: Fortress, 1981, xi.

13   Op. cit., 92.

14   Op. cit., 156.

15   Op. cit., 159.

16   Mark U. Edwards, *Luther's Last Battles*. Ithaca: Cornell, 1983, 3.

17   Op. cit., 4.

18   Op. cit., 208.

19   Ibid.

20   Hans Kueng, *The Church Maintained in Truth*. Edward Quinn, trans. New York: Seabury, 1980, 54.

21   Daniel Olivier, *Luther's Faith. The Cause of the Gospel in the Church*. John Tonkin, trans. St. Louis: Concordia Publishing House, 1982, 23.

22 Ibid.

23 Op. cit., 123.

24 Op. cit., 143.

25 Op. cit., 166.

26 Werner, op. cit., 346f.

27 James H. Pragman, *Traditions of Ministry. A History of the Doctrine of the Ministry in Lutheran Theology*. St. Louis: Concordia Publishing House, 1983, 13.

28 Op. cit., 18.

29 Cf. Lowell Green, "Change in Luther's Doctrine of the Ministry," *Lutheran Quarterly*, Vol. 18, May 1966, 173ff.

30 Robert Fischer, "Another Look at Luther's Doctrine of the Ministry," *Lutheran Quarterly*, Vol. 18, August 1966, 260ff.

31 Cf. Brunotte, *Das geistliche Amt bei Luther*. Berlin: Lutherisches Verlagshaus, 1959, 10-13.

32 Ibid., 13-18.

33 Ibid., 18ff.

34 Ibid., 21f. Cf. *Scottish Journal of Theology*, vol. 7, No. 1, Mar. 1954, 16ff. Cf. also Brian Gerrish, "Priesthood and Ministry in the Theology of Luther," *Church History*, vol. 34, Dec. 1965, 404ff.

35 Cf. "Vom Amt des Bischofs," *Schriften des Theologischen Konvents Augsburgischen Bekenntnis*, Vol. 9, Berlin, 1955, 6-12.

36 Brunotte, op. cit., 146f.

37 Cf. Joachim Heubach, *Die Ordination zum Amt der Kirche*. Berlin: Lutherisches Verlagshaus, 1956.

38 Lohse, op. cit., 187.

39 Hellmut Lieberg, *Amt und Ordination bei Luther and Melanchthon*. Goettingen: Nandenhoeck & Ruprecht, 1962.

40 Lieberg, op. cit., 235.

41 Gert Haendler, *Luther on the Ministerial Office and Congregational Function*. R. C. Gritsch, trans. Philadelphia: Fortress, 1981.

42 Op. cit., 19.

43 Elert, op. cit., 368.

44 Op. cit., 369f.

45 Op. cit., 371.

46 Ibid.

Chapter 3

Concluding Summary

In summarizing the views of these mostly European Luther scholars the least purpose of all is to claim a consensus or even wish to imply that a consensus was the desired end or purpose, as a kind of grand conclusion based upon shared viewpoints. In actual fact, however, there was little expressed disagreement on the theses, which, as stated (Part III, Chapter 1), were submitted prior to the dialogues. That the theses faithfully reproduced Luther's thinking was readily granted. Parts I and II also support this fact. Luther was a remarkably consistent theologian, whose views, early or late (so Aarts, *et alii, contra* Aland, e.g.), on subjects like church and ministry, are not difficult of portrayal, or first of all of understanding.

Needless to say, it was a reassuring sort of experience, drawn especially from the dialogues (Part III, Chapter 1), to see the generally consistent stance which the various scholars themselves evinced as regards their own theology on church and ministry. Were they illustrating, wittingly or not, the truth of the theological maxim or aphorism, *Quo proprior Lutero eo melior theologus*? Had Luther made us all, in part at least, closer in our thoughts on the two subjects than might have been anticipated?

It mattered little, moreover, that along with these discussions of Luther's theology, there had been a somewhat tabid and peccant interest in "Missouri's" internal struggle in the decade of the 70's. It was after all merely symptomatic of what had gone on throughout the Christian world, earlier to be sure, in the debate over the location of the authoritative Word in theology. The frank admission pointed to this as the real problem, locating the Word of God, in view of radical attenuating of Biblical authority during the past two centuries. To stand by while higher criticism threw a monkey wrench in the wheel of conservative Bible scholarship with cries of "fundamentalism," "hyperorthodoxism," "ultra confessionalism," "obscurantism," "repristinationism," "out-moded attachment" to things like six-day creation, the Jonah story, and rectilinear prophecy would have amounted to lese majesty and shameful apathy, if not total surrender. "Does the Missouri Synod think that it

360

somehow is the conscience of the church with special *summum jus* to speak for the rest of Christianity, specifically Lutheran theology?" This was probably the supreme slap or slur in contemporary put-down by opponents of strong conservative polemics. From this extreme of criticism there arose, on the other side of the spectrum, the plaedoyer that "Missouri" might somehow take the initiative in a renewed effort at an *addendum* to the *Formula of Concord* in our day, to rally the reft and disjoined forces of Lutheran theology, addressing the knotty problems troubling the church—especially on the subject of Scripture's authority as the Word of God, the challenge of higher criticism, the true nature of the church in this ecumenically confused age, and the proper basis for fellowship among the churches.

These were not inconsequential issues; the last century of happenings within the Lutheran church alone, apart from all other communions, has borne out the validity of this apostrophe to contemporary theology's quest for direction in our times. "Missouri" itself had entered the lists at the Bad Boll conferences, and, although it had come off reeling from this joining of issue or encounter with so-called scientific theology, it had so far managed to hold the ship on keel and on course. The question remained whether it could continue to stave off what appeared to most external observers as outsized odds.

Aside from this fascination with "Missouri's" grappling and jousting within its own ranks, there was remarkable calm evinced by the dialoguers on definitions and distinctions in connection with church and ministry in Luther's thought. Beyond question, for example, in the comments of Pinomaa and Oberman, was Luther's use of the distinction concerning the church's invisibility and visibility. Though this distinction is widely criticized, it is nonetheless a prevalent definition in Luther's thought. If we did not make it, we would indeed be separated from our Creed and all we confess therein concerning the church, Oberman pointed out. Strictly speaking, *stricte dicta*, the nature of the church must be described as invisible, Schlink agreed, and we do not yield to the charge that thereby we only believe in an invisible church which has no visible counterpart, located by the means of grace, Word and Sacrament. The latter church is a *corpus mixtum*; it bears the name "church" by virtue of believers present there. Thus broadly speaking, *late dicta*, it too has that name, and the local congregation is called church because of the holy ones, the believers, present there (Pinomaa, Schlink, Oesch, Poetsch, Mueller, Wachler, Hoffmann, Junghans, Peters, *et al.*) The opinion that *invisibilis* was not a good term was very strong among the theologians, since it seemed to suggest the inevitable unreality of the thing termed. Preferable were contrasting pairs like *ecclesia spiritualis* and *corporealis* (Aarts), *ecclesia spiritualis* and *carnalis* (Lohse), *ecclesia abscondita* (hidden) and *revelata* (Hägglund, Ebeling), *sichtlich* and *unsichtbar*, that which can be seen and that which cannot be seen (Peters).

Althaus preferred to use the terms "true church" and "empirical church." There is reason to object, however, that for Luther the terms *invisibilis* and *abscondita* were not actually equivalent (Oberman), since the first, which has to do with the church's very nature or essence (Mueller), is a present reality that has gone on before and is offered for faith's acceptance; while the latter has to do with the smallness of the church, with its suffering, persecution, cross-bearing in the world. Nor is this distinction just a resurrection of "old dogmatics," as Mahlmann charged.

There was general concurrence that the Word and Sacraments marked the church's presence on earth, the presence of the true church within the empirical. Evident was the *Volkskirche* kind of view towards baptism as marking those who were in the church (Heubach, *et al.*), though at times there was clarification that with baptism there must also be faith, as Luther stressed (Brunner). Since Luther's time opposition to the invisible nature of the church has been strong (Poetsch), but the Reformer did indeed employ the term and with it stressed that the church was a *communio sanctorum*, a communion or congregation, known only as to its totality and identity, as to who the holy and righteous really are, by God (Poetsch, Rengstorf, Oesch). On the other hand, where pietism is viewed as a positive factor in the church, and not negatively (Saarnivaara), the concept of the invisible church as the true church is unacceptable, because believers are held to be able to know each other by faith; the circle of believers becomes a well-defined entity, also to the discerning eye of fellow Christians and not God only.

God's mandate to proclaim the Gospel is closely tied to God's establishment of the church (Lohse). As Luther stated in the *Smalcald Articles*, the church through the preaching of the Gospel is like a magnet drawing believers into it (Baur). The Gospel has a clearly defined content. For the sake of the "holy and righteous,"

(Pinomaa) its constituents, the church has a binding obligation for and towards pure doctrine, for pure proclamation of the Gospel. As a result, the church's nature must be seen as closely tied to what the Gospel is (Rengstorf). Tragic is the fact that for many German churches, as well as others around the world, the Gospel of God's forgiveness for Christ's sake is no longer really known; a social gospel has taken its place (Brunner, Oesch, Poetsch). In a real sense one could rightly assert that there is but one thing, one sacrament or means of grace, which draws people into God's company of believers, and that is Christ (Peters). Put another way, Luther throws all else into the shade before *theologia crucis* (Poetsch). The figures or metaphors Luther found in Scripture for the church and how it came to be or exist, like Body, Bride, Fold, etc., all underscore the power of the constituting Word (Ebeling, Poetsch, Mueller, *et al.*)

Thus Word and Sacrament mark where the church is to be found (Peters, Oesch, *et al.*); it can be spotted in this way, even though the identity of its members may not be known with certainty, except by God. It does not follow that the church becomes visible in or through the means of grace, or marks. These marks can be stated in another, expanded way, as Luther does in his treatise on *The Councils and the Church* (Mueller). Here in addition to Gospel, Baptism, Lord's Supper, Luther adds confession and absolution, the calling of a pastor, worship or prayer, and cross-bearing. These all add up to *Lehre, Leben, Leiden*, all hanging on *theologia crucis* (Mueller, Poetsch).

It is because of Rome's departure from Word and Sacrament that Luther argues against its claim as church, though in his early years he had taken this stance first of all because of its pretension of identifying its empirical form with the true church itself, the *una sancta*. On the other hand, one can argue that Luther would never have agitated for *reform* of the church had he not still recognized the possibility of its existence within the Romanist organization; but when it failed to preach the Gospel, Luther contended that it had lost the right to its claim as church. (Lohse).

In similar manner, already in the early church, the apostle Paul recognized that even in the Galatian churches there were Christians, and that the church was present there because of the Gospel whose power could not immediately be negated by the incidental presence of "another gospel" (Brunner). Luther's failing,

according to his modern Romanist critics, was not that he wrongly
faulted the church of his day for its spiritual bankruptcy and failure
to proclaim the Gospel, as well as for its pretentious claim to
infallibility, but because he failed to regard and maintain due respect
for the "Peter office" exemplified by the papacy (Aarts, Pesch). The
Lutheran Confessions provide, in contrast, a worthy standard for our
day in the retention of pure Gospel loyalty and proclamation; there
must be a standard for orthodoxy faithful to the Scriptures; this the
Lutheran Confessions provide (Schlink, Brunner, Rengstorf).

We know that Luther agonized and struggled with this
whole question concerning Rome's place in the continuity of the
church on earth, the empirical church so-called. After all, "have we
not received Holy Scripture, Baptism, the Sacrament, and the pulpit
from them?"[1] This earnest probing of his own heart comes in the
series of sermons he preached on John's Gospel in 1537. "Do you
really imagine that you are the only one who is wise?" he asks
rhetorically.[2] He goes on: "What business have I to preach against
them as a pupil preaching against his teachers?"[3]   Sometimes
thoughts like these come charging into my heart, Luther confides to
his audience: "Oh, if only I had never started this and had never
preached a word! For who dares oppose the church?" He even
admits that "I find this church in the papacy too," that is, in the
Romanist organization. The answer to his heart-searching quandary
lies in Rome's betrayal of the Gospel. As the saying goes, "Not all
who carry long knives are cooks," nor are "all who lay claim to the
title 'church' really the church." They may be called that, but there
is often "a great difference between the name and the reality." The
Roman church had become unfaithful as regards Gospel preaching
is Luther's accusation. "They should have been God's people; but
they practiced idolatry so freely under the cloak of the name
'church' that God was forced to say: 'This shall no longer be My
temple and priesthood.'" So Luther says that he does not doubt that
"some of the papists are true Christians"; but he was also just as
convinced that some of them were not, because their idolatrous
practices had led to "a complete removal of Christ"; they had "cast
Christ completely aside."[4]

Moreover, church in New Testament usage, while most
often referring to the individual churches at given locations, should
also be seen as *ecclesia concordita*, that is, as church in the larger
fellowship of congregations (Poetsch). Though such convenanted

wider fellowship is not directly commanded by God, it is rooted certainly in New Testament example and conforms to the will of God. In such fellowship the guidelines are grounded on *fides quae creditur*, the content of Christian faith in its various articles, and not merely in *fides qua creditur*, the personal faith of believers or groups of them (Poetsch). A synod which is formed by congregations united in doctrine is a voluntary organization; yet it acts in the name of the *una sancta* when it deals with the *notae ecclesiae*, the marks of the church (Oesch). Congregations do not create a church when they constitute a synod in this manner. It is church as to its confessions, not according to its structure, a fundamental truth which needs to be remembered and respected (Oesch). Congregations may, of course, withdraw from a synod, but they ought to maintain fellowship when the bond of unity in teaching exists, for this is wholesome for all (Oesch).

The synod is rightly termed *ecclesia representativa*, since it performs those functions delegated to it by the churches or congregations. Walther, according to Prof. Oesch, accomplished in America something that was impossible in Germany with its territorial churches, which were *Volkskirchen*, people's or community churches. There everyone who was baptized was automatically, *ipso facto*, considered not only a part of the parish but also of Christ's church, whether professedly and actually a believer or not.

For Walther the writings and theology of Luther were the bearing point in theology by which he avoided the Scylla of hierarchical extreme, or high churchism, which elevated the territorial entity into a super-church, on the one hand, and the Charybdis of independentism, or extreme congregationalism, which repudiated the fellowship of the *ecclesia concordita*, on the other hand (Oesch). It is important to recall that the rejection of all hierarchy or organizational structure *per se* will under most instances end with extreme individualism, personalism, and subjectivism (Baur). A church or congregation then risks becoming schismatic, though this is not to say or claim that thereby it has become heretical (Schlink).

With the Peasants' War Luther saw that the congregations were not ready in most instances for self-government; as a result he accommodated himself to various temporary—at least so he thought of them—makeshift arrangements involving the magistrates, princes, consistories, and the like in the interest of competent guidance for the parishes (Mueller). This has resulted, however, in the present-day confusion of forms in Germany that range between the Romanizing view, which elevates the clergy into authoritative position in the churches, or the populist view, which ends with extreme laicism and downgrading of the pastoral office (Mueller).

Luther's early writings underscore *Gemeinde*, congregations, when he speaks of the church as gathered around the Word (Peters). His later writings do not negate this conception, but the emphasis goes in the direction of the *Amt*, or office of the ministry. The chief function of this office is the preaching of the Gospel by which believers are gathered and ministered to; the priesthood of believers thus yields and delegates its God-given authority in connection with the Keys to the called pastor, and seeks support and direction from the magistrates and princes (Peters). In any case, the congregations do not thus cease to possess what they have conferred upon the called pastor in his office, or *Amt*, to administer in their behalf.

Finally, too, it must be granted that the circle of believers extends more widely than the professing Christian church, or congregations; faith cannot be seen, and God alone knows those that are His; their works indeed can be seen and these do give evidence of faith; but God is able to gather His own wherever His Word is sown as seed-bearing fruit unto eternal life, even though a visible entity of believers, or congregation, is lacking (Brunner). Needless to say, this is an exception to the rule that regularly obtains, a rule which urges believers not to neglect the gathering or assembling of themselves together.

Luther's teaching on the church was well set by the year 1525; the same was true of his doctrine of the ministry (Aarts). The Keys indeed belong to all, but the office of the public pastoral servant belongs to the one who is called (Pinomaa). By the pastor's call into office he becomes, or is, *diakonos*, one who serves, not *sacerdos*, one who sacrifices or is the mediator; only Christ is that (Aarts). The pastoral office is distinctly ordained by God, with Christian believers electing qualified men (Saarnivaara). The ministry rests on God's specific command for office (Baur, Ober- man). This is very basic to a proper understanding of the office (Schlink). It is at the same time true that the office is a delegated one through the congregation. Luther never held the view that it evolved from the general ministry; congregations, in other words, do not create the office (Schlink). Hoefling and the Wisconsin Synod converged on the same track in holding that the pastoral office evolves out of the general priesthood (Oesch). In a way this is true, of course, but in a definitely restricted way, as stated above (Oesch).

It is good to stress both the general priesthood of believers *and* the special office of pastor (Mueller). Luther consistently, to the end of his life, taught both in their proper relation; he definitely respected the call by the congregation, also in his own case in Wittenberg at the Stadkirche (Mueller, Oberman). Luther preached at Wittenberg because he had a call to preach there (Juengel). In fact, it must be granted for Luther that both in his activity as professor and also as pastor, he saw his office(s) rooted in conferred authority (Aland).

When the Reformer speaks of the housefather performing the duties of pastor for his household, his comments must be seen as fitting the needs or situation to which he spoke. The situation(s) does not establish the principle, but vice versa, the principle indicates the manner in which each situation, or emergency, may be dealt with (Oberman). Under those conditions Luther was fully prepared to urge that the royal priests exercise the Keys, as the situation demanded. Thus proclaiming the Word, baptizing in cases of emergency, pastoral care, etc., were to issue forth from the royal priests as need dictated. Never, however, were they to compete with or usurp the pastoral office. Administering the Sacrament of the Altar remained for Luther an act belonging properly within the congregation, where there was pastoral care and discipline, thus not in each household or in *ad hoc* situations.

It would, therefore, be wrong to claim that Luther had what is know as a populist, or low, view of the pastoral office or ministry. This was true of certain Lutheran thinkers and leaders like Hoefling in Germany, Hauge and Hallesby in Norway. Had they known the Lutheran Confessions, they would not have succumbed to the notion which is so typical of the sects (Aalen, Oesch). It was also present in the thinking of Beyerhaus (Oesch). The pastoral office has very distinct duties, under God (Brunner), and a pastor is a pastor in so far as he is pastor of a congregation (Oesch). "I like the idea of a synodical president being called 'chief pastor' as little as I like the idea of our having life-time bishops in SELK" (Oesch re Independent Evangelical Lutheran Church).

The rite of ordination remained important for Luther as public manifesting of the call into the ministry and earnest petitioning of God's blessing upon the individual entering upon his vocation. But Luther never conceived of ordination as bestowing a special, permanent, ongoing *charisma* upon the pastor apart from a regular, proper call. Luther used the terms "call" and "ordain" in a synonymous, equivalent sense. In fact, the call remained for Luther the true ordination into the *Amt*, or office (Oesch, Wachler, Poetsch, Wisløff). In Germany and Europe in general, as well as in Lutheran circles in America, a "high" notion of ordination prevails. This was evident in the thinking of Schlink, Brunner, Heubach, *et aliorum*. It follows that they also took exception to Luther's judgment that an ordained man who is without a call, except for certain circumstances beyond his control, returns to what he was before. Luther held firm to the opinion that ordination did not bestow a certain lasting *charisma* or power. Nor did he, as a called parish pastor, see any reason to hesitate to officiate at the consecration of his old friend, Amsdorf, as bishop of Naumburg. Amsdorf had the credentials of a proper call, and he, Luther, had similar credentials from the magistrates acting for the people to perform the rite.

It is one of the curious phenomena in contemporary Lutheranism that the ordaining of women into the pastoral office should have impetus from two opposing poles, from the side of those favoring laicism or the power of the laity, and at the same time from the side of those professing to hold a high view of the office, clericalism. Obviously, both act in disregard for Scripture's clear injunction against that practice (Oesch). The argument that times have changed is hardly adequate to satisfy the conflict which is set up in violation of the Lutheran Confessions.

Finally, in assessing and summarizing the viewpoints, it should again be stated that agreement was widespread and virtually unanimous as to what Luther had in fact said and taught on church and ministry. Clear testimony of his own consistent, clear, limpid stance! The one additional thought that surfaced was the plea that there might be in our day something like an *addendum* to the *Formula of Concord*, to answer some of the aforementioned troubling questions in Lutheran theology today, particularly on Scripture's authority and the doctrine of the church (Oesch). It cannot be denied that the church has not confronted these issues with face-on penetrating, full-scale sort of engagement. Superficial skirmishing will not counter the threats coming from the higher-critical school of thought, on the one hand, and ecumenically superficial and emotional thinking on the doctrine of the church, on the other hand. It may, of course, be true that by this late date any effort involving the whole of the Lutheran church, or beyond that, of the whole Christian church, is too late. Perhaps the church is beyond mustering the style and vigor of the 16th century or that of the 4th. No less a scholar of church history than Hermann Sasse sadly opined that the hour was past. Not even a Luther *redivivus* could manage to rally the troops for such a major battle with any hope of triumph, it seems.

But the hand of God in the affairs of men, especially in behalf of His church and its eventual gathering of the faithful safely into the fold, Luther never doubted. For that reason his hope concerning the church and the high place of the pastor in his office as under-shepherd of the Savior never dimmed. In his thinking a blessed relation existed between the royal priests and the called pastors, based always, in his thinking, on the Keys themselves. By God's own mandate and purposing, there was to be a close, corollary relationship between the church, or congregation, and the called pastor or shepherd. Those to whom the Keys rightfully belonged must never opt to destroy or demean the office of pastor which God had established in their midst. "Of what use would the office of preaching and the ministry be, if the people could teach and admonish themselves?" Luther asked pointedly. "Christ could just as well have kept it and not purchased it so dearly. And why do we hold such an office if we do not want to carry on with teaching and admonishing" Luther asked of the pastors, just as pointedly in turn?[5] Things would then be worse than under the popes and lazy monks, or whatever other miserable state of affairs should afflict the Church. God be thanked, the church still stands; God will sustain it; God will supply His church with faithful pastors. This is God's promise.

Luther capsules this all succinctly in a sermon preached at Wittenberg, September 6, 1539, on John 3:34:

> John is speaking here about calling or sending, particularly about the sending of Christ. I have decided to discourse on this topic at some length. There are two ways of sending. First, God sent His messengers, the prophets and apostles, like Moses and St. Paul, directly and without the help of an intermediary. These men were called by God's word of mouth and without human agency. Such sending was done

only when God wished to inaugurate something new, as was the case when He sent Moses and the prophets. This exalted method came to an end in the New Testament with the apostles, who were the last to be called directly by God.

The other way of sending is indeed also one by God, but it is done through the instrumentality of man. It has been employed ever since God established the ministry with its preaching and its exercise of the Office of the Keys. This ministry will endure and is not to be replaced by any other. But the incumbents of this ministry do not remain; they die. This necessitates an ever-new supply of preachers, which calls for the employment of certain means. The ministry, that is, the Word of God, Baptism, and Holy Communion, came directly from Christ; but later Christ departed from this earth. Now a new way of sending was instituted, which works through man but is not of man. We were sent according to this method; according to it, we elect and send others, and we install them in their ministry to preach and to administer the Sacraments. This type of sending is also of God and commanded by God. Even though God resorts to our aid and to human agency, it is He Himself who sends laborers into His vineyard. [6]

NOTES

1   *LW* 24, 304; *WA* 46, 6.

2   *LW* 24, 323; *WA* 46, 22.

3   *LW* 24, 304; *WA* 46, 6.

4   *LW* 24, 304ff.; *WA* 46, 6ff.

5   *LW* 38, 100. *WA* 30², 597 in *From Admonition Concerning the Sacrament*, 1530.

6   *LW* 22, 482.

Index of Names

(Biblical names and principal figures frequently cited in the text - Luther, Melanchthon, Chemnitz, Walther are not included in this list.)

Index of Subjects

CPSIA information can be obtained at www.ICGtesting.com
Printed in the USA
242837LV00003B/4/P